AFTER GENOCIDE

MORE PRAISE

"*Adam Smith's* After Genocide *is a sincere and extremely readable account of its author's personal and intellectual experience in facing the unthinkable political endeavor which has acquired the name of genocide. Smith combines a deeply felt rendering of his family's fate during and after the Holocaust with a sober presentation of his own attempts to examine the efforts of international tribunals to deal with the perpetrators of genocide, its victims, and the societies affected by this massive crime. The book will cause many to think about the deficiencies of ad-hoc and permanent international criminal courts established so far and to search for more inventive solutions.*"
> —Dr. Vojin Dimitrijevic, professor of International Law,
> Union School of Law, Belgrade, Serbia, director of Belgrade
> Center for Human Rights, and author of *Reign of Terror*
> and *The Insecurity of Human Rights after Communism*

"*Adam Smith has made a vital contribution to the literature on justice for mass atrocity. Too often, legal scholars and practitioners have assumed that international criminal justice is either the solution or at least an important part of the solution for societies recovering from wholesale slaughter. Smith's detailed, thoughtful, and often compelling study counsels otherwise, urging closer examination and greater support for local responses. One may not agree with all of its conclusions, but this book should be required reading for those who study or engage in reckoning with mass atrocity.*"
> —James Cavallaro, executive director of the
> Human Rights Program, Harvard Law School

"*This is an admirable book. . . . There are many issues discussed by Smith and his detachment is great.*"
> —Alfred P. Rubin, Emeritus Distinguished Professor of
> International Law, Fletcher School of Law and Diplomacy,
> Tufts University

AFTER GENOCIDE

BRINGING *the* DEVIL *to* JUSTICE

Adam M.
SMITH

 **Prometheus Books**

59 John Glenn Drive
Amherst, New York 14228-2119

Published 2009 by Prometheus Books

Inquiries should be addressed to
Prometheus Books
59 John Glenn Drive
Amherst, New York 14228–2119
VOICE: 716–691–0133, ext. 210
FAX: 716–691–0137
WWW.PROMETHEUSBOOKS.COM

13 12 11 10 09   5 4 3 2 1

Library of Congress Cataloging-in-Publication Data

Smith, Adam M., 1974–
    After genocide : bringing the devil to justice / by Adam M. Smith.
        p. cm.
    Includes bibliographical references and index.
    ISBN 978–1–59102–684–6 (hardcover : alk. paper)
    1. Justice, Administration of—International cooperation. 2. International Criminal Court. 3. International criminal courts. 4. Genocide. I. Title.

K2115.S65 2008
345'.01—dc22

                                                                              2008046788

Printed in the United States on acid-free paper

To my family—past, present, and future.

CONTENTS

ACKNOWLEDGMENTS

Books, especially those that take several years to complete, are rarely solo enterprises. This one is no different. From the moment my ideas began to germinate in June 2004, until the final edits, I have relied on scores of people for their time, advice, support, and editing—sometimes all four from the same people. At Harvard, the International Legal Studies Office, the Human Rights Program, the Lewis Fund for International Law, the John Gallup Laylin Prize, the Chayes Fellows Program (and in particular its administrator Sarah Zucker), and the Kokkalis Program at the Kennedy School, provided critical funding for my adventures abroad. Particular thanks go to Ambassador Mary Ann Glendon, Jim Cavallaro, and Ryan Goodman. The enthusiasm with which they greeted my project, along with their thorough and constructive criticisms of it, kept me on track.

Outside the law school, dozens of people in the United States, Europe, Africa, Asia, and Australia assisted by providing me opportunities that expanded my understanding of the issues and/or by lending me their ear (and sometimes their couch). These included David Hein, Susan Wright, Aaron Presnall, Clifton Johnson, and David Kaye (and the staff of the US Embassy—The Hague), the Office of the Legal Adviser at the US Department of State, Justice Richard Goldstone, Ateesh Chanda, Joel Pulliam, the Honorable James E. Baker (and his chambers), Alan Gold, Michael Johnson, David Wadler, Julie Dam, Ken Anderson, Matt and Becky Price, and many others, some of whom wished to remain anonymous.

Additionally, I remain indebted to Alan Zuckerman at Brown University for his sage advice on writing and learning that predated this book but resonated as I wrote, as well as to Raufu Mustapha at Oxford University for guiding me and pushing me further.

My agent Scott Hoffman believed in my project even when I wavered. The staff at Prometheus Books, and in particular my editor Linda Regan and her insightful comments, gave the book the final polish and breadth it needed.

I was spurred to write by my family's history, and my greatest appreciation and admiration goes to them: my four grandparents who I was fortunate enough to have known but who have since passed, Cypa, Sol, Rose, and Otto, and members of their wider families whose circumstances denied me the privilege of meeting. My grandfather Sol filled in some of the background for this book but unfortunately did not live to see its completion. My uncle Paul's stories about wartime Budapest gave context to both this book and more importantly to my life. The support of my parents, my in-laws, and my sisters has been invaluable.

I cannot hope to express the depth and breadth of the thanks I owe to my Julie and my Izzy—their support, understanding, patience, and faith in me have been unending. And, the imminent arrival of our number two forced me over the finish line.

Naturally, while I could not have completed this book without each of these people, all errors remain mine alone.

A. M. S.
Washington, DC

LIST OF ABBREVIATIONS

CPA   Coalition Provisional Authority

DRC   Democratic Republic of the Congo (Congo-Kinshasa)

ECCC   Extraordinary Chambers of the Courts of Cambodia (the Khmer Rouge Tribunal)

ECOMOG   Economic Community of West African States Monitoring Group

ECOWAS   Economic Community of West African States

EU   European Union

FDLR   Democratic Forces for the Liberation of Rwanda

ICC   International Criminal Court

ICTY   International Criminal Tribunal for the former Yugoslavia

ICTR   International Criminal Tribunal for Rwanda

IFOR   Implementation Force (NATO)

IMF   International Monetary Fund

KFOR   Kosovo Force (NATO)

NATO   North Atlantic Treaty Organization

OHR   Office of the High Representative

OSCE   Organization for Security and Cooperation in Europe

RRRDR   Rassemblement pour le Retour des Réfugiés et la Démocratie au Rwanda (Rally for the Return of Refugees and Democracy to Rwanda)

RS   Republika Srpska (Serbian Republic of Bosnia and Herzegovina)

RUF   Revolutionary United Front

SCSL   Special Court for Sierra Leone

SFOR   Stabilization Force (NATO)

UN   United Nations

UNGA   United Nations General Assembly

UNMIK   United Nations Interim Administration Mission in Kosovo

UNPROFOR United Nations Protection Force

UNSC   United Nations Security Council

UNSCR   United Nations Security Council Resolution

UNTAET   United Nations Transitional Administration in East Timor

INTERNATIONAL COURTS
TIMELINE*

Nuremberg	1945
Tokyo Trials	1946
International Criminal Tribunal for the former Yugoslavia	1993
International Criminal Tribunal for Rwanda	1994
Special Panels in East Timor	2000
Kosovo International Judges and Prosecutors	2000
Extraordinary Chambers in Cambodia	2003
International Criminal Court	2002
Special Court for Sierra Leone	2002
Iraqi Special Tribunal	2003
Special Chambers of Belgrade District Court	2003
State Court of Bosnia and Herzegovina	2005
Special Tribunal for Lebanon	2007

*Dates refer to the commencement of court operations. Several of these courts were created by treaties or agreements that predated their operations by several years. The dates provided are those of the commencement of actual operations of the courts.

Chapter 1

FROM BUDAPEST TO BONDI TO BOSNIA

An Unlikely War Crimes Journey

On the evening of March 18, 1944, German commanders in Austria received the word to implement Operation Margarethe—the invasion of Hungary was on. Hours later, eleven German divisions, including armored trains, motorized guns, and Tiger tanks, crossed Austria into Hungary reaching Budapest at four o'clock in the morning. The Germans would occupy Hungary until near the end of the war in 1945.

For the Feher family—Otto, Rose, and nine-year-old Paul—the next year would be agonizing. The anti-Semitism of the Nazi occupiers was not a surprise to the Fehers, but that the family was specifically targeted was shocking and disorienting. Even before the Nazi arrival, the Fehers had done all that they could to be Hungarians first, and Jews second: Otto changed his name from the Semitic *Finkelstern* to the Magyar *Feher* (Hungarian for "White"); Paul was baptized and sent to a Christian school; the family never visited the grand Budapest synagogue on Dohány Utca; and they never hung a mezuzah on their door. Though Friday nights were often spent eating dinner with extended family, as per the Jewish tradition, no religion was ever discussed or performed.

Shortly after the invasion, Paul knew, even at his young age, that something extraordinary was happening. "I saw bodies floating down the Danube near our apartment," he told me years later. Family friends disappeared, and Otto, an executive at the state coal company, was removed from his job. Not before, however, the Gestapo took him out for an evening of beatings that left him with a permanent limp and no hearing in his left ear. The Gestapo put Otto into a work camp outside Budapest, while Rose and Paul, wearing yellow stars, waited for the nightmare to end. "You see up there?" Paul said, fifty years later, pointing to a second-story window in a fashionable part of Budapest near their former apartment. "Do you remember the Germans spitting on us, *anyu*?" he said, choking up and grabbing onto Rose's hand as though they were still in 1944 and on the run.

Otto was released from the work camp in the summer of 1944, as a part of a general "amnesty." It was clear that the amnesty would not last, and that the German and Hungarian Nazis were accelerating the deportation of the remaining Hungarian Jews, in a desire to forever "solve" the Jewish question. The Jews were soon ordered into a newly created ghetto—most of Otto's extended family complied, but Rose refused. It would be a fateful choice. The Nazis culled the ghetto shortly thereafter. Twenty thousand residents were brought to the banks of the Danube and shot; a large proportion of the remainder were shipped to Auschwitz. It is unknown into which group Otto's missing sisters and brothers fell.

The Fehers decided to run—they ripped off their yellow stars, left their comfortable apartment on the Danube, their live-in maid, concerts, and weekend chauffeured Mercedes rides in the country. Initially they fled to the countryside outside the city, to the farm of a non-Jewish couple who let them sleep in the barn for a few weeks. When the farmers became concerned about the potential repercussions for being caught hiding Jews, the Fehers fled again, this time back to Budapest where, thanks to renegade Swedish diplomat Raoul Wallenberg, they became "Swedes." The Fehers were given a place to stay in a Swedish safe house, and received legal reprieve from German threats of deportation.

The Wallenberg papers were a temporary lifesaver, but soon the Germans refused to respect the sanctity of either being Swedish or living in a diplomatic safe house—Jews were still Jews. The Fehers discarded the incriminating Swedish papers. Rose managed to conjure up German identification documents for the family. It was never clear how the seemingly frail woman I knew had managed to do this, and she took the secret to her grave. The anger and sadness in her eyes when asked to speak of the experience were enough to give me pause and to question whether I really wanted to know what she had to do in order to save her family.

The Fehers were bilingual in Hungarian and German, a product of the Austro-Hungarian aspects of Budapest and Otto's Viennese birthplace. Consequently, being taken for a German on the Budapest streets was not particularly difficult for either Paul or his mother; Rose's blond hair greatly aided the charade. Paul and Rose tried to use the new documents to establish a "normal" life amidst the chaos. It would not be so straightforward for Otto; according to the documents, he was a German soldier fighting on the Russian front. He had to go into hiding. German squatters had taken over their Danube home so the Fehers found another apartment, this one on the eastern side of Budapest; its coal cellar was its most important feature. It was in this cellar, out of sight behind a pile of wood and charcoal, that Otto hid until the end of the war. There were many close calls, and as the end of the war came into view, the Germans became even more insistent on searching for Jews—on many occasions coming into the apartment and then venturing into the Feher cellar, only to leave without uncovering Otto.

Even the end of the war would prove perilous for the Fehers. Their apartment abutted a railroad line that served as the front for much of the last weeks of the war. German troops had commandeered the balcony of the Feher apartment and erected a machine gun emplacement on it. Romanian soldiers working with the Soviet Army liberated the apartment in February 1945. The machine gun on the Feher balcony led the new occupiers to believe that German sympathizers, if not collaborators, lived in the building. The conquering soldiers rounded up all the men—including Otto who had left his hiding place as soon as the Germans departed—and marched them to a nearby field to be shot. Otto, who spoke French and some English, in addition to his two mother tongues, pleaded with the Romanians, trying to find a common language with one of his would-be executioners in order to explain the situation. His French finally worked. The soldiers believed the true yet almost unbelievable story, and he was released.

The war and occupation were over, and the Fehers were left to pick up the pieces. Despite their ordeal, they were lucky; of the two hundred and fifty thousand prewar Jews in Hungary, more than eighty thousand perished. The Fehers, like thousands of others, tried to recreate their former lives, even moving back into their old apartment. They had another child, Kati—baptizing her as well, "just to be safe." Kati would not even know that she was Jewish until her curiosity was piqued by a friend a decade later. Yet, in the end, it proved too hard to stay in Hungary; the memories were too raw, the future too uncertain, and so, in 1950, the Fehers left with a wave of immigrants bound for Australia. Otto and Rose were my grandparents, Paul my beloved uncle, and Kati (Katharine in English), is my mother.

Much less is known about the story of my father's family, the Polish side. Solomon Fox's mother died shortly after his birth in 1917, and his father, a deaf-mute porter, was unable to care for him. Solomon was adopted by his mother's brother-in-law, uncle Isaac Shmykowski. In the early 1920s, Isaac's prescience saw that his family would be better off away from the Pale. He moved his clan from their Warsaw home in 1924, when Solomon was seven. They were bound for South Africa; one wrong boat and two months later, the Shmykowskis found themselves in Brisbane, Australia, a world away from their initial target of Johannesburg, but fortunately even farther away from the terrors that would soon befall their native Poland. Isaac would become the "Most Reverend Isaac" and would help found Brisbane's Deshon Street Synagogue. In an assimilationist move, and to aid the spelling woes of any Australians who they encountered, Isaac soon changed the family name to "Smith." Solomon would go to school through age twelve before apprenticing himself to a local tailor, migrating south to Sydney with all of the newly renamed Smiths in 1939.

Tzippora Cajg, the daughter of a glazier, was the youngest of three and grew up in eastern Poland in the typical early twentieth-century shtetl of Zaklików. Already in the mid-1930s, with continuing anti-Semitism, the threat of impending war after Hitler's election next door, and with rumors of a Berlin-Moscow agreement to split Poland, the Cajgs thought it was time to leave. Though America was preferable, the family knew of people who had settled in Australia. The Cajgs sent Tzippora ahead to stay with an uncle who had recently arrived in Sydney. The other family members would continue working, raising funds for the voyage, and set sail as soon as Tzippora sent word. Eighteen-year-old Tzippora boarded a boat in Gdansk in late August 1939, bound for England and then onto Australia. It would be one of the last boats out of Poland before the German *Blitzkrieg* began on September 1.

Tzippora arrived in Sydney, and eagerly sent her family word to join her. They never did. And as rumors of the ruthless German occupation and the Polish work of *Einsatzgruppen* (Nazi death squads) slowly emerged from wartime Europe, Tzippora lost hope. With 90 percent of Poland's Jewish population decimated, and the Cajgs living so close to many of the concentration camps, the only conclusion that she was able to draw was the most obvious one. It would be twenty years before some of the truth emerged and Tzippora's fears were validated. Following a chance encounter with a fellow former Zaklików resident, she learned that the Jewish population of her native village had been exterminated. It would be another thirty years, sadly after her passing, that I would find out exactly what had happened. In early 2006, happenstance and the Internet put me in touch with a Zaklików survivor in Israel who knew Tzippora in Poland. He told me that on November 3, 1942, German troops rounded up Zaklików's Jews and locked them in the town's synagogue without any provisions. Days later, what was left of the group was deported en masse to the gas chambers at Belzec, east of nearby Lublin near the Ukrainian border. The Cajgs were among the deportees.

After arriving in Australia at the age of nineteen, Tzippora lapsed into a depressive state. Though depression did not prevent her from marrying Solomon in 1945, nor raising two children—my aunt Helen and my father Coleman—it remained with her for the rest of her life.

I grew up immersed in this history of loss. The Holocaust was all around me. My Hungarian grandfather passed away when I was very young, though his Gestapo limp remains etched in my memory. My uncle, especially as I grew older, did speak painfully of the experience, and even traveled to Budapest with me in the early 1990s. Yet, he divorced himself from other parts of his past—he changed his name to the decidedly Anglican "Farrer," and the only time he ever ventured into a synagogue was for my bar mitzvah and my sisters' bat mitzvahs. He never looked so awkward as when he was wearing a *kippah* (a skullcap). While my mother has long seemed ambivalent about her Judaism, she has remained deathly fearful of anti-Semitism in any of its guises and an avid, possibly addicted, reader of all things Holocaust and anti-Semitism—*I Was Mengele's Assistant, Hitler's Willing Executioners, IBM and the Holocaust*, the list goes on. I have always found her fascination with the topic odd and at times uncomfortable, yet strangely appropriate. My Hungarian grandmother refused to speak of the experience, and tried as hard as she could to avoid and even to erase her Judaism. I was never sure if she actually liked eating ham or was using it to buttress her gentile credentials. She was shocked when my mother decided to marry my father, a Polish, orthodox Jew—a mixed marriage if there ever was one.

My Polish family was far more outwardly Jewish than my Hungarian relatives, their own response to Holocaust losses. My father immersed himself in Judaism, involving himself in Jewish youth groups and Bible contests. According to my grandmother, he even contemplated becoming a rabbi—opting for medical school instead so that he wouldn't have to "sing for a living." Though my grandmother Tzippora was quiet and introspective for the entirety of the twenty-five years I knew her, my grandfather Sol filled in the silences and unknowns about what had happened in Europe with regular invective about the German "bastards" and the "bloody" Poles.

Even outside the family, I still could not get away from the Holocaust. Thousands of Jews had descended on Sydney after World War II, many straight from concentration camps or displaced person camps. They recreated a ghetto of their own, centered about Bondi Beach in Sydney's east, a place where I spent much of my childhood. As I look back, the combination of Holocaust survivors and Australian surf culture was bizarre, in part because the hot weather compelled short sleeves, forcing many to display their concentration camp tattoos as they drank coffee on the beach. It was hard not to stare at the numbers and letters and imagine what must have happened to them and their families.

Even after some of the immigrants became assimilated and successful, Germans remained persona non grata and the simple mention of Germany could spur outrage and denigration. One of the hardest tasks that my grandmother Rose was forced to endure was a demeaning, annual trip to the German consulate in the Woollhara neighborhood of Sydney (ironically in the heart of the Jewish zone). Every year she was forced to prove to the consul that she was still alive so that Germany would continue providing the nauseatingly small "survivor's check" that Berlin had authorized to atone for her wartime hardships. My uncle Paul refused to participate in any restitution scheme or accept any German apology. I remember as a young boy accompanying my grandmother on many of her annual visits. I am not sure if I ever saw such a chart, but I imagined the table the Germans used, listing the wartime "harms" endured (hiding, physical injury, concentration camp inmate, and so forth) with a corresponding neat arrow pointing to how much compensation each "wrong" merited. As a posthumous insult to my grandmother—and a fitting postscript to the indignity of the annual visits—the German government demanded refund of a small overpayment made to my grandmother in the months after her death.

It went without saying that, when mentioned, survivors spoke of Nuremberg in reverential tones, complaining only that the Germans did not deserve the quality of justice provided. I adopted this view of Nuremberg as my own. It solidified as I grew older, as I visited concentration camps, the Yad Vashem Holocaust memorial in Jerusalem, and studied Jewish communities lost throughout Europe. Nuremberg was the gold standard of how one deals with such crimes. The legacy of Nuremberg, in a very real, visceral way, alleviated some of the discomfort I felt toward the Holocaust.

The Yugoslav wars of 1991–2001 forced me to question the relationship I had with the Holocaust, as well as how I believed the world needed (or at least *I* needed) to address unconscionable pasts so as to face the future. The only memory I had of Yugoslavia before the war was the 1984 Sarajevo Olympics. I vividly remember watching Jayne Torvill and Christopher Dean's amazing ice dancing performance to Maurice Ravel's *Boléro,* and my grandmother Rose sitting behind me intoning in her distinct Budapest/Australian patois how "*é-lay-gaant*" she thought the skaters were.

My happy association of *Boléro* and ice skates to the Balkans was dashed in the summer of 1991, as stories of slaughter began to emerge. If the reports I read were only partly accurate, the brutality between Serbs, Croats, Bosniaks (Muslims), and others was terrifying. I was angered by what I saw and read and jarred by pictures that emerged of emaciated prisoners in what looked too much like concentration camps. At first, I was not sure what the correct response was, other than an urgent need to intervene to stop the war. But even on that topic, I was a little unsure. After all, my uncle was quick to tell me how nasty the Croatians had been to the Jews during World War II, doing the Nazi's "cleansing" work with relish and creativity. The Serbs, and in particular the various leaders of the Serbian Orthodox Church, also had a long history of callousness toward Jews. What I had read of the Bosnian Muslims ("Bosniaks") suggested that their leaders' relationships with the Nazis had been warm and that many had supported the Nazi goal for a *Judenfrei* Balkans.

Yet, as the scope of the calamity became clearer, my reticence to act quickly ceased. When the world reaction seemed to settle on a legal solution to the calamity—a continuance of the majesty of Nuremberg no less—I thought it seemed right. If Nuremberg provided justice to the Germans and the Jews, then this new court—the International Criminal Tribunal for the Former Yugoslavia—would do the same for the Serbs, Croats, and Muslims of the Balkans. So be it, and so it sat for ten years. As time passed, my belief in international solutions to the world's thorniest problems continued to grow, informing my professional life—sending me first to work at the World Bank, then the Organization for Economic Cooperation and Development (OECD), and finally to the secretariat staff of the United Nations. The more I worked in the international realm, the more I saw the power of law to set the foundation for growth and development, and to provide a means to right wrongs. I finally realized that if I believed in such law I needed to learn more about it—law school was the next, obvious stop. Yet, it was there that my perspective changed.

After my first year at law school, I spent the summer months in The Hague, working at the American Embassy's legal office, which is charged with managing the United States' relationship with the Yugoslavia tribunal. I was fascinated by the workings of the tribunal, and being at the embassy gave me unparalleled access both to the Court and its myriad personalities. Along with my colleagues, I met several times with the chief prosecutor, the president of the Court, the registrar, and lawyers and staff throughout the organization.

In the course of my meetings, I became troubled by aspects of what I saw. The pace of trials was glacial, the quality of defense at times questionable, and the extreme involvement of outside parties (nongovernmental organizations and governments) in the Court's work was jarring. My discomfort peaked, however, only after speaking with Balkan citizens, and those who had spent considerable time in the former Yugoslavia; I began to recognize a widening gulf between the Court's proud self-perception of its work and the decidedly more skeptical assessment that had developed among the very people it was trying to help. Those with experience in the region bemoaned many of the same problems I observed, along with others regarding the impact of the Court on the ground. I was still an unquestioned believer in the power of international criminal law as a tool of recovery after a violent conflict, so I decided to go the Balkans to see just what the problem was. Why did the tribunal not "take" when its Nuremberg ancestor had worked so well?

Since 2004, I have made several trips to the region, first to Belgrade, Sarajevo, and Novi Sad, and then a longer stay in Zagreb, back to Sarajevo, up to Ljubljana, and then to Skopje, Pristina, Podgorica, Brčko, Banja Luka, Tuzla, Mostar, Dubrovnik, Osijek, and many other cities and villages in between. I have spoken with scores of people, from the "official" community of government representatives, diplomats, and aid workers, and the "unofficial" community of academics, students, lawyers, victims, and perpetrators.

The first thing I noticed was that the separation between the Yugoslavia tribunal and the Balkans, which I had sensed in The Hague, was even wider than I had imagined. The Court has a troubling reputation throughout the region; few people were satisfied with the body, and even fewer trusted it. At various times in the court's tenure, as many as three-quarters of Serbs in Serbia and more than 95 percent of Serbs living inside Bosnia have expressed little faith in the Court.[1] Eighty percent of Croats and more than 50 percent of Bosniaks have viewed the Court as unjust.[2] Even those who might trust the Court nonetheless complain: some bemoan the slow pace of trials; others say that sentenced war criminals are coddled; and many protest about the politics of the Court's behavior, and are angered by what they see as a patronizing Court forcing the removal of cases, criminals, and justice from the region.

Despite the strength of people's concern about—and exasperation with—The Hague, the lack of knowledge of basic facts about the Court was also jarring, which represented yet another component of the distance between the tribunal and its people. This ignorance is hardly the Balkan residents' fault because the Court has established few outreach programs to the region. Balkan-based Court offices only opened a decade or more after the tribunal had been in operation; furthermore, the Court's governing statute was not translated into the local languages until the tribunal was already five years old. Consequently, though no less disconcerting, it is unsurprising that few people in the Balkans can articulate the Court's goals or profess an understanding of how the body operates. Fewer still are aware that the tribunal was designed as an ad hoc rather than a permanent court, and is set to close in 2010. The Court's budget, though a public record, is largely unknown on the ground, with gasps of amazement the common reaction when the truth is revealed.

As one Sarajevo law student told me, after he had recovered from the shock of how much the ICTY costs every year—an amount he had no inkling of until I showed him the accounts (nearly $280 million for 2006–2007)—"For that amount, the entire judicial system of the Balkans could have been reconstructed." And, indeed, this investment in The Hague—which will total more than $2 billion by the time the Court closes—made an additional aspect of the gulf between the Court and the region even starker. While the Court in The Hague is well appointed, well resourced, and as modern a judicial institution as one could find anywhere in the world, the justice systems in the Balkans remain languishing. The justice system in most of the former Yugoslavia—ranging from courtroom facilities, to legal education, to police reform—remains only minimally improved since the days following the civil war.

After realizing the extent of the separation between the Court and the region, my second discovery was more about myself—and Nuremberg—than about the Balkans. On my first visit, in my first meetings, I recognized the emotional scars of victimhood and, even more clearly, I recognized the Bosniaks' and Croats' feelings for the Serbs—they were eerily similar to the feelings I still harbored for Germans. I was compelled to recognize that Nuremberg, and whatever else followed, had failed to change my mind about Germans or Germany. Looking back I should have suspected this—an avid traveler in Western Europe, I studiously avoided Germany, felt a knot in my stomach when I heard the German language, and was uneasy about buying German products. It took meeting with Balkan citizens who had just been through their own horrors for me to realize that Nuremberg itself did not "take" in me. I did not feel that "justice" had been done. I am not alone. As evidenced by the partial walkout by members of the Israeli parliament when German chancellor Angela Merkel addressed the Knesset in March 2008, to continuing debates in Israel and the Jewish diaspora about whether Hitler's favorite composer, Wagner, ought to be enjoyed or even played, clearly Jews all over the world, and especially those close to the suffering of World War II, remain uneasy, uncertain, and at times unwilling to move on. I noted a similar feeling—if more intense as the harms were more recent—in my meetings with Croats, Bosniaks, and even Serbs, many of whom ardently and fearfully disdained the "other."

Additionally, I began to wonder what wider purpose Nuremberg had actually served. If the horrific stories I was being told and reading about the Balkans were true, it was all too evident that the long-term deterrent effect of Nuremberg had clearly faltered. If it had faltered in Europe—five hundred miles from the site of the Nuremberg trials—it made sense that its message of "never again" was even more muted in regions farther removed from both the Holocaust and the ensuing legal response.

I began to question whether a continuation of Nuremberg was the right answer.

While in the Balkans, I reflected on my relationship with the Germans and came to two sad conclusions. First, the real goal of a post-conflict tribunal had to be helping to create an environment for moving on. The past was painful, miserable, and, most importantly, unchangeable. The retrospective and at times paternalistic nature of The Hague's work did not seem to be helping the healing process in the Balkans. All of political life, and significant aspects of economic and even personal life in so many parts of the Balkans, were stuck in replaying the events of the 1990s or before, rather than focusing on tomorrow. Some in the Balkans recognized this, but the sometime-overbearing style of the tribunal and the caustic actions of some promoters of international justice made it difficult for those voices to be heard.

Second, I realized that there were two ways to create an environment that would help the aggrieved to move on. The first was the German model, in which reconciliation between Jew and German was essentially unneeded from a practical perspective. The Nazi attempt at "solving" their Jewish problem had been largely successful, and much of the Jewish population of Central and Eastern Europe had been killed or, like the Fehers, had decided to leave after the war. The likelihood of a Berliner having to live and work with Jews during the decades after World War II was very low. As such, it is not surprising that real reconciliation has been tepid at best and many Jews remain wary of Germany and Germans more than sixty years after the end of the war.

This ethnic separation is not the case in much of the Balkans. Some parts of the Yugoslav wars' "ethnic cleansing" programs—which I soon found had been conducted to various effect by all parties to the war—had worked; and much as Berliners found after World War II, many former Yugoslavs now lived in decidedly homogenous districts. But, in the heart of the region—in Bosnia, Kosovo, Macedonia, and parts of Croatia and Serbia—citizens still have to live with and work with a heterogeneous population. Consequently, a second model of "true" reconciliation was the only way forward.

While The Hague's inability to work toward reconciliation became ever clearer as I traveled more in the region, I nevertheless began to see hopeful signs—seemingly ignored by the international community—that there were growing local, Balkan attempts toward postwar justice and reconciliation. Even amidst a dilapidated local justice system that had received little support, far-sighted and brave politicians, civil society leaders, lawyers, academics, and others were overcoming their feelings for the "other" and working on reconstructing a life for themselves and their children. The more I dug in the Balkans, the more I understood both the problems of The Hague and the potential for other, domestically informed "solutions" to Yugoslavia's past. Many of these solutions were already being attempted in the shadow of The Hague. I found despair in the Balkans regarding how the international community treats or ignores the region. But I also found hope that the Balkan citizens themselves—operating *in* the Balkans—would be able to face the horrors not just of the 1990s, but also of conflicts with much deeper roots.

The personal aspect of this story is that in the hope I found in these regions, I began to have hope for my own feelings, which I recognized were still stuck in 1945. If these individuals could emerge from their pasts to focus on the future, perhaps I could as well.

It has been a hard journey questioning Nuremberg and my own feelings for the aftermath of World War II. It has created significant cognitive dissonance for me, challenging me to rethink understandings that I had never thought to doubt. In the course of this project, I have often surmised that my grandparents would not find my examination or conclusions to their liking. Nuremberg, and what it did for both publicizing the Holocaust and the German wrongs, was sacred. While my Balkan experience made me begin to question international justice, my views were solidified after studying African regions similarly scarred by recent violence and similarly subjected to international justice. Countries like Rwanda and Sierra Leone have also been pregnant with the possibility for local solutions to their tragic pasts—solutions also seemingly regularly shut down and shut out by the international community.

I began to believe that in the Balkans and war-torn parts of Africa, there was perhaps a wider, more universal lesson to be learned. I have come to believe that the best potential for making the hopes of Nuremberg and the aspirations of hopes of international justice a reality comes from a true acceptance of wrongdoing and a consequent desire to move on by the people most involved, and working toward these solutions in their homes, rather than continued vilification and ostracism from on high. Being assured that "never again" is really "never again" is what everyone desires, most of all those directly impacted by such violence. With ethnic tension still boiling in the Balkans, Rwanda, and Sierra Leone after years of international justice at work, and continued ethnic violence in many other parts of the world—with the new International Criminal Court playing a questionable role in adding fuel to some conflicts—we are clearly not "there" yet. I hope to serve my grandparents' memory best by providing an honest, heartfelt examination of how we may get from "here" to "there."

The story that emerged from my travels and the thesis of this book is that there are severe and at times irreconcilable problems with international justice. These problems have appeared in each of the world's attempts to provide such justice in the wake of atrocities. Just as importantly, the long-overlooked domestic systems in even the most shattered of states can almost always be leveraged to provide the "justice" needed by victims, perpetrators, and their societies.

What I had not expected was that the debate in the United States and elsewhere about international justice would be so heated. It was not just my grandparents who may have disagreed with my questioning of Nuremberg and international justice; an unexpectedly broad coalition had emerged from all walks of life that seemed as animated by this issue as I was. In order to get "there" I would have to understand, immerse myself, and be buffeted by the debate; this would be the next step on my journey.

Chapter 2

AN ODD, MISGUIDED DEBATE

Is it Really International Justice or No Justice?

Khrushchev's shoe, banged forcefully on his desk in the General Assembly hall of the United Nations, may have made a bigger initial impression. But in the annals of public displays at the UN, it would be hard to beat the lasting impact of Colin Powell's presentation to the fifteen-member UN Security Council on February 5, 2003. It was in Powell's fastidious, earnest presentation that Wednesday morning, replete with props (vials of anthrax no less), forty-five PowerPoint slides, and sober agreement from his flanks—the director of the Central Intelligence Agency and the US ambassador to the UN sitting stone-faced behind him—that Secretary of State Powell delivered the White House's urgent demand that the UN authorize the removal of Saddam Hussein from power in Iraq.

The secretary's relationship with the UN and the world community, if not the tone of his entire tenure in office, was overshadowed by that presentation. The presentation, and the military and political firestorm that followed it, arguably obscured an equally historic statement Powell made nineteen months later; this time it was before the twenty-one members of the US Senate Foreign Relations Committee. That afternoon, the committee was conducting hearings on the deteriorating situation in the Darfur region of western Sudan. Millions of civilians had been displaced by the fighting between Khartoum-backed Arab militias, the "Jingaweit," and African rebels. First-hand reports and wider surveys by the UN and others indicated that the Jingaweit was likely engaging in "ethnic cleansing," attempting to rid the oil-rich region of African interlopers.

It was a far less flashy presentation; no props, no PowerPoint, just a few aerial photos. Powell told the committee about the State Department's examination of the Jingaweit's actions. He spoke of the investigation he had authorized, in particular the interviewing of 1,136 refugees who were cowering in camps across the border in Chad. The refugees told stories of killings, rapes, atrocities, and concerted efforts to wipe out African villages. The secretary reviewed the evidence and made the jump that the international community had yet been unwilling to make, ascribing to the activities in Darfur the most serious label at his disposal: "genocide." "When we reviewed the evidence," Powell said, "we concluded—I concluded—that genocide has been committed in Darfur . . . and that genocide may still be occurring."[1]

The House of Representatives and the Senate both passed resolutions supporting Powell's assertion. Though some legal theorists quibbled, claiming that the attacks in Darfur did not exhibit all of the elements of the crime, and the absence of any subsequent bona fide effort by the United States and others to stop the genocide diminishes the impact of the secretary's designation, neither takes away from the importance of Powell's statement. The fact remains that Powell, and through him the United States, went further and faster than any other state to find a serious violation of human rights and to demand redress.

Though the war in Iraq and the wider War on Terror obscure this history, Powell's statement continued a longstanding trend in US politics and society, in which the Americans have been at the forefront of international human rights protection. During the US Civil War, the Union Army implemented the first modern code of conduct for soldiers, demanding ethical treatment of others on the battlefield and of prisoners of war. Americans were instrumental in establishing Nuremberg and the Tokyo Trials after World War II, with an American serving as the chief prosecutor in each and with the greatest support (financial and intellectual) for the endeavors coming from Washington, DC. Americans were also instrumental in the post–World War II strengthening of human rights rules around the world. After the Cold War, they played a central role in addressing the carnage in Yugoslavia and Rwanda.

To some, this long history of support for human rights and work toward both preventing abuses and punishing them if they occur made the George W. Bush administration's eight-year retreat from global justice galling. Many saw the Bush administration manifest a continuous and unprecedented neglect for human rights, with numerous examples: the infamous torture memos; the "legal" conclusion that the Geneva Conventions were "quaint"; and abuses at Guantanamo Bay, Abu Ghraib, and in various other countries achieved via the "extraordinary renditions" of suspected terrorists to states where they would be tortured on Washington's behalf.

Journalists, pundits, and human rights activists often append the Bush administration's categorical opposition to the International Criminal Court (ICC) to this list of wrongs. The Hague-based ICC is the first permanent international criminal court; all previous international judicial institutions—be they the tribunals at Nuremberg or Tokyo after World War II or the current courts prosecuting abuses that occurred in Yugoslavia and Rwanda in the 1990s—have been intentionally short-lived organizations, erected for a limited period to address crimes that occurred in a specific circumstance. In contrast, the ICC is a standing court charged with the prosecution of a litany of crimes: "war crimes," "grave breaches," "crimes against humanity," and "aggression." It does not spring from a particular war or battle. Rather, it is designed to be a permanent feature of the global landscape, deterring and punishing crimes. For many, the ICC is the ultimate marker that the international community is serious about protecting human rights and furthering a global culture based on the rule of law.

The ICC has been a long time in coming. Ideas for an international court percolated more than a century ago, bubbling more vigorously at the end of World War I, and again at the end of World War

II. Though put into hibernation during the Cold War, the global conversation resumed once the Berlin Wall fell. In 1989, the UN General Assembly asked the UN International Law Commission (ILC) to author a treaty for a standing international criminal tribunal. Over the following nine years the commission held several laborious rounds of negotiations and discussions and finally completed a draft document. During the summer of 1998, the document was presented to a diplomatic conference in Rome, and the attending states—consisting of nearly every country in the world—proceeded to negotiate, argue, and finally hammer out the statute that would govern the new institution.

During the Clinton administration, United States diplomats played a leading (some would again claim *the* leading) role in promoting the Court and finalizing its founding documents. The US delegation to the final talks in Rome was more than a hundred strong. By far it was the largest group in attendance. It was a high-profile, powerful interagency group, led by Ambassador David Scheffer, the recently appointed, inaugural ambassador-at-large for war crimes. Indeed, that Clinton had only created the position of ambassador-at-large for war crimes a few months earlier suggested his administration's growing concern for both the issue of crimes against humanity and the president's belief in the potential of institutions to deter and punish such crimes. Consequently, the White House empowered Scheffer to negotiate a strong, meaningful institution. Scheffer succeeded in his charge. While diplomatic conferences almost always serve to water down draft agreements, such weakening did not occur here. At the conclusion of the month-long conference, the end document was far stronger than the draft presented four weeks earlier. It was again primarily due to American insistence (and intransigence) that the document was as strong as it was. If not for the US delegation, the draft's definition of "crimes against humanity" would have been emasculated, due process guarantees in trials would have been dubious, and the institutional checks and balances would likely have been largely abandoned.[2]

Scheffer's work is all the more impressive given the extensive pressure he was under from Washington-based antagonists. Right-wing think tanks, academics, and others issued consistent criticism. The most legally significant venom came from North Carolina Republican Senator Jesse Helms, then the chair of the Senate Foreign Relations Committee (and thus an important player in the consequent ratification of any treaty), who was emphatic that the "American people distrust concepts like the International Criminal Court." "Why would Americans submit them[selves] to the judgment of an International Criminal Court a continent away comprised of mostly foreign judges elected by an international body made up of the membership of the UN General Assembly?" he asked. "It's not going to happen, my friends. It's not going to happen."[3]

Despite it all, the treaty was finalized in July and brought back to Washington, and on the last day of 2000, in the final month of his administration, President Clinton signed the ICC's treaty. But, barely a year into his first term, President George W. Bush had taken the brazen step of "unsigning" the treaty. His undersecretary of state (and soon to be UN ambassador) John Bolton declared it the happiest day of his professional life, later recalling his joy at being able to take a "big bottle of Wite-Out" to President Clinton's signature.[4] No treaty had ever been "unsigned," and though the international legal effect of his action was uncertain, how the new president felt about the Court was not. He was so predisposed against it that he was willing to engage in novel international legal action in order to remove this albatross from the necks of the American people. The media and international community cast rejection of the ICC as yet another outcome of the post-9/11 nativism, jingoism, and xenophobia that many argued had become the calling cards of the Bush administration. In the public's view, Colin Powell's association with the Bush decision to disown the Court, followed by Powell's active involvement in undermining the ICC (by securing special US immunity agreements from ICC member states), overshadowed the principled, pro–human rights stand the secretary would later take on Darfur.

A CLOSER LOOK — AN ODD DEBATE

The story of a Bush administration that turned its back on both traditional US leadership in international human rights and on wider progress toward international law has become gospel in some quarters. Yet, a closer look at the debates that occurred both in Washington and outside the Beltway about the ICC reveal that there was more (and less) to the Bush administration's rejection than was apparent.

First, regardless of John Bolton's views that the ICC was a "product of fuzzy-minded romanticism [and] not just naïve, but dangerous,"[5] it would be inaccurate to claim that the Bush administration's stance regarding the ICC was categorical. In fact, when the administration had the opportunity to land what might have been a devastating blow on the institution, it refrained from doing so. One of the primary means by which the ICC opens cases is via referral from the Security Council, a body in which the United States can exercise a veto. Yet, in March 2005, when Resolution 1593 was presented in the Council, passage of which would refer the situation in Darfur to the ICC for investigation, the United States chose not to kill the resolution via its veto. Instead, it abstained and allowed the resolution to pass. By making this choice, the United States empowered the nascent Court.

Second, it is a scantly reported fact that the arguments over the ICC have rarely been arguments between Republicans and Democrats. In fact, one could argue that the Bush administration's rejection of the treaty and the Republican Senate's failure to ratify the document in the eighteen months between Clinton's signing and Bush's unsigning were logical extensions of the criticisms that the *Clinton* administration had of the ICC.

It is noteworthy that at the Rome conference, when the finalized treaty came up for a vote by the assembled parties, the Clinton administration rejected it, despite its leading role in formulating it. One hundred and twenty states voted to ratify, but the United States, in accord with Libya and Sudan, were one of only seven attending states to vote against the final version. Adding to this confusion is the puzzling fact that there was no correlation among supporters (or detractors) between the level of human rights abuses perpetrated by states and the support by those states for the treaty. Thus, though China and Yemen voted against the document, states including Russia, Belarus, and Syria supported it.

Throughout the debates surrounding Rome, the Clinton administration officials played hardball. In one of the more brazen examples of their steamrolling negotiating tactics, Clinton's defense secretary William Cohen threatened to withdraw US forces from bases in the territory of states that did not support US proposals for limiting the Court. Later in the summer of 1998, as Ambassador Scheffer reflected on the document that had emerged in Rome, he told the Senate Foreign Relations Committee that the United States, in the end, could not vote for the treaty because it failed to address American concerns on core issues, ranging from the Court's power over nationals from states that did not sign the treaty, to the potential of politicized prosecutions; the final version, Scheffer said, led to "consequences that do not serve the cause of international justice."[6] Despite the lack of support, the document approved by the majority of the world's states was nonetheless sent to the White House for the president to either veto or endorse and pass onto the Senate for ratification. President Clinton did neither: he sat on the treaty for more than two years, refusing to sign or reject it. When he did finally sign it, he refused to send it to the Senate for ratification and added a written qualification to his endorsement that was as unprecedented as Bush's subsequent "unsigning" of the document. Clinton wrote that despite this signature he did "not recommend that [his] successor submit the Treaty to the Senate."[7]

Democrats and Republicans retained their alliance of convenience opposing the ICC even once it was clear that the treaty would never reach the Senate, let alone be ratified. And their opposition led to a surprisingly shrill, decidedly alarmist, one-sided debate. In May 2001, Congress passed the American Service Member's Protection Act, a classic "doth protest too much" bill designed to immunize all Americans from prosecution under the treaty, even if they committed crimes in the territory of a signatory state. The bill went further: it punished states that supported the ICC, mandating an automatic suspension of US military aid unless they provided written assurances that they would never extradite Americans to the ICC. Even more outrageous, it authorized the use of force to rescue Americans being held for trial by the ICC. This meant that Congress was authorizing an armed invasion of the Netherlands if the Court brought an American to the dock. This provision led some to call the measure "The Hague Invasion Act,"[8] and others to facetiously demand: "Where else will Bush invade?" "Will Bush invade Cambridgeshire?" an English newspaper queried. Secretary of Defense Donald Rumsfeld ignored the criticism and supported "The Hague Invasion Act" sobriquet. He argued that any attempt to turn a US national over to the ICC would be "regarded as illegitimate" and that, "We must be ready to defend our people, our interests, and our way of life."[9]

The bill passed both houses of Congress by huge margins: in the Senate, it received seventy-five votes (uniting the most unlikely of members: senators Frist, Santorum, and Domenici on the right, allied, perhaps for the first time with the likes of senators Schumer, Clinton, and Feinstein on the left); in the House, it passed with two hundred and eighty affirmative votes.

What has also been strange about the debate is how much the ICC and international justice raised concerns not just in Congress, or among the foreign policy/international law glitterati of Washington, or the academy but also among those who had rarely been at the forefront of the foreign policy debate. In short, the ICC and international justice have been subjects that "play in Peoria." Well before 9/11 brought the foreign policy debate to Main Street, local newspapers and their readers throughout the United States were animated and concerned enough to make their voices heard on the subject.

And so it was that in the August 1, 1998, edition of the Topeka *Capital Journal*, between discussions about the food at the Old Country Buffet and problems with the curb at the corner of Quincy and Eighth (the one in front of the bank) that Bob Zimmerman of Hoyt, Kansas, (population 571) proclaimed that President Clinton's seeming support for the Court was an "impeachable offense."[10] The Omaha *World Herald* penned an editorial on December 30, 2000, under the headline "No to a World Court" urging the United States to resist the "siren song" of internationalists and not join the body whose "high-minded sentiments" hid "an agenda hostile to US interests."[11] The Burlington *Free Press* published a letter to the editor a week earlier in which John Otis of Springfield, Vermont, argued that the Court was "but another dangerous step toward the degeneration of our Constitution, our national sovereignty, and our resulting dependency on global domination."[12] The Sarasota *Herald Tribune* published a letter under the headline "Ratifying ICC Treasonous," which posited that Clinton's signing of the treaty puts us "on notice that we are threatened by injustice for all."[13] The Kansas City *Star* criticized the "Flawed War Crimes Treaty,"[14] the El Paso *Times*[15] called the ICC the misguided goal of "one-world-order radicals," the Springfield, Illinois *State Journal-Register* proclaimed that "Sometimes Treaties are Worthless,"[16] the Bismarck *Tribune* warned that the ICC threatened to "Sell . . . Our Country Down the River,"[17] and Augusta, Georgia's *Chronicle*[18] published two editorials on the subject, under the headlines "Threat to the Constitution" and "Stop the Global Monster Taking Shape in Rome."[19] These were among the dozens of small, hometown papers that joined the chorus with editorials and letters to the editor, each more alarmist than the next.

Some opponents have not been satisfied with merely publishing their views. In Utah, the state House of Representatives—whose role in federal foreign policy is somewhat minimal—easily passed, on a bipartisan basis, a scathing rebuke of the ICC. It asked the Utah congressional delegation to rescind American membership in the UN as a whole in large part because of the sovereignty the ICC was supposedly stripping from the United States.[20]

Though the overall tone of the conventional wisdom may have been hyperbolic anxiety, there have also been loud voices outside Washington agitating *for* the Court. While some of the debate was measured—in 1995 the editorial board of the Roanoke *Times* simply argued that the world needed a new court "to deal with crimes against humanity"[21]—proponents regularly matched opponents with their own brand of histrionics, demonizing the United States while deifying the Court. Mary Helen Gerwin of Lebanon, Ohio, wrote that the United States' failure to support the Court made it the "biggest rogue nation of all."[22] Jack Kirkwood of Beaverton, Oregon, argued that there was "not a single valid argument why the United States should not cooperate with the International Criminal Court," since the body would "deter future genocide, war crimes, and crimes against humanity."[23]

As odd a topic it must be to rouse usually mild-mannered middle America and to ignore traditional political alliances to such a degree that Jesse Helms and Bill Clinton ended up as allies, the debate about the ICC and international justice continues to subvert traditional groupings further. Once one realizes that international justice is, at its heart, a form of globalization, the debate becomes even more aberrant. Frequent and vociferous "antiglobalization" critiques come from those who see globalization as a façade from behind which wealthy states impose "universal" (i.e., "Western") values on the rest of the world. Yet many of the very individuals and organizations that forcibly oppose globalization support an international court and an international justice system.

For instance, a key example of the antiglobalization critique arises in debates about economic development and in particular the utility of the World Bank's "Washington Consensus" in aiding growth in the developing world. Broadly, the Washington Consensus advocates that there is but one path to economic prosperity for poor countries: the broad removal of the government from the economy and the unshackling of state controls in order to allow capitalism to run more freely. This approach has, to be kind, only recorded modest success. Some of its more persuasive critics trace the Washington Consensus's difficulties to the fact that in its application the World Bank mandates homogenous solutions for heterogeneous problems, with often devastating results. It is in part the resulting inequity of the Washington Consensus that has led some to riot and has caused the annual World Bank meetings to become armed camps, with shouting protesters hurling abuse at the world's bankers and finance ministers.

What is odd about the often-raucous community of crusaders against the one-size-fits-all approach of development efforts is that in its membership is found some of the most ardent proponents of an international court. For example, London School of Economics professor David Held argues:

> There is, in fact, no single pre-ordained route or set of policy prescriptions to economic development. Knowledge of local conditions, experimentation with suitable domestic institutions and agencies and the nurturing of internal economic integration [are critical to economic growth].[24]

Yet, later in the same work he posits that

> all those who systematically violate the sanctity of life and human rights must be brought speedily and firmly before an international criminal court . . . that . . . can deliver justice.[25]

This duality of messages is also clear outside academia in the activist community. In a 2001 interview, Chilean activist Victor Hugo de la Fuente described his opposition to the Washington Consensus in a slightly different manner. He argued that the problem with the World Bank and the International Monetary Fund (IMF) is that they "attempt to impose capitalism and neoliberal globalization as the only system and path possible for humankind."[26] De la Fuente defended his objections to the Washington Consensus by stating that "antiglobalization provides for other paths [which is why t]oday more than ever it is necessary to have international bodies like . . . an International Criminal Court to help resolve conflicts and to prevent the law of the strongest from being imposed."[27] Antiglobalization activist Medea Benjamin concurs with de la Fuente, bemoaning how the IMF and the World Bank have "undemocratically" imposed their will on countries,[28] yet she too supports the notion of an international criminal court system.[29]

It seems ironic, if not mutually incompatible, to campaign against the homogenizing globalization mandated by the World Bank while militating for an international criminal court. After all, as undemocratic as the World Bank's imposition of neoliberal policies on the developing world has been, the International Criminal Court's imposition of justice from on high is every bit as antidemocratic. The ICC's judges are as answerable to victims and defendants as the World Bank's development economists are to those in poverty, which means not very answerable at all. Moreover, just as specific characteristics of a recipient nation may make certain development strategies more or less successful, this seems even more the case for justice: one size most certainly does not fit all. Yet, the ICC's justice, much like the World Bank's prescriptions, is being promoted "as the only system and path possible for humankind." The ICC will be the same court, with the same judges, applying the same law, no matter from where a defendant emerges or in what context crimes are perpetrated. Indeed, to many of its supporters, the Court's application of uniform laws is among its most important features.

But, the importance of cultural relativism when prescribing solutions is clearer in the realm of justice than it is in that of economic development. After all, while economic growth can actually be measured by some objective means, "justice" cannot. There is no GNP of justice; it is almost solely what one makes of it, and while many a political philosopher has made a career of this equivocation, anthropologists outside the ivory tower have long been fascinated by different societies' vastly dissimilar (and often incompatible) understanding of "justice." Observers of many parts of Africa have marveled at the ability of various groups to forgive and reconcile, even with those who ravaged them during battle. For instance, as the civil wars in West Africa raged through the 1990s, rebels brutalized, raped, tortured, and maimed; yet many of their surviving victims have nonetheless sought reconciliation with their tormentors. "You cannot disown your own blood. It is like the prodigal son," said Chief Tamba Kortu, of the village of Wondedu in eastern Sierra Leone.[30] Is it the task of an international court to tell them they are wrong, that they need "justice" against the brothers they have welcomed back into their fold?

The problem for supporters of international justice comes from what "justice" is: philosophers tell us that justice, in its least adorned guise, requires that people get what they deserve. And this means that justice, even based on "universal" human rights, is a concept that may significantly diverge between peoples. As Eleanor Roosevelt put it, "universal human rights" begin in

> small places, close to home—so close and so small that they cannot be seen on any map of the world. Yet they are the world of the individual person: the neighborhood he lives in; the school or college he attends; the factory, farm or office where he works. Such are the places where every man, woman, and child seeks . . . justice. . . . Unless these rights have meaning there, they have little meaning anywhere.[31]

Once one concedes that the "international" justice being implemented has a decidedly Western imprint, one can view it even more starkly than Roosevelt's quote may suggest. Comparative psychologists have long noted that "the values that are most important to the West are least important worldwide."[32]

With this in mind, how can antiglobalization proponents argue that differences between states, peoples, and cultures need to be validated when it comes to economic development, but not when it comes to providing justice? Justice must have meaning at home or it has little meaning anywhere. And one system of justice is as unlikely to provide justice to all peoples, as one mode of economic development is to provide wealth for all peoples.

One does not need to venture down the path of baseless moral or legal relativism to see how mandating a single judicial mold can be troubling. In the Yugoslav context, the procedural device of "plea bargaining" is a powerful example. Plea bargains are tools that courts in the United States (and in very few other countries) use, in which prosecutors reduce charges and/or agree to reduce the length of requested sentences in exchange for a defendant's cooperation—perhaps in the form of pleading guilty or in helping the prosecutor build cases against other indictees. Plea bargaining is based on a conception of justice that is concerned with the quantitative nature of the justice delivered ("How many people have been convicted") compared with the qualitative nature ("Was each individual wrongdoer justly convicted and did he receive a sentence commensurate with his wrong?"). Though this model is not formally a part of the legal practice of international courts, it has nevertheless been used by many of its prosecutors, resulting in more convictions but not necessarily better convictions. For example, plea bargaining has been used at the International Criminal Tribunal for the Former Yugoslavia (the ICTY). There, a plea bargain resulted in the conviction of Bosnian Serb "Iron Lady" Biljana Plavsic on charges of crimes against humanity (she played a leading role in the ethnic cleansing of non-Serbs from Bosnia); her sentence was only eleven years, with time reduced due to her agreement to plead guilty. Though her plea allowed the prosecutor to focus on bringing more indictees to justice, people on the streets of Sarajevo and throughout the Balkans (where plea bargaining was once unknown) felt that—no matter the number of extra defendants imprisoned due to Plavsic's deal—the shortened sentence was a perversion of justice and that the amount of jail time should more accurately reflect the seriousness of her crime, rather than her usefulness to the court.

Law is filled with examples like plea bargaining. There are different, often mutually incompatible methods for achieving justice, methods about which people can reasonably disagree but methods that for many can be the difference between a feeling that justice has been done or justice has been perverted.

THE ELEPHANT THAT SHOULD BE IN THE ROOM: AN UNASKED QUESTION

Supporters and detractors of international justice have by and large avoided a key question: "Is international justice effective?" In other words, "Does it work?" Though there is no easy way to measure "effectiveness," what is remarkable about the international justice debate is that it has rarely even been attempted. The discussion has hurdled this fundamental question in racing toward a conclusion that should never have been taken for granted. Only after an international solution can be shown to provide the "best" justice to victims, survivors, perpetrators, and their societies should there be a debate about whether to have another international court.

There are several reasons this question has not been asked in the American context. On Main Street, a key rationale seems to be that both supporters and detractors see international justice through the same lens as domestic justice and both broadly agree that domestic justice is "good." For supporters, that international justice provides the good of domestic law on an international stage is precisely why it should be championed; that domestic justice is good makes international justice more so. For detractors, the fact that international law is domestic law extrapolated is precisely the problem, as it ignores the unique building blocks—and Constitutional protections—that make US domestic law what it is. Neither side seems to acknowledge, however, how categorically different international justice is from its domestic cousin.

In the world of policy and government, where there is often a more nuanced understanding of the differences between international and domestic justice, there are two further reasons this initial question has been neglected. One reason is tactical and the other is substantive, and neither is persuasive. Strategically, it has made sense for supporters and detractors alike to avoid the question of international justice's efficacy, at least initially, if not permanently. For supporters, even inquiring about the effectiveness of international justice threatens the entire enterprise. An honest investigation may reveal difficulties, let alone nuances that would make international justice a tough sell. If the ICC and its justice is an unquestioned global good, the arguments are clearer. Many supporters have mutated the argument into the proposition "international justice or no justice," which has allowed them a broad brush to paint the ICC's detractors as "war-mongering," "isolationist," and "misinformed."

Meanwhile, when detractors even inquire about the effectiveness of international justice, supporters take the inquiry as a sign of openness to the endeavor. For those who see the ICC as a direct affront to American sovereignty, constitutional rights, motherhood, and apple pie, there can simply be no discussion. If the very topic is *verboten*, there is no need to discuss its practical merits or detriments. To even engage in such a debate is to concede some ground to supporters. For these reasons, this apparently staid, academic topic has managed to move the mild mannered to personal attack.

In short, investigating the effects of international justice requires a degree of nuance in the debate that neither side has been willing to concede. As a result, American politics has become stuck in a "prisoner's dilemma" resulting in a debate that has confused American allies, ostracized Washington in the world community, and added fodder to those who deplore the lack of intellectual depth in American national politics.

Again, it was the comparatively cerebral Clinton administration—not the Bush administration—that saw the most vociferous of these "nondebates." As a senior Clinton White House official told me, little debate on the merits of an international judicial system occurred, either leading up to the Rome conference or in the years between the treaty's completion and Clinton's signing. "Mentioning international justice sent everyone scurrying for the corners; there could be no discussion. Everybody just left the room," he recalled. Clinton's mealy-mouthed signing statement appended to the ICC treaty—in which he signed the document while simultaneously rejecting it—is a direct reflection of the uncomfortable *modus vivendi* the two sides forced on the White House. The Bush administration, in contrast, was not as equivocal but it too chose not to address the merits of any underlying system.

A substantive reason that this question has been avoided in political discourse is the difficulty of defining and measuring "justice," as mentioned above. Yet the difficulty in measuring justice seems a scant excuse for the whole American political establishment to simply forget the question of whether or not international justice is a good cause. Several government programs and policies are equally difficult to evaluate, yet questioning their effectiveness is a critical part of public debate. For instance, how does one measure "success" in education? Is it a certain pass rate on standardized tests? Is it the high school graduation rate? Is it literacy? There are competing definitions of success for education and indeed there is no reason to think that competing definitions of success could not be used to analyze the impact of international justice. To simply accept as received wisdom that international justice works is to put the institutional cart before the jurisprudential horse.

My purpose here is to turn the tables on the political discourse; though I will address, as needed, some of the arguments commonly raised by proponents and detractors alike, I will primarily be concerned with examining how international justice works—or does not work—on the ground. Thus the needed focus is not on whether international justice "cancels the sovereignty [the] republic stands for,"[33] or "erodes our borders by the acid of globalism."[34] The critical issue is not whether subscribing to international justice is needed for international harmony. Nor is the primary issue whether we should support multilateral institutions in an increasingly interdependent world.

The debate should be about the process and prospects of international justice, a system that is challenged by the mundane, such as its value for money, and the existential, such as its potentially negative impact on countries recovering from mass crimes and its "crowding out" of domestic solutions for rebuilding shattered societies. Some of the facts are stark: the international justice system achieves fewer than five convictions per year, and spends more than $20 million on each one. By some measures, this renders it the least efficient prosecutorial system in the history of recorded justice. And, while money and attention are lavished on the international stage, the international community has by and large not heeded the calls of the countries in which the crimes took place to assist them in rebuilding their own justice systems. The result is that in the target countries domestic justice systems are either nonexistent or drastically hobbled by a lack of resources decades after crimes have occurred. This in part speaks to an even more troubling characteristic of international justice: international justice consistently runs the risk of fomenting the very forces that led to atrocities in the first place, encouraging radicalism, and discouraging true reconciliation. This book will ask the question, why if the UN and the world community have seemingly definitively rejected the "tribunal" model for providing international justice, with senior UN officials decrying it as "politically and financially" nonviable, "costly, inefficient, and ineffective,"[35] and the world community more recently promoting different modes of postconflict justice, has the new International Criminal Court embraced so much of the old system?

Finally, the book will address the troubling separation between the international and the domestic in so many aspects of international justice. For instance, the advances in international law and human rights that the Yugoslavia, Rwanda, and other tribunals have produced are as trailblazing as they are heartening: individual responsibility has been established for the crime of genocide,[36] incitement to genocide has been deemed a war crime,[37] and rape has been found to be a form of genocide.[38] Despite this, it is often hard to see how this growth in international law has impacted the regions that gave rise to the violations on which the advancements were based. Nor, as importantly, is it clear how these advances have impacted other regions in which new crimes have continued to be committed. Further, there is the disconcerting fact that with few exceptions it is very hard to find consistent, vocal supporters of international judicial intervention among those for whom such intervention would seem to provide most benefit—the victims and survivors. It is telling that consistent support for such judicial intervention often comes primarily from outside the impacted regions.

The combination of all of these factors means that there is the real possibility that in its pursuit of international justice, the international community is leaving behind the states in whose name justice is being sought.

Chapter 3

LEFT BEHIND

The road from Sarajevo to Srebrenica is difficult to drive, even in the middle of summer. Road 19 stretches from the center of Bosnia and Herzegovina to its easternmost edge, winding up from the floor of the Sarajevo valley, between the five mountains surrounding the Bosnian capital, and down to the farming villages below. It has been largely repaired since the Yugoslav civil war saw tank treads, mortars, and mines ravage this vital thoroughfare. After three hundred kilometers of undulation, blind corners, and questionable paving, once the Serbian border is almost in sight, Road 19 meets the town of Milici; there the "main" road splits into an unnamed, still-smaller conduit, leading southeast toward the town of Srebrenica.

My wife and I had rented a car from the Sarajevo Holiday Inn early in the morning of July 11, 2005, and were not sure what to expect on the drive—our travels in formerly Communist Europe promised concrete, grey landscapes, and more concrete. It was cloudy and rainy as we left, seemingly confirming our expectations of what we would see. We did not expect, however, the streams, mountain passes, the occasional waterfall, and the verdant meadows extending to mountains that rose into misty skies. The scenes were straight out of the Brothers Grimm.

The environment made it easy to forget why we were here—to try to understand the brutal recent history of this country and its people. It all seemed so incongruous—the beauty of the surroundings, the friendliness of the people, and the seemingly painless mixing we saw in Sarajevo between Muslim, Croat, Serb, and others. Few places in the world can boast a mosque, synagogue, and Orthodox and Catholic churches in the same neighborhood, let alone within two hundred yards of each other. At the eastern edge of Ulica Ferhadija, Sarajevo's main walking artery, sits the Eternal Flame, lit to honor all those Sarajevans who died in World War II and dedicated to "South Slav" unity, seemingly irrespective of ethnic or religious persuasion. Meandering down Ferhadija to the east, one can tell to the meter where Christian Bosnia ends and Muslim Bosnia begins—the street name changes from "Ferhadija" to "Seraci," Central European polished cobblestone gives way to rougher, Turkish pavement, and the Sarajevo Cathedral and Viennese coffee shops are replaced by the Gazi Husrev Bey Mosque and ćevapi stalls. Despite the change in mindset, religion, and lifestyle between the two zones, the boundary is easily and frequently crossed; washing down a lunchtime burek (a tasty pastry available in cheese or Halal meat) with a cappuccino is a favorite pastime. "Tourist" Sarajevo, which is much, though far from all, of downtown, has been largely repaired, making one doubt, if only for a moment, how severe the recent conflict really was.

Yet there are reminders of the violence, and they quickly return you to your senses. Ten minutes out of Sarajevo, near the top of the first hill to the city's east is a large sign wishing drivers a welcome to Republika Srpska (Serbian Republic—RS), one of the three entities into which Bosnia and Herzegovina was split following the 1995 Dayton Peace Agreements. RS—if only in its name—is an all too clear reminder that the desires for ethnic homogeneity remain. The welcome sign itself is a marker of separation—the Serbs religiously use Cyrillic, while the Croats and Muslims use Latin characters. We were no longer going to "Srebrenica," we were now driving to "Сребреница." That made our Latinate map a bit harder to read, and we opted to follow a friendly wave from a car hopefully going the same way.

Much like almost any area of the Balkans, the picturesque scenery before us belied a horrific past. The region between Sarajevo and Srebrenica had the particular misfortune of playing host to interethnic and internecine fighting between all three of the major factions—Muslims, Croats, and Serbs—during the war. Driving farther into RS, we saw Mount Bjelasnica to the south, the site of the Olympic downhill races during the Sarajevo Games of 1984. While this symbol represents a peaceful time in the past of the formerly unified Yugoslavia—one of its last before the wars—it is also a reminder of what eventually became of the venues that hosted the Mahre brothers and Bill Johnson on the slopes, as well as the performances by Katarina Witt, Scott Hamilton, Jayne Torvill and Christopher Dean on the ice. The fighting had stained all these sites that had once been so full of hope. Billboards depicting the Olympic mascot, Vucko the Wolf, were riddled with bullet holes. The athletes' village in Dobrinja became a death trap, with residents of the once-stylish high-rises trapped in their apartments for months on end as rockets slammed into their buildings. The bobsled run was transformed into an artillery position before becoming littered with landmines. And the skiing facilities where Jure Franko won Yugoslavia's first Winter Olympic medal (a silver in the giant slalom) and "handicapped skiing" made its Olympic debut became a military base that was destroyed during a Serb retreat in August 1993. Back in Sarajevo, "Kosevo Stadium," the main Olympic venue, was converted into a makeshift morgue and today remains surrounded by a sprawling graveyard. Though *Sports Illustrated* dubbed the 1984 Games "the sweetest Winter Olympics of . . . all,"[1] the decay of its symbols proves the limits of such imposed togetherness.

Driving on, each village tells a sadly similar, almost numbing story. Mokro, at mile fourteen, was where Croatian security forces in October 1995 set upon the Serb inhabitants, raping and slaughtering dozens. Twenty-five miles farther east you pass Sokolac, where its once famed three-hundred-bed psychiatric hospital was so neglected and mined for parts during the war that 142 patients died or froze to death during the winter of 1992. We stopped for fuel at Vlasenica, a town that Serbs enthusiastically decimated after being whipped into a frenzy of fear amid rumors of a planned "jihad" against them by the town's Muslims. There were 18,699 Muslims in Vlasenica before the war, about 60 percent of the town's population; today, there are none.

Milici, for which we initially missed the turnoff because we could not decipher a road-sign ("Милиħи"), is home to a bauxite mine—a critical source of hard currency during the war. The town was a bitterly fought over because of this asset. It is most infamous as the location of one of the forced labor "concentration" camps operated by the Serbs; pictures of the camps' emaciated inmates so resembled those of the Nazi camps that the international community was shocked into action. Milici was also a site where Muslims killed and mutilated Serbs. In Simici, just south, a Croatian priest was shot in the head in September 1995, and five hundred meters farther is the village of Podravno that was burned to the ground by Muslims in September 1992, killing at least thirty-four Serbs. And so on, until Srebrenica. . . .

Srebrenica itself is relatively nondescript, having entered the popular consciousness solely as a synonym for the massacre that occurred there. It was the events at Srebrenica that finally cemented the addition of the phrase "ethnic cleansing" into the world's lexicon. In July 1995, Srebrenica was serving as one of the first UN-authorized "safe areas," providing protection to Muslims who were unfortunate enough to be living in the midst of an increasingly jingoistic Serb Bosnia. The Yugoslav civil war, which had erupted with Croatia's declaration of independence on June 25, 1991, and resulted in the steady disintegration of the entire country into seven, separate units, was coming to a steady close. The Dayton Treaty, which concluded the northern part of the war, was to be signed later in the year (Kosovo in the south would not flair up for another few years), and the independence of Croatia and Slovenia were faits accompli. Yet, many in the Serb leadership, both in Belgrade (Serbia "proper") and in the field ("Serb Bosnia"), remained bent on preserving and establishing a "Greater Serbia" that would link "Serbia" with regions in which Serbs had historically lived. Croatian independence subverted this goal, as did Croatia's simultaneous reclamation of "Serb" land. And it was never clear if the average Serb desired such an outcome. "Greater Serbia," however, continued to be the blight of non-Serbs in the middle of eastern Bosnia, a region traditionally home to a majority Serb population. As a result of UN and wider international complacency, unconscionable failures by the Dutch troop battalion who had been stationed in Srebrenica to protect it, and the tenacity of Bosnian Serb president Radovan Karadzic and his commander Ratko Mladic, Bosnian Serb troops moved into Srebrenica. With little resistance, they wiped out any semblance of a "safe" zone for non-Serbs.

Once they controlled the region, the Serbs set about "ethnically cleansing" the area. Serb forces destroyed the city's two mosques, defaced Islamic holy books, and perpetrated a mass killing on a scale that had not been seen in Europe since the end of World War II. In the space of a few days, centered around July 11, 1995, Bosnian Serb soldiers systematically and brutally killed 8,500 Muslim men and boys, forcing many to watch the slaughter of their sons or fathers. The attackers raped, assaulted, and otherwise abused thousands of Muslim women and girls.

While Srebrenica was just one of many senseless acts of the war, it is unique—and not simply because of the scope of the massacre. It is emblematic, not only of the war itself, but also of the aftermath of the war and, in particular, of the diplomatic reaction to the conflict. The international community did not engage in a unitary response to the Yugoslav crisis; initially it deployed the whole arsenal of international tools to attempt to placate and diffuse the situation. Various world leaders implored for "cooler heads to prevail," and the UN General Assembly and Security Council passed resolutions demanding a "cessation of violence." Dozens of negotiated ceasefires were made and broken. Arms embargoes were next, followed by wider sanctions, and then mandates for UN peacekeepers to be deployed to physically separate the warring parties.

Though each of these responses was important and demonstrated that the Yugoslav conflagration was not going unnoticed in the world community, the judicial response to the crimes became the centerpiece of international reaction to the crisis. For the first time since Nuremberg in 1946, an international war crimes tribunal was formed—under the aegis of the UN—with the goal of bringing justice and law to a region that evidently lacked both. It was a creative response that encapsulated the hopes of a post–Cold War (and pre-9/11) world. In May 1993, the International Criminal Tribunal for the former Yugoslavia was born in The Hague. An "ad hoc" court, the tribunal was designed to close once its tasks—and presumably the dispensation of justice—were complete.

In the Balkans, there was some early local support for the tribunal from all sides of the conflict. However, as the tribunal became more established and concentrated more of its operations in The Hague, residents of the former Yugoslavia began to sense that the body did not know the scope of its assigned "tasks" and many residents began to bridle as they saw the tribunal pursue justice with little reference to their needs. Balkan citizens soon expressed increasing dissatisfaction that they were standing on the sidelines rather than being active participants in the justice that the tribunal was ostensibly providing for them. As a result, over time an often-devastating disjuncture developed between the "justice" provided by the tribunal and the "justice" called for on the ground. If there is one consistency among the heterogeneity of the Balkans, it is that there is no group in the region—either the alleged perpetrators or their victims—that uniformly feels that the tribunal has delivered "justice." Many, in fact, doubt whether justice has even been the goal of the enterprise. Far from justice, for locals, the continuation of ethnic animosity since the tribunal's founding—and perhaps because of the tribunal—has led to even more sobering admissions. A senior UN official in the Balkans bluntly admitted to me that while the tribunal has taken some of the Balkans' "biggest thugs" off the streets, it clearly has not repaired Yugoslav society. "The ICTY has failed; ironically the Balkans are probably more likely to Balkanize now, than at any time since the war ended," he said. With Montenegro's separation from Serbia in June 2006, Kosovo's controversial declaration of independence in February 2008, and continued rumblings in various corners of multiethnic Bosnia, he may well be right.

Though officially only a part of the international response to the Balkans, the tribunal quickly became the focus of all international efforts, with almost all other aspects of international involvement—ranging from political redevelopment, to economic investment, to European integration—funneled through The Hague process. Everything became contingent upon the success of the Yugoslavia tribunal and the "cooperation" of the Balkan states with the body. As such, the disjuncture between the international community and the realities on the ground—a separation that directly allowed the Srebrenica massacre—became both the hallmark and Achilles' heel of the international reaction to the war in Yugoslavia.

At no time has this separation been clearer—or more debilitating—than during ceremonies that marked the ten-year anniversary of the massacre, held at Srebrenica in July 2005. We drove the three hundred kilometers from Sarajevo to attend the commemoration. From driving to the site, to the content of the ceremony, to its aftermath, the entire venture can be seen as a parable for the limits of the international response. Few things provided a clearer case of international hubris in the face of domestic suffering. And, within that unfortunate cadre, few things better exemplified the problem than the Audi A8.

Rather than the Mercedes S-Class, favored by leaders in the Middle East and Africa, or even the hulking Zil, the famed Soviet limousine still used in parts of Eastern Europe and the former Soviet Union, the car of choice for ferrying ministers of state around the former Yugoslavia is the black Audi. This is not just any Audi—it is the colossal, twelve-cylinder "A8," fitted with tinted windows, incomprehensibly wide tires, and diminutive flags waving from both sides of its front hood. These are fearsome, four-thousand-pound automobiles, just a turret short of being full-fledged tanks. Though the car already gives an impression of impenetrability, no minister or visiting dignitary ever rides in such a vehicle without a phalanx of police escorts, serving as ice breakers for the traffic ahead and a warning for those behind to give appropriate wake. When driving along a major thoroughfare, the A8 shrinks even the most massive, Communist architecture back to size. Being forced to make way for such a convoy on the streets of Sarajevo, Belgrade, or Zagreb is annoying; being forced to do so on the winding, impossibly narrow roads of rural eastern Bosnia is infuriating, dangerous, and a recipe for confrontation.

It was in these automobiles in the early morning of July 11, 2005, that diplomat after diplomat, politician after politician, raced toward Srebrenica, along the increasingly hazardous roads. Up to one hundred thousand Bosniaks were also trying to get to Srebrenica, driving from all corners of the former Yugoslavia in cars that were anything but the black Audis. In a cavalcade of derelict Communist engineering, they traveled in tiny, anachronistic Zastavas, Ladas, Dacias, Skodas, and the occasional East German Trabant, along with huge, rusty tour buses chartered for the occasion. The goal of the majority of these visitors was simply to pay their respects; for many, however, the purpose of the commemoration was far more personal. They came to Srebrenica to rebury family members whose bodies had been unearthed from one of the mass graves that dotted Srebrenica's outskirts. Their reburial would serve as the centerpiece in the commemorations. Everyone was to converge on a tiny plot of land outside Srebrenica, in Potocari, that was to be christened a "Peace Park."

The narrow, bumpy roads, damp rain, and questionable logistics at the Peace Park, conspired to turn the event into a mess. The parking lot, thanks to the morning's rain, consisted of a muddy bog that trapped any cars unfortunate enough to park in it—as we attempted to do. Security checks were chaotic and random—local, national, and international security forces were present, and were uncoordinated among themselves let alone with the sundry guards who had arrived with the dignitaries. Physically getting into the park was a laborious process, with the line quickly turning into a mosh pit. Exacerbating the problem was the fact that while the Bosniaks were driving to the site, they were told by countless police—who were present every two hundred yards all the way from Sarajevo to Srebrenica—to stay on the correct side of the road. The same officers dutifully, however, waved the politicians' black Audis to the empty, left side of the road. After a time, some Audi convoys went to the left side even before being officially invited to do so, confident in their diplomatic immunity to stop any intrusion on their way. With sirens blaring and flags waving, the politicians and diplomats streaked by the Bosniaks.

The result was that while many Bosniaks did make it to the event, tens of thousands were stuck in a virtual parking lot ten miles long, stretching from the outskirts of Potocari toward the Road 19 turnoff. While some seemed bemused by the delay, content with shrugging their shoulders, getting out of their cars and chain-smoking their way on foot, others were not so complacent. Anger boiled on the road, involving us in a minor riot as we attempted to return to Sarajevo. Indignant Bosniaks blocked the road, refusing to allow any cars to pass. We were the lead car in the block, and tempers—mine included—rose. "Why are you stopping us?" I asked. "We went to pay respects, and now you are making it impossible for us to get home. *We* didn't make it so you couldn't attend." One aggrieved Bosniak—who had driven "for hours" to get to Srebrenica—expressed his sympathy with our predicament but asked, "What else are we supposed to do? We have no other power. How else will 'they' get the message?" He pointed with his cigarette dismissively down the road to Srebrenica, his ash falling onto our car.

It was only after an hour of waiting and arguing, having our car pounded upon by angry fists, and finally insisting that the strikers let through an ambulance blaring behind us, that we escaped the blockade. Hundreds of cars behind us remained stuck. We learned later that many people at Srebrenica did not get back to Sarajevo until the next day. "They," of whom the protestor spoke, were the motley international officials from nearly fifty countries: including the US ambassador-at-large for war crimes, Pierre-Richard Prosper; the president of the Yugoslavia tribunal, Theodor Meron; the UN high representative to Bosnia and Herzegovina, Baron Ashdown of Norton-sub-Hamdon (known to locals as the "Viceroy of Bosnia"); and presidents and diplomats from all of the surrounding states and much of the European Union. "They" managed to get to the Peace Park—through creative and bullying driving or even helicoptering in—seemingly eager to congratulate themselves on a job well done and to be interviewed by the likes of Christiane Amanpour in the process.

And, the international community had much to be proud of. The international community had stopped the Balkan wars and in the process resurrected the moribund international criminal justice system. Standing in the Peace Park on the morning of July 11, 2005, it seemed that in large part due to the success of the Yugoslavia tribunal, the world was poised to enter into an era of true "international criminal justice," with the recently enacted Rome Treaty on the International Criminal Court leading the way.

But just as in the peacekeeping and peacemaking throughout the Balkans since 1995, the average people of the Balkans were left out. The ten-mile traffic jam was as much a sign of the poor planning surrounding the ten-year anniversary as it was a metaphor for the very real feelings of the average Balkan citizen. The international community had left them behind. The Hague process, of which the Yugoslavia tribunal was the centerpiece, was as foreign and impenetrable to the average Balkan as the Audis streaming past them.

Bosniak anger was not just at the failed organization of the anniversary event; it was a much wider, deeper frustration at the whole process. Though they may have found "peace," they did not have the stability, let alone the justice that The Hague process had promised. But how could they have? No one had ever asked them what they wanted or needed in order to feel that justice had been done.

Events barely a month later in Croatia made this breakdown even clearer and showed the degree to which Croatian feelings and understanding of recent history diverged from that of the international community. The Croats had also been left behind, though in a different manner. In August 2005, Croatia marked the ten-year anniversary of "Operation Storm," the military campaign widely recognized as one of the most "successful"—measured numerically and absolutely—

instances of ethnic cleansing of the Yugoslav wars. Twenty thousand Serb homes were torched, and over two hundred thousand ethnic Serbs fled from Croatia during the operation. Croat general Ante Gotovina's leadership in Operation Storm led to his indictment by The Hague. To many on the scene, the difference between this operation and Srebrenica was not only its massive scale, but also the "the degree of Western hand-wringing that [only] the latter . . . elicited."[2]

Though there were no international dignitaries at the Croat event, the proceedings attracted all of Croatia. Thousands of Croats gathered in Knin, the Dalmatian town on the Zagreb-Split railroad line that had served as the nerve center of the Serb community that had been marooned in an ethnically chauvinist, independent Croatia since 1991. Croatia's leaders mounted a great viewing stand. Twelve formations of Croatian Armed Forces units passed in review and US embassy officials reported to me that "everything that could fly" in the country was conscripted to provide for celebratory flyovers of the battlefield. In paroxysms of patriotism, "with banners, songs, and rousing speeches,"[3] leaders of Croatia spoke warmly of the brave soldiers who had reclaimed "Croatia for Croatians."

Croatian prime minister Ivo Sanader, a relative political moderate, proclaimed "[Operation] Storm . . . a magnificent action planned with the aim of liberating Croatian territory."[4] Though there was some veiled comments about "shameful acts" against Serbs that may have been committed, his tone was clearly of a black and white nature, and it was clear on which side the Croats and the Serbs each lay. Newspapers declared the "patriotic war . . . clean as a whistle."[5] Vladimir Seks, the speaker of the Croatian parliament intoned that the operation was "luminous [and] as pure as driven snow," the critical act in ridding Croatia of "Serb terror." "The truth [of Storm's glory] will not be darkened by anyone," he said, speaking over the booming applause that interrupted him a half-dozen times during his brief speech.[6] The city fathers of the town of Split, along the Adriatic coast, hung a huge poster of its favorite son, General Gotovina, framed by the words: "He is a hero. What are you?"[7] That the international community had branded Operation Storm a "war crime" and indicted Gotovina as a war criminal was ignored.

While the Bosniak and Croatian examples of the summer of 2005 are perhaps the clearest signs that Balkan citizens were out of step with the international community's wishes and beliefs—the former believing that justice had not been done, the latter believing that no justice needed to be done—one can see a similar disconnect throughout the former Yugoslavia between what the international community has tried to promote since 1995 and what exists on the ground. In Serbia, the tribunal's indictment and trial of nationalist leaders was meant to render them and their ideas illegitimate in front of their people. In this, the trials spectacularly backfired. Up until former president Slobodan Milosevic's death in March 2006, Serbia had the dubious distinction of having two of its largest political parties run by indicted war criminals: Milosevic's Socialists and, to his right, Vojislav Seselj's Radicals. Far from their parties losing their popular support, throughout both Milosevic's and Seselj's trials, their parties and their attendant philosophies only grew in strength. In September 2005, polling revealed that if elections had been held the Radicals would have won the balance of power—Radicals who have remained committed to a "Greater Serbia." Milosevic's death and "martyr" status only emboldened reactionary politics in Serbia.

In December 2006, thirty thousand Seselj supporters marched in Belgrade in support of their incarcerated leader. Though Seselj's Radicals lost in the February 2008 presidential elections, it was hardly a rejection of nationalist politics. His party won half the popular vote and the reformist leader who was elected, Boris Tadic, nonetheless remained beholden to a right-wing prime minister and parliamentary leader. Elections in May 2008 seemed to tip the balance further toward the reformists but the conservative parties nonetheless succeeded in winning more of the vote. Indeed, Milosevic's old party continued to hold the balance of power. Politics had stalemated and the conservative and reformist blocs had developed seemingly irreconcilable positions. The conservatives celebrate indicted war criminals and wish to turn their backs on the West and recapture Kosovo; the reformists see their future in the West, in Brussels as a part of the EU, and want to close the book on "Greater Serbia." The July 2008 Karadzic arrest and extradition to The Hague served to harden this schism. The Radical Party called the arrest "horrible," and another indication that Serbia was set to "disappear."[8] The reformist leadership, meanwhile, hailed the arrest, claiming it a critical step in Serbia's march toward the EU. The impasse led Ljiljana Smajlovic, the editor of Belgrade daily *Politika*, to lament, "Serbia is not going to be a stable or happy country in the next year."[9]

In newly independent Kosovo, Ramush Haradinaj enjoyed similar support, both before and perhaps especially after he was indicted for war crimes committed during the 1999–2000 Kosovo conflict. Few Albanian Kosovars believed his arrest was right. "It is unjust that Ramush and his friends, who are patriots, have been taken to The Hague knowing they defended our homes, liberated us, and brought freedom to Kosovo," said Hakif Hyseni, watching the tribunal on TV in a Pristina café.[10] Haradinaj served as Kosovo's prime minister prior to being called to The Hague, and then again *after* the tribunal allowed him to return home while awaiting trial. And, he was only one of the region's war criminals *qua* elected officials. In November 2007, Hashim Thaci, a former leader of the Kosovo Liberation Army, an organization that has had several of its other leaders indicted for war crimes, was overwhelmingly elected as Kosovo's prime minister. The Serbs in Kosovo presciently feared his platform of declaring independence, and refused to participate in the election. Since Kosovo's unilateral declaration of independence in February 2008, the situation between Serb and Albanian Kosovars has only deteriorated. But, in truth, even before the surge in Serb-Albanian violence that accompanied Kosovo's assertion of independence, interethnic violence had plagued the region, despite The Hague's work, and despite the presence of nearly twenty thousand NATO troops in the province.

There have been some brutal highlights in Kosovo. During 2005, an international mission—the Organization for Security and Cooperation in Europe (OSCE)—was bombed three times.[11] The OSCE attacks followed a bloody 2004 during which violence centered on the town of Mitrovica. There, following an alleged shooting of a Serb teenager and the retaliatory drowning of several Albanian children, 22 people were killed and over 500 others were injured, while 27 churches and monasteries were destroyed, and 4,100 citizens were displaced; NATO quelled the violence only after deploying an additional 1,000 solders.[12] More recently, Serbs attempting to return to their homes in the province have been attacked by Albanians—often with the knowledge or participation of officials. And the Serbs themselves have bolstered "hard-line Serbian radio stations," demanding the reintegration of Kosovo into Serbia at any price.[13]

In a sense, Kosovo's declaration of independence represents the final failure in reconciling the Albanian and Serb Kosovars. It is noteworthy that in the postindependence conflict, justice has been a flashpoint for discord among Kosovo Serbs. Anger and violence has been directed against the Mitrovica courthouse in northern Kosovo that the UN took over in 1999. Nikola Kabasic, a Serb judge at the courthouse until 1999, put his argument succinctly. Pointing to the UN-fortified court a few weeks after Kosovo had declared its independence, he stated that the Serbs will continue their "protest until that building is a court which belongs to the people who live here and who have a right to have a judiciary from their own community."[14] Neither side is in any mood to back down.

Though Kosovo and Serbia have been at the center of recent violence, over the past fifteen years most of the former Yugoslav states have seen riots and disturbances break out over war crimes trials and related matters. Ethnic-based violence—and attempts at such violence—have been distressingly common. In spring 2005, a car bomb was discovered outside the Office of the High Representative (the international community's chief representative in Bosnia) in Sarajevo and two bombs were discovered at the Srebrenica memorial a week before the ten-year anniversary commemorations. In Macedonia, a similar story of frozen conflict can be told: the ethnic enmity between Macedonians and Albanians that had led to the final "war" during the dissolution of

Yugoslavia remains and has also arguably strengthened. With few exceptions, "anti-Albanianism" remains the key to mainstream political success in the country; parties can't come to power without playing the "Albania card." Macedonian nationalists continue to persecute and discriminate against Albanian residents of the country. Despite the requirements of the EU-negotiated peace, efforts at providing greater recognition and rights to the Albanian minority have stalled. Violence and rhetoric have predictably escalated, with calls from Albanian political leaders for the secession of Western Macedonia in hopes of creating an ill-titled "Greater Albania." Well-founded accusations of Macedonian police violence against Albanians have arisen, and, even more troubling for stability, before February 2008 a spiraling of inter-Albanian violence regarding views on the correct disposition for Kosovo emerged.

Despite the international community's nearly $2 billion investment in international justice, the result on the ground has arguably been a mainstreaming of radicalism, as well as an entrenching of the very ethnic animosities that led to the brutal wars of the 1990s. War has not reignited, but true peace, at least for Serbia, Bosnia, and Kosovo, remains in the distance. In what some have deemed "The Hague Mania" that has swept over the region, true reconciliation between countries and between peoples may have been the latest victim of the 1990s war.[15]

THE BALKAN BANDWAGON

The Yugoslavia tribunal ignited a phenomenon and forged an industry out of a subject—international criminal law—that had been moribund, esoteric, and decidedly theoretical. Even in the ivory tower, prior to the ICTY, international criminal law scholars had been viewed as eccentric idealists, with the field dominated by those few old enough to remember Nuremberg or young enough to be mesmerized by it. Mainstream law reviews all but shunned the topic and in the decade before the ICTY's establishment, an article on the subject was a novelty; in many years the major legal publications published no pieces about international justice.[16] By the early 1990s, scholars believed that the potential of international justice actually coming to pass was so unlikely that they began excising material on the subject from legal textbooks.[17]

"International justice" was even more derelict outside academia, with newspapers and magazines demonstrating scant interest in the topic. Throughout the 1980s and early 1990s, it was rare for a major publication to devote ink to war crimes, crimes against humanity, or international justice, even as the trials of the Argentine junta and the Dergue in Ethiopia broke new ground, and even as the Cambodian Civil War, the Iran-Iraq War, and the West African civil wars exacted appalling tolls on civilians around the world. From 1984 through to the launch of the ICTY in May 1993, the *Wall Street Journal,* for instance, published two articles about "international justice."[18] The *New York Times* did slightly better, publishing nearly seventy articles on the subject in the decade prior to the Yugoslavia tribunal; even at the Gray Lady, however, articles appeared sporadically and the newspaper failed to publish more than ten such pieces in a given year until 1991. It was not just in the United States that coverage was so meek; the *Times of London* had similar figures, regularly publishing one or two articles per year throughout the 1980s and early 1990s.[19]

Since May 1993, when international justice established its home base in The Hague, the change has been remarkable. In academia, not only have major academic law reviews taken to the topic with alacrity and fecundity, publishing hundreds of articles on the subject, but also The Hague has been a catalyst for new law publications focused on international justice and international law. Since 1993 it has become increasingly common for American law schools to produce a specialty law review on international issues; this is also so at law schools around the world. Interest in international criminal justice can be credited for a good part of this growth. Student enthusiasm about the subject has led to a new generation of international law scholars; "war crimes research clinics" have become widespread. At Harvard, the first year law curriculum—famous as the subject of *The Paper Chase* and *1L*—was overhauled, for the first time in more than century. In addition to torts, contracts, property, and criminal law, students now must take a more "modern" course, with "international law" selected as one of the few additions.[20] The proceedings that began at The Hague in 1993 helped catalyze this change.

Given its near nonexistence prior to the Yugoslavia tribunal, the change outside academia is even more extreme. The press has become interested; in the decade after 1993, the *New York Times* published twice the number of articles on international justice than from 1983–1993; readers of the *Wall Street Journal* saw a *twenty-five-fold* increase in the number of stories that newspaper covered. As discussed earlier, the public at large also became interested in international judicial issues, demanding action or inaction on the subject as evidenced in newspaper editorials, letters to the editor, and even local legislation. International justice has even given rise to new professions in both the national and international spheres. Since 1997, the United States has had an "ambassador-at-large for war crimes," a high-ranking position that reports directly to the secretary of state. A whole generation of what could affectionately be described as "international court groupies" has emerged with the same names and faces traveling from court to court. The new prosecutor at the Khmer Rouge tribunal, for instance, earned his stripes at international courts dealing with Rwanda, Kosovo, and East Timor; the chief of defense in Cambodia has spent time at the ICTY and the Sierra Leone Court. Civil society engagement represents the most extreme and voluble change, and the number of nongovernmental organizations centrally concerned with international justice has skyrocketed. What was once the province of a few—Human Rights Watch, Amnesty International, and the like—expanded to include hundreds, if not thousands, of groups. So many NGOs have become enamored of the subject that there were actually more such organizations accredited to the Rome conference that debated the ICC statute (236) than there were national delegations

(159), which were actually charged with the negotiation. Several of the NGO delegations were larger than some government delegations.[21]

The cast on board—the ivory tower, Fleet Street, civil society, and even the wider public—would seem to have been rendered complete by the more than a half-dozen states and regions who have also joined the trend since 1993, asking for institutions similar to the ICTY to address their violent pasts. And the international community responded favorably to several of them. The United Nations provided the ICTY a sister court eighteen months after its creation, the International Criminal Tribunal for Rwanda (ICTR), which was established to address the 1994 carnage between the Tutsi and Hutu ethnic groups in that country. Six years later, the UN changed its course slightly and became enamored with sharing responsibility for post-atrocity justice; "hybrid" courts (part UN/international, part domestic) were formed, with the UN injecting international law and personnel into East Timor (to address the violence associated with its independence from Indonesia). This was followed by similar "hybrid" systems established in Kosovo in 2000 (where international judges were inserted in the aftermath of Milosevic's incursion in 1999); Sierra Leone in 2002 (to address the crimes committed during that country's civil war); Cambodia in 2003 (to prosecute the Khmer Rouge atrocities perpetrated in the 1970s); and concerning Lebanon in 2007 (to investigate and try those responsible for the 2005 assassination of former Prime Minister Rafiq Hariri).

Though all of these instances are worthy of comment, the key exemplars of international justice on which this work will focus are the freestanding tribunals—the ICTY, ICTR, and the oddly named "Special Court for Sierra Leone" (SCSL).[22] This is not solely because they have been the most intensely studied of the impositions of international justice but also because it is the establishment of an independent tribunal rather than attempting to resurrect a country's justice system—as was the goal in East Timor and Kosovo, for example—that is most similar to the new International Criminal Court. To see how the ICC will work, and consequently how international justice is poised to work in the future, it is imperative to see how the international tribunals that have epitomized "The Hague Process" have functioned.

Unfortunately, in the wake of each court established subsequent to the Yugoslavia tribunal, in Rwanda and then in Sierra Leone, we see circumstances similarly troubling to those in the Balkans, encouraging one to question whether international judicial efforts have provided the goods claimed by proponents. In all of international criminal justice's iterations, we see victims and perpetrators, states and communities most impacted by abuses (even those who originally asked for tribunals and international assistance), being left behind.

RWANDA

In Rwanda, the international community's imposition of a postconflict tribunal was met with dismay and dissatisfaction by a society struggling to recover from the brutality of more than eight hundred thousand ethnic killings in 1994. The Rwanda tribunal, curiously placed in Tanzania, has played second fiddle to the Yugoslavia tribunal (for much of its life it even shared the same prosecutor), has operated on a shoestring budget (it is said that its initial Web site was put together by an intern at a dollar-an-hour internet café), and has received only sporadic cooperation from the Rwandan government and even less cooperation from Rwanda's primary victims' groups. Questions have abounded about judges' qualifications and bias, and at least a half-dozen prosecutors have been dismissed for incompetence.

The former colonial power, Belgium, can be blamed for exacerbating the ethnic tensions that led to the massacres of 1994. The country's primary ethnic groups have long been the majority Hutus and the minority Tutsis. The Belgians practiced a "divide and conquer" approach. Brussels empowered the Tutsis, disproportionately providing them the plum administrative, commercial, and academic positions throughout the colony. Yet when Hutus rose up in the years before independence to complain about this inequality, the Belgians supported the uprising. In retrospect, this 1959 minirevolution, which led to as many as twenty thousand Tutsi deaths and the forced departure of as many as two hundred thousand Tutsis from Rwanda, was a foreshadowing of the even more horrific events in the early 1990s.

When independence came in 1962, a Hutu-dominated Rwanda was created alongside a seething Tutsi diaspora. The Tutsis became increasingly militant over the decades, finally fomenting a civil war in 1990 when the Tutsi-created Rwandan Patriotic Front launched an offensive against Kigali. The civil war itself was bloody, leading to a fragile peace agreement in 1993. A year later, when President Habyarimana's (a Hutu) plane was shot down, killing all onboard, a vicious Hutu-led genocide against Tutsis and moderate Hutus began; in the space of one hundred days (April to July 1994) as many as eight hundred thousand people lost their lives. Tens of thousands of Rwandans were involved, with machetes used as a primary tool for slaughter.

Four months later, the UN established the ICTR. Much like the ICTY the Rwanda tribunal has operated to bring to justice those responsible for the genocide. And, much like the Yugoslavia tribunal, it is not clear that the Rwanda tribunal has succeeded in punishing the perpetrators of the 1994 bloodshed or in truly deterring a repeat. That the tribunal is an illustration of the international community's neglect of Rwanda is fitting, given that the Rwandan genocide itself was in part allowed by the international community's neglect. In what is now a well-trodden tale, the international community was deaf to the requests of UN peacekeepers on the ground in Rwanda and to the warnings from various observers, about the impending attacks. The UN left its forces outnumbered, impotent in the face of the mass onslaught. While able to witness the carnage, it was unable to stop it.

Once the genocide ended, the new government, now dominated by Tutsis, was supportive of some judicial response to the atrocities. Yet, here too, Rwanda would be left behind. Though Kigali was initially supportive of an international tribunal, once it became clear how international the process would be, and how detached from Rwandan perceptions of justice it would operate, Rwanda became cool, if not hostile, to the Court. In fact, in a sad irony, the Rwandans were holding a rotating seat on the UN Security Council when the approval for a "Rwandan" tribunal came up for a vote. Rwanda was the only state to vote against it; Rwanda remains the only state *ever* to vote against the establishment of an international court in the Security Council.[23] And yet the court proceeded, even as leading Rwandan politicians and academics worried that the "Western School" of justice to be employed by the tribunal would prove harmful to the prospects for Rwanda's national reconciliation.[24]

Rwanda is somewhat unique in the annals of postconflict justice because despite the viciousness of the 1994 genocide, it is one of the few states recovering from mass crimes in which many members of competitor ethnic groups are being forced to once again live with one another. Regrettably, the court's legacy both for interethnic relations and regional stability is troubling. Hutus and Tutsis have hardly reconciled. Inside Rwanda, survivors have been brutally assaulted—many fatally—in a series of isolated but steady attacks in recent years. Perpetrated by Tutsis and Hutus alike, killings and disappearances have continued with "hundreds and possibly thousands of people 'disappeared'" across Rwanda.[25] Privately, many Tutsis admit that they cannot shake the feeling that it is only the government's sometimes-suffocating control over dialogue and events in the country that prevents Hutu extremists from killing again. "I fear that, inside, they are not satisfied," whispered one.[26] And, killings have continued, of judges and witnesses participating in local trials, along with reprisal killings of "alleged perpetrators, their friends, family, and bystanders—risking a new round of violence."[27]

The situation on Rwanda's borders is as dire. Hutus and Tutsis have changed places: Hutus are now proving militant in the diaspora and Tutsis are now attempting to hold them off in Rwanda. The result has been the formation of Hutu militias on Rwanda's borders that have mounted frequent attacks and issued constant threats. This has led the

Rwandan government to complain to those states that have been harboring the Hutu forces. In 1996, and again in 1998, Rwanda actually invaded its neighbors aiming to flush out the Hutu militants. The latter invasion, of the Democratic Republic of the Congo, triggered the deadliest war since World War II, with nearly four million killed—thus far—as almost all regional states have become embroiled.

Though many in the international community are unaware of the continuing violence on Rwanda's borders, and others are blinded by Rwanda's healthy economic growth, the country and wider region remains on the brink. Rwanda's leaders have resorted to the establishment of a "progressive dictatorship"[28] while continuing to nervously eye Hutu rebels in surrounding countries. Despite the overall growth of the economy, Rwandans are mired in poverty; annual per capita income is a paltry $230, well below the global poverty level. Given the confluence of these factors, it is not a surprise that many Rwandans hold an overwhelmingly negative view of international justice.[29] Meanwhile, Rwanda's own justice system is in shambles, never having received even a tiny fraction of the financial or personnel support provided the comparatively flush ICTR.

SIERRA LEONE

By the time Sierra Leone requested a tribunal in 2000, the international community had cooled to truly international justice, with many frustrated by the cost of the ICTR and ICTY, coupled with their modest judicial output and uncertain benefits. As a result, though the UN again set up a court, it opted for a new model, an international tribunal "lite." The Special Court for Sierra Leone (SCSL) was the first freestanding tribunal in the "hybrid" model. It was designed to be simultaneously a local body (housed inside the country, applying local and international law) and an international entity, formed under the auspices of the UN, employing nonlocals to serve as key figures in the court (such as the prosecutor and several judges).

However, even in Sierra Leone, for reasons of financing and international politics, the welcomed local characteristics of its court have been often subsumed by the international. The result has been the development of a court much more like those in Tanzania and The Hague than initial supporters would have wanted. An unfortunate consequence of this international "overhang" imbued into the newly streamlined version of international justice has been that the Sierra Leone court has all of the weaknesses of its predecessor courts and few of the strengths. A key change was in its funding. The Yugoslavia and Rwanda tribunals have been funded largely by "mandatory" contributions from UN states, but a condition imposed by the UN Security Council on the establishment of the Sierra Leone court was that its funding would be "voluntary." This system has led at least one defendant to complain that a fair hearing was doubtful given that benefactor states could influence the court by deciding to withhold funds.[30] Though there was no proof that this has sort of bullying has occurred, it is evident that "voluntary" assessments have often fallen short, meaning that court leaders have had to spend inordinate amount of time traveling the world, "cap in hand," rather than working to dispense justice. The current prosecutor, Stephen Rapp, has said that he spends 40 percent of his time on the road, outside of Sierra Leone, trying to shore up the court's finances.[31] Despite this effort, reports of the "imminent collapse" of the court due to funding difficulties have been nearly constant since the earliest days of the court's operation.[32]

These structural weaknesses under a façade of seeming strength parallel those of Sierra Leone as a country. The immaculate grounds of the multimillion dollar international courthouse in Freetown and the impressive pronouncements and indictments emanating from the building belie a country too weak and uncertain to even let the court hold its most important trial—of former Liberian strongman Charles Taylor—in the country, for fear of destabilizing the state and wider West Africa. Many Sierra Leoneans see the court as an expensive waste, unable to improve the country, and sacrificing stability and growth for what only the international community views as "justice." The same wartime factions that the international community has tried to dismantle remain, and in various quarters are stronger than ever. Some seasoned observers have even noted that far from forestalling a return to violence, "the continuation of the Special Court could create the conditions for another civil war."[33]

The atrocities committed in Sierra Leone, which perhaps most famously included the forced conscription and drugging of children, compelling them to commit the war's signature crime—mutilation— had complex roots. Control of the country's vast diamond reserves were a primary cause of the initial conflict, but crimes were also based in part on other factors: ethnicity, an ill-defined revolutionary ideology, frustration with a military dictatorship, and forces outside Sierra Leone (emanating from Liberia to the south, Guinea and Côte d'Ivoire to the north and east, and even as far afield as Britain and Libya). In spring 1991, a small band of Sierra Leonean rebels, the Revolutionary United Front (RUF), began attacking eastern villages in the country from bases in Liberia. The Freetown government proved ineffectual at repelling the attacks, such that by 1995 the RUF—under the leadership of Foday Sankoh—was knocking on the doors of Freetown. The first of several negotiations began between the civilian leadership of President Ahmad Kabbah and the RUF. After further confusion brought on by a 1997 coup, the "humanitarian" intervention of Nigerian forces in ECOMOG (the Economic Community of West African States Monitoring Group) as well as additional negotiations and amnesties, the warring parties signed a peace accord in 1999. UN peacekeepers were deployed in April 2000, but they were unable to fully quell the violence. Indeed, violence returned to such an extent within a few months of their arrival that foreign states deployed forces solely to evacuate their own nationals. Another peace was declared, again violated, but this time by forces from Guinea in the north, which attacked RUF bases inside Sierra Leone. Yet further agreements were made and President Kabbah (who had returned to office) proclaimed final "peace" in January 2002.

The Special Court began operations shortly thereafter, and since then both local and international observers have come to the same conclusion—Sierra Leone has made limited progress in addressing many of the issues that gave rise to the conflict: endemic corruption, weak rule of law, and the inequitable distribution of the country's vast natural resources. It is an extremely dangerous situation that threatens the return of conflict. Diamonds are key to Sierra Leone's growth, and while there have been some needed reforms in the sector, they have largely failed to reach the mass of impoverished diamond diggers who were among the rebel's most "enthusiastic recruits" during the war. Wider respect for law remains low, while impunity continues to characterize much of society. Elections in July 2007 were a potential flashpoint. While they succeeded without disintegrating the state, they were far from peaceful. Numerous house burnings and the stoking of ethnic tensions were a part of the campaigns.

Though it would be inaccurate to claim that today's Sierra Leone is in the same condition that it was in when civil war began in 1991, "most of the problems that existed before the war, [and that fueled the war,] remain."[34] As the *International Crisis Group* put it: "[w]hile Sierra Leone is no longer a failed state [its] . . . core institutions remain untested."[35] Or, as *The Economist* noted in December 2008, the ". . . roots of conflict . . . still go deep [and u]ntil they are tackled Sierra Leone will remain a fragile state at best."[36] That there was such fear that the Taylor trial could return the region to violence is indicative of just how perilous the country's, and West Africa's, stability really is. Grinding poverty (Sierra Leone is by many measures the poorest country in the world), state corruption, the maintenance of strong ethnic identity, and the pervasive feeling of continued injustice more than six years after the court was established remain the hallmarks of Sierra Leonean life today.

Unfortunately, the destabilizing impact that international justice can have has not been limited to these cases. Even the *threat* of international judicial intervention has often seemed to have negative effects. On this score, in the Sudan and Uganda, many claim that the nascent International Criminal Court has done more harm than good. Many of the ICC's problems in these regions have stemmed from its structure. The ICC has replicated many of the serious problems of the international justice system seen in Yugoslavia, Rwanda, and Sierra Leone, and in doing so has subverted long-held, respected indigenous tools for forgiveness and reconciliation. More critically, it has banished one of the most potent tools of the peacemaker—the offer of amnesties for crimes in exchange for peace. In the eyes of some observers on the ground and elsewhere, the court's activities have been a spur to continue fighting. Even governments that originally requested the court's presence have now begun to have second thoughts or have acted in ways to limit the ICC's reach. Most famously, Ugandan president Yoweri Museveni, who asked the court to investigate abuses committed by a rebel group in his country's north, proceeded to negotiate with the group, with amnesties from ICC indictments an important sweetener in his offer.

ARE COURTS THE ONLY ANSWER?
NO, BUT THEY ARE SPECIAL.

> If the only tool you have is a hammer, you tend to see every problem as a nail.
>
> —Abraham Maslow

Gary Bass, the author of *Staying the Hand of Vengeance*, concludes his incisive book about the politics of war crimes tribunals by asking, "Do war crimes tribunals work?" He replies that they might not be effective but "they have the clear potential to work . . . much better than anything else diplomats have come up with at the end of a war."[37] In light of the difficulties of international tribunals, and perhaps even more so the problems that the tribunals highlight in the international criminal justice system at large, this might not be true. It neglects the negative effects of some of the courts—a former US ambassador to both Yugoslavia and Croatia has commented that it is only once the Yugoslavia tribunal has closed can rehabilitation really begin;[38] and it also appears to undervalue the successful reconciliation and justice achieved by many other states that have opted to pursue postwar reconstruction primarily outside the courtroom.

In Spain, for instance—ironically, the same country that demanded former Chilean dictator Augusto Pinochet's extradition to answer for his human rights abuses in a trial—the end of its Fascist period in 1975 resulted in explicit amnesties rather than trials. Any serious pursuit of trials waited until the end of 2008, more than three decades after Franco's death. In South Africa following the end of Apartheid, perhaps the most famous nonjudicial solution was developed: its Truth and Reconciliation Commission was manifestly *not* a court, trading "truth" for "prosecutions," doling out thousands of amnesties in exchange for former regime leaders testifying about exactly what happened during their reign. Even against those who were denied amnesties, trials have been few and far between.[39] Throughout Central and Eastern Europe, the end of Communism—and its associated five decades of mass human rights abuses—also did not see many trials. Rather, other than a few high profile trials (of note were those of a few former East German "Stasi" security officials conducted in Germany[40]) states preferred nonjudicial solutions, with the favorite in Eastern Europe being "lustration," whereby former Communist officials were deprived of the ability to ever again hold state jobs.[41] This model of removing abusers from their ranks was also seen in El Salvador. Intriguingly also operating under a UN mandate and beginning just two weeks before the Yugoslavia tribunal was set up to judicially punish war criminals, the international community instructed El Salvador to simply purge its military of human rights abusers, rather than try them.[42] Finally, in Chile, the country's decision to forego trials immediately after the departure of Augusto Pinochet in 1990 may have resulted in a formalization of the military's impunity (thus leading to significant outrage in the ranks when Spain demanded Pinochet's extradition eight years later). But the Chilean decision was also a recognition of political realities and the fragility of Chilean society. Significant doubt exists that the gains Chile managed to achieve by removing Pinochet would have come to pass if Pinochet had been immediately brought to trial. Nearly twenty years later, a much-strengthened Chile is now returning to this chapter and has begun prosecutions of the junta.[43]

Regardless of the variety of these cases, and the imperfections in each, it would be hard to claim that any of them definitively failed. Especially in the wider sense, in each instance, democratic societies replaced nondemocratic ones, and pledges to never again engage in the monstrosities of the past have largely been upheld. Moreover, it would be difficult to say that those "responsible" for the crimes in each society—and thus, those who would presumably be tried if judicial proceedings were selected—are no less punished simply because their verdict was not rendered quickly in a court of law. The explicit exclusion of people from civil and political society mandated by lustration, and the power of shaming, active in all of these states, are powerful penalties. Finally, though evidence on the subject is mixed, victims may be far better served by nonjudicial remedies.[44]

Despite this, "most commentators assert that criminal prosecution is the best response to atrocities," and other options—such as truth commissions, amnesties, or other alternatives—should only be used when prosecutions are not possible.[45] The Rome Treaty that formalized the International Criminal Court is even more direct on this matter, stating that its chief prosecutor will take up a case of purported crimes if a state has shown itself unwilling or unable to prosecute a person charged with the crimes under the treaty's purview.[46] That trials have achieved a clear primacy in the manner in which the international community seeks to address postconflict realities is evident. It is illustrated no more clearly than by the fact that the treaty for the ICC has now been signed by more than two-thirds of member states of the United Nations.[47]

Increasing global convergence toward international justice does not mean that amnesties, truth commissions, lustrations, shamings, or a host of other localized "solutions" are actually not more promising alternatives in many postconflict situations. Each situation must be addressed on its merits; the decision to pursue one path or another is highly fact dependent and no case is like another. Yet, despite this, because of the growing international acceptance that trials are preferable, we will focus here on legal or judicial responses to mass crimes.

Additionally, concentrating on trials makes sense in postconflict states because trials are unique in the ways they can aid in the redevelopment of a state. More so than the alternatives, they can provide definitive justification and closure to painful histories whereby victims can be vindicated and a new class of political leaders can rely on legal justification for their power and departure from the past. Finally, trials are worthy of focus because they are exceptionally difficult to stage, requiring sophisticated knowledge and infrastructure, coupled with dispassionate practitioners capable of applying law to facts. In many postconflict states, it does not appear as if any of these requirements have been present. Trials are so hard to "get right" that many people claim that they simply cannot be done in situ in the wake of atrocities. If trials are to occur, they need to take place outside the afflicted region, and operated by those unrelated to the conflict.

Yet, given the challenges that international tribunals have encountered in following this prescription, if law is to be the solution to humanitarian crimes, then another, more satisfying and effective way of approaching them is needed. Where to find this solution is revealed, in part, by the Bass quotation above. He qualifies his belief that war crimes trials are promising, by stating that they are "better than anything else *diplomats* have come up with." That is exactly correct: diplomats, and not the aggrieved parties or the local systems, have devised international justice. Bringing local systems into the justice equation, very early in the postconflict era, seems to have more promise for the establishment of true reconciliation and the dispensation of justice. It is increasingly evident that the only way that justice can be dispensed in an environment so torn, and so charged, is via the inclusion, rather than the exclusion, of those most impacted.

A potent example comes from Rwanda. In late 1994, only months after the summer's genocide had mercifully ceased, Robert Press from the *Christian Science Monitor* likened Kigali's main prison to an eighteenth-century, trans-Atlantic slave ship: prisoners arrested on suspicion of participation in the killings were everywhere, sleeping body-to-body in cramped cubicles atop triple tiers of wooden bunks, with little food and almost no provision for hygiene. The Kigali prison, built in 1930 to hold eight hundred, was bursting with more than five thousand.[48] By the beginning of 1995, almost twenty thousand people had been arrested. These new inmates had been rounded up and stacked into cells throughout the country, with little hope that the local justice system—itself decimated by the killings—would be able to address each case. A survey in December 1994 revealed that the entire country had only thirty-one investigators and five judges to work on the genocide cases.

The situation was rightly called a humanitarian nightmare but few voices, and none in the international community, recognized the potential amid the dismay. There was little question that most of the people incarcerated were guilty of playing some part in the murderous rampages over the summer; the only question was what to do with them in a country with scant resources and an all but nonexistent judiciary. Rwanda needed help to right its judicial system and process prisoners and cases. Government officials admitted their incapacity and begged for international help. In an effort to publicize the dire situation, the justice minister welcomed foreign journalists into the prisons, and invited scores of human rights monitors into the country—both unique steps on the continent. With the assistance of foreign scholars, the Rwandan government drafted and passed new legislation to aid in the processing of prisoners, and to accord them greater rights. However, Rwanda needed aid—chairs, tables, and computers, let alone expertise—to effectively implement the law. The new government begged for funds and some were promised at a 1995 donor conference. Very little, however, was delivered.

Instead, diplomats arrived in Rwanda, trying to convince leaders that aid would flow if they would agree to an international court. An American emissary met with the new Rwandan leader Paul Kagame and urged him to request a court. President Kagame was unenthusiastic: "[His] message for the envoy was clear and simple. He was not convinced any UN court would be helpful to Rwanda. When Rwanda needed assistance stopping the genocide, the United Nations did nothing." He continued, "We have done this entirely by ourselves. . . . The United Nations would be too slow." It would take a long time to launch an international tribunal, and "we need early and viable justice," he told the American representative. "We need the people of Rwanda to see this justice for themselves."[49]

In the end, the international community missed its chance, as the UN plowed ahead with its plans for a Rwanda tribunal without Rwandan support. Rwanda was so chastened by the international community's actions it even withdrew its initial request for assistance. Instead, the human rights-weary Rwandan government saw no choice but to release the vast majority of its detainees—as many as fifty thousand inmates were released when it became clear that Rwanda would receive insufficient aid to process them.

This was the first time, but would not be the last, that the international community missed an opportunity to help Rwandans deal with war crimes on their own.

Real local trials subsequently occurred in Rwanda, as they have in almost all postconflict states. It may seem counterintuitive that the states in which such flagrant abuses took place, and ethnic animosity remains so raw, that real, just trials could be staged. Some of the trials that have occurred have clearly smacked of the inequality and ethnic bias of which the international community seems so concerned. The trials have been far from perfect. In Rwanda, critics note that no Tutsis have ever been brought before a domestic court. While true, critics fail to note that no Tutsis have ever been brought before the international court either.

In the former Yugoslavia, local justice has also been troubled. Some truly absurd cases have emerged. In Bosnia, the Supreme Court upheld the guilty verdict of a "murderer" even after his two "victims" were found alive and well *and* others had already been charged for their "deaths."[50] Yet, the experience of the former Yugoslavia is also instructive. Since the start of the war, let alone following its conclusion, such blatantly unfair trials are hardly the norm.

The lessons of Rwanda and Yugoslavia are that neither an international nor national judicial "solution" will be perfect; yet, it would be unreasonable to think that in the wake of so great a social upheaval as genocide or mass crimes, such a solution would be possible. The question reduces to: "Which is the best of imperfect options?" In this, it is increasingly apparent that a greater focus on the local is almost always a more promising starting point than a focus on the international.

And this does not mean that the international community has no role. Rather, in both Yugoslavia and Rwanda, "real" trials could have been better and more numerous, but it is hard to blame the Yugoslavs or Rwandans for all of their shortcomings. The international community, until very recently, has shown little interest in supporting domestic efforts. When the international community put its muscle and will behind trials in the Balkans, as elsewhere, such trials were successfully held. In short, the international community has had a critical part to play, but not necessarily the one in which it has been cast.

Retrieving our car from the mud—with the help of a Bosniak who had traveled from Connecticut for the Srebrenica commemoration—we headed back to Sarajevo in the early afternoon. After our "participation" in the riot, it was relatively smooth sailing. Traffic had thinned and other than our continued difficulty with Cyrillic, retracing our steps was uncomplicated. However, the drive was made more emotionally trying by the commemoration. The 614 coffins that we had seen reburied brought home the horrors of Bosnia's recent history, making our academic understanding of the various massacre sites we passed on Road 19 come alive. We turned on an English-language radio station for some news of the trouble that we had just left. No mention was made then, or even the next day, of the traffic jam or the fact that thousands of Bosniaks were unable to get into the park for the commemoration. The following morning, we checked the *International Herald Tribune*, which we were sure would feature news of those thousands who had been thwarted in their attempts to reach the ceremony. Nothing. Again, the international community had left behind those who had experienced the events.

I had to keep wondering, "What next?" How does the world community help the Balkans to "catch up" and rejoin the journey to peace and reconciliation that the world has tried to foster? Was this wave of international grieving that we saw at the Peace Park enough?

For many Serbs the answer was clear. Despite the commemoration, a popular newspaper in Belgrade "reported" that the Srebrenica massacre was a case of "pure fabrication."[51] As late as December 2005, polls suggested that many Serbs refused to believe it ever happened. The evening prior to the commemoration saw several Serbian television stations broadcast pictures of badly hurt Serbians from the various Balkan wars, with a clear message: "the others are the bigger criminals."[52] Clear-eyed Serb observers like former Deputy Prime Minister Zarko Korac recognized that "many more steps will have to be taken before we can confront the fact that atrocities were committed in our name."[53]

For Bosniaks, the commemoration, perhaps unsurprisingly, seemed to harden their ethnic animosities. "The question is what will happen after 11 July," asked Ruzdija Adzovic in the daily *Jutarnje Novine*, "after a good night's sleep how many . . . officials will think about Srebrenica?"[54] Talk of reconciliation and peace would have to wait until another day.

For Croats the matter was also self-evident. The government-owned paper, *Slobodna Dalmacija*, opined that even with the world's attention, the state of ethnic relations in the Balkans shows that "evil obviously hasn't been eradicated. And, what's worse, justice seems even more helpless."[55]

The minarets and cathedrals that punctuate Sarajevo's skyline took on a decidedly different flavor when we returned in the late afternoon. While they represented the potential for true multiethnic living when we departed, they seemed more static, monolithic, and unyielding on our return. My hope would not return until we once again ventured down Ferhadija. The kebabs were still there, and yards away so too was the tasty gelato. People mingled on the streets, played "giant" chess in the park, and walked from one part of Sarajevo to the other. It became clear that it was here, on the ground, that reconciliation and justice could be nurtured, and perhaps could have always been fostered. By focusing on the minarets and cathedrals, some soaring hundreds of feet into the sky, the action and interaction of the people below had been neglected. It was on the street, and likely *only* on the street, that people could be assured that they would no longer be left behind.

Chapter 4

THE POLITICS OF HELL[1]

What Happened?

Sixteen thousand two hundred and sixty-six days, and tens, if not hundreds of thousands, of war crimes separated the post–World War II international justice effort and its resurrection in 1993. More than forty-four years passed between the final gavel at the Tokyo Trials and the passage of United Nations Security Council Resolution 827—the resolution that established the International Criminal Tribunal for the former Yugoslavia, and revived the practice of international criminal law after a Cold War-induced hibernation of nearly five decades.

The scope and majesty of the task that the international community set for itself was remarkable. After more than a generation in abeyance, the precedent and promise of the post–World War II Nuremberg and Tokyo Trials was finally to be realized, with legal right trumping the military might that had done such injury throughout the Balkans. The process seemed uncomplicated: a respected international prosecutor would be chosen, and he would employ the world's best and brightest legal minds to develop cases and try defendants before a similarly talented bench of global jurists. The world would no longer watch silently as tyrants flaunted their impunity. Victims would be respected, perpetrators would be prosecuted, and justice would be served.

With such a noble goal, a daunting question emerges. How did one of the bravest, most optimistic, and amazingly expensive assertions of post–Cold War global power—the provision of justice to those aggrieved by atrocious crimes—slip into a system in which so many doubt justice is being done, so few survivors, perpetrators, and other residents of postconflict regions are satisfied with "their" justice, and which in several instances may well be exacerbating the very problems it was designed to fix in Yugoslavia, Rwanda, Uganda, and elsewhere? This troubling outcome has by and large not been the result of the people who have toiled in these courts. With very few exceptions, the prosecutors, investigators, judges, and defenders have been talented professionals striving to make the system work. The difficulties have arisen due to the structure of the system itself. And this structure was a direct result of the international community's reactions, or failure to react, to the first major post–Cold War crisis—the Yugoslav war. In responding to the Balkan situation, the international community followed a script that would be replayed most clearly in Rwanda, and in some ways in each of the subsequent cases where international justice has been attempted.

To say that the world was stunned by the events in the Balkans in the early 1990s is a drastic understatement. The savagery of the war, echoing the Holocaust of the 1940s and the Armenian genocide of the 1910s, seemed anachronistic to a world emerging from a fifty-year Cold War and embarking upon a democratic "new world order." Yet, on the very doorstep of Europe, which was joyously celebrating the end of Communism and the long-awaited re-fusing of its East and West, conflict erupted. Fascism and nationalism—two of the most feared "isms" that were thought to have been put down after the Cold War—proved very much alive in the Balkans. Cajoled by charismatic politicians who owed much of their style and rhetorical flourish to the influence of Hitler and Mussolini, the region quickly slid into chaos. With calls for ethnic "purity" and *lebensraum**, the Serbs, Croats, Bosniaks, Albanians, Slovenes—along with a smattering of other groups— jointly propelled toward war.

---

*German for *living space*. Hitler's desire for more of such space for the German people was one of his stated justifications for Nazi territorial expansionism during World War II.

Yugoslavia, a federal, multiethnic conglomeration, quickly fractured, with Slovenia and Croatia the first to go, both declaring independence in June 1991. While the Slovenian "war" of July 1991 was barely a conflict at all—lasting ten days and resulting in few casualties—the reaction to Croatia's declaration of independence by the rest of Yugoslavia, the Serbs who lived in Croatia, and the international community would ignite a campaign of bloodshed that would cost more than three hundred thousand lives in the following decade, while displacing millions more. Federal Yugoslavia, under the control of a Serb-dominated government headed by Slobodan Milosevic, rejected Croatia's independence. Meanwhile Germany—working against the conventional diplomatic and political wisdom among its European and North American allies—proceeded quickly to validate Zagreb's claims, recognizing Croatian sovereignty in December 1991. With the history of Nazi influence in Croatia during World War II, the murderous rampages of the German-allied Croatian nationalists against the Serbs during the 1930s and 1940s, the seeming resumption of the German-Croatian alliance was enough to trigger a knee-jerk Serbian reaction; they steeled themselves for a fight.[2]

Caught between Croatia and Serbia were the Bosniaks and Kosovar Albanians, largely Muslim and historically tolerated minorities. With the Croatian and Serbian conflict quickly inflamed with talk of reclaiming historically Croatian and Serbian lands from other parts of the Balkans, both the Bosniaks and the Kosovar Albanians entered the fray. In large measure, they did so to protect the integrity of whatever territory and rights they had managed to amass under the comparatively benign reign of long-time Yugoslav Communist leader Marshal Josip Broz Tito (who remained in power from the end of World War II until his death in 1980).

Thus began a multisided conflict replete with national armies, allied rebel groups, "fronts," paramilitaries, and various affiliated and splintered factions producing an alphabet soup of acronyms that made it difficult for almost anybody to follow exactly what was happening in the region.

The result of this confusing conflagration was that world leaders, starting in late 1991, regularly expressed their moral outrage at the events in the former Yugoslavia, but refused to do anything more than make hortatory statements. In the waning days of his administration, President George H. W. Bush's secretary of state James Baker famously warned his boss against American involvement arguing that "we don't have a dog in that fight."[3] It was only in 1993, following the publication of pictures of Balkan prison camps, that the world community was shocked into paying real attention. This shock led to a linguistic framing of the situation that proved deleterious at the time and continues to haunt the resolution of lingering issues. The language surrounding the situation "shifted from that of moral imperative [whereby the United States and European powers would be compelled to act] to that of an amoral mess."[4] The situation officially became described as a "Problem from Hell." The genesis of this description as an official policy statement sheds light on why such framing would prove so damaging to the prospects of actually doing anything to aid Yugoslavia.

This statement was uttered by President Bill Clinton's first secretary of state, Warren Christopher. With mounting exasperation, Secretary Christopher described the Balkan situation in the early 1990s as horrific, evoking the "'futility' imagery of tribal hatreds."[5] Recalling the "centuries of conflict" between the warring parties, he argued that "the hatred between all three groups . . . is almost unbelievable. It's almost terrifying . . . that really is the Problem from Hell."[6]

Though his claim that the region had been embroiled in such conflict for centuries is belied by history,[7] and was quickly repudiated, Christopher's view quickly became the American administration's view, and then that of the Europeans. The entire Balkan region was quickly baptized as "Hell on Earth" with the appellation stretched to cover more than just the figurative battlefield. Milosevic, his wife, and his children were dubbed "the family from Hell."[8] Svetlana Velickovic, the popstar wife of Serb warlord Arkan, was dubbed "the bride from Hell."[9] In his indictment before the Yugoslav tribunal, Radovan Karadzic was accused of "masterminding massacres"[10] that were "scenes from Hell, written on the darkest pages of human history."[11]

Dubbing the dire nature of the situation, and the depraved character-istics of the players, in such descriptive terms did not mean that United States (or Europe) would actually do something about the problem. Instead, that it was a "Problem from Hell" gave the world community cover. The wars were "somehow inevitable," and the situation was *so* intractable, and *so* horrendous, that intervention would be futile.[12] By categorizing the Balkans as Hell, it placed the situation beyond the ken of decision makers; it was a perfect excuse *not* to act.[13] The stage was thus set for the bloodshed to continue, almost unabated.

However, while claiming that the situation was hellish led to non-action, the same description led to *overaction* after the international community had been shamed and sickened into addressing the fallout of the war. If the Balkans really were "Hell," the "devils" in the region could not possibly act to provide justice to those who had been injured by the conflict. The international community took over—explicitly in Bosnia and Herzegovina, with the arrival of a UN appointed "Office of the High Representative," and in Kosovo with the establishment of the UN Interim Administration Mission in Kosovo (UNMIK), and implic-itly in Serbia and Montenegro, Croatia, and Macedonia, where interna-tional actors (a combination of powerful states, NATO, and the EU) used their leverage to exert control over those polities.

The Hague-based, UN-backed International Court fit neatly into this political model that attempted to balance a risk-averse interna-tional community with an increasingly human rights-focused global citizenry. Though it was born with much fanfare and supporters were quick to focus on the growing importance of human rights in the global commons, a coterie of detractors quickly emerged. They saw in the Court a troubling lack of desire to actually stop war crimes. This view was expressed even at the highest levels of the UN, the Court's institutional parent. Ralph Zacklin, at the time the UNs chief legal officer, wrote that it was evident that the Court was an "act of contri-tion"[14] on the part of the international community. It had been un-willing to exert the needed efforts, and undertake the needed risks, in order to really help those on the ground. Robert Kaplan, the author of

Balkan Ghosts, bemoaned that this would not be "the first time . . . that a call for a war crimes trial has been offered as a substitute for genuine action."[15] And, it wouldn't be the last.

The UNs postmortem regarding Rwanda makes it painfully clear how little political will existed to stop the carnage. But political will was somehow mustered after the fact, so long as there was minimal risk. UN member states "dithered and failed to act"[16] to head off the clearly imminent violence in Rwanda, and yet fell in line behind an international judicial solution to the problems after the conflict subsided. The same "ancient tribal hatreds" formula was recycled, again lending "a patina of logic to indifference . . . saying that there is little that outsiders could do, even if they were willing."[17] "Hell" reemerged, this time in the African Great Lakes: "Rwanda's Descent into Hell" became an all too common cliché, and an all too common title for reports by NGOs and governments. *Shake Hands With the Devil* was the title of the book written by the commander of the UN force in the country during the violence and the Pulitzer Committee in 1995 awarded its international reporting prize to Associated Press reporter Mark Fritz for his coverage of Rwanda, due in part to the "vivid detail" in which Fritz "described scenes of hell."[18]

And in Sierra Leone, the wars of West Africa—which engulfed Sierra Leone, Liberia, and to a lesser extent Guinea and Guinea-Bissau—were also allowed to fester with little international involvement throughout the 1990s, with "hellish" imagery similarly abounding. "Hell's Other Name is Sierra Leone," intoned the *Chicago Tribune*—"how else to explain what is happening to the people of Sierra Leone, except as the work of monsters?"[19] Peter Penfold, the British high commissioner in Freetown, was called the "hero of Hell City" for securing the rescue of eight hundred Europeans from a besieged hotel in the Sierra Leone capital.[20] It was only in 1999 that UN peacekeepers, or the "blue helmets," were put on the ground to enforce peace; the Special Court soon followed.

✳

INTERNATIONAL LAW AS A "SOLUTION"— WHERE HAS IT FALLEN SHORT?

The international political actors who gave birth to the Problem from Hell devised a judicial solution in line with how they saw the problem—the international criminal tribunal. It became widely accepted that a court was the most appropriate response to the grave crimes of the Balkans, and the UN Security Council in February 1993 voted unanimously for its establishment.[21] Despite the breadth of its support, and forthcoming investment from the UN and individual states, the Yugoslavia tribunal would quickly fall prey to differing conceptions of just what its goal was supposed to be. This same lack of clarity would befuddle each of the subsequent attempts at international justice. Regarding Yugoslavia, at each instance, the aims of the tribunal seemed obviated by events on the ground, necessitating the development of a compromised identity and purpose. It was this perpetual philosophical framing and reframing that continued to plague the tribunal in the eyes of its prime constituents in the Balkans. The same malleability has been seen in the subsequent tribunals, also much to the chagrin of their constituents.

At its inception, there were two primary competing versions of the Yugoslavia tribunal's purpose. Each saw the tribunal, and international criminal law in general, as responsive to a different set of problems. The first, and in many ways the most favored argument for the tribunal, rested on its deterrent potential. On the ground in the Balkans, already in 1992 there were journalists and other observers who implored the world community to establish a court so as to prevent further crimes. Past crimes would be punished, but the real good was to be achieved by the abatement and even avoidance of future crimes. Language to this effect played a large role in official pronouncements regarding the tribunal's establishment, as well as in the body's founding statute.[22]

The difficulty with deterrence as the Court's raison d'être was made clear within months of the tribunal's establishment in 1993. Crimes were continuing in the former Yugoslavia and, by all accounts, were worsening. Territorial divisions, fragmentation, and ethnic cleansing picked up in the months following The Hague's inception. Almost all of the most infamous crimes of the war took place after the Court was founded: Srebrenica and Operation Storm in 1995, and perhaps most clearly, the Kosovo invasion in 1999, all occurred long after the Court was in session and its deterrent force was supposedly in effect.

Though some adherents of the deterrence model remain resolute—arguing the difficultly proven notion that even if some crimes continued to occur, the gravity of others was lessened due to the threat of judicial punishment—the other competing philosophy behind the Court picked up strength as the deterrence model faltered. This school saw the tribunal, and again international criminal justice in general, as a tool toward promoting reconciliation and peacemaking in the wake of conflict. This was a much more sullen, realist perspective of the war in Yugoslavia, all but taking the commission of crimes as a given, and leaving it for the Court to establish a foundation for peace and stability ex poste. Roused by the mantra "no peace without justice," this camp saw the ICTY as the crucial first step in returning the Balkans to their prewar prosperity. As Grant Niemann, the lead prosecutor in the tribunal's first case put it, the Court was "created not only to administer justice . . . [but with the] expectation that it will contribute to a lasting peace in the country that once was Yugoslavia."[23] It would provide a full, unbiased recounting of wartime events and thus provide citizens with a starting point from which they could both address the past and face the future. The Court would be a tool for reconciliation.

Despite the attractiveness of this model, this school also faltered. It became apparent very quickly that the Court was not aiding reconciliation. An early and key indication of this inability came less than a month after the Court's 1993 founding. In mid-June, the most comprehensive peace plan yet negotiated for the region, the Vance-Owen agreement, was declared "dead" by one of its coarchitects, Lord Owen. The warring parties were in no mood to reconcile. Indeed, far from aiding reconciliation, the Court became a weapon brandished by each of the parties. Croats, for example, provided The Hague reams of evidence of Serb wrongdoing, while Serbs did the same. Even if each side initially supported the Court's work in its pursuit of justice, such support was limited to the Court's prosecution of the "other." Any mention of the Court's focus on Serb or Croat acts led to anger by Serbs or Croats and made the potential for reconciliation even more remote.

After the failure of the Vance-Owen agreement, several more peace plans would come and go until the Dayton Peace was finally solidified in late 1995. Even at Dayton, it is not evident that the Court had a positive impact on the peace agreement, a fact illustrated by the unwillingness of any of the parties—Croatia, Serbia, or Bosnia—to consistently assist the tribunal in its subsequent work after Dayton. Moreover, had any of the interlocutors at Dayton been told that they might be indicted by the tribunal, the Dayton deal might not have received any of their support.

It became plain that neither the deterrent nor reconciliation arguments behind the Court were persuasive. The consequence of this conclusion was a philosophical reassessment by the Court's backers. If international justice did not deter further crimes or reconcile warring factions, to what set of problems was international justice the clear answer? There was no agreement on what such a problem looked like. Thus, the question was changed to one that almost all of the Court's backers could support: it was not to ask *what* was the problem that the tribunal solved, but rather *where* was the problem that it solved. On this there was widespread agreement, and this was unaffected by realities on the ground in the Balkans or anywhere else crimes took place. There was accord that any problem that existed did so on the *international* plane. These were international crimes committed and thus international solutions were the only viable way to resolve them. As Antonio Cassese, a former ICTY judge, contended:

> For the very reason that war crimes are violations of . . . international law, an international judge should try the international offences. He is the best qualified.[24]

Over time, this philosophy only strengthened, with the Court becoming evermore hegemonic over the Balkan states, reviewing, authorizing, and in many cases disallowing domestic trials on war crimes.

While the Court as deterrent and the Court as peace builder were certainly troubled, if not flawed, conceptions, at least they were both directed at the states in question. This new understanding all but completely removed the problem from domestic purview. It was as though the crimes themselves had been perpetrated on the international plane, rather than in the destroyed homes, torched businesses, and decimated places of worship *in* the Balkans.

This increasingly paternalistic philosophy led to an even greater concentration of Court operations and power in The Hague and away from the battlefields, with Balkan citizens becoming an afterthought in the process. Public relations and outreach of the Court in the region were perennially underfunded. Court offices in Balkan capitals either did not exist or had only skeleton staffs. And, perhaps most galling to the citizens of the region, outside the Court's translator corps, the tribunal refused to employ any Balkan citizens. The same was true until very recently in Rwanda. This ostracism from the judicial process has compounded a more pervasive emasculation of almost all government and civil society functions. To take Bosnia as an example:

> After fifty years of Communism, five years of war, and the last decade of international control, the state has a legal and political order that is decidedly not its own. From the country's new internationally imposed criminal code—which, by a strange twist of legal fate, is modeled on the criminal law of the state of Alaska—to its thoroughly compromised national symbols, which include a national anthem "sung" without any words, [there is limited] local ownership [of] the state.[25]

The Yugoslavia tribunal is often seen as yet another slight to the country's attempts to attain some domestic stake in the operation of the state. It is little wonder that the Court's reception has been so cool.

It is true that more recent iterations of international justice have attempted to reform some of these difficulties and "return" some of the crimes to the locations in which they were committed. The "hybrid" courts such as in Sierra Leone, for instance, have operated usually within, or as a part, of domestic justice systems. Importantly these courts have been negotiated with the target state, rather than imposed on them. Despite this difference, the UN and the international community have proven particularly bad at nuance; the international component of these "mixed" courts has almost always trumped the local, overshadowed domestic participants, and again often rendered "justice" without concern for local needs or views about what "justice" looks like.

While the current status of those countries in which international justice has been attempted is distressing, a closer examination of the pinnacle of war crimes justice—at Nuremberg—suggests that perhaps we should not be so surprised with these troubling outcomes. As much as the international community has largely failed to do with its current tribunals, after World War II the Allies were manifestly unable to use international trials as a tool to alter the hearts and minds of the German public. Far from furthering a sense of guilt among the populace—due to either their participation in or simple neglect to stop any of the atrocities perpetrated by their government—the international trial at least in part appeared to solidify defensiveness about the National Socialist era.

Evidence for the initial failure of the trials to capture the "hearts and minds" comes from disturbing public opinion polls conducted by the Allied occupation forces in Western Germany. In October 1946, the month that the first major Nuremberg proceedings concluded, and thus in the immediate wake and publication of the scope of Nazi crimes, "large numbers of postwar Germans [nonetheless] . . . continued to [publicly] express . . . characteristic" National Socialist perceptions.[26] Thirty-three percent of respondents maintained that "Jews should not have the same rights as those belonging to the Aryan Race"; 37 percent denied that the "extermination of the Jews and Poles . . . was not necessary for the security of Germans"; and over half of respondents argued that the German territories that the Hitler regime had annexed—in search of *lebensraum* for the greater German nation—should be a part of Germany proper.[27] Throughout the second half of the 1940s, support for National Socialism remained widespread.[28]

Even more troubling is that the strength of these views actually *increased* over time, such that during the 1950s it was clear that a "declining percentage of . . . respondents, averaging only about a third . . . rejected National Socialism outright. An increasing percentage, averaging about half, thought it merely a good idea badly carried out."[29] At that time, only one in ten Germans supported the prosecution of war criminals.[30] In Bavaria, traditionally the most conservative region of the Western zone, more than half of respondents were even favorably disposed toward introducing elements of the Nazi program in order to reduce unemployment and other social ills.[31] In short, by the middle of the 1950s it was clear that

> if the aim of the Allied occupation was to turn Germans against the entirety of the National Socialist era, to force individuals to recognize the part that they had played in bringing the regime to power or sustaining it, then surely the Allies' reeducation program [of which Nuremberg was a centerpiece] must be deemed a failure.[32]

Some went as far as to claim that the Allies' international justice program "turned the masses away from the hoped-for democratic beginnings and invited comparisons to the lawlessness of the Nazi era."[33] Germans eventually saw the light, but it is noteworthy that, according to polls, they only began to do so in the late 1950s, which was the same time that Germans began to pursue numerous, even if imperfect, domestic prosecutions of their own against the Nazis.

In Tokyo, the postwar situation was even worse than in Germany, and continues to be to this day. Victims of the Empire of Japan are still waiting for a comprehensive mea culpa. The Tokyo Trials of major war criminals, the Asian sister court to the Nuremberg proceedings, were even more meekly run than Nuremberg. Many major leaders and instigators of the war were either not punished or given quick amnesties. Even in the few cases that trials and true punishments eventuated, many convicted war criminals went straight from prison back to parliament and the government, reelected by a thankful populace uninfluenced by any of the horrors these leaders were shown to have committed during World War II. Particularly egregious examples of such postincarceration embrace included that of the former head of Unit 731—the infamous group within the Japanese military that engaged in medical experiments on POWs. He was not only unpunished but ironically became the president of the Japanese Medical Association. Four years after he was paroled from his war crimes conviction, Mamoru Shigemitsu, the Japanese foreign minister at the end of World War II, regained his post as Japan's top diplomat.

These were the unheralded legacies of the post–World War II international legal efforts that have been obscured by history, and thus were neglected in the lead up to the modern international criminal courts. However, criticisms of Nuremberg were present at the time and shortly after the trials were held. United States Senator Robert Taft of Ohio speaking in October 1946, a few months after Nuremberg had concluded, questioned whether the proceedings would really do any good for Germany or for the United States. He argued:

> About this whole judgment there is the spirit of vengeance, and vengeance is seldom justice. The hanging of the eleven men convicted will be a blot on the American record which we shall long regret.[34]

His was not the popular sentiment.[35] Indeed, Taft's statements were so politically risky, so out of accord with seeming popular consensus—and caused such a firestorm—as to earn him inclusion in John F. Kennedy's *Profiles in Courage*. In that book, which was first published a decade later, Kennedy remarked that Senator Taft's "conclusions are shared, I believe, by a substantial number of American citizens today. And they were shared, at least privately, by a goodly number in 1946."[36]

The international community's failure to look at how Nuremberg and Tokyo fared on the ground makes the international community's continued failures to do so in the latest international justice a continuation of the trend—a trend that vilified Senator Taft and stamped down Nuremberg dissent in the 1940s.

In a very real sense, the Politics of Hell, practiced in the world capitals and in UN headquarters in New York and Geneva, have led to a new sort of "Hell" in the many places where international justice has tried to respond to violence and violations of international law. It is not a "Hell" of war or genocide, but rather a "Hell" of neglect. The Politics of Hell obscures the Problem from Hell by reverting to generalities and broad brushstrokes to explain highly complex situations and, just as importantly, it obscures real solutions to the problem. It is time to listen, to see how international justice plays out on the ground, in what Eleanor Roosevelt would call "the small places, close to home," the world of the "individual person" seeking justice.

Chapter 5

FALLING ON DEAF EARS
[PART I]
International Justice from the Ground Up

Paul Rusesabagina, the latter day Oskar Schindler, who earned acclaim
for harboring Hutus and Tutsis in his Hotel des Mille Collines during
the 1994 Rwanda genocide, is angry and scared. Looking across the border
toward Tanzania and the International Criminal Tribunal for Rwanda
(ICTR) operating five hundred miles away in Arusha, Rusesabagina—
whose story became famous in the film *Hotel Rwanda*—sees a tribunal
that has failed to listen to its constituency in Rwanda. Rusesabagina is concerned that unless the ICTR changes its tactics immediately and markedly,
most of his countrymen will see it as a biased tribunal that, instead of
resolving the devastating fractures in Rwandan society, will exacerbate
them. He implores the tribunal and the UN to hear the people in whose
name justice is purportedly being done, the "millions of Rwandese who
have no one to speak out for them."[1] The tribunal has not listened.

It is not surprising that the ICTR has been unreceptive to requests
from Rwanda. Ever since Rwanda voted against the creation of the tribunal when it came up for a vote in the UN Security Council, Rwandan
leaders and many private citizens like Rusesabagina have looked with
suspicion at the work of the Tanzania-based body. The suspicion seems
mutual. Rwanda has regularly demanded concessions from the tribunal
and argued vigorously for the indictment or nonindictment of poten-

tial suspects. In the several cases in which the tribunal has ignored Rwanda's pleas, the Rwandan government has sporadically severed all relations with and orchestrated mass protests against the tribunal. In February 2004, more than ten thousand people protested in Cyangugu, a town in southwest Rwanda, following the acquittal of two defendants at the ICTR—demonstrators carried placards branding the Rwanda tribunal "revisionist," and the UN "useless."[2]

This history has made the ICTR immediately and understandably circumspect when Rwanda presents it with yet another complaint or demand, and the tribunal often refuses to act. The summer of 2006, however, saw Rwanda launch a particularly trenchant protest against the tribunal. The protest concerned twelve suspects in the 1994 genocide. The problem that Kigali had was not that the suspects were missing from the tribunal's indictment list—a common claim made by the government—but rather that they were on the tribunal's payroll. Instead of prosecuting suspected *genocidaires*, the tribunal was paying them.[3]

Incredibly, this was not the first time the tribunal was similarly accused. There was the case of the investigator who worked for the tribunal for six years; he may well still have been with the tribunal if not for the fact that in 2001, on a trip to the Butare region of Rwanda to prepare a case, a survivor recognized him and lodged a complaint. And there was the case of the lawyer, Callixte Gakwaya, who was on the original list of genocide suspects prepared by Interpol, but nonetheless was appointed as tribunal-funded defense counsel in February 2006. This led one exasperated Rwandan official to lament that the "if the ICTR wants, it can prosecute him, but not employ him."[4] A further case of a tribunal-employed genocide suspect emerged in 2008.[5]

How a tribunal established to prosecute genocide could come to employ suspected perpetrators is distressing. Of even greater concern is that in so many of these cases, including that of the dozen suspected perpetrators named in summer 2006, the tribunal refused to immediately act.

Though Rwanda's concerns have been ignored in other equally distressing cases—such as when members of the tribunal staff were suspected of complicity in the murder of a witness against a war criminal[6]—the "good" news for Rwanda is that faced with the potential for permanent severance of its relationship with Kigali, the tribunal finally acted, and the 2006 complaint was addressed. The dozen suspects were thrown out of the tribunal (though it is not clear if they were then pursued for prosecution).

The ICTR needs cooperation from the state of Rwanda in order to function. Consequently, Rwanda has had leverage to ensure that its interests have been heard and respected. For the millions of regular citizens in Rwanda, Sierra Leone, and throughout the Balkans who have no such powers, having "their" international courts redress their grievances has been a regularly impossible task. It is true that some of their complaints, much like some of those made by the state of Rwanda, have been misguided. For instance, as we will see, the common claim that the international courts are more prone to find guilt than domestic courts does not hold up under scrutiny. However, some complaints have clearly deserved the same attention that Rwanda's concerns about ICTR employees merited; and yet, in all too many instances, locals have not just been ignored, but often belittled, with concerns dismissed as irrelevant, ill informed, or reflective of a pernicious ethnic bias that all residents of the region presumably have. Serb Vojin Dimitrejevic underscores the separation between the courts and their target countries, lamenting that things may "look quite different to people sitting in The Hague, to foreign legal experts, and to the prosecution," than they do to the people on the ground.[7]

Examples of the "deafness" of the international judicial system to the concerns of the locals are numerous and often astounding. In the Balkans, the story can be told of "its" tribunal's seeming disinterest for the thoughts and needs of the 24 million residents of the former Yugoslavia. The statute for the tribunal was not even translated into Serbo-Croatian until the institution was five years old. Even once outreach in the Balkans began, funding lagged, with financing coming not from the tribunal's main budget but rather from the sporadic generosity of states themselves. This resulted in a timid, erratic effort and, to many observers and residents on the ground, indicated a fundamental "lack of attention . . . paid to ordinary Bosnians, Croats, and Serbs."[8]

Even in Sierra Leone where the situation is significantly better—largely because the Special Court for Sierra Leone is located in the Sierra Leone capital, Freetown—true conversation between its court and its constituents is lacking. Learning from the previous tribunals, the Special Court promised early outreach to those affected, and made far-sighted accommodations for the many Sierra Leoneans who could not afford to make the trip from inland Sierra Leone to see the proceedings in Freetown. The Special Court has regularly ventured out, holding town meetings in Sierra Leone's provinces and districts, and produced regular radio broadcasts to supplement in-person meetings. The result has been a comparatively high level of local support, at least for the *idea* of the court. Yet, even here, despite the well-meaning efforts and some noteworthy successes in communicating to the populace, the dialogue has essentially been all one way—from the Court down. A principal obstacle for the Special Court to be effective in its role has been the view of many in the country—"including its most obvious constituency: human rights and reform-oriented NGOs"[9]—that despite its unique provenance and ostensible domestic "ownership," it is nonetheless an imposition, either by the government itself, or by the international community. Notably, Court prosecutions are done in its own name, not in the name of the people of Sierra Leone. Many have simply taken to referring to the Special Court as "Kabbah's court" (the former president who initially requested the institution) rather than as a judicial body of and for the people of Sierra Leone.

WHAT ARE THEY SAYING?

Disenfranchised subjects of international justice are a diverse group, making many claims about their courts and the quality of justice being provided or denied. Some of their concerns and complaints are self-serving and certainly fit into the rubric of being based on bias or misinformation rather than fact. However, there are real failings in international justice, and such failings are not only evident from on high but also in the homes, businesses, and streets of the states for whom international justice has been prescribed. In short, some of the complaints are not only valid but potentially devastating, both to the people trying to recover from mass crimes and for the practice of international justice. Almost all complaints can be categorized as falling under three broad claims that correspond to the three stages of a trial: the initial indictment, the trial itself, and the trial's aftermath. "Subjects" of international justice say that the various international courts:

1. Prosecute the wrong people for the wrong crimes.
2. Are unfair in the prosecution of defendants.
3. Further destabilize target states by, most benignly, failing to provide support for developing domestic justice systems and, most devastatingly, fomenting new bouts of violence.

Though some of the complaints are unfounded, a closer analysis of these concerns reveal that a large majority of the most often heard claims are about actual, serious problems. Perhaps most troubling is that even if the international community heeded the concerns it would have limited ability to rectify them.

THIS "ILLEGAL" WAR CRIMES COURT: PLUS ÇA CHANGE?

The defendant was an experienced soldier, having risen up in the service of his state as its leader's territorial ambitions expanded. He had finally been given command over a large swath of occupied territory and proceeded to do his state's bidding, murdering those who resisted, and encouraging (or at least not discouraging) mercenaries from several states to rape and plunder in the name of his sovereign. It was only through the work of a coalition of outside nations, sickened and angered by his actions, and eager to stem the contagion of instability that his leadership had wrought, that he was finally removed from office, incarcerated, and put on trial. An international court, with a multinational bench of judges was assembled, and representatives from the many peoples whom he had abused gathered to witness the case. The chief prosecutor set out the charges, including rape and murder. However, the defendant refused to recognize the legality of the Court; it had no jurisdiction over him, he said, and it was only his state, in whose name he had worked, that could try him.

This vignette, with surprisingly similar players and geostrategic facts, has played out before the judges at Nuremberg and the Tokyo trials, repeated before the Yugoslavia and Rwandan tribunals, the Special Court for Sierra Leone,[10] the Special Panels for Serious Crimes in East Timor, the Iraqi Special Tribunal, and will almost certainly repeat itself once more at the Khmer Rouge tribunal, the Lebanon tribunal, and before the International Criminal Court. The facts that led to a trial and the court proceedings themselves, including the predictable parries by a defendant refusing to recognize the legality of an international court, are made all the more eternal when one notes that this "modern" vignette describes the story of a war crimes trial in 1474, some 450 years before Nuremberg was even contemplated. Charles the Bold, Duke of Burgundy, had appointed Peter von Hagenbach governor of Breisach (a fortified town on the Upper Rhine) and asked him to secure the region. Governor Hagenbach had taken to his task with brutal enthusiasm. Once he was removed by a military coalition raised by the Archduke of Austria, rather than being immediately dispatched he was brought before a panel of nearly thirty judges from the various states and independent towns surrounding Breisach. It was a "real international court"[11] and one that Hagenbach was unwilling to recognize.

While there are some differences between Hagenbach's trial and modern iterations, including that upon his verdict and sentence to death there was a competition among eight candidates who wished to do the honor of chopping off the defendant's head,[12] Hagenbach's refusal to recognize the legality of this court provides it a distinctly modern, if not timeless, flavor.

Ever since the Hagenbach trial there have been two forms of illegality that have raised defendants' and observers' ire about international courts: the illegality of creating a tribunal, which has largely been resolved, and the illegality of a purely political body dispensing supposedly apolitical justice. In either sense, this initial complaint boils down to an assertion that international courts prosecute the wrong people precisely because international courts are themselves illegal.

> *The UN Security Council has seized power it does not possess, corrupting the Charter of the United Nations, placing itself above the law.... The Criminal Tribunal for Former Yugoslavia is illegitimate and its creation a corruption of the United Nations.*[13]
> —Slobodan Milosevic, The Hague, August 2001.

Of all the modern indictees, Slobodan Milosevic was probably the most articulate, if verbose, in analyzing why he believed that UN tribunals were illegally created, a belief shared by many in the Balkans. Milosevic's claim was that an international court like ICTY could only be created via a multinational treaty or amendment to the UN charter. The establishment of such a body, which exercises jurisdiction over and above national sovereignty, was too great a leap for the UN Security Council alone to make. He has not been the only one to raise this argument. During the Security Council debates about the Yugoslavia tribunal, the UN secretary general himself noted that "in the normal course of events" an international treaty ought to be used to form such an entity, though he worried that such a process would take too long and there was "no guarantee" that it would be ratified.[14] Even among states on the Security Council, where the resolutions creating the tribunal were eventually passed unanimously, there was significant disquiet that echoed Milosevic's claims. China stated that it did not endorse "the legal approach involved" and that "it [was] the consistent position of the Chinese delegation that an international tribunal should be established by concluding a treaty so as to provide a solid legal foundation."[15] Brazil, which occupied one of the rotating seats on the Security Council, justified its eventual vote for the tribunal as a "political expression of our condemnation of the crimes . . . not . . . an overall endorsement of legal formulas involved in the foundation of the . . . tribunal." The "most appropriate means [to create such a tribunal] would have been via a convention."[16]

Milosevic's claim also seemed to have a basis in logic, as it appeared to be on par with the wider accepted wisdom of the global legal community. If an international court could be created using so simple a tool as a Security Council resolution, why did the world community go through the labors of the decade-long negotiations leading to the Rome Treaty of the International Criminal Court? There may have been a desire to assure real inclusiveness in such a body that compelled the international community to address the ICC outside the confines of the selective Security Council. Moreover, there may have been concerns about a veto by one or more of the Security Council's permanent members, although in the early 1990s this was far less likely than it has become since 2000. Still, at the very least, this claim is deserving of a long-overdue response. What did the extended negotiations at Rome provide the resulting ICC that a well-phrased, persuasive Security Council resolution could not?

Unfortunately though, even if logic accords with this argument, and Chinese/Brazilian complaints aside, law does not. International law, both inside and outside the criminal domain, is constructed via a dichotomous process of written agreements—treaties, conventions, and so forth—together with widely, if not universally, accepted long-standing state practice, otherwise known as "customary international law."[17] A fundamental building block of this customary portion of international law concerns the establishment of legitimacy by an international tribunal. The world has long recognized the "international law principle . . . granting all international adjudicative bodies 'competence de la competence'—that is, the power and the duty to determine the legality [and scope] of its own jurisdiction."[18] In its first judgment,

Prosecutor v. Tadic, the Yugoslavia tribunal did just this, perhaps unsurprisingly, holding that it was a legally constituted body with jurisdiction to rule and assess punishment on matters discussed in its statute.[19] The Rwanda tribunal ruled similarly in *Prosecutor v. Kanyabashi*.[20]

Consequently, though perhaps insufficient to mollify the claim of illegality—especially as voiced by nonlawyers, those unfamiliar with international legal processes, and even some states such as Kenya and Burundi, which have cited the "illegality" of the Rwanda tribunal to justify their intermittent noncooperation with the body—legally speaking, Milosevic's argument fails. Interestingly, amongst the earliest proponents of the ICTY's *legality* were Milosevic's ethnic brethren, Serb academics. While recognizing the difficulty of implementation, both Konstanin Obradovic and Vladan Vasilijevic—amongst the leading figures in Yugoslav international law circles at the time—held that the tribunal was "legal," at least in how it was envisioned in February 1993.[21]

The legality of international justice can be put to rest. This is especially so regarding the more recent tribunals that were negotiated by states (such as those in Sierra Leone and Cambodia), rather than imposed on them. If Milosevic's concerns, and those of China and Brazil, were based on the Security Council's abrogation of state sovereignty, such sovereignty implies that a state can consciously cede its sovereignty if it wishes. Sierra Leone and Cambodia have explicitly done so, by negotiating their tribunals with the UN and agreeing to invite the international community to play a part in war crimes justice.

Yet, here too, there is some complexity that reveals that the complaint of illegality remains not *entirely* without merit. Even if the tribunals are legal, it is not clear (or legally irrefutable) that their structures are similarly legal.

Modern international criminal law before the Yugoslavia tribunal had only existed at the Nuremberg and Tokyo trials, which were organized according to their own internal logics. International law, however, continued to develop from 1945, even if its criminal piece lay dormant. Public international law at the International Court of Justice, private international law at scores of permanent and ad hoc arbitration tribunals, and human rights litigation at the European Court of Human Rights and the Inter-American Court of Human Rights have all progressed in the ensuing fifty years.

The international courts that emerged before the Yugoslav and Rwanda tribunals developed certain characteristic structures and processes that were so commonly abided by as to arguably take on the weight of "customary international law." And, if the Yugoslav and Rwanda tribunals are to gain legitimacy by reference to customary international law, it seems logical that their structures and processes should similarly adhere to customary law. In this regard, it is possible to contend that the ICTY and ICTR, and, to a lesser extent, courts in Sierra Leone, Cambodia, and East Timor, have contravened at least two bedrock principles of international law as it had come to be practiced prior to, and outside, those tribunals. And, though the international community has seen the error of its ways in some regards—making amends when it came to devising courts after the ICTY and ICTR— the International Criminal Court marks an almost complete return to the structures and processes of these initial tribunals.

The first legal principle concerns the balance between universal ideals and domestic norms. Courts that rule on matters of human rights for a diversity of states have long realized the need to balance universal norms (as manifest in human rights treaties and customary international law) with the particular needs of constituent states. This has been the case with the European Court of Human Rights, where judges hear disputes arising from any of its forty-seven member states, which range from Turkey to Ireland, Portugal to Russia. The result has been the development of the doctrine of "margin of appreciation," which refers to "the latitude a government enjoys in . . . applying provisions [of] international" law and agreements.[22] The "margin" is the deviation from some standard "average" allowed by multinational courts out of respect for "cultural, historical, and philosophical differences" of each member state. In the European context, it recognizes that "what is right for Spain may not be right for the United Kingdom."[23] The "margin" makes sense for many reasons, not the least of which is that it encourages a state to accept the court's rulings, knowing that the state's particular national "story" has played a part in the decision. This is not what international criminal law usually advocates: international criminal courts provide a single answer to legal questions, and uniformity across states—in interpretation and punishment—is one of the avowed goals (and often-cited benefits) of international justice.* As we have seen, this is not only in direct opposition to the conventional wisdom in other international arenas that have moved away from universalist solutions, such as development policy, but is also contrary to the developed practice of the international tribunals that operated between the end of the post–World War II trials and the establishment of the Yugoslavia and Rwanda tribunals.

The second manner in which the ICTY and ICTR could be held to violate standing international legal practice is in the makeup of their judicial corps. Noticeable for their absence are judges from any state in which crimes were committed or states from where the accused come. In almost *every* other aspect of international law, ranging from multistate commercial dispute settlement, to state-on-state litigation, participants in proceedings have a role in selecting some of the judges who hear their case.[24] In such cases, judges chosen by parties to a dispute rarely make up the sole vote, nor usually even a majority; however, they are present, and it is their task to bring the local perspective back to the judges' chambers, enlightening other jurists of the specific, cultural, historical, or societal contexts critical to the case. As early twentieth-century American statesman Elihu Root contended when discussing litigating cases before international courts:

> Nations should be able to go before [an international] . . . Court with the certainty that their case will be fully understood. For this

---

*It is true that some laws have no "margin of appreciation"—they are completely non-derogable. These are the so-called *jus cogens* norms and they include many of the crimes under the jurisdiction of international criminal tribunals (such as genocide and crimes against humanity). However, even if no margin exists in defining the crime, the margin speaks also to the punishment of infractions. And, even if *jus cogens* violations are found, this does not necessarily mean that the same punishment is appropriate; local norms and the exact conditions under which a crime occurred should be relevant, for the same reasons that "margin of appreciation" is important in the interpretation of other laws.

purpose there must be . . . a judge of their nationality on the Court, who must sit on a footing of complete equality with the others."[25]

It is true that in some international courts, parties cannot choose judges. However, in those cases, such as in the European Court of Human Rights, states impacted by a decision have the right to intervene in the proceedings in order to directly provide judges with country-specific information.[26]

At the Yugoslavia tribunal, the failure to include Balkan judges is especially odd in light of two facts. First, shortly after the tribunal commenced, the International Court of Justice (ICJ)—which also sits in The Hague, about a mile away—began hearing matters closely related to those being heard at the ICTY. As the official legal arm of the UN, the ICJ's primary duty is to hear cases between states, and by statute it ensures that a "hometown" judge for each side sits on the bench, either as a permanent judge or a judge specifically chosen to hear a particular matter. The ICJ was the site of two sets of cases involving states impacted by the Yugoslav wars: Serbia and Montenegro brought the first cases—complaints against participant NATO member states involved in the bombing of Serbia—in 1999.[27] Bosnia and Herzegovina brought the second set of cases, seeking reparations from Serbia for the Yugoslav war. In each proceeding, at least one member of the adjudicating bench was of each party's choosing.

That the ICJ deals with matters between states and that criminal tribunals try individuals is an important difference. However, it does not explain why the longstanding tradition of "hometown" judges should be abrogated. This seems especially the case when dealing with mass, state-orchestrated war crimes. In such cases, many, especially in defendants' home regions, perceive prosecutions to be against state policies (rather than specific individuals), making them de facto very similar to ICJ matters. This is certainly true in Serbia where a large proportion of the population has long felt that the Milosevic trial was really an indictment of the entire state—a view that many observers outside Serbia have echoed.[28] Any *legal* distinction between the ICTY and ICJ cases is moot on the ground.

Moreover, again in the Balkan case, the ICTY has never managed to explain why Balkan judges have been excluded from the proceedings, nor to convince Balkan citizens of the necessity for doing so. For Yugoslavs old enough to remember the judicial system under Tito, this is still more exasperating. Ethnic bias was sadly common in Tito's "forced" republic.[29] Consequently, when matters were brought to trial, it was a rule of practice that neither a coethnic nor a non-coethnic could serve as the sole jurist. Group benches were consequently very common.[30] Potential judicial ethnic bias was handled via inclusion rather than exclusion.

Again, though the subsequent Special Court for Sierra Leone has rectified some of these concerns by including locals on the bench, the same is not true for the ICC, which represents a return to the true "justice from on high" that has caused so much concern at the earlier tribunals.

Even if strictly speaking the argument that international courts have been illegal is untrue, the concern about illegality—in light of the courts' structures among other factors—remains. This perception is a real problem for courts eager to make their mark on peoples recovering from mass crimes. Instead of seeing a return of law, for many, these courts are simple manifestations of politics, often practiced at the expense of justice. And, it is in politics that many on the ground also sense "illegality."

THE POLITICS OF JUSTICE—THE JUSTICE OF POLITICS

Bruno Rakic leans over his strudel, cigarette dangling from his lips, ash dripping dangerously close to my coffee: "That tribunal in The Hague, politics, not law, is its master." We are sitting in the "Hot Spot," a café across the main drag, Vasa Carapica, from the University of Belgrade's law faculty. If it were not for Rakic's invective, it might be easy to mistake our *kaffeeklatsch* as taking place in almost any coffee shop in the West—the Starbucks aesthetic has clearly permeated the Serb entrepreneurial class. Rakic's argument is not so much that The Hague is "illegal," just that it is "*not* legal." Politics, not justice, is the end goal of the enterprise.

Rakic may not be the most sympathetic, nor the most unbiased, of the Serbs crying foul at the Yugoslavia tribunal. A close associate and unofficial Belgrade lawyer of former president Milosevic, Rakic evidently has a political axe of his own to grind. However, what is most surprising about Rakic's views is that they remain mainstream in Belgrade and among Serbs living throughout the Balkans. It is "unbelievable how negatively" the ICTY is viewed by the average Serb, said Rakic. Surveys conducted by the American embassy in Belgrade, working alongside several local and international NGOs, support this claim, revealing that up to 75 percent of the population of Serbia (only 65 percent of whom are ethnic Serbs) view the tribunal with contempt, with a similar majority emphasizing that such trials that should occur need to be undertaken at home, not in the Netherlands.[31] And, even more surprising is the degree to which other groups—Bosniaks, Croats, and Albanians—agree with this assessment. [32] Rakic's belief that "politics controls The Hague" process is amongst the most widely held.

Using slightly different terminology, former Liberian leader Charles Taylor, who has been arrested and is facing trial before the Special Court for Sierra Leone, made a similar argument. Taylor justified his refusal to participate in the proceedings against him not on the grounds of the Special Court's purported illegality, but rather its illegitimacy due to its political overtones:

> I cannot participate in a charade that does injustice to the people of Sierra Leone and Liberia and the people of Africa, and a disservice to the international community in whose name this court claims to speak. . . . I choose not to be the fig leaf of legitimacy for this process.[33]

The same criticisms can be heard before the Rwanda tribunal—a defense lawyer arguing that the tribunal is "a political court;"[34] in Freetown—a major Anglophone African daily asking whether the Special Court enforces "law or politics?"[35]; in Dili, East Timor—where UN politics was supposedly determinative in providing justice at the Special Panels[36] and defense counsel stated that the Special Panels were a sham political body;[37] and increasingly in Phnom Penh—where some have questioned the political independence of the Khmer Rouge tribunal.[38] The argument often heard on the ground is that because the tribunals are products of political will that they prosecute anyone is unjust, or at least politically rather than judicially motivated.

Are they right? Are these courts really "political" rather than "legal?"

In a sense, the answer is self-evident: *all* courts are at least partly political. The Yugoslavia tribunal, for one, has even partly embraced the political moniker: former tribunal president Gabrielle Kirk MacDonald admitted as much, stating that even while serving she knew that she presided over "a political court."[39]

However, in reality, the argument that politics controls these institutions is too broad. And, it is certainly inaccurate especially when speaking of their initial establishment. For the majority of the tribunals formed after the Yugoslavia tribunal, it is hard to say that there was much true discussion of any sort, political or otherwise. Once the Rubicon of actually giving the international community permission to construct a court had been crossed, subsequent courts, even if fraught with logistical and domestic difficulties, from an international political perspective were much easier to justify and involved little arm-twisting, political wrangling, or backroom dealing. Even regarding the Yugoslavia tribunal, the "political" criticism is somewhat unfair. The search for real "justice" rather than political advantage was a concern early on in discussions about creating a court, and was clearly a goal of many of the diplomats and others who, from late 1991, began thinking about a Balkan tribunal.

In coming to this conclusion about the motives of those who created the Yugoslavia tribunal, historical context is critical. Since Nuremburg, attitudes about international justice had been rising and falling. In the early 1990s, they were ascendant again. These were halcyon days for internationalists and those who believed in the potential of international institutions and, in particular, of international justice. The "End of History"[40] foretold by the apparent mending of the great schism between East and West, led many to believe that "universal" solutions to conundrums such as providing postconflict justice were at hand.

The world was quickly becoming more welcoming to the idea of instituting international justice in the wake of mass crimes. With this predisposition, the crimes in the former Yugoslavia cried out for such international, judicial attention. The first concrete demand for a tribunal covering the Balkan situation was made in May 1991 by a Yugoslav journalist, Serb Mirko Klarin, writing in *Borda*, a prominent Belgrade newspaper.[41] In a piece titled "Nuremberg Now," he called for the quick creation of an international tribunal to try crimes against peace and humanity occurring in the region.[42]

Though other calls for war crimes trials emerged shortly after Klarin's, it would be another year before those outside the Balkans began to seriously contemplate Klarin's request. In mid-1992, the French government took up the charge, inserting the creation of an international tribunal into the final "Decision of the London Conference," a multinational meeting that had been called to assess the best means to address the quickly deteriorating situation in the former Yugoslavia. The German government revamped and elucidated the French proposal, presenting it to wide acclaim before the UN General Assembly in September 1992. A sprint to draft a statute for the tribunal ensued, and the statute was debated before the UN Security Council on May 25, 1993. Council deliberations were civil, and focused primarily on the horror of the crimes in the former Yugoslavia and the urgency of responding to them. As noted, some Security Council members expressed reservations, but in the end, passage was unanimous. Explaining its vote, China made clear that its consent to the tribunal was a not an "endorsement" but rather was a "political position."[43]

It is possible to sense, as China did, some politics in these early maneuvers arguing for and establishing the tribunal; yet, it would be disingenuous to argue that "politics" and wider third-party political advantage were the primary forces driving the process. Following the end of the Cold War and the end of the first Gulf War,[44] widespread support abounded for such a tribunal. The Europeans took the lead in proposing an international tribunal. Europeans—and to a lesser extent North Americans—were alarmed at the crisis on the continent and appeared manifestly and increasingly guilty that they had not acted forcefully to stem the Balkan carnage. The continent's political leaders were compelled to recognize that "collectively they [had made] . . . a mess of [the] . . . crisis."[45] Germany in particular—reunified in October 1990, months before the outbreak of Balkan violence—sought to use the establishment of a tribunal to make amends for these mistakes and to demonstrate the newly enlarged country's noble intentions, clearly divergent from the country's outlook the last time all of Germany was unified. Both the German public and officialdom were sensitive to the increasingly frequent comparisons made in the early 1990s between Balkan "ethnic cleansing" and the Holocaust.[46]

While politics would soon permeate the process, the lead-up to the tribunal's founding was refreshingly devoid of outward political machinations. Rather, the tribunal seems to have been born of the same optimistic, universalist humanism that pervaded the UN and much of the world during the first years after the Cold War.

Once the mold had been set with the ICTY, each subsequent tribunal involved less and less true political debate—an irony in itself, as some of the more reluctant supporters of the Yugoslavia tribunal had conditioned their vote on an explicit understanding that the Yugoslavia tribunal was to be ad hoc, and their support did "not constitute any precedent."[47] However, when the idea for subsequent tribunals emerged, it was clear that the ICTY precedent was the basis for action—seemingly similar problems resulted in resort to the same legal approach. Smoothing the path further in the case of the Rwanda tribunal was the sentiment that if the Security Council did not provide a tribunal similar to the one provided for the Balkans, it would be accused of Eurocentrism or worse. Sensing some foot dragging in the council, Rwandan prime minister Faustin Twagiramungu in May 1994 made this accusation clear, asking whether it was "because we're African that a court has not been set up?"[48]

States had become cognizant of the awful crimes committed in regions where international justice was to be deployed. And finding a "threat to international peace and security" in mass crimes—the necessary trigger for UN Security Council action—was a much easier conclusion to make once the Balkans, and then Rwanda, had blazed the trail. It is neither naïve nor overly optimistic to claim that in each instance, tribunal creation was based on achieving some sort of justice—even if the Security Council had to be coaxed and guilted into providing it—rather than because it was seen to provide some political advantage.

"PERCEPTION" OF POLITICS

Unfortunately, regardless of the relative political "purity" of the historical record, tribunals have regularly been unable to shake the appearance that they serve the wider political aims of some states rather than the aims of justice. This too has fomented a widespread view in the target states that the tribunals have been political rather than legal enterprises. Such a view is notable in Sierra Leone, where the Special Court has been viewed by many within and outside the country as an implicit arm of US foreign policy that Washington has used for furthering a host of ends having little to do with the wars of West Africa.

To some, the Special Court is an American-imposed instrument specifically designed to thwart the International Criminal Court. Intellectuals within Sierra Leone are well aware of the US opposition to the ICC. They recognize that the United States would greatly prefer the establishment of tribunals similar to that in Sierra Leone to address mass atrocities. The Americans, who have been by far the largest funders of the Sierra Leone court, have done little to dissuade the notion that the court was designed as much to provide justice in West Africa as it was to provide further proof that the ICC is unnecessary. In a February 2002 interview, Pierre-Richard Prosper, then US ambassador-at-large for war crimes, made clear the favor with which Washington views the Sierra Leone "model" in contrast to the ICC:

[Unlike the ICC,] [h]ere we reached an independent court through an international agreement that shares the responsibility between the Sierra Leone government and the . . . United Nations. It fits our global philosophy [unlike the ICC].[49]

Concerns about Washington's dual purposes behind supporting the Special Court for Sierra Leone hardened after Sierra Leone signed the ICC treaty in 2002. Especially galling for some was that Freetown followed its ratification of the ICC treaty by signing an agreement with Washington guaranteeing that Sierra Leone would not surrender any US nationals to the ICC. This led a columnist for a Freetown daily to question the independence of Sierra Leone and the rationale behind his government's actions:

First, we ratify . . . the International Criminal Court . . . [then], we turn around . . . to condone a country rebelling against the Court at a time when we are prosecuting our own citizens [for] . . . similar crimes. Is it that the government values Americans more than Sierra Leoneans?[50]

The seeming American imprint was not helped when the Special Court appointed an American, David Crane, to be its first chief prosecutor. Crane was an experienced military lawyer, well-versed in the laws of war; his professional background made him a powerful choice. Yet, even before he began investigations and trials, it was Crane's background as a longtime US Army lawyer, and his straight-shooting, decidedly American style of speech and analysis that unwittingly solidified the impression of an American court dispensing American justice in Freetown. When the court began issuing indictments, members of Crane's own office became frustrated that the prosecutor's sound bites were obstensibly being made for an American audience or a wider international constituency, rather than for Sierra Leone.

For instance, throughout his three-year tenure at the Special Court, which corresponded with the ratcheting up of the Bush administration's "War on Terror," the prosecutor regularly referred to terrorism, claiming of Sierra Leone and West Africa that "al Qaeda is here" and he gave several interviews around the world alleging links between al Qaeda and Charles Taylor. Notably, he stated before a Security Council press gallery that "al Qaeda has been in West Africa. It continues to be in West Africa, and Charles Taylor has been harboring members of al Qaeda."[51] To be fair, there is some circumstantial evidence of such a link.[52] However, not only has definitive proof of such a link not been released by the Special Court but it is not the Special Court's mandate to investigate Middle Eastern terrorism. Prosecutor Crane admitted as much, justifying his repeated comments about al Qaeda by stating that even if the group fell outside his mandate he was not "going to be shy about passing information onto appropriate international and national [crime-fighting] organizations to give them lead[s] and tips."[53] Though fears of al Qaeda muscling into the Sierra Leone diamond business had been rife in the country—"Diamonds and al Qaeda? Everyone talks about it on the streets in Freetown"[54]— Crane's justification rang hollow for many in Sierra Leone. Locals saw in Crane's focus on al Qaeda a clear attempt to, at best, increase American interest in the work of the court, and, at worst, to use the court as a resource for intelligence gathering for the War on Terror.

Crane denied working for the American government and his departure in 2005 (replaced with British barrister Desmond de Silva, who had experience practicing law in Sierra Leone) momentarily dampened the concerns. American Stephen Rapp, however, replaced de Silva in December 2006, resurrecting the accusations. Regardless of the plausibility or remaining strengths of the "local suspicions of extrajudicial US objectives . . . they [have] undoubtedly affect[ed] the Sierra Leone people's sense of ownership in the process."[55] For some participants in international justice, such concerns, whether in Sierra Leone, Rwanda, the Balkans, or elsewhere, are not so far fetched. As Judge Howard Morrison, a British barrister who served as a defense lawyer before the ICTR, noted,

> . . . the reality is that . . . there are huge vested interests [in international justice]. There are vested interests in people who want . . . the

Balkan cases determined in a certain way, there were vested interests in the people who want . . . the cases of Rwanda to be sorted out in a certain way, the Great Lakes and the Congo are rich pickings.[56]

SELECTIVE PROSECUTION

One of the supposed shortcomings of international criminal justice commonly pointed to, and in which people see truth in Judge Morrison's statement, concerns international courts' "selective prosecutions." People see the hand of international politics in the absence of specific leaders in the dock, and in the overrepresentation of some specific groups in the dock. Complaints about selective prosecution have been rife wherever international justice has been implemented. Again even if it has been untrue that states have pressured tribunals to prosecute some and ignore others, in several courts the facts are interesting, if not suspicious.

More Than One Devil Dancing on Water

"Why," asks Sierra Leonean journalist Aminatta Forna, the author of *The Devil that Danced on Water*, "if [Liberian leader Charles] Taylor has been indicted . . . why not Gaddafi or Blaise Campaore of Burkina Faso, both of whom have been linked to plans to destabilize the entire region over the past decade?"[57] Forna's question is a reasonable query for anyone even tangentially familiar with the recent history of West Africa. However, it is only Taylor, and in all likelihood will only be Taylor, who has to face justice. In this, many people in Sierra Leone and elsewhere see injustice.

The Charles Taylor indictment and arraignment has been rightfully celebrated throughout the world and even in much of Africa. The crimes of which Taylor has been accused are monstrous by any standards: the indictment includes murders, sexual slavery, wanton violence, the use of child soldiers, and abductions. The question is not whether Taylor should be indicted but why other leaders remain untouched.

The keystone in much of West Africa's troubles throughout the last two decades of the twentieth century was Libyan leader Moammar Gaddafi. During the 1980s, he ran military training camps in Libya that became "the Harvard and Yale of a whole generation of African revolutionaries."[58] Charles Taylor was one of Gaddafi's star students. Taylor's role in West Africa was to help Gaddafi execute a larger plan to economically capture West Africa by expropriating its natural resources, and to politically capture the region by forcibly destabilizing the states whose leaders were unamenable to his aims. As such, Gaddafi was directly implicated in the Sierra Leone civil war. His role is even mentioned in the Special Court for Sierra Leone's indictment of Foday Sankoh, the leader of Sierra Leone's primary rebel group, the Revolutionary United Front (RUF).[59] Similarly, even though when asked Prosecutor Crane maintained that Burkina Faso was not "off the hook," West Africa observers question why so little attention has been paid to Blaise Campaore, Burkina Faso's president and a fellow Gaddafi student. Campaore had met Taylor while both were training under Tripoli's protection and the Burkina Faso leader provided critical assistance both to Taylor in his devastation of Liberia and to the RUF in its war in Sierra Leone. The United States, if not several other major states, was long aware of Campaore's critical role in fomenting West African violence and instability. In the early 1990s, Washington requested that Campaore cease his support for Taylor and the RUF; when Campaore refused to do so, Washington withdrew its ambassador to Burkina Faso in 1992, publicly complaining about Campaore's misdeeds in the process.[60]

While Campaore's and Gaddafi's absence on the Special Court's docket is politically troubling, what is legally difficult to swallow was the centerpiece of the Taylor indictment: it charged that Taylor was part of a "joint criminal enterprise" bent on reaping diamond wealth and committing horrific crimes in the process.[61] "Joint criminal enterprise" has a specific legal definition: it is a means of assigning individual liability for actions taken by a group of which the individual is a member. The indictment claims that Taylor and the RUF were a part of such a joint criminal enterprise, thereby pinning culpability for many of the RUF's crimes on Taylor. However, after Prosecutor Crane had departed the Special Court, he noted that Taylor was a part of a "joint criminal enterprise" "aided and abetted by . . . Gaddafi . . . and Campaore."[62] Thus, the prosecutor seemed to believe that the enterprise extended beyond the RUF and included the Burkinabé and Libyan leaders. For some reason these leaders were not included in the indictment. Based solely upon what is known in the press and on the street (let alone by investigators and intelligence agencies), it would seem logical that both Gaddafi and Campaore should be indicted, with a trial focused on whether their participation and complicity equated to their membership in the "joint criminal enterprise" that did so much damage to Sierra Leone.

Though Campaore's absence is perplexing, to many, Gaddafi's absence is unsurprising and reflects the realist nature of global politics. This became particularly evident following two events in the second half of 2003. First, in August 2003, Gaddafi finally accepted responsibility for the 1988 Pan Am 103 Lockerbie bombing, and agreed to pay compensation to each affected family. And second, in December 2003, Gaddafi concluded an agreement with the United States and the United Kingdom pledging to cease Libyan development of weapons of mass destruction. As a new Arab "friend" of the West in a region where the West can always use more allies, it would have been distressing to the United States and the United Kingdom—who fund so much of the Special Court—for the institution to indict their nascent ally. Consequently, it was likely an untenable option.

While Taylor's cosupporters of RUF remain absent, there were war crimes committed on all sides of the conflict. Such acts were perpetrated by the Sierra Leone government and even by the international forces that came to stabilize the country. Yet despite these well-accepted facts, a key leader and an entire group are also absent from the Special Court. It is true, and much to the Special Court's credit, that some senior members of the sitting government have been indicted, notably Hinga Norman, deputy minister of defense during the civil war; even more to the court's credit, Norman is considered a national hero by many for his fight against the RUF and Taylor-backed forces. The Special Court was under great pressure not to indict him.[63] However, Norman's boss, former president Ahmed Kabbah, has not been indicted—and will not be—despite that fact that a government commission found that he should be held liable for the acts of his agents on the ground, and that he was both aware of the war crimes being committed by his troops and that he had often authored the orders that Norman was indicted for implementing.[64]

The group that has been absent from the Special Court is any member of the Economic Community of West African States Monitoring Group (ECOMOG), the Nigerian-led intervention force that arrived to help the Sierra Leone government withstand the rebel attacks in 1997. The group was "responsible for serious abuses, including summary executions . . . use of child soldiers, and indiscriminate bombings against civilians." In one particularly gruesome operation in January 1999, ECOMOG forces "stormed a hospital, [and] proceeded to drag wounded rebels from their beds, and execute them on hospital grounds."[65] ECOMOG also engaged in looting to such a degree that the acronym ECOMOG took on a different meaning in Sierra Leone: "Every Car Or Moving Object Gone." However, far from being investigated, let alone indicted for their behavior inside Sierra Leone, the very statute of the Special Court provides the group explicit cover, stating that the "transgressions by peacekeepers" fall outside the court's "primary" jurisdiction. The home states of the ECOMOG soldiers were to take responsibility for their punishment—no ECOMOG soldier has ever been charged with crimes committed during the Sierra Leone operation.*

The Yugoslavia tribunal, again because of the unequal amount of

---

*Theoretically, the Special Court *could* take jurisdiction over such soldiers, but it would have to be asked to do so by the Security Council or a state *and* the state from which the peacekeeper defendant came would have to be "unwilling or unable genuinely to carry out an investigation or prosecution." *Statute of the Special Court for Sierra Leone*, article 1. Needless to say, such circumstances have not eventuated.

attention allayed on the body, is probably home to the most famous case of selective leader prosecution, for which Slobodan Milosevic once more serves as the primary exhibit. And, like Taylor, the question is not whether Milosevic should have been indicted but why others have not been similarly called to book. The other wartime leaders of the former Yugoslavia have been strangely absent. As Bruno Rakic, Milosevic's Belgrade lawyer, complained, "If justice, rather than politics, is at the heart of the tribunal, why have only Serb leaders [Milosevic and Karadzic] been indicted? Why not [the other regional wartime leaders,] Croatian president [Franjo] Tudjman, [Bosnian-Croat leader Mate] Boban, or [Bosnian president Alia] Izetbegovic?"

Croatia's president Tudjman, who authorized and led the Croats in expelling and killing Serbs during 1993's Medak Incursion and 1995's Operation Storm—maneuvers that have since been recognized as war crimes—as well as a host of other acts he commissioned with the aim of homogenizing Croatia,[66] remained unindicted when he died of stomach cancer in 1999. To many, the lack of a Tudjman indictment was a gross unfairness, limiting the ability of the ICTY to claim that it is an "impartial arbiter of justice."[67] Apparently an indictment had been prepared against Tudjman, though it was never issued, leaving him to die a national hero untarnished by any official accusations.

Alia Izetbegovic, the nationalist leader of Bosnia and Herzegovina, was similarly unindicted when he died in 2003, despite having ignited the Bosnian portion of the war with his unilateral declaration of independence in April 1992, and further fueling the flames of ethnic hatred while commanding Bosniak units during the conflict. Many of the acts in which Izetbegovic was almost certainly involved resulted in the indictment of several of his generals, but not of their leader.[68] Despite pressure from Bosnian Serbs, and their claimed collection of sufficient evidence to establish an indictment against Izetbegovic—evidence passed to the Yugoslavia tribunal—Izetbegovic, like Tudjman, died a national hero with no legal claims made against him. It is not clear whether an indictment of Izetbegovic had even been prepared. There were claims made on the day of his funeral that he was under investigation;[69] however, far from being internationally vilified, at his death in October 2003, representatives from dozens of states paid their respects, and officials from NATO and the EU publicly called him a "national hero" in his country's "war of survival" during the 1990s.[70] Even if an indictment was now possible based upon investigations, due to the impermissibility of in absentia prosecutions, the ICTY would be unable to prosecute him. To the disbelief and consternation of many Serbs and others, upon both Izetbegovic's and Tudjman's deaths, the Yugoslavia tribunal publicly announced that all investigations into their wrongdoings—let alone preparation for indictments or trials—were suspended.[71]

Slobodan Milosevic was evidently not so "lucky." That he out-survived his adversaries and to many in the West subsequently came to represent all that went wrong in the Balkans, explains part of why the Serb leader was indicted. In addition to the decidedly non-justice-related facts that he was the only one left and that he was unpopular among major states, there is much about the timing and style of the Milosevic indictment and subsequent trial that appears politically, rather than judicially motivated. In this, Rakic seems correct. Milosevic may have been objectively "worse" than the other wartime leaders, having had a hand in more bloodshed and destruction; yet Izetbegovic and Tudjman also engaged in awful crimes. Given this, analyzing why Milosevic was indicted while his contemporaries were not, one can only conclude that the ICTY, and the wider international community, could "afford" to indict him, but not the other leaders.

The timing of Milosevic's indictment is critical to this supposition. Enough damning evidence had been amassed several *years* before his indictment was released in May 1999. (Milosevic was actually named in the original list of potential prosecution targets in December 1992, six months prior to the establishment of the ICTY,[72] and a US House of Representatives resolution calling for his indictment was passed overwhelmingly—complete with substantial testimony and evidence—in September 1998[73]). But, that Milosevic's indictment was only issued in 1999—after Milosevic had lost considerable support at home and, more importantly, after he had betrayed the promises he had made to the international community by intervening militarily in Kosovo—raises questions that only "politics" can answer. Quite simply, though before Kosovo he was "more valuable for a settlement in the Balkans [if he stayed] in Belgrade than in The Hague,"[74] after Kosovo he was of no further use in the international community's Balkan strategy. Until Kosovo, while other forces for change and stability were courted in the region, diplomats remained focused on Milosevic as "the key to any solution for Balkans unrest."[75] Or, in the view of another observer, "the reality is that Kosovo is for Milosevic what income-tax evasion was for Al Capone—an offense that prosecutors [could] nail him on."[76]

Both Tudjman and Izetbegovic, meanwhile, were not involved in Kosovo, and proved to be vital allies in the international community's efforts in the region. Tudjman, for instance, was "very shrewd," publicly supporting the American proposals regarding a settlement in Bosnia, leading the Clinton administration to embrace him (even after it was clear that his forces had engaged in war crimes).[77] Izetbegovic played his cards very carefully as well, in the view of some by acting as a clear proxy for United States and NATO interests in his unwavering negotiations with the Serbs.[78] Concerns for political popularity and utility, rather than strictly justice, were at play. The "tribunal's hit list of wanted men nicely dovetailed with the [leaders] in the region that the West . . . preferred to see out of the way."[79]

The specific timing of the issuance of the Milosevic indictment is also intriguing. Though the document had long since been completed, the tribunal's issuance of the document curiously occurred at the same time as the planned commencement of Russian-led negotiations with the Serbs that were being held to end the NATO bombing of Belgrade. The NATO bombing was launched in March 1999 and was designed to arrest Milosevic's advances into Kosovo. At the time of the Russian-led discussions (May 1999), NATO states wished to continue their offensive. The predictable result of the timing of the indictment was that once it was released on May 27, 1999, peace efforts were scuttled, and a peacemaking trip to Belgrade by the Russian envoy Viktor Cheno-myrdin was canceled. The NATO bombing campaign, however, continued for another two weeks. It was widely assumed that NATO states played a role in coordinating this fortuitous timing.

The likelihood that the Milosevic indictment was timed to frustrate the Russians makes sense in light of the Russian-American competition regarding the ICTY. The Russians have long been cool to the tribunal, concerned about the continued erosion of Moscow's influence in its Slavic "backyard." Russians saw the Yugoslav crisis with decidedly different eyes than did the West, focusing more on the plight of Serbs seemingly attacked from all sides, than on their purported victims.[80] This explains the more recent Russian rejection of Kosovo's independence and its support of Serbia in securing its rights over its former province. The 1999 NATO bombing—which was conducted without UN authorization *because* of the near certainty of a Russian veto if the matter had been raised in the Security Council—had shaken the Russians. Moscow's attempts to reenter the region by playing peacemaker were unwelcome by the United States and its NATO partners. Asking the tribunal to issue the indictment when it did made sense for the United States, removing not only the Russian variable, but also focusing world attention on Milosevic's crimes (and especially those in Kosovo), rather than on the increasingly globally unpopular NATO bombardment of Serbia.[81] By May 1999, global negative sentiment surrounding the bombing was on the rise, especially among the non-NATO permanent members of the UN Security Council—Russia and China (the latter whose Belgrade embassy was mistakenly bombed during a NATO air raid, killing three).[82] These pressures were enough to lead the ICTY prosecutor to open an official war crimes investigation into NATO's action.[83] The prosecutor found no war crimes and ceased the investigation.

It is true that the ICTY prosecutor is independent and thus could have issued the Milosevic indictment when she thought justice demanded it. Moreover, there is no evidence that the prosecutor at the time, Canadian Louise Arbour, was influenced by her government's membership in and support of the NATO campaign. To the contrary, it was she who opened the war crimes investigation into the NATO bombings. However, that the ICTY answers to the UN Security Council makes it seem that the scheduling of the release of Milosevic's indictment was directed by political, rather than judicial, forces. This is certainly the view in the Balkans and objectively it must be admitted that the coincidence of political value that certain states received from both the timing of Milosevic's indictment, and the absence of indictments against Tudjman or Izetbegovic, is too great to genuinely believe otherwise.

"Not a Tutsi in Sight"

A closely related complaint to the presence or absence of various leadership figures as defendants in the international courts is the specter of larger group bias. In this regard, the Special Court for Sierra Leone is a distinct standout, with its defendants coming from all sides of the conflict. This is all the more noteworthy because when President Kabbah asked the Security Council to create a court, he explicitly requested the establishment of a body to try the rebel forces and no one else. However, the UN demurred and only consented to a court if it had jurisdiction to "prosecute persons who bear the greatest responsibility for serious violations" regardless their political or national affiliation.[84] With the important exceptions of Gaddafi, Campaore, and Kabbah, the Special Court has done just that.

The same cannot be said for the Rwanda tribunal. Much as in Sierra Leone, the Rwandan government that asked for a tribunal wished only for a body that would try the "criminal elements" chased out by the victorious, current, Tutsi-led government. Again the UN refused and at least officially created a tribunal with jurisdiction over all parties to the conflict. The UN had little choice: its own Commission of Experts had reported that "individuals from both sides to the armed conflict in Rwanda . . . perpetrated serious breaches of . . . law," and "both . . . [committed] . . . crimes against humanity."[85] Despite this, there have been *no* Tutsis even indicted by the ICTR, let alone prosecuted. That the current government in Kigali is Tutsi controlled, and that the Rwanda tribunal relies on its cooperation to function (providing access to witnesses and crime sites), has led some to surmise that leaving Tutsis off the indictment list was a logical and pragmatic strategy. It was this discrepancy that led Paul Rusesabagina to pen his letter to the secretary general, convinced that if the "tribunal ends its functions having only considered one side of the problem, most . . . [Rwandans] would see it as a biased tribunal, and instead of resolving the Rwandan unity problem, it would have worsened it." As a Hutu-led group—Rally for the Return of Refugees and Democracy in Rwanda—put it:

> [P]artial justice cannot bring durable peace to Rwanda. It is going to heighten ethnic and political tensions. Prosecutorial partiality and bias against Hutus in indictments and the interference of the [Tutsi-dominated current] . . . regime in their defense make the ICTR appear as a victor's tribunal instead of being an international impartial tribunal.[86]

In the former Yugoslavia, it is the Serbs who have the biggest claim of bias, though again at the international level support for the ICTY was in some cases predicated primarily upon the creation of an "impartial [tribunal] . . . [that will] in no way . . . act as . . . retaliation against the Serbs."[87] Yet, Serbs complaining of bias certainly seem to have a point.

From very early in the discussions about having a tribunal, Serbs were not blind to what they saw as the international forces for justice teaming up against them. It was already clear in mid-1993 to the secretary of the Yugoslav State Commission for War Crimes and Crimes of Genocide—the national commission Belgrade established to investigate such crimes—that the ICTY was "meant to punish [only one] . . . state and its people."[88] Yugoslav deputy prime minister and foreign minister Vladislav Jovanovic voiced doubt that it would be possible to form an impartial tribunal, precisely because its establishment had been urged by those who had been exclusively accusing Serbs of crimes in the Balkans.[89] Belgrade's human rights minister Momcilo Grubac warned that prejudices and prejudgments regarding perpetrators and defendants threatened to turn any potential proceedings "into political trials of nations and not of war criminals, which would greatly discredit justice and humanity."[90] Even Prince Alexander Karadordevic, the Yugoslav *dauphin* who is normally silent on political issues, released an impassioned letter to UN secretary general Boutros-Ghali imploring the UN to assure that the tribunal be a fair court.[91]

The Serb focus, however, only intensified as plans for the tribunal solidified. In August 1992, the German foreign minister Klaus Kinkel addressed the government in Belgrade:

> I appeal to the Serbian leadership. Realize that you stand at the crossroads. One of the roads leads back into the community of nations. . . . [The] other leads to absolute isolation and impoverishment. . . . Those responsible for the devastation will be held accountable.[92]

As evident by Kinkel's statement, the Serbs were becoming the clear focus of attention. Kinkel was even clearer in a contemporaneous comment in which he said that his government wanted to put "Serb leaders on trial for war crimes."[93] By the time of the tribunal's actual formation, the UN itself had "labeled the Serbs the worst offender."[94] Consequently, almost immediately after its establishment, there were loud claims emanating from Serbs in the Balkans that the tribunal would be no more than a tool for Serb persecution.

The numbers of indictments leveled against the Serbs in the early days of the tribunal (and the nonexistence of indictments against members of other ethnic groups involved in the war) served only to further confirm fears of prejudice against the Serbs. Of the twenty-three indictments issued over the first two years of the tribunal's existence, only seven were against non-Serbs (all against Croats in connection with a single military campaign in Lasva Valley).[95] By December

1995, even this balance had deteriorated: fifty-two people had been indicted, forty-five of whom were Serb (nearly 90 percent). By February 2006, observers noted that this trend had strengthened further:

> Not one ethnic-Serb defendant has been cleared and released [from the Tribunal], compared with at least four Croats, one Bosnian Muslim and one Kosovo Albanian. More than three-quarters of guilty verdicts and almost two-thirds of indictments have been against Serbs.[96]

More troubling for Serbs and some observers was that this seeming prejudice exacerbated the perceived bias of wartime coverage in the West. Following a particularly brutal round of Croatian-orchestrated "ethnic cleansing" of Serbs, General Charles Boyd, the deputy commander of the US European command during the Yugoslav conflict, reported that the inhuman practice of forcibly ethnically homogenizing a region seemed to "evoke condemnation [from the West] only when it is . . . committed by Serbs, not against them."[97] For example, it was far from clear why

> the expulsion of Serbs from Croatia in 1991 and 1995 was labeled a 'population transfer' and even justified by the logic of nation-states, while the expulsion of Muslims by Serbs in 1992–1996 from an area of Bosnia and Herzegovina that the Serbs claim for their state was labeled genocide.[98]

While the strength of the claim that the Serbs are the target of the tribunal remains among both Balkan-resident and diaspora Serbs, a closer examination of the tribunal's work suggests that the reality of tribunal bias is not clear-cut. First, other ethnic groups—and in particular, Croats—were also mentioned by the UN and others very early in the ICTY's operations, and alleged to have committed violations.[99] US secretary of state Christopher, to much public outcry, maintained that all sides shared guilt,[100] and, in December 1992, his predecessor Lawrence Eagleburger had presented a multiethnic list of potential defendants that a planned tribunal should target.[101] A May 1993 UN report, authored by former Polish prime minister and UN special envoy Tadeusz Mazowiecki, held that "Croatian forces [had] . . . carried out a deliberate and systematic policy of 'ethnic cleansing' against Bosnian Muslims."[102] Additionally, the report found that "forces of the Muslim-dominated Bosnian government have also committed atrocities against Croats, including arbitrary executions and torture."[103] Perhaps unsurprisingly, the singling out of other ethnic groups, such as the Croats, led to an ICTY backlash among those groups, which also suddenly claimed prejudice.

Yet, despite the existence of these cross-ethnic accusations and recriminations, and even though crimes were committed by all sides of the conflict, those claiming an anti-Serb bias at the tribunal neglect the fact that a majority of the crimes committed in the former Yugoslavia during the 1990s, and thus under investigation by the tribunal, *were* committed by Serbs. In Bosnia alone (the site of a disproportionate percentage of the military violence), the UN's Commission of Experts concluded that 90 percent of the crimes were the responsibility of Serbs, 6 percent Croats, and 4 percent Bosniaks.[104] A leaked report from the US Central Intelligence Agency (CIA) also claimed the 90 percent figure.[105]

These distressing figures are not because the Serb people are necessarily "worse" than the Croats, Bosniaks, or Albanians. Though there are some who disagree, arguing that the Serbs were "Milosevic's Willing Executioners,"[106] collective guilt is always hard to ascribe. There were other elements at work beside "evil" that continues to subvert Serb wishes to establish the numerical "equality" in indictments and convictions between ethnic groups. First, Serbia was the largest of federal Yugoslavia's six republics. The Serbs were the plurality ethnic group in the former Yugoslavia (36 percent of the population), and, given their historic presence in many corners of the country and their prime roles in running the federal state both under Marshal Tito and the regimes that followed the marshal's death, they were also the most dispersed of the competitor ethnic groups. For Tito, this dispersion was by design; in an effort to restrain Serbian nationalism, he redrew internal boundaries early in his tenure so as to strand Serb minorities in each of the Yugoslav republics and outside Serbia itself.[107] Because of Tito's resettlement plans, at the time of Bosnia's declaration of independence in 1991, there were only five hundred thousand fewer Serbs than Muslims in the new state.[108] In other parts of the former Yugoslavia, the population movements were more recent; one of Milosevic's first acts upon ascending to the Yugoslav presidency in 1990 was to flood Kosovo with Serbian technocrats, removing any Albanians from positions of political or economic authority.[109]

The combination of all of these factors meant that there were simply more Serbs in more places in the former Yugoslavia. Consequently, even a small proportion of Serb wrongdoers was enough to overwhelm, geographically and numerically, a similarly small proportion of wrongdoers hailing from the other smaller and more geographically concentrated ethnicities.

Second, and more importantly, once Croatia, Slovenia, and Bosnia declared independence in 1992, the rump state of Yugoslavia consisted essentially of Serbia. Consequently, Serbia and Serbs had access to the Yugoslav state's impressive store of weaponry and military know-how, and as a result were able to wreak more destruction than the nascent, irredentist states that had broken off. As a marker for this inequality in military resources, it is telling that though less than 40 percent of the population of the federal Yugoslavia, Serbs made up nearly 80 percent of all commissioned officers in the Yugoslav Army.[110] The capacity for Serb-induced violence—and ability to commit crimes serious enough to warrant the tribunal's attention—far outstripped that of any of the other groups. The simple issue of unequal military capabilities among the former Yugoslav states—a distinct advantage held by the Serbs through much of the war until arms embargoes against Belgrade exacted their toll by 1995—goes far in explaining the discrepancies in indictments and investigations.

Even though the perception of bias is troubling and certainly limits the ability of any court to do its work, based upon the facts on the ground, it would be hard to claim that the ICTY has truly been inequitable in its dealings with the Serbs. Similarly, the Special Court for Sierra Leone has managed to toe the same line, indicting more rebels because more violations were committed by rebels. However, even though the majority of the crimes in Rwanda were committed by Hutus, the abject absence of any Tutsi to stand before the Rwanda tribunal is troubling, goes against the UN's own findings on the subject, and certainly seems like bias, regardless its source.

Timing is Everything

However, even if claims of bias in Sierra Leone and the former Yugoslavia seem overblown, a brief foray into the painfully fluid histories of almost any of the groups targeted to receive international justice shows there is more to the concern of bias than might meet the eye.

"If you're lucky they go back to the Second World War, but sometimes you begin in the 14th century."[111] So began almost all the meetings the Yugoslavia tribunal's first prosecutor, Richard Goldstone, had with representatives from the post-Yugoslav states during his tenure. In the Balkans, as in all of the states in which international justice has been implemented, history is very much alive, informing and creating the present. The ability for people to become animated, even enraged, about a slight endured a century ago or even half a millennium ago is perhaps shocking to the postmodern conscience. It is, however, a reality that plays not just into postconflict reconciliation but almost always serves as at least part of the spark to the conflicts themselves. The modern international criminal tribunals have *never* taken into account the full scope of national and ethnic histories. Largely for reasons of pragmatics, all international courts have been radically temporally constrained, only allowed to prosecute crimes that occurred after a specific date. Some international courts have even narrower jurisdictions, empowered solely to prosecute crimes committed in a specific area and by specific people. This "selective historical approach"[112] almost by definition serves to dispose courts favorably toward some groups at the expense of others.

In all too many instances of modern international justice, subject aggressors and defendants have come from ethnic groups and peoples who have been perpetually in flux, moving into and out of power, at one time serving as the *genocidaire*, at another time the victim. The seesaw between the Hutus and Tutsis both in Rwanda and its neighbor Burundi is a stark case of this phenomenon. The two countries are historically linked, and during the colonial period were actually treated as a dual kingdom, "Ruanda-Urundi," which Germany occupied in 1890. The main ethnic groups in both states are the Hutus and Tutsis, with the latter a relatively small minority in both (less than 20 percent). In both states, prior to colonialism and under a comparatively benign German mercantilism, the Hutu and Tutsi coexisted, at times establishing a fragile *modus vivendi*, and at other times positively living with, doing business with, and even marrying one another.

To be sure, there was a divide and sporadic tension between the two—a result of the fact that most political power was held by the minority Tutsi populations. Germany lost its African colonies after World War I and Belgium took over. In both countries, the Belgians worked to emphasize and harden the Tutsi-Hutu divide, using it as a tool of administration and, in so doing, favoring the Tutsi in government, education, and commerce.

Tensions in the colony began to boil as independence neared; in 1959, in what is now Rwanda, violence erupted with the Hutus carrying out a "social revolution" rebelling against their Tutsi overlords. They succeeded and, in so doing, massacred fifty thousand Tutsis while driving as many as two hundred thousand Tutsis into exile.[113] In Rwanda, the Hutus would manage to maintain power for nearly thirty years, with significant episodes of anti-Tutsi violence in 1963, 1966, 1973, and every year from 1990 to 1994.[114] In 1962, independence arrived and the Rwandan and Burundian states were formed. In Burundi, it was the Tutsis who managed to seize power, though their rule was far less secure. Ever since 1962, Rwanda and Burundi have developed a devastating codependence in which ethnic violence in one has precipitated reprisals in the other—true "neighbors in Hell."[115] The violence, on both sides of the border and perpetrated by both peoples, is numbing.

In 1961, Rwandan Tutsi refugees in Burundi attacked Rwanda, an effort they would repeat ten times over the next six years. During these years, some twenty thousand Tutsi were killed by Hutu reprisals and more than three hundred thousand were forced to flee abroad. In the wake of this first attempted invasion, the Hutus engaged in still more mass violence against any Tutsis remaining in Rwanda. Thousands of Tutsis were killed. In 1963, the Tutsis in Burundi again attempted to invade Rwanda, and the Hutus brutally repelled them once more. In retaliation, the Hutu prefect of Gikongoro district in Rwanda ordered a local genocide of the Tutsi population; more than ten thousand were killed.[116] In Burundi, in 1965, a failed coup by Hutus led to reprisals that resulted in more than five thousand Hutu deaths at the hands of Tutsis.[117] In 1972, the Burundian king was assassinated by Hutus, who, in their momentary ascendancy, also killed as many as two thousand Tutsi.[118] Once the Burundian Tutsis regained the upper hand, they organized a culling of the Hutus, a genocide that would have eerie similarities with the crimes that were to be committed twenty years later by the Rwandan Hutus themselves. In a period of a few weeks in April 1972, as many as two hundred thousand Hutus were killed by elements of the Tutsi-dominated army and raging Tutsi youth groups who constructed lists of Hutus and systematically sought them out for slaughter.[119]

After a brief era of seeming democratic rule in Burundi, during which Hutus assumed some power, a Tutsi-led coup in 1988 and rumors of Hutu attacks on Tutsis led to still more ethnic bloodshed, with the primarily Tutsi Burundian army murdering as many as twenty-five thousand Hutus. In 1990, a Tutsi-led rebel group attacked Rwanda, this time successfully enough to force the Hutu-led government to sue for peace. A fragile peace was maintained until April 1994 when President Habyarimana, the Hutu president of Rwanda, was killed in a plane crash. The Tutsis took the brunt of the blame for his death and elements of the Hutu majority used the killing as the *causus belli* to justify their attempt, once and for all, to remove the Tutsi presence from Rwanda. After one hundred days of violence and madness, as many as eight hundred thousand Tutsis had been murdered, along with an unknown number of thousands of moderate Hutus. Tutsis and Hutus changed places, two million Hutus became refugees and though there was a titular unity government in Rwanda (complete with a Hutu president), the Tutsis were back in power.

Clearly, there is much on both sides of the ethnic and political border about which international justice ought to rightly investigate and likely prosecute. However, as its title may suggest, the "International Criminal Tribunal for Rwanda," is legally constrained, with jurisdiction only over "serious violations" that occurred in Rwanda and committed by Rwandan citizens in neighboring states. And, by statute, the tribunal can only investigate those crimes that took place between January 1, 1994, and December 31, 1994. The deck has seemingly been stacked against the Hutus, with no recognition for the times in recent history, in both Burundi and Rwanda, where Tutsis held sway and exacted equally frightful crimes on their Hutu brethren. Even the Rwandan Tutsis, who were benefited by these constraints, disagreed with this limited jurisdiction, contending that it would hobble the tribunal's ability to "fully capture within its prosecutorial scope the criminal activities that culminated in the genocide of 1994."[120]

This same switch in identity of abusers and abused has resulted in a similar complaint often made by older Serbs regarding the Yugoslav tribunal. Whereas the Serbs may have had the military advantage during the 1990s, this was not always so, especially vis-à-vis the Croats. During World War II, the Croatian nationalist group, the Ustasha, under the quisling Ante Pavelic, nominally ruled Nazi-occupied Croatia.[121] These Croat separatists, owing much of their philosophy to, and operating under the direct patronage of both Mussolini and Hitler,[122] sought to "purify" their state and set upon exterminating its non-Croat inhabitants—largely Serb, but also Jewish and Romani— "with a brutality that shocked even the Germans."[123] As in the case of the Tutsi-Hutu cycle of violence, though the horrors perpetrated by the Ustasha in the 1930s–1940s do not mitigate those perpetrated by the Serbs fifty years later, they do raise the question often repeated in Serb areas of the Balkans: why was the Yugoslavia tribunal designed to be so constrained? The ICTY was only given jurisdiction over crimes committed in the former Yugoslavia since 1991. This is especially troublesome because this history of violence and counterviolence and "the belief that crimes . . . perpetrated in World War II and before had gone unavenged," was "[o]ne of the tools used by Serb and Croat leaders to spur their followers to commit atrocities."[124] By being limited as such, given the political realities on the ground in the Balkans during the 1990s, it is an easy, and in some minds inescapable, conclusion that the tribunal was indeed erected primarily to prosecute Serbs. If there is no statute of limitations on war crimes, a fact largely agreed to since 1968,[125] many Serbs have long asked why the crimes of the Ustasha were not similarly under international scrutiny?[126]

True, there were only few, aging members of the group remaining when the Yugoslavia tribunal began operations. However, there were some, and interest and ability in pursuing such crimes is manifest by the November 1999 conviction in Croatia of Dinko Sakic, the commander of the notorious Jasenovac concentration camp during World War II,[127] and the May 2005 launch of an investigation by Croatia against Milivoj Asner, a ninety-two-year-old who had served as an Ustasha police chief from 1941 to 1942 in the eastern Croatian town of Pozega.[128]

On the Serbian side, the crimes of the Chetniks, a group of militant Serb nationalists that began World War II as "a legitimate resistance force [to the Axis occupation] . . . [but] degraded quickly into something far less honorable,"[129] matched the Ustasha in both venom and nationalism. They also flirted with the German and Italian fascists during World War II—often at the expense of Croats, Muslims, and other non-Serbs—and would similarly be open for judicial examination.[130] In addition, not to be left out, various Bosniaks also had an infamous role in World War II: the Waffen SS-Handschar Division, a Nazi unit recruited from the Bosnian Muslim population with the aid of the virulent anti-Semitic propaganda of Hitler's ally Husseini, the Great Mufti of Jerusalem, was implicated in numerous attacks against Serbs, Jews, and Romani throughout the war.[131] Bosnia's president Alia Izetbegovic was once a member. During World War II, each side was equally uncompromising and brutal, which is evidenced by the devastating fact that of the 1.7 million Yugoslavs who perished in World War II, nearly half were killed at the hands of fellow Yugoslavs.[132]

By expanding its jurisdiction to include periods in which the Serbs were not dominant, the tribunal would have recognized the historical and cultural context of the 1990s conflict. This would have sent the Serbs (and Croats and others) a powerful message of equality before the law, making the simple existence of the tribunal—let alone its judgments— much more acceptable in the region. It is telling that before the tribunal was established, a strong plurality of Croats believed that local war crimes trials dealing with acts of the Ustasha ought to have been held.[133] That number quickly dissipated after the ICTY began operations.

In Sierra Leone, the conflict was far less strictly intraethnic, but the Special Court's jurisdictional constraints similarly serve to pervert the possible pool of defendants. The Sierra Leone civil war began in 1991, yet the Special Court, for fear of overloading the prosecutor, is limited to investigating crimes committed after November 30, 1996, within the "territory of Sierra Leone." Both limits are troubling. Given that appalling acts of violence occurred before November 30, 1996—the date of the signing of the first peace accords—many view this cutoff as arbitrary, if not absurd. Moreover, significant concern regarding this date has been raised in the Sierra Leone countryside; prior to November 1996, fighting and atrocities remained largely in rural areas. It was only after that date that the fighting reached Freetown. Some have argued that the constraint implies that only the atrocities that occurred in Freetown matter.[134]

Further, as is made clear by the indictment of Charles Taylor, the Sierra Leone civil war was not a conflict bound by the country's borders. The war was closely related to the destruction of Liberia, and had direct connections to states throughout the region including Libya,

Nigeria, and Guinea. The geographic limits of the Special Court means that many "with blood on their hands" are out of bounds, and the leaders of all too many of the warring factions "who participated in tremendous atrocities" will not be held to legal account.[135]

PROSECUTING THE WRONG PEOPLE AND THE WRONG CRIMES: TROLLING FOR THE BIG FISH

While the politics behind the Milosevic indictment and prosecution are complex, and at least somewhat legally questionable, there are few people even in Serbia who question whether their former president ought to have been in the dock (even if at home). Even hardliners like Milosevic advisor Rakic soften somewhat when asked to consider the validity of a Milosevic prosecution had both Tudjman and Izetbegovic ended up in the same situation. Yet, despite the broad acceptance throughout the Balkans for a Milosevic prosecution of some type, there is a great deal of confusion regarding the Yugoslavia tribunal's other targets. To most, it is unclear what links the indictees, and why some are targeted, while others have been ignored.

These complaints have a great degree of merit.

At the outset of its work, though it was evident that not everyone who committed a crime could possibly be brought to The Hague, it was unclear exactly who should be the target of inquiry. The tribunal was under the direction to convict those "most responsible"[136] for crimes, a nebulous standard to say the least. The initial list of potential defendants included some very low-ranking "henchmen" such as twenty-one-year-old conscript Borislav Herak.[137] The first person to appear before the tribunal, Drazen Erdemovic (who pled guilty) was also a young, rather unwilling soldier in the Bosnian Serb army.[138] The first actual prosecution was of Dusko Tadic, a karate expert/failed café owner about whom the *Philadelphia Inquirer* penned a piece headlined: "As War Crimes Trial Opens, A Minor Figure Looms Large."[139]

These early prosecution choices—which were based on the availability of defendants rather than any desire on the part of prosecutors to focus on junior officials—caused consternation in the Balkans and even among the tribunal's biggest supporters outside the region.[140] Many argued for the tribunal to quickly indict and try truly senior figures behind the crimes committed during the war.[141]

The tribunal settled down after *Tadic,* and subsequent prosecutions have been of those considered in the regional parlance to be "big fish." Though the post-*Tadic* strategy of indicting generals, high political leaders, and other "important" figures has certainly yielded success, it has in the opinion of many people in the former Yugoslavia nonetheless brought the wrong people to book. From Sarajevo to Skopje to Zagreb, the victims in the region seem pleased that foot soldiers like Dusko Tadic are no longer viewed worthy of the tribunal's attention. "We can take care of them ourselves," one Sarajevo survivor told me. The truly senior officials, meanwhile, are often objects of derision, but are usually felt to have been only proximately responsible for the crimes. "Prosecuting them does not really help us," the leader of a victims group argued. The people who many victims wish to see in the dock are precisely those who the ICTY is overlooking: the middle-ranking officials who had a direct hand in ordering and often taking part in violations.[142] There is insufficient capacity in The Hague for such a diffused focus.

Providing further evidence that a one-size-fits-all approach to international justice can fall short, the Special Court for Sierra Leone faces a different set of complaints about the seniority of its indictees. Here, NGOs speaking on behalf of victims have likewise attacked the mandate of the Special Court, which has, from its inception, sought solely to prosecute those who "bear the greatest responsibility" for abuses. The Special Court has interpreted this phrase to mean "the masterminds of the war," focusing their attention on leaders such as Taylor and Sankoh. However, throwing post–World War II international justice on its head, many in Sierra Leone have suggested that it is direct perpetrators, rather than those who "just" gave orders, who are actually the *most* responsible.[143] Victims often wish to know why it is that a commander is in custody, rather than the man who actually cut off a hand or burned down a house.[144] And thus, local conceptions of justice often run counter to international goals.

Show Me the Money

Clearly, residents of states receiving international justice often have difficulty swallowing the choice of who is prosecuted by their international courts. Similarly they often have difficulty understanding the types of crimes being prosecuted. For instance, in Sierra Leone, people on the ground are frustrated that the Taylor trial focuses only on his war crimes and not on other acts that so negatively impacted Sierra Leone. In particular, many wish that Taylor's startlingly brazen thefts from the people of Liberia would be addressed.

In 1980, twenty-three-year-old Charles Taylor, a native Liberian armed with an American education (an economics degree from Bentley College in Waltham, Massachusetts) returned home eager to make his mark and, as it turned out, his fortune. He signed up with the new administration of Samuel Doe, the US Army-trained master sergeant who had orchestrated a coup earlier that year and who personally and savagely executed the former president, William Tolbert Jr., by stabbing him fifteen times and disemboweling him. Though it seems that Taylor's sole "business" experience was a brief stint as a gas station attendant in suburban Boston, the Doe government gave him a position as a procurement officer, entrusted with substantial money to purchase goods for the Liberian state. Taylor rose quickly, within several months operating as the government's chief procurement officer—a position that he expertly leveraged in order to steal nearly $1 million, siphoning it off into a New York bank account, his "sticky fingers earn[ing] him the nickname 'Super Glue.'"[145] Taylor had gained a taste for graft; this was only the first, and one of the smallest instances of his subsequent pilfering of the Liberian state. The Doe government pressed charges against the young Taylor, compelling him to flee the country. Taylor returned to Massachusetts in 1983 and the Liberian warrant for his arrest was executed by US marshals in 1984, who arrested Taylor in an apartment in Somerville, Massachusetts, in 1985.

In a story straight from central casting, Taylor, while awaiting extradition, escaped from a Massachusetts state prison in September 1985, "using a hacksaw blade to cut off one bar . . . [he then] slid [down] about twenty feet on sheets tied together."[146] Four others escaped with him, but they were each captured. Taylor disappeared into the ether, with the police showing little interest in pursuing their quarry; in a sickening irony, the authorities said that they were unconcerned, as Taylor had "no history of violence."[147] Taylor eventually wound up in Libya, was trained by Gaddafi, and, with his freshly minted revolutionary credentials, returned to Doe's Liberia in December 1989. He led an armed uprising against his former patron, catalyzing both the ruinous Liberian civil war and his eventual rise to the presidency. He held the presidency for almost exactly six years, and during that time resumed the activities he had so nearly perfected while a procurement officer. He seized foreign aid monies provided to the destitute masses (masses that he had no small part in making destitute) and he traded with the rebels in Sierra Leone, receiving their diamonds in exchange for weapons. Once the UN levied sanctions against him, he became creative, commandeering the Liberian maritime registry (the sole steady flow of income into the country) and making the lucrative timber industry his own personal account. All the while, he developed a taste for chauffeur-driven luxury automobiles (driven in dozen-car convoys), fine white suits (accessorized with a cane), tennis, and multiple cell phones. It is still unknown how much money Taylor managed to steal, though it seems evident that his claims of penury made before the Special Court (thus allowing him to receive a court-supported lawyer) are false. During Taylor's last four years in power alone, at least half of the government's $200 million in revenues disappeared. All told, from his days as a procurement official to his final exit from power in March 2006, it is thought that Taylor removed as much as $3 billion to foreign accounts—an amount that is about equal to the annual gross domestic product of the entire country.[148] As Taylor amassed his fortune, Liberia, and wider West Africa including Sierra Leone, slipped further and further behind—what were once comparatively stable and even promising states became verifiable basket cases. At various points during Taylor's kleptocratic rampage, each state occupied the last or second to last spots in the global rankings of country wealth and human development.

This story of Taylor's financial excesses may pale in comparison with the two hundred thousand people whose lives were lost in the bloody wars he instigated or propagated. However, this, combined with the poverty he all but forced on West Africa, also provides an opening for a potentially unique form of war crimes prosecution in which courts would recognize that more often than not, war profiteers are war criminals—and vice versa. For residents in target regions, this is as intuitive as it is baffling that international courts have not focused on such crimes. This complaint about international justice is not that the wrong people are being brought before courts, but the wrong crimes, or at least an incomplete list of such crimes, are being reviewed by courts.

This complaint is warranted. The Special Court for Sierra Leone, along with the Yugoslavia tribunal and all of the other international criminal courts, are limited by statute from taking advantage of these local concerns for fiscal crimes. All international tribunals have been unable to prosecute "quotidian" wrongdoings such as financial misdeeds. Some purists even condemn the potential prosecution of financial or other criminal wrongdoings in light of the more serious crimes committed.

As Aaron Presnall, the president of an economic development NGO in Belgrade and long-time observer of Serb politics, noted to me, prosecuting financial crimes first, as a way to get to war criminals, is not only a wise strategy but also one that would have resonated on the ground. For instance, in the Balkans, while there remains some resistance to prosecuting war crimes, there is very little resistance to, nor sympathy for, the more "common criminals" involved in organized crime who have succeeded in bilking the former Yugoslav states out of millions of dollars in aid and investment. It is these criminals who are the most troubling to residents of region. Many of these "common criminals" began their pilfering during the Balkan wars, aided by their ruthlessness and willingness to commit war crimes.

The Milosevic case provided the perfect opening for such a model, but the Yugoslavia tribunal had its hands tied. When Belgrade finally arrested Milosevic, and before he was extradited to The Hague, Serb authorities indicted him on several domestic crimes including "embezzlement" and "abuse of power." The Serbs did not indict him for war crimes.[149] However, it was the domestic charges that damned the former president in the eyes of the people whom he had misled, and which finally managed to quell significant protest against his detainment. Even staunch opponents of the ICTY, such as Milosevic's successor Vojislav Kostunica expressed willingness to see the former president stand trial on war crimes, in addition to (*and subsequent to*) his trial for domestic financial transgressions.[150]

In Rwanda, there was little money to be made and consequently there have been few voices urging an accounting for financial crimes. However, in Sierra Leone, where diamonds were a key factor in the war, there was immense war profiteering. To his credit, Prosecutor Crane immediately saw the connection between the capture of wealth and the perpetration of mass crimes in Sierra Leone. He sought to bring charges against representatives of the business community who profited due to the conflict. This was one of Prosecutor Crane's primary goals and many expected that he would be able to "open a new front in the struggle against crimes against humanity by attacking the financial networks that underwrite them."[151] Yet, indicative of how limited the bounds of international criminal justice actually are, despite the intimate connections between profiteering and crimes, the prosecutor was unable to establish the needed link between the businessmen and the crimes that fell within the tribunal's jurisdiction. This greatly limited not just the tribunal's ability to try those deserving of attention but also precluded a potential path to it gaining greater acceptance in the population.

❋

The various views of the legality, politics, process, and limitations of international justice have not endeared the system to those in the very regions most affected by the crimes to which it has been directed. Unfortunately, even for those on the ground who have come to accept both the scope of crimes and the list of defendants who are indicted, the actual process of trials has produced still more discord.

Chapter 6

FALLING ON DEAF EARS
(PART II)
"Unfair and Unhelpful"

From the Balkans to West Africa, from Southeast Asia to the African Great Lakes, survivors, perpetrators, and observers regularly claim that even those international prosecutions brought against the "right" people for the "right" infractions are nonetheless unfair.

"Unfairness" is a varied complaint when it comes to justice and is often made by those who wind up on the wrong side of judicial decisions. However, in the context of international tribunals, the complaint is far more nuanced and rarely a simple objection made by "sore losers" in the system. Concerns are diverse and relate to how trials are conducted before international courts. Many are incensed about the distance between the target states and "their courts," angry that prosecutions have occurred in foreign countries, using foreign modes of justice, and before foreign judges and lawyers. Yugoslavia's "court may as well be on another planet," one Balkan law student told me.

Other aspects of "unfairness," widely believed, concern the purportedly blatant bias in the proceedings, with complaints pointing to systemic inequalities in the manner in which justice is dispensed; these accusations range from the inadequacy of defense resources, to unclear rules of procedure, to the slow pace of trials, to an unhealthy reliance on outside states.

As in the complaints regarding bringing the "wrong" people to trial, some of these typical grievances are similarly not based on fact. Unfortunately, this has not made them any less resonant. Moreover, many of these objections are accurate, and though the international community has addressed some of them, the vast majority of concerns have remained neglected. Such is the case with the first, commonly cited concern about the process of international cases: distance.

DISTANCE

The population must feel this is justice in Rwanda, not foreign justice.[1]
—Pasteur Bizimungu, President of Rwanda (1994–2000)

While the Serb siege of Sarajevo from April 1992 to February 1996 captured the world's attention, the Croatian siege of the ancient town of Mostar in May 1993 was arguably equally horrific. Thousands were killed as Croatian forces bombed the eastern section of the city inhabited by Muslims, following their rampage with mass executions, rapes, and ethnic cleansing of any Muslims found in the city's western sector. Actions in Mostar rightfully served as the basis for at least six indictments before the Yugoslav tribunal. There were Bosniak survivors, many of whom were gratified that the international community was taking interest in their plight. Some even wished to see justice in action in The Hague, in order to personally witness those who did them such injury receive their punishment. This proved rather difficult.

In order to visit the tribunal, a survivor from Mostar would have to undertake a one thousand four hundred and fifty-five kilometer (about nine hundred miles) journey though a half dozen countries. Averaging one hundred kilometers an hour (about sixty miles an hour), and perhaps a bit faster on the German autobahn portion of the drive, it would take about fifteen hours to drive straight through. To fly would be somewhat faster. But there are no nonstop flights from Mostar, or even Sarajevo, to The Hague, and the Dutch capital does not even have a commercial airport of its own. Consequently, most would drive the one hundred kilometers to Sarajevo and take Lufthansa or Austrian Airlines, stop in Munich or Vienna, and connect to Amsterdam. From there, Dutch rail departs three times an hour to Den Haag ("The Hague" in Dutch), about a twenty-minute train ride away. At Den Haag Centraal train station, one takes Tram Line number 10, in the direction of Scheveningen. Disembark at Churchillplein, and walk across the street to the Court. Without any delays, the door-to-door journey would take eight or nine hours.

The physical distance that a survivor must travel is arduous enough, but there are more hurdles to such a trip, hurdles that have made the trip to The Hague impossible for the vast majority. First, the victim would need to secure Bosnian travel documents, a task whose cost could easily be beyond the means of the many who live in, or near, poverty. A passport costs about $30, but with so many Bosniaks living on some kind of welfare, passports for an individual victim, let alone for his entire family, are out of the question.[2]

After securing a passport, Bosnians would then need to lay their hands on a Dutch visa.[3] The prospect of their visa applications being accepted can be much improved by the tribunal's sponsorship—which is regularly provided to witnesses and family members of defendants. It is much more difficult to secure for victims who are not traveling to participate in a trial. Visas can cost up to $60 each, and can take up to three months to process; moreover, visa applicants need to show the purchase of a plane ticket (approximately $400 for a flight between Sarajevo and Amsterdam); accommodation (approximately $100 per night plus food and incidentals); and, sufficient resources in Bosnia to encourage their return. These requirements are also often impossible for many to meet, primarily because of their cost. The average Bosniak only makes about $400 per month,[4] rendering such a trip out of reach to all but a few.

For a Rwandan survivor wishing to observe "her" justice at the ICTR in Arusha, it is an equally difficult journey. Though it is barely five hundred miles from Kigali to the tribunal, it is a difficult seventeen-hour road trip, with no regularly scheduled public transport. The

UN has operated a twice-weekly, small air shuttle (seven passengers), to ferry investigators or witnesses between the two cities. However, the average Rwandan will not get a seat. Similar hurdles regarding travel documents and accommodation costs also limit the possibility of Rwandans taking the trip.

As a consequence of these obstacles, few from Rwanda or the Balkans have managed to see their tribunals, placing some doubt in the international community's commitment to public trials. Many domestic systems—and the international community through the Universal Declaration of Human Rights and other instruments—place significant importance on the ability of members of society, and especially victims of crimes, to be able to witness justice dispensed.[5] As the trials have receded from local media interest, "justice" has disappeared into a foreign vacuum.

Of all the complaints raised in the Balkans and Rwanda, the physical distance between the tribunals and the location of the crimes they have prosecuted is the broadest-based objection, equally made across all sectors of society, and by both victims and defendants. The distance could have been overcome in one of two ways. First, the tribunals could have made it easier for Rwandans and Balkans to travel to their respective courts. The other option would have been to bring the tribunals to the people, either physically by hosting hearings and trials in the region or "virtually," by establishing effective and robust outreach programs. Unfortunately, despite some initial discussions about holding local hearings, none have occurred and neither court has initiated effective outreach. While history will be critical of many aspects of these tribunals, their failures in grassroots outreach will likely be recorded as one of their gravest mistakes. Some aspects of the lack of outreach are stunning. For instance, as mentioned before, it was not until 1998—five years after its establishment—that the Yugoslav tribunal translated its decisions and other relevant documents into Serbo-Croatian or other local languages. Operating in English and French, the ICTR was similarly delinquent in translating tribunal documents into Rwanda's majority language, Kinyarwanda, which has on several occasions been the only language spoken by those indicted or witnesses. Even today, the requirements for working at the Rwanda tribunal include an ability to converse in English or French (but not necessarily both), and *not* Kinyarwanda.[6] Unfortunately, even when translations have been attempted, they have at times left much to be desired. At the ICTR, in one trial, "mass graves" was repeatedly translated as "masquerade."[7] In the Special Panels for East Timor, in one case a defendant recounted in his native language, Tetum, about his "hitting" a victim; a court translator correctly rendered his answer into English, but due to the translator's linguistic background he failed to sufficiently articulate the "h." When the answer was translated into Bahasa Indonesia (the language of the judges), the defendant was said to have admitted to "eating" the victim.[8]

In the Balkans, the public relations and outreach budget of the tribunal has been largely nonexistent in the region, and permanent local offices of the tribunal in the region did not, in many cases, even appear until the tribunal was more than a decade old. The absence of any reliable information from the tribunal itself has "fueled suspicion and hostility" regarding the tribunal throughout the region.[9] Moreover, even though tribunal offices in major Balkan cities are now open, they are usually understaffed and their prime responsibility is *not* outreach to the affected populations. Rather they are charged with liaising with the local government on matters related to official cooperation with the ICTY. There have been few comprehensive programs geared toward bridging the gap between the ICTY's work and the people in whose name the tribunal purportedly exists.[10]

During the period between the establishment of the Yugoslavia and Rwanda tribunals, the international community realized some of the shortcomings of having physical distance between people and their judges. This was part of the reason behind the localized justice instituted in Sierra Leone when its Special Court emerged in 2002. And, in Sierra Leone, outreach was an early and vigorous component of the Special Court's activities. In the first several months of the Special Court's operations, the chief prosecutor and registrar held public meetings throughout the country. "Outreach Teams" remain a central part of the Special Court's staffing structure, and the organization even developed innovative outreach strategies to communicate with the hinterland, especially in areas where radio and newspapers did not regularly reach. These strategies often leveraged technology: a centerpiece has been weekly thirty-minute video summaries distributed throughout the country's fourteen provinces via mobile video units.[11] The contrast with both the Yugoslavia and Rwanda tribunals is striking. In the Rwandan case, "apart from the opening [of] an information center in Kigali in 2000 [some six years after the tribunal's establishment], [as of a decade after its founding, the ICTR had] carried out no action of this type"; in the ICTR's defense, there simply has been insufficient funds to do so.[12]

The irony of distance, however, is that even in Sierra Leone, complaints regarding "physical" distance between victims and other interested parties and their Special Court remain common. This is largely because the Special Court for Sierra Leone is in Freetown, and despite the outreach efforts, the Sierra Leonean population remains heavily rural, and there is inadequate infrastructure to economically transport countryside dwellers to Freetown on a regular basis to see the proceedings. Moreover, there have also been "actual" distance problems about which complaints have been heard. Early arraignment of defendants did not take place in the comparatively accessible Freetown facility, but rather were held in Bonthe, a remote town on Sherbro Island, a forty-minute helicopter ride from Freetown; only about a hundred people witnessed some of these early proceedings. The vast majority, however, were a combination of journalists, court staff, and international NGO representatives. The only locals were the few residents of Sherbro interested in attending.[13] Only a "tiny percentage of Sierra Leoneans" has ever seen their Special Court in action.[14]

The removal of the Charles Taylor trial to the Netherlands worsened the situation, placing Sierra Leoneans wishing to observe the proceedings in very similar circumstances as those in the Balkans and Rwanda. Sierra Leoneans face the same, and arguably greater, logistical hurdles to seeing the Taylor trial. The distance between West Africa and The Hague is greater (more than three thousand miles), a return ticket more costly (more than $2,000 from either Freetown or Monrovia to Amsterdam), and the difficulty of obtaining a Dutch visa is exacerbated by the absence of a Dutch embassy in either Freetown or Monrovia. The combination of these factors makes it highly likely that other than direct witnesses, and the select few that the Special Court will bring to The Hague, only a tiny proportion of the people Charles Taylor has been accused of abusing will manage to personally witness his trial. The Special Court's laudable desire to bring local journalists and NGOs to The Hague is a positive step, but clearly not the same as allowing actual victims and survivors the ability to be in the courtroom.

"Mental Distance"

Moreover, even if the physical distance was overcome, tribunals could do little to bridge the "mental distance" between the court's victims and perpetrators and the trials themselves.[15] The international tribunals have removed themselves intellectually and spiritually from the realities of the local communities. In Sierra Leone, Ansu Lansana, the leader of the People's Movement for Democratic Change (a political party), lamented that "despite geographical proximity" Sierra Leoneans are "psychologically detached" from their court.[16] This psychological distance arrived early in the case of Sierra Leone, with the public pronouncements of its first prosecutor serving to confuse, enrage, and alienate many Sierra Leoneans who quickly came to believe that the prosecutor failed to grasp the complexities of the situation. For example, early in his tenure, Prosecutor Crane intoned that:

> To put it very simply . . . [in my] thirty years of public service, I have never seen a more black and white situation in my life, of good versus evil. Fundamentally the cause of this war was to control a commodity and that was diamonds.[17]

Yet, as one observer noted, "[r]educing the conflict to its business dimension and . . . oversimplifying the root causes of the civil war risk[ed] undermining the credibility of the prosecution in the eyes of many Sierra Leoneans."[18] The average Sierra Leonean—let alone the average Sierra Leonean victim—saw more nuance than did the foreign prosecutor.

In Rwanda, the "rampant ignorance of the history" of the conflict and the 1994 genocide, combined with a "casual insertion of names"[19] into indictments led to one of the more devastating manifestations of this psychological detachment. In the spring of 2002, Leonidas Rusatira, a Hutu general in the Rwandan army during the genocide, was charged with genocide and arrested in Belgium on the orders of the Rwanda tribunal. The problem was that he was "known to everyone as the person who opposed [the genocide]. He [was one of] the first signatories to a letter to the Rwandan Armed Forces denouncing the genocide."[20] In July 1994, he had even called for the creation of an international tribunal to try those responsible. Evidence even existed that during the genocide, far from participating, he used his position to try to shield Hutus and Tutsis alike. His arrest shocked observers, leading some to claim that it manifest a "grave dysfunction in the office of the prosecutor."[21] Three months later, as was all too clear at the moment of his arrest, the prosecutor withdrew the indictment conceding that there was insufficient evidence to hold the general.[22]

While the ICTR prosecution has over-charged, it has also under-charged: crimes of sexual violence, despite being on the forefront of the minds of the countless victims of such violence, have never been fully and consistently incorporated into the investigations or strategy of the prosecutor's office.

Indicative of even more psychological detachment between the ICTR and Rwandans was the fact that it was not until June 2006—nearly 12 years after its founding—that the tribunal made a definitive ruling that there was no question (either legal or factual) that genocide had occurred in Rwanda during 1994.[23] Rwandans were shocked that it took so much time to put the "question" of genocide to rest and viewed the delay as yet another example of how removed the Rwanda tribunal was from Rwandan realities.

The Yugoslavia tribunal has engaged in an additional manner of separating itself from the Balkans in its trial strategy, especially in regard to its most famous defendant, Slobodan Milosevic. Ignoring pleas from Balkan experts and even many commentators from outside the region, the prosecutor launched a massive sixty-six-count indictment against the former president, separating his malfeasances into those committed in Kosovo, Croatia, and Bosnia.[24] The difficulty with this strategy was two-fold. First, the prosecutor opted to try the Kosovo indictment first, which led to confusion in the Balkans given that the events that made up the bulk of the Kosovo indictment happened long after those for which Milosevic was indicted in Croatia and Bosnia. For Serb academic Vojin Dimitrijevic, it helped turn the trial into "a postmodernist play," with its "final act [shown] first."[25] The trial strategy failed to resonate with those in the region.

The second problem with the indictment was that in the prosecutor's desire to demonstrate just how bad a man Milosevic was, she created a monstrous case. It took two years for the prosecution to present the sixty-six counts against the defendant, and Milosevic died after spending a year presenting his defense. The prosecutor could have put together successive prosecutions of smaller counts against him,[26] which would have resulted in initial guilty verdicts and, importantly, his likely rapid delegitimization after a first verdict branding him a "war criminal." But, the prosecutor refused to split the case.[27] The "all or nothing" approach that the prosecutor preferred—amassing 466 days of hearings over 4 years, nearly 300 prosecution witnesses, and costing more than $200 million[28]—resulted in precisely "nothing" when Milosevic died on March 11, 2006.[29] This led to significant disquiet, with both Milosevic supporters and detractors united in their belief that the increasingly distant tribunal had failed.

One final aspect of this spiritual remoteness present in an extreme fashion in the Rwanda and Yugoslavia tribunals, and to a lesser degree in the other international judicial attempts, could easily have been improved. Because of the tribunals' hiring practices, the population of the target states has been effectively "other-ed" and kept physically away from the tribunals. With very few exceptions, outside the translation corps and defense counsel, Balkan citizens have not been allowed to hold employment in *any* position in their tribunal. Not only are there no Balkan judges or prosecutors, there are not even any support personnel from any of the former Yugoslav states. For nearly the first decade of the ICTR's existence a similar prohibition was in force and no Rwandan could "occupy a post of any importance in the judicial chambers, the Prosecutor's Officer, the Registry or . . . the Defense Office."[30] When the Prosecutor's Office finally appointed three Rwandans as advisers, it was described as tantamount to "a small revolution."[31] Rwandans remain barred from other, more substantive positions in their tribunal.

There was logic behind these prohibitions; they were instituted in order to stem leaks, to ensure the security of information, and in many cases the security of endangered witnesses. Yet, leaks have nonetheless been rampant at both institutions, with such leaks almost invariably traced back to organs of the tribunals and states "cooperating" with the courts.[32]

Far more problematic for both the Yugoslavia and Rwanda tribunals than simply whether this employment rule has been effective is that it has created even more distance between the tribunals and the people they are serving. It assumes a likeness among all Balkan and Rwandan citizens, painting indicted war criminals, victims, and even uninvolved citizens with the same brush of bias. Again, among Balkans and Rwandans, it is a clear illustration of the assumption that Balkan and Rwandan citizens all hold an immutable ethnic bias and thus cannot be trusted to work toward an impartial, unethnically informed justice. Hiring those from affected populations by finding ways to properly vet potential employees, or following Tito's model and ensuring that opposition groups are equally represented in sensitive organs of the tribunals, could have gone a long way toward building both more equitable tribunals and greater trust on the ground.

The Special Court for Sierra Leone attempted to right the balance. It was designed to have locals and internationals play parts in all aspects of its work. And, at least compared with the Rwanda and Yugoslavia tribunals, the court has done this successfully. However, even here, there are complaints about the imbalance between national and international staff in posts of responsibility.[33] At several times in its tenure, Sierra Leoneans have been demonstrably underrepresented both on the bench and in the management levels of the Special Court. To some extent, the Sierra Leonean government has at times contributed to this imbalance by appointing foreigners to some of the key posts left to its discretion, such as that of assistant prosecutor.

As in Rwanda and Yugoslavia, "the ownership is not there" for Sierra Leoneans, bemoaned John Caulker, who runs a victim-focused NGO.[34] Consequently, in Sierra Leone, feelings such as those expressed by Charlie Hughes (the director of a Freetown-based NGO promoting democracy) are common; he argues that the "ordinary man sees [the] ... court as something from the outside that has little meaning. ... [The] court [is] ... an expensive waste that won't really change the country in terms of poverty and other serious problems."[35]

BIAS

> *Fairness is what justice really is.*
>
> — Justice Potter Stewart

Justice Stewart is not alone in linking fairness with justice. Throughout the regions where international justice has been practiced, concerns about unfair process and proceedings have led many to believe that justice is an afterthought, if not an impossibility in international criminal process. The perceived unfairness within the international judicial system is multifaceted, and ranges from perceptions of outright bias against defendants regarding a "rush to convict" to the widespread belief that defendants are provided subpar counsel and insufficient protection of their rights. More nuanced critiques also exist, concerning the nature of the legal process itself. Accusations of unfairness have resulted in diplomatic disputes, the shutting off of state cooperation with tribunals, and, in the case of the Rwanda tribunal, a strike by defense lawyers protesting against unfair treatment of their clients.[36]

In each of the claims of bias, there has been a significant measure of truth; for instance, the striking ICTR defense lawyers' grievances included assuring their clients the right to bail and to know the identity of prosecution witnesses—both central rights in most legal systems. These rights had been limited in the ICTR. Further, some of the most strident criticisms about the international system come not from aggrieved parties or concerned defendants—who might be predisposed one way or the other—but rather from scores of observers and academics on the outside. Many have penned reports that describe the rights of the accused before such tribunals as "on the road to disaster," and they have lamented that there has been "relatively little interest in the rights of the accused before the international criminal courts [where] fair trials are often all but impossible."[37] Some have claimed that the motto of international criminal courts is simple: "When in doubt, convict."[38]

While this concern for fairness is significant, and often stated, the concrete statistics of the tribunals' prosecutions, especially when seen in comparison with domestic systems, suggests that at least in regard to hasty convictions, the complaint is overstated. Though measuring conviction rates is as much an art as a science, as of the beginning of 2008, 151 accused had appeared in proceedings before the Yugoslavia tribunal. Only 53, or 35 percent, had been found guilty.[39] At the Rwanda tribunal, 34 cases had been completed, resulting in only 6 sentences, or 18 percent. In comparison, though some states such as the United Kingdom have conviction rates below 60 percent,[40] criminal prosecutions in many states that purport to be concerned with trial fairness often exceed 90 percent. In France, for instance, the country's two highest courts have conviction rates between 90 and 95 percent,[41] in Japan conviction rates in criminal trials regularly exceed 99 percent,[42] and in Australia, nearly 80 percent of the criminal cases the government brings result in conviction.[43] Even in the United States, which has the world's most extensive system for protecting defendants' rights, fully 90 percent of litigated criminal cases result in guilty verdicts.[44] Though there are important differences among domestic systems and between domestic systems and the international tribunals—thus potentially limiting the significance of such comparisons—seen in this light, there does not appear to be a systemic or systematic bias toward conviction in the tribunals.

"Inferred" Bias

However, there is more to this concern of fairness than simple conviction rates or "legal" definitions of impartiality. For both the Yugoslavia and Rwanda tribunals, there is the issue of the perception of bias, and in particular how extradition of indictees to The Hague and Arusha has been viewed. This "inferred" bias is brought about by the locations of the tribunals, which for many have been troubling. For the Balkans, removing criminals to Holland—even if to an international court—is worrying to many sides of the conflict. To begin, The Hague was the site of some of the early failed negotiations between constituent states of the disintegrating Yugoslavia—the bad blood from these 1991 discussions contributed to further violence. For Serbs who remember the 1999 NATO air raids on Belgrade, depositing indictees with a key participant in these bombings is akin to handing them over to the enemy. The Dutch were prime players in the NATO bombings, and were one of the many NATO states sued by the Serbs for alleged war crimes committed during the attack. Many wonder how Serbs can get a fair trial in The Hague when the same nations that paid for the NATO bombing against Serbia in 1999 are underwriting and hosting the trial.[45] The Dutch/NATO relationship leads to a further perception of bias. Statements and actions of major figures in the NATO alliance concerning Serbian—and especially Milosevic's—culpability, and the close military and political alliance between the United States and the Netherlands, similarly leaves many Serbs (and others) feeling that the Dutch-based tribunal is necessarily predisposed against them. Many recall US secretary of state Madeline Albright's statement in June 2000, as the United States doubled aid to anti-Milosevic forces to $25 million: "As far as US policy is concerned, we want to see Milosevic out of power, out of Serbia, and in The Hague."[46]

For Bosniaks and other Muslims, the Dutch played a more tragic role in the Yugoslav conflict. The Dutch were directly involved in Srebrenica, the site of one of the signature massacres of the war. It was a Dutch battalion that was tasked with ensuring the integrity of the UN "safe zone."[47] However, it was Dutch ineptitude and missteps that played a substantial part in allowing the horrors that occurred. Reports after the fact, which were so damning as to lead to the fall of a Dutch government, singled the Dutch forces out for failing to stop the killings.[48] Consequently, extradition to Holland for Bosniaks, or simply going to the Netherlands to be a witness, evokes difficult and conflicting feelings among this population regarding whether the Dutch will once again prove unable to protect them.

The situation is not much better for Rwandans. That the tribunal is a UN court is difficult enough. After all, it was the UN in Rwanda that played the role of the inept Dutch battalion at Srebrenica. According to British charity Oxfam, the "international community, and in particular the . . . United Nations, through their . . . supine inactivity and callousness. . . . contributed to the slaughter in Rwanda."[49] The shoestring UN force in Rwanda, under the command of Canadian lieutenant-general Romeo Dallaire, began with few resources and during the genocide had even less. When the killing began, Dallaire appealed for reinforcements, but sadly saw the most capable members of his multinational force, the Belgians, withdraw entirely. His further requests to the UN were turned down, initially by the secretary general and then by the larger Security Council. Far from being strengthened, as the killings commenced, Dallaire's 5,500 soldiers were drawn down, reduced to a skeleton group of 270. This was not the first time the international community failed to intervene in a Tutsi genocide: in the early 1960s, UN observers in Rwanda similarly stood by as Tutsis were massacred and expelled by the Hutus.[50]

Given this recent and more distant tradition of UN inaction, it is not surprising that Rwandans have expressed concerns about the UN's ability to protect both defendants and witnesses coming to Arusha, concerns that have tragically been validated. Several tribunal witnesses have been harassed or even killed, and local Rwandan groups with names ranging from *Associate Ceceka* ("Keep Quiet") to *Ntubavemo* ("Don't Betray Them") have launched organized efforts to discourage Hutus and Tutsis from testifying.[51] Though the tribunal has tried to protect witnesses, most everyone agrees that the structure of Rwandan society makes the bulk of these measures "illusory."[52]

For the Rwanda tribunal even to be in Arusha, Tanzania, is another sensitive point. Given that "a historical precedent haunts" Arusha, much as one does The Hague, the international community can be said to have had an odd knack for selecting emotionally charged sites for its tribunals.[53] Just as The Hague was for the Balkans, Arusha was the site of an ill-fated agreement—the Arusha Accords of 1993—that tried to stop Rwanda's slide into civil war. And, much as The Hague agreements in the former Yugoslavia did, the Arusha Accords in themselves may have sown the seeds for further violence. The extremist Hutu coalition, under President Habyarimana (whose death would spark the genocide), strongly opposed the power sharing arrangements proposed at Arusha, an intransigence matched by the Tutsis, who hardened their positions as well. In the wake of the Arusha Accords, the Hutu militias that would be the prime players in the genocide began to form.

Tanzania is also an odd choice as a site for an independent tribunal. There has historically been some tension between Francophone Rwanda and Anglophone Tanzania, its much larger neighbor. In recent years, the tension has focused on Rwandan refugees. For two years after the 1994 genocide, as many as two hundred thousand primarily Hutu Rwandans lived in squalor in Tanzania, as unwelcome refugees. The refugees were forcibly repatriated in 1996, with Tanzanian troops using batons and tear gas to force them back into Rwanda.[54] In addition to the refugee issue, there is a sensitive Anglophone/Francophone linguistic divide throughout Africa. Usually a contest between states, the linguistic divide emerged *within* Rwanda after the Tutsis returned to power. This has made Tanzania's Anglophone status relevant. The current Tutsi leaders primarily grew up in exile, largely in Anglophone countries.[55] Rwandan President Paul Kagame's family, for instance, moved to British Uganda in 1960. Tellingly, Rwanda's 1991 constitution, passed by the Hutu-led government, recognizes only Kinyarwanda and French as national languages; the 2003 constitution, adopted once the Tutsis returned to power, added English to the mix. Kagame himself, the president of a country that is still officially Francophone, does not even speak French.[56] Consequently, for Hutus to be arraigned in an English-speaking country strengthens perceptions of an uneven playing field.

Discomfort with the choice of Tanzania as the tribunal's host also derives from the crosscutting loyalties of East and Central Africa. In 1979, Tanzania aided the Ugandan National Resistance Army (of which Rwandan Tutsi refugees made up one-fifth of its membership, and in which President Kagame was a colonel) in removing Ugandan dictator Idi Amin from power.[57] It was the Ugandan Army that then aided Kagame in his 1991 invasion of Rwanda, which removed the Hutus from power. Consequently, Kagame can directly thank Tanzania for his eventual ability to secure power in Kigali. Seen from this vantage point, extraditing a Hutu to Arusha is akin to sending a Serb to The Hague. The location of the tribunals alone has been enough to spark the "bias" controversy.

CORRUPTION, INCOMPETENCE, AND INJUSTICE

In the regions, however, another issue detracting from a sense of fairness stems from repeated charges of corruption in the international tribunals, and its partner in crime, incompetence. Many have asked:

"How can the tribunals handle the grave issues of justice, if they cannot administratively handle themselves?" Regarding corruption, there have been recent high-profile instances of UN corruption and impropriety—most notably the Oil for Food Scandal which broke in 2003, and revelations of widespread sexual abuse of refugees by dozens of UN peacekeepers in the Democratic Republic of the Congo in 2005, followed three years later by accusations that these same peacekeepers were involved in arming militias and smuggling.[58] Even though these recent difficulties have had nothing to do with the tribunals, that the Yugoslavia and Rwanda tribunals are officially UN courts has meant that their reputations have been dragged down with that of the wider organization, further sullying the confidence that locals may have had in their tribunals.

However, at least in Sierra Leone, there have been comparatively few accusations of corruption in their Special Court. Some defendants, such as Hinga Norman, have accused the Special Court of corruption, though his claims were not substantiated. In contrast, in 2002 the UN internal watchdog—the Office of Internal Oversight—found corruption and mismanagement in both the Yugoslavia and Rwanda tribunals, concluding that the "legal system at both UN tribunals . . . [was] abused," often via kickbacks provided to detainees by their court-appointed lawyers.[59] The Rwanda tribunal, for instance, pays defense lawyers as much as $110 per hour, and defendants often ask for kickbacks from attorneys seeking to handle their cases. Unfortunately, whistleblowers within the tribunals have been treated harshly.[60] Some attorneys have been disciplined and even fired due to corruption, though by all accounts such practices continue. In some cases, the UN rules on staff retention have made it difficult to dismiss offenders. An infamous case occurred in 2002 when an employee in the Rwanda tribunal's legal aid department was moved to the transport department, but not fired, even though UN investigators had found him guilty of corruption and racketeering.[61]

This inability to remove offenders contributes to a larger perception of incompetence. Though there are justifiable concerns regarding the competence of defense lawyers (discussed in greater detail below), the more serious concern regarding bias for Rwandans and Yugoslavs is the competence and professionalism of the tribunal's own staffs, from the judges, to the administrators, to the prosecutors. Questionable antics of a few have been attributed to the entire enterprise, leaving many to doubt the potential for fair trials. Unfortunately, the Rwanda tribunal has proven especially fertile ground for such behavior. For instance, in May 2004, Melinda Pollard, a Rwanda tribunal prosecutor, was found to have been disbarred *twice* by her home jurisdiction, the state of New York, and was practicing law without a license, in contravention to the requirements imposed on lawyers acting before the UN court. She was disbarred for the first time due to dishonesty and fraud, and the second time for perjury.[62] When she appeared before the judges in her home jurisdiction to argue against her disbarment she claimed that even if she had behaved improperly, her work as a UN prosecutor did not "present any threat to the public," neglecting, of course, the potential threat she posed to defendants she prosecuted, let alone to the integrity of the tribunal.[63] Pollard's case came on the heels of a troubling 2001 during which six prosecutors were fired from the Rwanda tribunal due to incompetence. And the Pollard case was unfortunately followed a year later by a series of disturbing cases. In May 2005, allegations of a sex scandal at the tribunal's office in Kigali emerged, as well as allegations that some ICTR staff members were pressuring witnesses at the tribunal to recant their testimonies. A month later, the case of Bongani Dyani erupted. Dyani was a South African tribunal staff member working for the prosecution. He fled Arusha after it was revealed that throughout his one-year tenure at the ICTR he was a wanted fugitive in South Africa, charged with attempted murder and aggravated robbery.[64] Each of these instances has led people to question the tribunal and the wider Hague system.

People on the ground have also doubted judicial impartiality and professionalism. Several examples are often cited: in November 2002, Rwanda tribunal judges laughed out loud as a defense attorney cross-examined a witness who repeatedly had been gang-raped over a period of weeks; during her tenure, Yugoslavia tribunal president Kirk Mac-Donald called Serbia a "rogue" state (hardly instilling confidence in Serbs that her decisions on Serb defendants were not preordained); similarly, another ICTY president, Antonio Cassese, was so public in his premature pronouncement that certain Serbs who had not yet appeared before the tribunal were guilty, that leading human rights campaigner Geoffrey Robertson suggested that "in many domestic legal systems," Cassese would have been disqualified from serving as a judge in those cases.[65]

Troubling potential conflicts of interest have also been handled strangely. Here the Special Court for Sierra Leone receives as much attention as the others. In the trial of former Sierra Leone politician Hinga Norman, the defendant sought the disqualification of Austrian Judge Renate Winter. A central component of the Norman trial was the legality surrounding the use of child soldiers. The UN Children's Fund (UNICEF) worked extensively on this issue and made submissions to the tribunal on the topic. Judge Winter enjoyed a long association with UNICEF. The concern for Norman was that Winter's intimacy with UNICEF and her clearly held views on the subject of child soldiers implicated her ability to dispassionately hear the case. Yet, the motion for disqualification was dismissed. In another curious move, the Special Court appointed Geoffrey Robertson, the same lawyer who had objected to Cassese's putative bias, as president of the tribunal despite the fact that Robertson was explicitly held to be biased, or at least potentially so. Robertson had published a book in 2002 that railed against the Revolutionary United Front (RUF), the key rebel group in Sierra Leone, the leadership of which was under trial at the court. Robertson's judicial peers ruled that he could not hear any RUF cases, but could remain on the bench. This was an odd solution given that one-third of the cases before the court involve the RUF.[66]

Inequality of Arms

The concern of "unfairness" is more than just one of perception; there are other, more legally substantial bases for the complaint of unfairness. A key concern addresses what lawyers refer to as the "equality of arms" between the tribunals' prosecutors and defendants, a principle that "goes to the heart of the fair trial guarantee."[67] Concerns about such equality are present in every legal system (both domestic and international) and derive from the fact that a criminal trial is not a contest between equals. States' investigative and litigation resources dwarf those of all but the wealthiest and most powerful of defendants. Even if resources are equivalent, the states' power to incarcerate, and the fact that judges, jurors, prosecutors, and investigators all represent the state's interests, means that the playing field in a criminal courtroom is far from level. These factors explain a good part of the high rate of conviction in many domestic systems.

This fundamental unfairness has long been understood in many domestic justice systems, with states establishing specific structures in an attempt to reconcile the primacy of ensuring a fair trial with the reality of inequality between the parties: the provision of competent counsel to defendants, the mandate to provide defendants of exculpatory evidence amassed by the state, the requirement that defendants be permitted to confront their accusers, and the presumption of innocence—and its correlate requirement for the government to surmount a high burden of proof.[68]

Yet, while these elements of mitigation are often successful in many domestic systems, they have translated poorly into the international criminal realm; in the tribunals many have identified a substantial "imbalance" threatening the veracity of trials,[69] and Milosevic, Taylor, and others have often complained of a glaring inequality in arms. One seeming exception to this failure, apparent in the relatively low rate of convictions at the tribunals, is the presumption of innocence. Tribunal defendants are entitled to this presumption, even if it is not as robust a right as that in many domestic systems. The problem with the presumption, however, is that the tribunals have never fully elucidated just what the presumption is, and exactly how much the prosecutor must prove in order to overcome it.[70] Moreover, even if the base presumption exists, at times it has not even been clear that it is the prosecution that bears the primary burden of proof. The unclear rules by which trials are run—a result of the odd mix of the "oil" of Anglo-American common law, with the "water" of Continental civil law systems—has resulted in perpetual uncertainty in many areas. Though it seems that common law rules have begun to predominate, on central issues related to trial management and even judgments, the status and rights of the defendant continue to be uncertain. And it is in this regard that defendants and others have been right to express concern.

Uncertainty is a key manner in which "arms" are unequal. The reason for this uncertainty is the newness of international justice and the absence of history and settled practices that provide perhaps the greatest protection for defendants' rights: predictability. The unpredictability of the international courts has also been a common complaint.

JUDICIAL EXPERIMENTATION

Milosevic again provides some of the clearest articulation of this concern. The former Serb leader had hoped to make a statement on August 30, 2001, in which he was to complain that the tribunal was "without helpful precedent, common tradition, or relevant experience."[71] The tribunal wisely forbade him from using the proceedings as a soapbox. Nonetheless, the statement was subsequently leaked to his supporters, and has since been borrowed from and repeated by some of the Balkans' most astute legal thinkers. It is another aspect of unfairness, and one of the most procedurally damning of the common complaints heard in target regions. Essentially, this complaint alleges that the international criminal justice "system" unleashed on the people of the former Yugoslavia, Rwanda, Sierra Leone, and elsewhere was unformed and evidently rushed. Further, this complaint also suggests that it was an "experiment," with any resulting "justice" a product of arbitrary, ad hoc rule making rather than dispassionate legal reasoning. Interestingly, this complaint mirrors one made in 1946 by Robert Jackson, the chief prosecutor at Nuremberg. He observed that a chief obstacle to success at his tribunal was the lack of a "beaten path" for international criminal law.[72] This remained true fifty years later at the establishment of the Yugoslavia tribunal; there was no "time to perfect a solution."[73] Implementing such an admittedly rudimentary system has hardly endeared the system to the people.

The list of what international criminal justice did *not* have at its resumption in 1993 is substantial. As a fundamental complication, the new cadre of international lawyers had to contend with the absence of any practicing international prosecutors prior to 1993 on whom to model their work. For a profession such as law, in which vocational training has usually consisted of the apprenticeships of young lawyers to senior practitioners,[74] the dearth of international prosecutors meant that new international prosecutors had no precedents upon which to draw from in answering even the most basic questions, ranging from organizing their office bureaucracies to structuring cases.[75] Moreover, many practitioners quickly found historical exemplars, such as the prosecutors at the Nuremberg and Tokyo trials, "uniquely ill-suited"[76] as guides. The political situation in occupied Germany and Japan made Nuremberg and Tokyo trial prosecutors arms of the occupying state, able to wrest cooperation from anyone in either country and with free reign to gather evidence and investigate. This was not the case in the Balkans, Rwanda, or Sierra Leone.

That there was no precedent or common tradition, as Milosevic claimed, was undeniable, and none of the lawyers or judges had any direct experience in the provision of international criminal justice. Moreover, there were no rules of procedure and evidence. The tribunal's statute simply directed the tribunal's judges to author such rules as they saw fit.[77] This tabula rasa approach has been followed by all subsequent tribunals and has continued to cause difficulties in international courts. The consistency with which tribunals' rules have changed has been one of the few constants. The regulatory fluctuations have made practicing before the tribunals, let alone effectively defending a client, an adventure. As of the middle of 2008, the Yugoslavia tribunal's rules had been substantively revised on forty-two separate occasions, with each revision often adjusting a half dozen, if not more, of the approximately 130 rules (in addition to subrules) that make up the code of trial practice and regulation.[78] Such flux has been present in more recent tribunals as well, with proceedings in Sierra Leone initially hampered precisely by confusion from the bench concerning rules and procedures.

The instability in the rules has regularly left even highly qualified defense lawyers confused and indignant. One such aggrieved lawyer was American law professor Anthony d'Amato, who was engaged to defend Serb physician Milan Kovacevic in 1997. D'Amato recalled that in late 1997 he had received his client's indictment, discussed the charges and trial strategy with Kovacevic, and was almost ready for trial. Shortly before the hearing, he was presented with an amended indictment with dozens of altered charges. D'Amato had been given no notice of these additions, nor had he received any information about new charges prior to their appearance on the new indictment.[79] He would have had no time to prepare adequately for the hearing if these additional charges were to remain.

In this case, what the prosecutor had done was within the rules if only because there was no rule that barred the practice. According to the regulations in force at the time, an indictment needed to be sent by the prosecutor to a judge who must approve it before the indictment could be served on a suspect. The rules were clear about this requirement, but did not address the question whether a similar procedure, taking place close in time to trial, would suffice for amending indictments. Such ex parte proceedings (held with only one side present before a judge) would be manifestly unfair, as it could mean that defendants would have no time to review any new charges before being called upon to refute them. D'Amato complained and the rule was altered in the same manner rules are always changed: in a private hearing among judges, with no formal comment from outside the bench.

The rule that affected D'Amato's client was rectified, and that it was done quickly, shows the flexibility and responsiveness of an otherwise slow-moving ICTY bureaucracy. But it also serves as a note of caution, and perhaps evidence that complaints about unfairness heard in the Balkans and Rwanda and elsewhere may be largely true. It is unknown how many other similarly detrimental rules have *not* been challenged; it seems highly likely that the existence of unchallenged, unfair rules may have unjustly injured other defendants, especially those who did not have counsel as experienced and forceful as D'Amato.

While the instability of the tribunals' rules of procedure and evidence have often made it hard to determine what rights and responsibilities befall advocates and judges, the most serious "black box" still burdening The Hague system is the unclear, uncomfortable compromise between running the tribunal in accordance with common law and civil law principles. This presents logistical and ethical quandaries for lawyers, judges, and defendants.[80] In general, it can be said that common law systems, also known as "adversarial" systems, are based on custom or precedent, while civil law systems, also known as "inquisitorial" systems, rely primarily on written legislated code. It has never been clear just how much of each system is actually represented in international tribunals. With many prosecutors from common law jurisdictions (US, UK, Australia) and most judges from civil law states (in Europe, Asia, and Africa), the conflict can be serious because several of the differences between the two are critical in criminal trials. Officially the tribunal claims to operate under them both,[81] a difficult, and at times, impossible task given their incompatibility on central issues, such as the right to remain silent.

There is a fundamental difference in the manner in which the two systems organize the courtroom. In civil law jurisdictions, the judge often plays the role of lead questioner of witnesses and lawyers; there is rarely a jury. It is the judge who makes it the "inquisitorial" system, and in many civil systems the judge can even call her own witnesses (a practice that has been common at the tribunals). In common law jurisdictions, especially in criminal cases, the judge plays a retiring role, letting the lawyers battle before a lay jury. It is the lawyers who make it the "adversarial" system. The judge's role in common law trials is primarily to keep order during the proceedings and to explain to the jury the law on which it is to assess the facts.

At its most benign, the clash of civil and common law jurisdictions makes for awkwardness in the trial process. It has not been an unusual sight at either the Yugoslavia or Rwanda tribunals for a common law prosecutor questioning a defendant or witness to be interrupted by a civil law judge who rephrases the question or summarizes the answer. As such acts are unknown in common law jurisdictions, and are frowned upon in most, the grimace of the common law prosecutor, upset with the "unwarranted" interruption from the bench, is often palpable.

The problems with this procedural disjuncture have been evident in several instances. First, the relationship between civil and common law practice, and the growing influence of common law at the tribunals have arguably come to impugn one of their primary purposes. Several supporters of the Yugoslavia tribunal, and especially many of the tribunal's Balkan champions such as Vesna Terselic of the Croatian NGO, Documenta, claim that the tribunal's primary benefit is that it will help establish truth and a historical record. However, the common law system is architecturally disadvantaged in attaining this end, especially in comparison with the civil law system. As Australian jurist Anthony Mason notes of the difference:

> [Civil jurisdiction] courts are said to have as their object the investigation of the truth. Within the adversarial [or common law] system. . . . the function of the Courts is not to pursue the truth but to decide on the cases presented by the parties.[82]

American academic Alan Dershowitz puts it even more starkly, arguing that in the common law system,

> [a] . . . criminal trial is anything but a pure search for truth. When defense attorneys represent guilty clients. . . . their responsibility is

to try, by all fair and ethical means, to prevent the truth about their client's guilt from emerging.[83]

This elementary difference in philosophy has often stymied trial judges in basic questions of courtroom management. For instance, can a defendant choose to defend himself, even if that choice leads to significant delay? Pro se cases (proceedings in which a defendant acts as his own lawyer) are not unknown in either civil or common law. However, when this issue arose at the Yugoslavia tribunal, it became evident that the tribunal's statute was ambiguous; moreover, common law and civil law suggest different solutions. In most common law systems, limiting a defendant's pro se rights is difficult. This is not so in many civil law countries. The judges were flummoxed, and after delaying proceedings for several months, the three judges—composed of two common law and one civil law judge—deferred to civil law (including rules pertaining in Serbia) in holding that counsel could be forced on the defendant. Ironically, the appeals bench reversed the holding, clouding the situation once more.[84] The civil law and common law split can clearly influence trial strategy and potentially even outcome.

In this regard, critics and defendants have bridled at what some see as the "potpourri" approach the tribunal has used to finding precedents for its actions—many believe that the tribunal simply decides what it wants to do and then cherry picks precedent, from national or international code, civil or common law, in order to justify its actions. It is not just the tribunals' choosing between "common law" and "civil law" as it sees fit, but rather, the tribunals' picking law from almost any jurisdiction in order to provide support for its behavior. The most infamous example of this exercise was the widely reported instance in which Yugoslavia tribunal prosecutor Louise Arbour defended charges made against her office that it had improperly seized documents from the Bosnian government. Arbour claimed that the seizure was compatible with the domestic laws of at least one state: Paraguay.[85] Not only is this South American country as divorced from Balkan realities as one could be but it also seems to provide dubious legal justification: its judiciary is said to be corrupt and its constitution allows lengthy detention without trial.[86] Even if the story of Arbour's resort to Paraguayan law is apocryphal, it has shades of truth and it remains gospel to many.

DEFENSE COUNSEL—"BOSTON LEGAL VS. BALKAN LEGAL"[87]

While legal diversity managed to enrich and embolden the prosecutor's office, such diversity among lawyers who have appeared before the tribunals—and in particular the defense counsel—has added still further grist to the contention that the tribunals have been unfair to defendants.

Defense counsels are critical to the protection of defendants' rights. Yet, in each of international justice's iterations, defendants and citizens of postconflict regions have complained of substantial problems with the quality and effectiveness of defense advocates. The truth behind this complaint is not so simple. Indeed, while cases of defense lawyer corruption have not helped the situation, and though there have been some true incompetents who have appeared before the tribunals, the majority of defense counsel—especially in recent years—have been seasoned, effective lawyers. However they have nevertheless been stymied by a legal infrastructure that makes the international courtroom fundamentally imbalanced.

Solely from the perspective of inadequate resources, the perception of ineffective defense counsels seems valid. The defense in all international tribunals has been hobbled. At the Yugoslavia tribunal, though there have been improvements since the first trials—in which defense counsel were paid $26 per hour—there remains a significant funding gap between prosecution and defense: for the biennial period 2004 and 2005, the defense budget was $29.5 million, while the prosecution's budget was $99.9 million. Such "dramatic" underfunding can be seen throughout international justice, with its hopeful nadir seen at the Special Panels for East Timor. There, insufficient defense support directly impacted fairness: largely because of defense budgetary constraints, the defense did not call a single witness for any of the Special Panels' first fourteen trials.[88]

For both the ICTY and ICTR, unequal resources is *legally* untroubling since judges at both tribunals have held that "equality of arms" solely means equality of rights, rather than of resources. Yet, even in the Special Court for Sierra Leone, which has embraced the commonsensical notion that equality of arms relies in part on an equality of resources, the reality of the situation is anything but equal. As James Cockayne of the International Peace Institute noted, prosecutors in Freetown investigate cases with court vehicles, dedicated drivers, security personnel, translators, and professional international investigators. Defense team staff, meanwhile, are not formally permitted to use court transport, have no dedicated drivers or security, and must find their own translators and investigation staff, with only national (as opposed to international) level salaries for those staff covered by their budgets. The prosecutor's budget takes up a large proportion of the Special Court's endowment and the defense receives less than 5 percent of the funding accorded the prosecutor. Prosecutors have, until recently, been given five times the office space assigned to the defense. Finally, bureaucratic rank also speaks to inequality, with the Special Court's prosecutor accorded the rank of UN assistant secretary general, while the head of the defense is "many rungs lower."[89]

With this in mind, Charles Taylor's' complaints about unfairness in his trial before the Special Court for Sierra Leone appear more reasonable. Taylor has written to the Special Court complaining that his lawyer lacks the resources to mount an adequate defense, pointing out that his counsel works virtually alone while prosecutors have a team of nine lawyers. The Taylor defense team was given an international investigator only in March 2007—a full year after his arraignment—and a local investigator in Liberia only in May 2007. Though it is difficult to understand how Taylor—who stole so much—can now claim indigence and be forced to rely on the Special Court's generosity for his defense, his claims are nonetheless troubling. "It is not justice to emaciate my defense to an extent that I am unable to launch an effective defense," Taylor wrote. "It is not justice to throw all rights to a fair trial to the wind in a headlong rush to trial."[90]

Even if financial resources were equilibrated, the tribunals could nonetheless be faulted in their provision of competent defense lawyers. Initially, the Yugoslavia tribunal was an unfortunate victim of the long dormancy of international criminal law, with no practicing lawyers on whom to model. However, a new generation of international prosecutors gained their footing while a dearth of effective international defenders remained. A yawning gap in quality between defense and prosecution emerged—a gap that has been replicated in other international tribunals. The reason for this is several-fold. First, defense counsels are usually temporary participants in the international justice system, with engagements limited to a particular case. They have had limited ability to establish expertise via repetition. The second reason relates to how foreign the international system has been to defense counsel. Few of the Balkan lawyers who appeared before the ICTY in its early days had even read the Nuremberg transcripts (as they are not widely available in Serbo-Croatian), let alone practiced courtroom advocacy in the manner required by the tribunal.

This in itself creates the perception of, if not an actual, a priori imbalance: in trials, the primarily Western European and North American prosecutors regularly advocate before their cocitizen judges on the bench, using laws and procedures written by their Western compatriots. The creeping encroachment of common law practice further ostracizes civil law Balkan attorneys, who already seem foreign to the judges (given the absence of Balkan jurists on the bench), and who already are nonconversant in the laws and regulations of the tribunal (which were similarly written without Balkan input).

Judge Patricia Wald recalled that in the early days of the ICTY, Balkan-trained lawyers were particularly unfamiliar with the process of cross-examination, a staple of common law systems, but a rarity in civil law. She remembered that "[s]ome [lawyers were] quick learners," but others "painfully awkward. . . . sometimes arguing with or even criticizing . . . witnesses." The tribunal has operated a training course for these lawyers, but Wald noted that "candidly, it is not easy to acculturate lawyers in a wholly new legal system in a few days of lectures or even simulated exercises. . . . I frankly found many ICTY defense cross-examinations painfully unhelpful to my own judgment."[91] Although the tribunal now requires defense counsels to have at least seven years of experience in criminal law, prior to 2004 it required counsels to have only "reasonable experience in criminal and/or international law"—a requirement that the tribunal interpreted generously. In practice, many attorneys who appeared before the ICTY had little criminal defense experience, and even less knowledge of international law.

There has been one further problem with regard to criminal defense lawyers: the UN courts have at times limited the ability of defendants to choose their own counsel. This is in direct opposition to many domestic systems where the choice of counsel is sacrosanct. Yet, in a classic case of defendants' rights bumping up against the UN bureaucracy, the UN requires "national diversity" in all its institutions. If too many lawyers from certain countries were engaged in defending individuals, citizens from those countries were barred from defending others. The UN has even removed appointments on this basis. Thus in October 1998, the Rwanda tribunal stated it was "temporarily refraining from assigning any Canadian or French defense counsel," because of the number of attorneys from those states already in the defense counsel pool. Rejecting the choices of the accused, and the fact that Canadian lawyers, and especially Quebecois lawyers, are perhaps uniquely qualified to handle the mixed civil law/common law system, and the ICTRs bilingual English/French operations, the tribunal wished to "maintain a geographic balance."[92]

Defendants were understandably displeased about the decision, which had the effect of suspending some lawyers who had already been appointed; 25 of the 32 individuals being detained in Arusha went on a hunger strike. They protested the discrimination against their lawyers and complained about the quality of counsel who had been assigned in their place.[93]

Even if the recruitment, training, and funding of defense lawyers were improved—as it has over the ensuing decade and in the more recent tribunals—the effectiveness of defense counsels has been further harmed by the corporate structure prevalent in the tribunals. Unlike the prosecution staff, who sit in a large number of office suites within the tribunals' buildings, the defense counsel are physically and "spiritually" separated. At the ICTY, physically the defense cannot even freely enter the main tribunal building. In the UN system, identification badges, and in particular their color, "make the man"—in The Hague judges and prosecutors have blue access badges, while the defense attorneys have rather ominous, stop-light red, access badges. These badges literally limit their movements into and around the tribunal building that has dozens of locked access points (only openable via the swipe of a "correct" badge).

This "spiritual" gulf between defense and prosecution extends to social relationships outside the tribunal. Defense attorneys are often largely excluded from even nonlegal relationships. In the case of the ICTY, The Hague is a small, diplomatic town, and it is rare for a week to pass without some official reception. Important figures from the city's many legal institutions are almost always invited to embassy or government functions, including prosecutors, judges, and other tribunal officials. Defense lawyers are rarely invited. The close, supportive, and convivial relationships that arise due to this informal contact between only some members of the tribunal can give the impression of collusion between judges and prosecutors. One hopes that defense counsel are not invited simply because their comparatively short tenures at the tribunal means that they do not have time to make it onto the various embassy and official guest lists. Regardless of the reason, the defense teams' access to judges and administrators is much more limited than that of prosecutors'. In Freetown and Arusha, the situation is similar, with the prosecution permanently stationed at the courts, while defense counsels are usually itinerant.

Whether based on the "spiritual" gap or more concrete shortcomings, the international community has recognized the problem of defense lawyer quality. A 1999 expert group that reviewed ICTY operations flagged the "misgivings regarding the qualification of some assigned counsel" expressed by both judges and lawyers at the tribunal. The report concluded that the combination of segregation, insufficient resources, and inexperience has meant that all too often "shockingly poor" lawyers have represented defendants[94]—lawyers who at times have not understood basic concepts (such as a "guilty plea") let alone had the ability to explain them satisfactorily to their clients.[95]

Incredibly, a year after the publication of this report that bemoaned defense lawyer inexperience, in a case of the international community's right hand not knowing what its left is doing, the UN decided to try an "experiment." It created the Special Panels for East Timor—an internationalized domestic court system in East Timor to address the crimes that occurred during East Timor's movement toward independence in the late 1990s. The UN decided to assign verifiably inexperienced local defenders to cases, pitting them against primarily international prosecutors. The defense lawyers were clearly overmatched and uncertain of the process, leading to cases in which witnesses were not produced, prosecution testimony was not questioned, and defense counsel publicly challenged their own clients. It was only midway through the Special Panel's tenure that the UN conceded that the experiment had failed. Unfortunately, the damage to the trials that went before had been done.[96]

TRIBUNALS NEED STATES FAR MORE THAN
STATES NEED TRIBUNALS

The relationship between the tribunals and the states in the international community also provides a source of unfairness. This unfairness derives primarily from the utter dependence of the tribunals on the states. There are several examples of this dependence, but none more directly impacting justice and fairness than the requirement that tribunals provide defendants all evidence it possesses that could demonstrate a defendant's innocence or mitigate his guilt (so-called exculpatory evidence). However, though explicitly provided in each tribunal, this right has often been honored in the breach, a direct result of the limited powers held by international courts.

The comparison with domestic systems is stark. In domestic courts, though investigators and prosecutors may chafe at turning over hard-won evidence to the defense, they are accountable to the court and are compelled to disclose this evidence under pain of potentially forfeiting their case and/or being held in contempt. The same is true for those people who hold information; if they are unwilling to provide it to the court, they can be subpoenaed and can also be held in contempt.

In the tribunals, though defense lawyers have been ruled in contempt,[97] it is far from clear that prosecutors can also be held in contempt for refusing to share information with the defense.[98] The result is that there is little incentive for prosecutors to proactively reveal any evidence to the defense. Two fundamental facts of international criminal justice further define and create impotence in the face of recalcitrant providers of evidence. First, the tribunals' mandates create an unhealthy reliance on member-state cooperation. The tribunals' temporal jurisdiction is one example of this. The Yugoslavia tribunal is charged with prosecuting crimes that predate its creation—born in May 1993, it is responsible for punishing crimes committed "since 1991." The Rwanda tribunal was formed in November 1994 and has jurisdiction over crimes that have occurred since January of that year. The Special Court for Sierra Leone was created in 2000 but with jurisdiction over all relevant crimes since November 30, 1996. While all of the tribunals may have developed the capacity to track crimes that occurred after their birth, in order to fulfill their missions effectively they have required access to detailed information collected prior to their existence. Even for more recent crimes, all tribunals have relied heavily on information sources outside their control, to gain further evidence and an understanding of events. Given the subject matter of its cases, the vast majority of such assistance and information comes from governments "friendly" to the tribunals.

Of the international tribunals currently in operation, only the one in Sierra Leone has been able to count on consistent cooperation from its target state. In the other cases, governments have only been of sporadic assistance, regularly turning cooperation on and off as domestic political conditions demand. In the Rwandan case, the "friendly" state most critical to the success of the tribunal has been Rwanda itself; without Kigali's cooperation, the tribunal would simply have ceased to function. Consequently, given the current Tutsi government, the tribunal has been largely unable to obtain evidence concerning Tutsi wrongdoing during the genocide. Attempts by the ICTR to pursue Tutsis have invariably failed. The most recent formal attempt was made in 2000, when Carla Del Ponte, at the time the joint prosecutor of both the Yugoslavia and Rwanda tribunals, announced that she would open investigations into alleged war crimes committed by members of the current Rwandan army, largely made up of Tutsis. Her announcement set off a "merciless protracted game of chess," between the Rwandan authorities and Del Ponte that only ended in August 2003 when the UN stripped Del Ponte of her prosecutorial role at the ICTR.[99] Rwanda has continued to make life difficult for the tribunal. On several occasions, it has supported genocide survivors' associations in their efforts to impede any Rwandans (Hutus or Tutsi) from testifying in Arusha if the content of their proposed testimony was not to their liking.[100]

For the Yugoslavia tribunal the situation is more complex. "Friendly" governments important to ICTY operations include both those formed out of the breakup of Yugoslavia, as well as other governments active in the Balkans during the conflict. The records and archives of the entities that emerged following the fall of Yugoslavia have been critical to ICTY success. The friendliness or animosity of these states to the ICTY mission has directly influenced the scope and quality of charges that the tribunal has been able to assign against indictees, and has often directly determined the outcome. At times, this unfriendliness has been rather odd; the Yugoslavia tribunal, in December 1995, was forced to release an indicted Bosniak soldier who was suspected of killing Bosnian Serbs because Serbia refused to release evidence needed to justify his detention.[101] Some found it strange that Serbia's distaste for the tribunal would extend to sacrificing a potential case against an individual accused of killing fellow Serbs. Serbia was not alone in this unyielding, yet seemingly counterproductive, animosity toward the tribunal. The Croatian general Tihomir Blaskic was prosecuted during a period of intense Croatian recalcitrance toward the tribunal. Croatian president Franjo Tudjman categorically refused to cooperate with The Hague. As a result, Zagreb's archives were ruled off limits to prosecutors and defendants. Based on the material available, the trial court convicted Blaskic of genocide and other crimes against humanity, sentencing him to forty-five years.[102] By the time of his appeal, the situation on the ground in Croatia had changed. Tudjman had died and Zagreb had softened its stance regarding cooperation with the ICTY. Consequently, the defense was able to provide thousands of state archive documents to the appeals chamber. Although there is some question as to the impact of this new evidence on the outcome, the appellate judges proceeded to overturn much of the tribunal's findings, reduce his sentence by thirty-six years, and release him for time served.[103]

Other than the local "friendly" states, the other states crucial to the tribunal's work have been those outside the region that have provided the funding, evidence, and personnel needed by the tribunal. In the former Yugoslavia, throughout the 1990s, Western powers feared a destabilized Europe and became more interested in the region. This interest was often expressed via expanded embassies and more vigorous on-site monitoring through increased intelligence service personnel and satellite surveillance. The result of this activity is that traditionally tight-lipped organizations—the major intelligence services of the West—became the owners of amongst the most detailed and sophisticated information on almost all aspects of the conflict. This intelligence included information about central elements necessary to build a prosecution case for war crimes and defend such a case; for instance, the presence of mass graves can often be most clearly seen via satellite imagery. The stock in trade of intelligence agencies is keeping secrets and consequently it is not surprising that the tribunal has had some difficulty in prying open their archives for cases.

While Balkan governments and Western intelligence have had different reasons for uncooperative behavior toward the tribunal—a desire to stymie the tribunal's work and a concern for the protection of classified information, sources, and methods, respectively—the results have been the same. The tribunal has been very constrained in gaining full information or even full access to witnesses, and, most critically, there is little that the tribunal can do to force any government to act.

This constellation of factors has allowed governments to provide evidence when they see fit, and when they see political advantage. To many, this process was all too clear in the Milosevic case. As Michael Posner of the Lawyers' Committee for Human Rights put it, "[Cooperation is] like a spigot . . . [States] . . . turn it on and off as it suits their purposes."[104] There is no other way to explain why Britain provided information on the prosecution of Slobodan Milosevic only in 2000, when it almost certainly had evidence—"stacked a mile high"[105]—several years before. Before 2000, Britain thought it could work the Serbian leader toward regional peace; after his Kosovo actions, any hope of rehabilitating Milosevic was dashed.[106] Similarly, once the Clinton administration "went to war against Mr. Milosevic, it began releasing satellite imagery of mass graves . . . and providing classified intercepts to the tribunal."[107] Milosevic was not the only "beneficiary" of such intransigence. The United States proved equally unwilling to aid the tribunal in providing satellite photos to investigate Croatian actions during the war.[108] State cooperation has been so uncertain that the Yugoslavia tribunal was forced to adopt its "Rule 61" procedures whereby, in public hearings, prosecutors could recertify their indictments and make it even clearer which countries had failed to provide evidence. One of the hopes of this process was to shame the international community into providing assistance.[109]

The second root of the disclosure problem is a function of the broader inequality between states and the tribunals, apart from the provision of evidence. Though member states are mandated to varying degrees to work with the tribunals, international courts and states are far from equal partners. Rather, the courts regularly come to states from an administratively, politically, and economically subservient position. The issue of how much the tribunals can compel states to carry out directives became a minor cause célèbre in Croatia in 1997 after The Hague demanded the country produce evidence.[110] Zagreb refused and Croatia was vindicated when the tribunal held that "the ICTY cannot issue binding orders" to states compelling any action.[111]

It is not just legal weakness that hinders the tribunals. The needs of the tribunals vis-à-vis member states are as significant when it comes to investigative assistance and financial management. These needs include even the most prosaic of ministerial functions such as the apprehension of indictees and the housing of convicted war criminals. The result of this foundational inequality between states and the tribunals is the perpetuation of further unfairness to defendants even if "friendly" governments agree to provide information to the tribunals. For example, in contrast to the majority of domestic systems, providers of information, even *after* they have given evidence to the tribunal, can maintain control over the information's dissemination. Thus, the tribunals' various rules of evidence and procedure are clear in their demand to the prosecutor that she disclose "to the defense any material which . . . may suggest the innocence or mitigate the guilt of the accused." Nevertheless, the reality is that this requirement is seriously constrained, especially if confidential or classified information is at issue.[112] In its relevant portions, the tribunals' rules hold that if "the prosecutor is in possession of information which has been provided to the prosecutor on a confidential basis," neither it nor its source needs to be disclosed.[113] Though there are limits to the prosecutor's ability to hold back such information and what she can do with the information, the defendant's right to both know the full scope of the evidence against him, and to effectively confront his accusers, is limited.

Member states have kept tight control over their classified information. In one case during the summer of 2004, the prosecutor divulged information to the defense that had been provided by a member state on a classified basis. This resulted in a furor. The state, for a time, ceased all cooperation with the tribunal. It was only after high-level meetings between the state's ambassador to the Netherlands and the prosecutor, and repeated contrition on the part of the prosecutor, which meant the establishment of further checks on the ability of the tribunal to use information, that the member state relented and resumed its sharing role.

This clear inequality between tribunal and state is the core of many complaints heard on the ground.

THE TRIBUNALS AS EXPENSIVE INSTITUTIONS

While international tribunals need state cooperation in order to function—with almost no facet of its operations possible without state assistance—state financing is perhaps the clearest and, for those in the devastated regions recovering from mass crimes, among the most controversial aspects of the needed state support.

Though some residents are not aware of how much their courts cost, others raise frequent objections about the amount of money devoted to the international justice system. However, one of the most persuasive complaints about the tribunals' costs comes not from impacted regions, but from within the UN itself—from the UN's former chief legal officer, assistant secretary general Ralph Zacklin. In a decidedly undiplomatic article, Zacklin deemed The Hague process "costly, inefficient, and ineffective."[114]

Many in the UN were furious at Zacklin's remarks. Yet, it is hard to quibble with at least the financial aspects of his conclusions. The courts have been monumentally expensive. The yearly ICTY budget from 1993 to 2007 expanded a thousand-fold, from $276,000 to more than $276 million; at various times in its tenure, the ICTY alone has accounted for 10 percent of the UNs entire annual operating budget. In all, from 1993 through 2007 the ICTY cost $1.2 billion, and is on pace to cost as much as $2 billion by the time it completes its mandate in 2010.[115] Judicial productivity, however, has seemingly not matched the expense. The average cost per conviction at the tribunal has been estimated at nearly $30 million, more than fourteen times the average cost per capital conviction in the United States.[116]

The Rwanda tribunal is somewhat less costly, though it is projected to also have spent more than $1.4 billion by the time it finishes operations in 2010. In 2004, the Rwanda and Yugoslavia tribunals together constituted 15 percent of the total UN budget.[117] Even the cost of the Special Court for Sierra Leone, which was designed to be a more "streamlined" version of international justice, has ballooned; its unique international/domestic nature, headquartered in a relatively inexpensive city and close to the scenes of the crimes, was designed to be "cheaper, faster, and leaner." Before the Taylor trial, there were some doubts whether this new streamlined approach would provide the needed financial and judicial benefits. Once Taylor was captured and transferred to The Hague, however, it immediately became clear that any true streamlining and cost cutting as compared with the ICTY and ICTR was going to be impossible. The Special Court was already having difficulty dealing with its caseload, all the more troubling given that at the time it had just ten detainees. The original budget was very ambitious and called for only $54 million over three years; since the Special Court's opening in 2002, that amount has more than tripled, and the Special Court's initial three-year mandate has morphed into eight years.[118] With the removal of Taylor to The Hague, the Special Court has been forced to duplicate much of the infrastructure it houses in Freetown (in terms of staff, accommodation, and office space), in a far more expensive city.

The Dutch received a significant windfall when the Yugoslavia tribunal decided to set up in the Netherlands, and now the Special Court for Sierra Leone has done the same. The vast majority of the funding for both the ICTY and now the Special Court, and a substantial portion even for the ICTR, flows straight to The Hague. Though understandable, to many it is upsetting that the "selfless task" of international justice has produced such financial gains in an already wealthy state. Since the Yugoslav war, the once comparatively well-off citizens of the Balkans have seen their economic fortunes crumble. The three states most heavily involved in the ICTY (Bosnia and Herzegovina, Croatia, and Serbia) have an average GDP per capita of approximately $6,000, less than one-fifth of the per capita income of the average Dutch citizen.[119] The economies of Sierra Leone and Rwanda make the situation even starker.

The financial flow to the Netherlands has become all the more troubling since during the time when the budget for international justice has been markedly increasing, target states have had to scale down or cancel efforts to improve their own judicial systems due to a lack of funding. For example, police reform in Bosnia was long stalled and the training of judges in Serbia was pared due to financial shortfalls. Meanwhile in Rwanda, the once grand hopes of international support for its local justice system have long since dissipated. Balkan citizens and others see that money for "their" justice is clearly available and donor states have evidently been generous to the cause. Yet, the financial stakes have gone to The Hague and Arusha rather than to their countries.

Though the financial aspect of this arguably misdirected investment has caused significant irritation in the region, a more insidious component of this investment has only recently begun to be voiced. More than the financial capital developed in The Hague, the past decade has seen the development of substantial amounts of human and intellectual capital also developed in The Hague. Judges, lawyers, and administrators have resurrected international criminal law, and due to the long-standing service of many staff members, a heavy concentration of expertise has also developed in The Hague. An unfortunate component of this phenomenon is that this expertise is not being transferred to the Balkans, or any other region that is actually addressing war crimes and humanitarian law violations. Rather, upon closure of the tribunals, other than the few lawyers who will continue working in the field at the ICC, the expertise will return home with the staff members, predominantly to the United States and the United Kingdom (for prosecutors) or throughout Europe and the industrialized world (for other staff members). It will largely not go to the very places where it could be put to most practical use.

The situation is again somewhat different in Sierra Leone. The Special Court has made training of Sierra Leoneans a part of its mandate, and at the very least when the court is done, the internationally funded courthouse will remain. Yet, even here, there have been unintended consequences. In building the courthouse, the Special Court usurped land from the Sierra Leone Prison Service, some of which was to be devoted to a new training school.[120] Further, the court has lured domestic legal experts away from the underserved domestic system, with promises of higher pay and better conditions. Indeed, the experience that the court is affording some of Sierra Leone's leading lawyers may ironically lead to a reduction, rather than an increase in local expertise. Some Sierra Leoneans, armed with court-provided international legal educations and experience, have decided against returning to the domestic sector. They have begun looking elsewhere, outside the country, for opportunities. The Special Court may have unwittingly initiated a brain drain that could leave Sierra Leone with an absence of home grown experience and understanding of the judicial issues of greatest concern.[121]

The other difficulty for Sierra Leone is to justify the amount spent on justice when so many other needs are unmet. This is especially the case because of the location of the Special Court. The gleaming courthouse seems so out of place among the destitution of the rest of Sierra Leone. Court finances have become a combustible political issue. Many echo Marianna Kallon, a local war victim whose leg was cut off during the violence: "The money they have spent for the Court is [worth] nothing. . . . My foot is gone, and it's not coming back. [It would have been better to use the money] . . . to educate my kids." Her primary use for the court is as a place to beg for spare change.[122]

"*JUSTICE DELAYED, JUSTICE DENIED?*"

Justice can be a lengthy affair—no more so than international justice, which deals with invariably complicated, evidence-filled, and resource-rich cases in an environment not conducive to efficient decision making or courtroom management. Yet, the slowness of the international tribunals has become so much a part of any description of the bodies that a cottage industry among observers has developed, with each competing to find the best metaphor to describe just how slow the process is: some say that international justice proceeds at the pace of a "plantation snail,"[123] while others opt for a more syrupy view claiming that the tribunals move "at a molasses pace."[124] The point is clear: these are slow trials, and in their slow pace many see yet another example of unfairness, if not injustice.

While trials themselves can be numbingly slow, it is not just the courtroom proceedings that take time. There is often a significant delay between an initial detention and the start of a trial. Take the Rwanda tribunal as an example: by the time that tribunal was in its fifth year in 1999, it had indicted forty-eight people and tried and sentenced five of them. In total, as of the beginning of 2008, the ICTR had completed only thirty-three cases; in fourteen years, the tribunal has completed an average of just over two cases a year. In the US system the "average murder trial" takes about two weeks; in Australia the length is similar. While the cases before the tribunals are far from average murder trials, it is hard to justify the fact that "average" ICTR case can take as much as ten or twenty times as long (if not more).

Further, though the cases are complicated, much of the delay comes from the system itself. Absent judges can lead to a case being paralyzed for days or weeks; unclear rules of procedure can lead to time-intensive interlocutory appeals; and the necessity for mass translation involves still more administrative time.[125]

The delays in bringing detainees to trial—let alone the tempo of the trials themselves—have often been so lengthy at the Yugoslavia tribunal that some have raised questions whether the tribunal was violating the guarantee for speedy trial provided in the European Convention on Human Rights.[126] At the Rwanda tribunal the average defendant has been detained for more than four years in Arusha before his trial has begun. The delays themselves, and the frequent death of detainees while awaiting trial, have been used as justification for noncooperation of states with the tribunals. The Yugoslavia tribunal has lost five detainees, with Slobodan Milosevic the highest profile. Two have died while in the Special Court for Sierra Leone's care, a substantial proportion as there have only ever been twelve detainees.[127]

Some of these delays are more troubling than others—both for the tribunals and their legitimacy—because they came after guarantees that detainees would be brought to trial quickly. For the ICTY, Croatia made many of its "voluntary" surrenders to the tribunal with the explicit proviso that defendants would be dealt with within six months. That The Hague was unable to process the cases so quickly has been a further cause for Balkan citizens' mistrust of the system. Some have claimed that the "broken promise" to start trials within six months could rightly be viewed "as a deception which justifiably arouses suspicions in the objectivity, reliability, and unbiased nature of th[e] Court."[128]

There is one other, more far-reaching result imposed by the delays that are seemingly inherent to The Hague system: despite the strength and widespread nature of many of the concerns mentioned above, the longer the courts drag on, the worse they fare in popular conscience, both in their target regions and elsewhere. Historically, this is not surprising: surveys conducted by the occupying authorities in West Germany in 1945 to 1946, indicate that by the end of the first phase of Nuremberg, which lasted barely eleven months (November 1945 to October 1946), German interest and confidence in the proceedings had waned markedly.[129] As with the modern courts, the start of the Nuremberg proceedings was met with great interest, with a January 1946 survey revealing that nearly 80 percent of respondents followed the trials. However, there was rapidly declining interest.[130] And the longer the trials progressed, the more pronounced the German concerns became for both the fairness of the proceedings and whether the people accused were actually guilty: whereas three-quarters of the respondents felt that the accused were guilty when asked in January 1946, by August, only 50 percent of Germans believed this was the case.[131]

SERVING TEN YEARS IN SWEDEN? OR THIRTY YEARS IN MALI?

Even once convictions have been rendered, concerns of unfairness abound. This is largely because of the vagaries of sentencing at the tribunals, which is essentially an unknown and undefined process. Judges only have the broadest guidelines regarding sentencing; the actual sentences rendered suggest that judges have almost unchecked discretion in imposing sentences. Judges have but one firm limit: the death penalty is unavailable. The result has been a remarkably inconsistent sentencing practice, with the appellate judges regularly admonishing trial judges to be more uniform, holding that justice has at times been compromised due to inconsistent sentencing.[132]

If the differences and inconsistencies in sentences within a particular tribunal are troubling, a comparison of sentences meted out by different tribunals is even more so. The Rwanda tribunal, for instance, has regularly imposed punishments far more severe than those for similar crimes judged at the Yugoslavia tribunal. For example, the ICTY sentenced General Radislav Krsitic to forty-six years for genocide; the ICTR "issued life sentences (at times multiple life sentences) to [defendants convicted of similar crimes] such as Jean Kambanda, Alred Musema, and Jean-Paul Akayesu."[133] ICTR sentences have been more severe for "lesser" crimes as well. Until recently, it was thought that the difference in severity of penalties was a function of differences in the criminal codes and sentencing schemes of Rwanda and in the states of the former Yugoslavia (which are meant to serve as a rough guide to judges when they impose penalties). That both tribunals have explicitly held that judges are not bound by any of the domestic schemes[134] makes the sentences of both tribunals considered separately, and especially side-by-side, troubling in their seeming arbitrariness.

Yet, the manner in which convicted defendants are handled often means that the resulting punishment, even if facially similar, is nonetheless different, and perhaps unconscionably so. Without facilities for long-term incarceration, the tribunals rely on member states to incarcerate prisoners.[135] The first problem with this is that holding prisoners in states outside their home states may impose further "hardships [upon a prisoner] . . . resulting from linguistic differences, cultural differences, and less frequent family visitation due to distance."[136] The second difficulty comes not from the discomfort that prisoners would feel but rather from the potential "excess" comfort. Prisons in the participating states for the Yugoslavia tribunal—all Western European—are substantially more pleasant than similar accommodations in almost any Balkan prison. Assumptions on the ground concerning just how much more comfortable are at times outlandish but no less persistent. For instance, it is conventional wisdom among many Bosniaks in Sarajevo that Bosnian Serb leader and convicted war criminal Biljana Plavsic's incarceration in Sweden includes her access to all that makes Swedish prisons hospitable, including "tango lessons and birthday cakes."

Disposition of prisoners under the Rwanda tribunal's sentencing agreements also have the makings for disproportionality. The states agreeing to host ICTR prisoners include Sweden, Italy, and France, along with Benin, Mali, Swaziland, and Tanzania.[137] Though prisoners are guaranteed a certain minimal level of prison conditions—and as of mid-2008 all prisoners have been detained in African prisons—the difference between serving a stint in Paris or Rome, compared with a similar time served in Porto Novo, Benin (where "prison conditions are harsh, marked by poor diet and inadequate medical care"),[138] or Bamako, Mali (where "inadequate food" is common in prisons),[139] are significant enough to doubt whether the penalties are even comparable. This inequality of post-trial care continues for the Special Court for Sierra Leone; if Charles Taylor is convicted of crimes he committed in Sierra Leone, he will serve his sentence in the United Kingdom, where prisons are far more convivial than detention facilities in either Sierra Leone or his home country of Liberia.

THE TRIBUNALS AS IMPERIAL INSTITUTIONS

In a sense, it would be in keeping with the model of international criminal justice for Taylor to serve his time in the United Kingdom. Britain was the colonial power in Sierra Leone for centuries. And to many, the entire international justice system represents a rebirth of the colonial system in a different guise. If the justice provided is to be colonized, then it makes sense for the penalties to be as well. In short, as a Bosniak judge in Sarajevo put it, "The Hague process is a return of colonialism . . . [it is] legal imperialism without concern for local conceptions of justice and law."

A trip to Sarajevo is a voyage back in time. It is not just the medieval streets and ancient churches, temples, and mosques. The entire political organization of the city and the country appear to have regressed to the time when Bosnia and Herzegovina were a simple vassal state of the Ottoman Empire; people then paid fealty to the emperor's local pasha, unable to move without Constantinople's assent. After the Dayton Treaty, which created an omnipotent UN-appointed high representative, the international community assumed this role. And in May 2008, the EU assumed a portion of the UN mantle. Regardless whether a UN or EU representative, like the emperors before him, he holds final say and sway over essentially all matters of state in the country. The names and allegiances may have changed since 1914, but the same basic political, economic, and judicial impotence of the local polity remains.

While the Bosnian case is extreme, this same weakness can be seen throughout the Balkans, even in the fully independent states of the former Yugoslavia. In Serbia and Croatia, at the behest of The Hague, new criminal codes have been promulgated—also in line with foreign, Anglo-American common law principles—while in Macedonia the ICTY is also pushing reform of its judicial system.

Few would argue that the post-Yugoslav states could not benefit from some institutional reforms. The eruption of the civil war, let alone the fifty years of Communism, led to justice systems in need of repair. Yet, the reform conducted under the watchful eyes and direction of the ICTY has completely overtaken the states, especially on the issue of war crimes. The ICTY has had full authority over local judiciaries to allow cases to be heard, to stop such cases, and even to overturn verdicts and/or have cases removed entirely. The frustration that many Balkan residents feel over their lack of local control comes from the fact that Yugoslavia was not a retrograde, failed, or dysfunctional state. The country had a highly industrialized economy, a cosmopolitan citizenry who could travel freely in the West and East, and a functioning civil society and political system, including a judiciary.

The civil war evidently fractured these institutions, but they had not been destroyed, and more importantly, there were Yugoslavs in the new Balkan states who had worked and practiced in the antebellum system. The system was eminently salvageable had the international will to do so been present. Yet, in large part through the ICTY's actions, the former Yugoslav system—and indeed the experiences of those who worked in it—was declared moribund. Thus, it is perhaps unsurprising that

> a [2003] survey . . . revealed that Bosnian judges and prosecutors felt marginalized by the ICTY because of . . . criticisms of the Bosnian legal system made by the international legal community . . . [which,] Bosnia's legal community felt . . . was 'an attack on their professional identity.'[140]

The study's authors note that "[against] this backdrop, many . . . legal professionals felt increasingly powerless and devalued both as citizens and as professionals."[141] This is hardly fertile ground for the Yugoslavia tribunal to make a difference.

Again it is the common law/civil law clash that has defined the perceived colonial judicial project. With the exception of Sierra Leone, which has a British common law legal heritage, each of the target states for international justice has been a civil law state. And, yet, while the common law/civil law clash has not been resolved and has created many problems for the international tribunals, domestic courts have been asked to be receptive to ICTY cases and their investigatory materials despite the fact that they may have been obtained in a manner disallowed under local civil law. In short, common law practices have begun to usurp civil law domestic systems. One of the clearest outcomes of this schism was the passage of the "Alaskan" criminal code in Bosnia that was promulgated at the international community's urging.* New criminal codes have also been passed in Croatia and Serbia, also at the behest of The Hague. The Yugoslavia tribunal has thus helped push an Anglo-American justice system upon a region more comfortable with civil practices. As a result, many Balkan legal professionals complain that they have little understanding of either the ICTY system or of the new Anglo-American components of their own systems.[142] And there may be longstanding repercussions to this ignorance given that the absence of knowledge extends to the legal academy; there are few Balkan professors who are capable of teaching "their" new law.

Similar changes have been forced on Rwanda, with a primary sticking point the Rwandan government's desire to maintain the death penalty. As preparations to wind up its operations began to take hold, the ICTR decided to transfer some of its cases to Kigali. However, the ICTR insisted that prior to any transfer, Kigali had to repeal capital punishment. This was a bitter pill for Rwandans, especially in light of the fact that it was largely due to Rwanda's insistence on keeping the death penalty that led to the tribunal's decamping to Tanzania. Throughout the ICTR's operations the barring of the death penalty has been a frequent point of tension between Rwanda and Arusha. It often resulted in the death penalty for the lower-level perpetrators who were prosecuted in Rwanda, while their superiors in Arusha received less serious punishments.

---

*It was an Alaskan lawyer who had the primary hand in drafting the text that became the criminal code.

Other than influencing the development of target states' law via legislative "suggestions," international justice has shown two more direct aspects of legal hegemony, and even "imperialism." With the exception of the Special Court for Sierra Leone, since their foundings, both the ICTY and ICTR have limited the attempts of both the post-Yugoslav states and Rwanda to address war crimes on their own, especially if their methods were viewed counterproductive to the tribunals' goals. For instance, though the process of lustration—professional ostracism of those involved in a past regime's wrong-doing—proved largely sufficient in punishing former regime leaders during the transitions of most Eastern European states following the collapse of Communism,[143] any attempts to impose lustration in lieu of trials was quashed in the Balkans (by a combination of the ICTY and the High Representative). Further, the ICTY's refusal to try defendants in absentia, while perhaps positive from the perspective of protecting defense rights, is nonetheless out of accord with common practices in Europe, and especially in the former Yugoslavia.[144] Yet, not only does the ICTY refuse to permit such trials, but it does not view the trials in absentia that have taken place in the domestic systems of the various Balkan states as "real" proceedings.

Additionally, for almost the entire history of the Yugoslavia tribunal, ideas for a Balkan Truth and Reconciliation Commission have percolated both inside and outside the region.[145] Such a commission would formally give up the goal of "full" prosecution, trading amnesties with the vast majority of potential indictees in exchange for complete information from those responsible for crimes. Though many scholars and observers have come to believe that truth commissions may be superior to trials, at least in establishing an incontrovertible record of what actually happened,[146] the idea of such a Bosnian commission, especially the one long proposed by Bosnian parliamentarian Jakob Finci, remains a dream more than a decade after it was first proposed.

In sum, in ways big and small, the legal footprint of international justice has been as oppressive as residents in target regions commonly claim. This had made it difficult for the post-Yugoslav states, Rwanda, and Sierra Leone to truly develop postconflict legal cultures and systems of their own.

The concerns heard on the ground about international justice are not only loud and consistent, but often valid. Anger over seemingly selective prosecution is in many cases well founded; unease that politics plays too great a role in the process of international courts appears equally so; disquiet about aspects of unfairness and bias in the tribunals is in several regards also justifiable; and frustration about the colonial imposition that "international justice" has become is similarly defensible.

It is as yet unclear whether the new International Criminal Court will proceed down the same path as these earlier tribunals. But, early indications are that it may as well.

Chapter 7

THE INTERNATIONAL CRIMINAL COURT AND THE LIMITS OF INTERNATIONAL JUSTICE

The Number Ten tramline in The Hague starts at Scheveningen, a North Sea beach town just west of The Hague. Its pronunciation (*s'CHay-fuh-ninger*) so befuddles the average non-Dutch speaker that Dutch resistance forces in World War II used stating its name as a test to see if someone was a German spy. Departing the shibboleth, the tram rolls southeast, clacking past the Yugoslavia tribunal on its right, then the International Court of Justice, and the Permanent Court of Arbitration. After about twenty minutes, it comes to its final stop on Maanweg, just inside the city limits in the Binckhorst area, across the street from the International Criminal Court. The Number Ten "Courts Local" makes tangible The Hague's well-deserved reputation as the "capital of international law" and bolsters the intellectual, philosophical, and emotional links between the international courts in the Dutch capital.

We will examine here the ICC and international criminal justice in its most recent and arguably most favorable guise, and ask the question that was so neglected by the US government (and indeed by many other governments) when the ICC treaty was up for debate in 1998: Will it work? Several of the complaints heard about the international judicial institutions created since the early 1990s have some merit and represent real failings in the system; citizens from the Balkans, Rwanda, Sierra Leone, and elsewhere are in many ways right to question the "justice" provided to them by their tribunals. The question that logically follows and has become more critical with the commencement of the ICC is: How many of these concerns are a function of the growing pains associated with the rebirth of international criminal justice and how many are intrinsic to the international imposition of criminal justice?

THE ICC AS INTERNATIONAL CRIMINAL JUSTICE

The ICC is a permanent, international criminal court, marking a break from the ad hoc courts that have made up the collection of international criminal institutions until now. The Court's caseload, deemed "situations," emerges from one of three sources: a state party to the Court (a "member state") can request an investigation, the UN Security Council can refer situations to the prosecutor; or the prosecutor can begin an investigation on his or her own initiative. In the cases in which situations are referred or requested, the prosecutor is charged to begin investigation unless he determines that there is no "reasonable basis" to proceed. Management oversight of the Court, which includes the election of its eighteen judges, the prosecutor, and other senior posts, falls to the Assembly of States Parties, the body to which all member states belong.

Though ICC staff will be among the first to assert that their organization is only a part of the delivery of justice to postconflict zones, the ICC model is nonetheless a good proxy for the entirety of The Hague "system." After all, the Rome Treaty that authorized the creation of the ICC was the focus of the world's diplomatic and legal attention for much of the 1990s. And despite the presence of notable holdouts, as of the end of 2008, 108 states had ratified the treaty. A further forty had signed the treaty and were waiting for their parliaments to formally implement it.[1] As such, the treaty broadly represents the state of the world's thinking on the issues of international criminal justice and how the international system ought best respond to serious violations of humanitarian law.

At first glance, two characteristics are noticeable about the Court. First, the ICC looks very similar to the Yugoslavia and Rwanda tribunals. The structures are parallel—with a similar separation between the Office of the Prosecutor, "chambers" (the judges), and a "registry" (which performs many of the Court's administrative functions). Judges are similarly elected, though out of a pool comprised of all members of the Court, rather than from the UN at-large (as in the Yugoslav and Rwandan cases). Also, as the Court is permanent, judges and prosecutors will be permanent, and consequently like the ICTY and ICTR will similarly not hail from the same countries from where defendants and victims will come. Though there are differences and improvements in operation and law that differentiate the ICC from the older tribunals, it is clear that the ICC is a direct institutional, legal, and political progeny of the Yugoslav and Rwandan bodies.

The second issue is the irony, if not misfortune, in the timing of the ICC's founding. From the perspective of learning from history and other institutions dealing with mass crimes, the ICC was founded at a highly inopportune time. The Rome negotiations occurred in July 1998, when the Yugoslavia and Rwanda tribunals were still in relative infancy. Further, July 1998 was a full two years before the first "hybrid" court (in East Timor) came on line, and four years before the Special Court for Sierra Leone emerged. As such, the ICC, frozen by a hard-fought treaty, will be largely unable to implement many of the lessons derived from those more recent institutions. In 1998, the international community was still enamored of the "tribunal" model of "pure" international justice; it had yet to fully comprehend the difficulties of the system, and consequently it had yet to depart from that model as the most appropriate means for dispensing international justice. Since

1998, thinking and practice toward international justice has progressed—conventional wisdom has questioned the "distant" justice provided by foreign-based tribunals; it has seen the benefits of providing justice often in the country itself. Similarly, the requirements of imposing justice for mass crimes by reference to only international law and adjudicated by only international judges has been diluted, with all tribunals formed since 1998 including roles for local jurists and lawyers, paying heed to local laws in addition to international code. The result of these developments is that by the time the ICC opened in 2002, it risked being an anachronism at birth. "We had moved beyond 'The Hague System,'" a senior international lawyer in The Hague told me. The ICC represents a return—and potentially a regression—to the ancien régime.

The ICC's Movements Forward

Evidently, some of the easiest corrections that the ICC could have undertaken—and in some cases already has done—involved the complaints heard regarding inefficiencies and managerial missteps of the international tribunals. The ICC may exacerbate some inefficiencies, due partly to the fact that the new Court answers to an unruly Assembly of States Parties made up of each member of the Court with an equal voice, rather than the comparatively streamlined UN Security Council. The ICC, however, has taken care to directly address some of the major shortcomings of its forbearer courts, such as problems with meek outreach, poor public relations, and the sluggish speed of proceedings.

A key improvement concerns the strongly held belief that the novelty of the ICTY and ICTR led to unpredictability in courtroom procedure and unfair processes and decisions. One of the main contributions to such inconsistency, however—the uncertain fusion of civil and common law tradition in the Court—is set to continue. The ICC's first prosecutor, Luis Moreno Ocampo, is from Argentina, which is a civil law country; many on his staff and several judges hail from common law jurisdictions. But the ICC has addressed this concern explicitly and implicitly. Explicitly, the ICC's first chief judge (known as the Court's "president") is Philippe Kirsch, a Quebecois jurist who has professional experience in both the civil law practiced in his Francophone province and the common law practiced in Anglophone Canada. Moreover, the implicit, and in the long run more substantial manner in which the ICC is addressing this weakness is by taking advantage of developed practice. Over their histories, the Yugoslavia, Rwanda, and Sierra Leone courts have solidified their procedures and codes of practice have emerged (some written, some unwritten). This, along with the fact that three of the ICC's first cadre of eighteen judges have experience on the Yugoslavia or Rwanda tribunal (with one having spent time as the president of the Rwanda tribunal, and another as vice president of the Yugoslavia tribunal),[2] will greatly improve predictability for litigants and consistency in courtroom management, determination of guilt or innocence, and sentencing.

An additional area in which the ICC has at least theoretically internalized some of the criticisms is regarding its "complementarity" provisions. The Court, unlike the ICTY and ICTR, is not designed to supplant domestic jurisdiction. Its charge is to only prosecute when domestic courts have not. Though there are problems with the undefined nature of this provision, the doctrine behind it speaks directly to the concerns of legal "imperialism" that have so vexed many Balkans, Rwandans, and others since "their" courts were established. Yet, even so, there is a chasm of difference between waiting to *see* if domestic justice works, and actually *helping* domestic systems work. Prosecutor Ocampo has on many occasions conceded that his organization is not designed nor funded to aid in such capacity building.

The ICC also appears to have addressed two problems on the defense side: inequality in resources and skills. The ICC has adopted a broad set of rules regarding both the qualifications required for defense counsel as well as the resources provided for the defense. The ICC requires defense counsel to have at least ten years of experience, not just in law, but specifically in international or criminal law. The

Court has also developed an Office of Public Counsel—completely autonomous from the administrative arm of the Court—charged with protecting defendants' rights during investigation, a protection many thought overlooked in the earlier tribunals.

The ICC has also responded—or at least potentially responded—to the issue of unequal resources between the prosecution and defense. The Court covers "all costs reasonably necessary" for an "effective and efficient" defense, which includes salaries for counsel and staff, and even for investigation, translation, and travel. The Court also requires parity between the salaries of prosecution attorneys and those paid to defense lawyers.

There are two final areas of improvement, one not yet realized and the other already in existence. Regarding the former, one of the benefits of having a permanent, international criminal court, as opposed to the ephemeral, explicitly ad hoc variety, is that there will be a certain degree of coalescing and a limitation on the confusion that has often arisen from the existence of multiple international courts with unclear inter-relationships. This has been most notable in the interchanges between the Yugoslavia and Rwanda tribunals. It was never clear whether the decisions of one were binding on the other. Further, this was even more evident in the uncertain relationships between the Special Panels for East Timor and international precedent. The Special Panels were criticized for being run with limited reference to wider international legal developments, and especially those emanating from The Hague and Arusha.[3] But it was never clear whether the Special Panels, or any other international court were compelled to recognize precedent from other institutions. With a single, international court, such uncertainty will be reduced, as will the existence of turf wars between "competitor" international courts that have at times erupted. A particularly distasteful episode of such infighting actually occurred with the ICC, which was approached by the Special Court for Sierra Leone when the Freetown tribunal decided to move the Charles Taylor trial to The Hague. The Sierra Leone court wished to lease an unused courtroom from the ICC, and the ICC agreed but only at exploitative rates. After heated, lengthy negotiations—and the development of a considerable amount of bad blood—a compromise was finally reached.

A second area of improvement springs from the Rome Treaty's concern for women. For the first time an international court has been mandated to have a bench composed of a "fair representation of female and male judges."[4] This has resulted in the appointment of eight females to the bench, with a woman holding the first vice presidency.[5] In comparison, as of 2008, of the twenty-five total judges appointed to the ICTY bench, only four were female, and only two of the permanent judges were women.[6] On the ICTR, there were only two women on the bench, and only three in Sierra Leone.

The Problems That Remain Unsolved

While there are clear improvements that the ICC has instituted, other problems remain that have yet to be, and likely cannot be, rectified. Unfortunately, the makeup of the ICC's staff, and in particular the shared professional histories of many, may make it difficult for the new Court to forge a new path. In terms of staff experience, the linkages between the Yugoslavia tribunal especially and the ICC are greater than just a tramline. The Yugoslavia tribunal has become a font of wisdom, procedure, and legal process for the ICC, and in a sense for international justice writ large. With this flow of intellectual capital has come personnel, an increasing number of whom are departing the ad hoc UN tribunal, paying the €1.60 tram fare for the trip south and taking up permanent positions at the ICC. It makes a great deal of sense for the ICC to take advantage of such an easily accessible pool of expertise, and as mentioned there are benefits for predictability of relying on those with expertise in the process of international justice. However, doing so has also meant that the ICC may be saddled with the same difficulties encountered by the Yugoslavian, Rwandan, and other international courts—the new ICC employees may bring unhelpful assumptions and procedures with them.

It is understandable both why the ICC would want to hire personnel from the Yugoslavia and Rwanda tribunals, and why such employees would wish to leave their current employment. Ever since the announcement that the ad hoc courts will complete their trials by the end of 2008, and then close once appeals have been heard in 2010, morale has plummeted. Rolling hiring freezes instituted in response to financial shortfalls have meant that even many longstanding employees cannot be given long-term contracts. Choosing between the insecurity of repeated six month contracts—with the possibility of termination at the end of every period—and the stability of the long-term contracts at the ICC, the choice for many has been obvious.

There are several other problems that the new Court will have difficulty in fixing. One of the key concerns of many, and the background for several of the citizen-derived complaints in the target regions, is the perception that international justice is too foreign to understand the culture, sensitivities, and the critical histories that usually factor into the crimes over which the ICC will exercise its jurisdiction. In truth, though perceptions of the Yugoslavia or Rwanda tribunals as distant, ignorant forces remain (again, exacerbated by the essential absence of Balkan or Rwandan staff on the respective tribunals), one of the benefits of narrowly focused courts has been the build-up of institutional expertise and knowledge of the subject matter. At the Yugoslavia tribunal, for instance, this was aided by the creation of an in-house "history" department made up of academic experts on the region. Though a small and not an entirely diverse group—one of its former members told me that at several points in its history, its membership was comprised solely of graduates of Yale's Slavic Languages and Literature program—the benefits it has provided in aiding prosecutions and in helping the whole institution to understand the complex events on the ground have been significant. At the ICTR, a slow profusion of Rwandan experts, some even from Rwanda, has also begun to grace the tribunal's halls.

It seems a difficult task to ask a court theoretically concerned with crimes committed anywhere on the globe to have such a geographically, let alone nationally focused research arm. Yet such institutional expertise already seems imperative. Though the ICC's first four investigations involve a small part of Africa—Uganda, Sudan, the Democratic Republic of the Congo, and the Central African Republic—the cases are bewilderingly complex. To take the Democratic Republic of the Congo, one of the court's initial "situations," as an example, in order to effectively prosecute cases the ICC will have to become familiar with the "confusing set of actors" who have been accused of committing crimes. Some observers have doubted:

> whether the prosecutors . . . will be able to keep straight the [various groups involved in the conflict, which include] FAC, RCD-ML, RCD-N, UPC, APC, RCD-Goma, MLC, FNI, May-May and FRPI militias [let alone dozens of additional political parties, movements, and unnamed armed groups], and the various ways in which Kinshasa, Rwanda, and Uganda and their respective armies [have] supported or undermined them.[7]

Even if separate research departments could be created for each case, there would remain the problem that judges and prosecutorial staff would be static. No intimate local knowledge or experience would be present or truly capable of being developed in either the prosecutor's office or on the bench.

With an absence of longstanding, dedicated in-house expertise, the likelihood of errors in both prosecutorial strategy and even in judgments seems high. For instance, on the most basic level, the ICC has the task to only prosecute those "most responsible" for crimes. Though it may be possible for an outsider to examine an organizational chart of a military faction and discern who deserves punishment, the reality and perceptions on the ground as to who is "most responsible" is much more nuanced than those gained from afar. This is especially true for those unfamiliar with the particular environment in question. Thus, even the ICC's most basic mandate may be impossible to fulfill, following the ICTY, ICTR, and Sierra Leone courts down a path of prosecuting the "wrong" people, at least in the eyes of residents within the target states. The new Court is also prevented from pursuing those who many in a target region believe to be the most culpable and deserving of punishment (such as those who have committed mass financial indiscretions). Consequently, there is a likelihood of more situations like Milosevic's massive indictment—which many in the Balkans found unwieldy, counterproductive, and misdirected.

This situation is aggravated by the same "temporal" constraints that were imposed on the ICTY, ICTR, and Sierra Leone courts, which have angered so many in the Balkans, Rwanda, and West Africa. The ICC is empowered to investigate and prosecute only those crimes that occurred after its official inauguration in July 2002, and even then, only in specific areas. Yet the conflicts at issue—and certainly the roots of the conflicts—extend back decades. For instance, in one of the ICC's other initial cases, dealing with the rebel forces under the "Lord's Resistance Army" (LRA) in Uganda, the conflict that gave rise to the alleged crimes dates from 1986; the situation in the Democratic Republic of the Congo dates from at least 1990. Yet, the first decades of these conflicts—which were replete with mass violations—are off limits. Bringing only the current powerful, offending parties to judgment, and only looking at particular regions, without reference to prior abuses perpetrated by the group that may currently be victimized, is a recipe for establishing a perception of bias and perhaps immediately making whole sectors of society enemies of the process.

Continued Problems of State-Court Relations

The importance of the ICC maintaining good relationships with and enjoying the confidence of its member states represents an additional concern held over from the older international criminal courts. It is highly unlikely that the current international justice system can overcome this problem. The fundamentally unequal relationship that exists between the current tribunals and states similarly exists between the ICC and states in the international community. The impact this will have on the provision of evidence to the Court—both for the prosecution and defense—is significant. The ICC will almost certainly be hindered by the same problems of state cooperation in terms of evidence and investigation that have dogged the Yugoslavia and Rwanda tribunals. As one participant at the Rome conference put it, "[t]he diplomats . . . failed to establish a procedure for the production of evidence that will lead to . . . fair and effective trial[s]."[8]

Given the important, and largely uncontrolled, role that states will have in almost all facets of the ICC's work, the potential for improper political influence is high. The ICC and its founders are well aware of the potential for such influence and have attempted to structure the Court to insulate many of its components—and the prosecutor especially—from such pressure. The prosecutor's isolation, which has him answerable only to the full membership of the Court (the Assembly of States Parties), rather than just to the UN Security Council, accounts for much of the United States' reticence in joining the ICC.[9] The United States' privileged role in the Security Council—being one of only five permanent, veto-wielding members—would not be replicated in the ICC.

Despite this thoughtful design, it would nonetheless be naïve to believe that the prosecutor, or any other part of the Court, will be fully protected from political influence. The ICC's need for state cooperation and assistance in all aspects of its operations assures at least a modicum of political control over the institution. At a minimum, the prosecutor will be limited in his choice of targets for investigation. The likelihood of his investigating any major power, or even any close ally of a major power, is remote. In light of such geopolitical realities, it is not a surprise either that the first spate of cases were all referred to the prosecutor from the Security Council or member states (rather than emerging from the prosecutor's own initiative), nor that each of these first cases emerge from poor, weak states. They unfortunately all happen to be in Africa. Throughout Africa there has developed a concern that Africans are serving as the laboratory for the ICC's nascent justice—a not dissimilar feeling that has been expressed by many in the Balkans and Rwanda concerned about being guinea pigs in the earlier international judicial experiments. The focus on Africa has also led some to ask if the ICC is really just going to be the "International Criminal Court for Africa," rather than a true global body.[10]

It is not just evidentiary issues that require ICC fealty to state interests. It must be remembered that there is no standing ICC police force to go along with the standing Court. It needs states to accomplish any of its coercive functions, from investigation, to arrest and detention, to final sentencing. Without member-state support, the Court cannot do its job. Its current investigation in the Ituri region of the Democratic Republic of the Congo is an important example.[11] The region is inordinately volatile. Thus, when the ICC issued indictments against various leaders, it was forced to surreptitiously rely on UN peacekeepers operating in the region to detain suspects. Given the ICC sensitivity of some members of the Security Council—primarily, though not only, the United States—any publicized use of UN-authorized peacekeepers to do the ICC's work would be politically problematic for both the Security Council and the Court.

The Court's impotence relates directly to the question of not just which states it will be able to investigate but also who in the end it will be able to actually prosecute. Again, selectivity will likely rule the day. The Ugandan case is worrisome in this regard. Yoweri Museveni, the pro-Western president of Uganda, invited the ICC into his country for the limited purpose of prosecuting members of the Lord's Resistance Army rebel group. To its credit, the ICC accepted the invitation but made it clear that it would be investigating *all* violators of international law. However, it is curious that it has yet only trained its sights on the rebels. Many have asked why the ICC has not focused on Museveni himself. After all, according to the UN, Museveni's misdeeds are very similar to those for which Charles Taylor is currently being prosecuted by the Special Court for Sierra Leone.

In December 2005, the International Court of Justice, the UN's primary judicial organ, ruled on a matter between the Democratic Republic of Congo and Uganda. The DRC had brought the case to protest Uganda's occupation of parts of its territory and its treatment of Congolese civilians in the process. The ICJ's ruling cast Museveni as a Charles Taylor of East Africa, sending his forces on foreign escapades in order to plunder mineral wealth, extending logistical, military, and other support to rebel groups in a neighboring state.[12] Moreover, the ICJ continued,

> by the conduct of [his] armed forces, which committed acts of killing, torture and other forms of inhumane treatment of the Congolese civilian population, destroyed villages and civilian buildings. . . . trained child soldiers, [and] incited ethnic conflict, [Museveni] violated . . . obligations under international human rights law and international humanitarian law.[13]

Despite his misdeeds, one can only surmise that Museveni has escaped legal scrutiny because he invited the ICC to Uganda to investigate the LRA. If the ICC were to turn its attention to him, he would likely insist that it depart. This also raises the difficult question whether Museveni is using the ICC to do his dirty work and help him get rid of his LRA headache. After all, the Ugandan courts have not been emaciated by the violence; LRA actions are confined to a relatively small swath of northern territory. Though the Ugandan court system has less than robust judicial independence, it nonetheless ranks on most global surveys somewhere near the middle. And, more importantly, the history of political interference in Ugandan justice suggests that only particular kinds of cases—usually those questioning the validity of the government's leadership—invite political attention. It seems evident that the domestic courts, either as they stand now or via a proposed Special High Court to address war crimes, could handle any trials that arise.[14] With this in mind, some have made the justifiable claim that Museveni has been using the ICC opportunistically, and for political ends—his invitation to the Court was based on his desire to outsource difficult domestic political issues by casting them as international judicial matters. In short, the Court "has taken over judicial responsibilities that Uganda could and should have fulfilled itself, but wished to hand off out of political self-interest."[15]

The "complementarity" provision in the ICC charter provides the prosecutor some cover of legitimacy in his decision not to pursue certain states and certain issues and individuals within some states. The provision holds that the ICC will only engage in prosecution of matters in which member states are unable or refuse to mount an effective prosecution of those charged with the crimes for which the ICC has jurisdiction.[16] What counts as a state "refusing" to prosecute, and what makes a prosecution "ineffective," remains undefined. For instance, in the Uganda case the "inability" that the ICC has found appears to refer solely to a lack of desire, which in itself has led some observers to question whether the ICC in pursuing the Uganda case is violating the spirit, if not the letter, of its own statute.[17]

Even once a trial begins, the ICC will face the same difficulties regarding reliance on "friendly" states—both those involved in the conflict in question and third parties—to provide evidence to build cases. The same restrictions emanating from classified information—and the likely resulting unfairness to defendants created by unequal access to exculpatory and other information—will almost certainly continue. Finally, upon conviction, the ICC will again face the same needs with respect to member states housing prisoners. Thus it too runs the risk of actual or perceived unequal sentences depending upon where prisoners are located.

Continued Structural Problems with Defense Counsel, Bench, and Investment

While the ICC has recognized some of the shortcomings associated with the defense counsel function in the prior courts and has made moves to address it, the ICC will be unable to ameliorate some of the more fundamental concerns. The ICC efforts, however, are praiseworthy. These include regular "defense seminars," consultations with experts on issues related to defense (such as rights and presumptions), and the early establishment of a list of qualified defense counsel who can be brought into the tribunal when needed.

Yet, the structure of the Court continues to fundamentally exclude the defense from the institution. Though it is not certain given that the ICC is moving in 2014 to permanent, purpose-built facilities elsewhere in The Hague (at the former Alexander Barracks near Scheveningen), it seems likely that the Court will mimic its ad hoc ancestors and keep the defense physically outside the Court, and perhaps less cared for than the Court's other components.

Further, one set of parties, not even a formal part of the Court, already seems set to receive greater respect from the ICC than the defense—the victims. Even before the ICC, David Scheffer—the US ambassador-at-large for war crimes during the Clinton administration—admitted that to practice postconflict justice in today's world is "to practice victims' justice."[18] Rupert Skilbeck—the former director of the defense bar in Bosnia's new domestic war crimes court and now working on defense issues at the Khmer Rouge tribunal—told me that he believes that international justice has shifted the balance of concern from fair trials to victim assistance. The ICC appears poised to continue the trend, and has been lauded for the establishment of a Victims Trust Fund to aid those most harmed by the crimes tried by the Court.[19] While an important addition to international criminal justice—especially as tangible support for victims has often been lacking—the trust fund is a further example of the balance in international justice toward victims, as opposed to fair trials and defense rights. Compensating victims is important, but it is uncertain whether the Court itself should be playing this role. In Chile, for instance, similar compensation has been offered to victims of the military junta that ruled that country from 1973–1990, but the money is being offered outside the justice system that is trying the regime's leaders.[20] Having the ICC involved in the process of monetary distribution gives an odd flavor to justice by implicitly casting the Court's lot on the side of victims and victims' rights rather than on the side of justice and fair proceedings.

Unfortunately, an additional problem with the defense, present at the current tribunals, looks to be exacerbated by the permanence of the ICC. The unequal access that prosecutors have to the bench—due in large part to the small size and intimacy of relations in The Hague—will probably continue with the ICC. Moreover, as the ICC is a "permanent" institution, the permanence of convivial relations will likely be even stronger between prosecutors and judges, and thus more able to survive inevitable turnover of personnel.

Difficulties with the ICC judges are twofold. First, due to the selection process of judges, which is regionally determined, and the "plumness" of positions on the Court for both the individual judge and his or her appointing country, the process of nomination and election of judges has already become highly politicized. It involves as much diplomatic horse-trading and pork barreling as concern for the caliber of the nominated individuals. Though such stories in the ICC remain anecdotal, the politics of ICTY judicial selection have become famously acidic. The 2001 elections of ICTY judges, for instance, were noted for their extreme politicization marked by the "amount of money spent on campaigning, as well as [the fact that] political considerations were . . . much greater factors in the outcome of the elections than [were] the qualifications of the candidates."[21] Such politics has long been a disconcerting and unhelpful part of judicial selection in many international tribunals, and no evidence exists that the ICC could limit its impact on its bench. Unfortunately, the judicial politicization appears to be extending to other parts of the Court. For instance, in the fall of 2005 South Korean president Roh Moo-hyun spent considerable energies during a tour of the Americas soliciting support for a South Korean lawyer to fill a seat at the ICC. Several senior ICC officials have bemoaned the resulting insistent requests—some forcibly heeded—from officials in member states to appoint their chosen candidates to various posts.[22]

The ICC's structural problems regarding misinvestment and misplaced creation of physical and intellectual capital are exactly the same as those at the ICTY and ICTR. The ICC promises to be yet another significant financial and intellectual boon to The Hague and the Netherlands. This explains why there was such fierce competition among states to house the new Court.[23] Already, before the commencement of any trials, or even complete staffing, the 2008 budget of the Court is more than $150 million, an investment made in a country that hardly needs it.[24] The average GDP per capita of the four states where the ICC is currently undertaking investigations is barely one-thirtieth of the Netherlands.'[25]

Some argue that if the world is to establish a permanent international court, it is important to have it in a country with at least a modicum of wealth, stability, and infrastructure in order to assure its operation. Yet, in light of the Special Court for Sierra Leone in Freetown, this is unpersuasive. Moreover, the ICTR was initially placed in Rwanda itself,[26] before being moved to Tanzania, a country with barely $700 per capita income.[27] This combination of factors suggests that the threshold requirements to be an appropriate home for an international court are fairly modest.

Some contend that security concerns dictate that such a Court must be in a stable region, away from the areas of conflict. Yet, again, that the ICTR was set to be in Kigali questions this logic. Further, consistent statements from ICC officials that the Court will try to hold at least some hearings in the Democratic Republic of the Congo similarly makes one question how much security is really at risk and whether or not any risk that does exist could be appropriately managed.

As in the Yugoslavia and Rwanda cases, one can only wonder what improvements and reforms toward justice and sustainable peace could take place in the target countries if some of the ICC budget were diverted to the countries under investigation. But, a much more devastating aspect of the ICC investment is that it will again likely concentrate the development of human capital in the wrong people. The ICC's lawyers and staff—primarily from the developed world—will gain great expertise in humanitarian law and dealing with postconflict proceedings. But those who really need such expertise reside in the very countries targeted by the Court, citizens of which by design are largely excluded from gaining any of this vital experience.

MACRO-LIMITATIONS OF THE HAGUE PROCESS

In addition to structural issues and those implicating fairness and acceptance by the countries receiving international justice, there are two further disquieting limitations in regard to The Hague process: it may lead to continued conflict and it could crowd out local justice and other initiatives critical to ensuring that states do not slide back into violence. Unfortunately, these concerns appear to have been more reinforced by the ICC than they were by its predecessor courts.

The first limit concerns the determination that a given problem is a "Problem from Hell." As we have already noted, such a determination has led to dual errors of too little involvement of the international community in stopping conflict and an overinvolvement of the international community in postconflict justice. In today's world, it seems that the formal labeling of a conflict as "hellish" is no longer needed. Rather, that the ICC has taken up a conflict to investigate, especially if the situation was officially referred to the ICC by the UN Security Council, is a clear enough message to ensure no action regarding the ongoing crimes and "overaction" in legally addressing the violence after the conflict is over.

Such has been the sad case of the Darfur tragedy. After much diplomatic debate and political hand wringing, in March 2005, the Security Council officially referred the Darfur situation to the ICC to begin investigations.[28] This move seems to have been a salve for the international community. Even though many states, including permanent members of the Security Council have followed the United States' lead and declared the situation one of "genocide,"[29] very little additional action has been taken by the UN or independent states on Darfur. Not only has the international community done little, but also it failed for over a year to fund the modest efforts that were being undertaken. The African Union put together a small, "gravely insufficient" battalion of troops to guard refugee camps in Darfur, where so many killings were taking place.[30] However, with no money forthcoming to aid in their mission, and amid threats of the African Union disbanding the battalion because of insufficient funds, private groups in the US and elsewhere began the unprecedented task of soliciting *private* donations to pay for the soldiers' deployment—pejoratively deemed the "Adopt-a-Peacekeeper" program.[31] The amount of money required was paltry, and the risk for the states outside of Africa in the venture, essentially none. Yet, nothing happened and even if recent moves have been more promising, the crimes continue. The most plausible conclusion one can draw from this unfortunate state of affairs is that the inaction on the part of the international community is because states are satisfied that their referral of the situation to the ICC, and potential future prosecution of those responsible, is action enough. International justice, or even the potential for such justice, is once more serving as a replacement for the more difficult, costly, and dangerous task of actually trying to stop further crimes. In this case, however, international inaction is even more troubling, given that the added risk is mitigated by the fact that the international community could outsource much of the hard work and risk to willing participants in the African Union.

The second macroproblem with international criminal justice is the second half of the "Problem from Hell" conundrum. Just as international justice allows too little to be done during a conflict, it compels too much to be done after. International prosecutions crowd out local law and initiatives—judicial and otherwise—seeking solutions of its own. Regarding law, static, international rules of procedure and law often do not mesh with diverse situations in dissimilar countries. In a different context, this led Ken Flemming, a senior Rwanda tribunal attorney, to ask, "How can we assess truth in [states as diverse as] Colombia or Afghanistan with but one rule of evidence? We simply can't."[32]

Concerning local initiatives, various prosecutors have proved hostile enough to a Balkan Truth and Reconciliation Commission to quash any progress. They have similarly ignored the success of Eastern European lustration and South America's many models of postjunta justice. In East Timor, observers have likewise lamented that international solutions allowed no space for true, local reconciliation, leaving the actual sources of the conflict that led to the crimes unresolved.[33]

In its current African work, ICC prosecution has the real potential of not just limiting the official peace efforts but also of derailing promising traditional means of reconciliation. In parts of Uganda, where anthropologists have long remarked on the unparalleled capacity of citizens to forgive, ceremonies of contrition are perfect examples of "justice" in local eyes that may be thwarted by an insistence on more "universal" conceptions of redress. *New York Times* reporter Marc Lacey describes one such ceremony, odd to Western eyes, and potentially "insufficient" to count as an "effective" prosecution under the ICC's Rome Treaty:

> Twenty-eight young men and women who had recently defected from the [LRA] rebels lined up according to rank on a hilltop. . . . They had killed and maimed together. They had raped and pillaged. One after the other, they stuck their bare right feet in a freshly cracked egg. . . . The egg symbolizes innocent life, according to local custom, and by dabbing themselves in it the killers are restoring themselves to the way they used to be. Next, the former fighters brushed against the branch of a pobo tree, which symbolically cleansed them. By stepping over a pole, they were welcomed back into the community.[34]

A similar set of non-Western issues arose in East Timor where international justice took on the appearance of Western justice cloaked in international robes. There, local beliefs held that "justice" required a restoration of the "socio-cosmic order" that existed before the crimes occurred, rather than a definitive Western judicial outcome. In East Timor, such restoration is often accomplished via paying compensation, rather than incarceration—the preferred Western-style punishment that the Special Panels for East Timor meted out.[35]

Even if bizarre by the standards of "more exacting" Hague justice, it is hard to argue with the impact of traditional processes. Moreover, such fluid "justice" makes a good deal of sense in many conflicts, including the former Yugoslavia and those currently waged in the four states under ICC investigation. In such conflicts, as in many modern conflagrations, the line between victim and killer can be blurred. The criminal trials that make up the core of The Hague process seek definitive justice rather than address the ambiguous realities of modern states mired in and emerging from civil conflict. In many postconflict situations

> there is no wholly defeated side [nor wholly victimized side]. In such cases, partially vanquished factions often see trials and other retrospective penalties as unjust retribution rather than the reestablishment of law. [If] effective post–civil war transitions . . . make national reconciliation a priority [—the stated goal in all cases— such a task is self-defeating] . . . if certain groups feel maligned by the process itself.[36]

It is unclear if and how local/traditional notions of justice, forgiveness, and reconciliation can comport with the rigors of The Hague process. Thus far, despite Prosecutor Ocampo's public assurances that he will include concerns for such traditional processes, it seems that the modern and the traditional might be irreconcilable.

Peace v. Justice

Unfortunately, ICC operations toward "justice" may also prove irreconcilable with "peace." The debate between peace and justice is a hackneyed discussion in the international criminal justice world, with many supporters of international justice claiming that it is a red herring. They posit that there are few cases in which the trade-off actually has worked (i.e., cases in which justice has been explicitly delayed or rejected and peace has been secured).

While this may be true, there is a critical difference between the ICC and the Nuremberg model of the past. In all cases in which the ICC is investigating and has issued indictments, the conflict out of which alleged crimes have emerged is continuing. At Nuremberg, the Allies had fully placated and occupied Germany; there was little chance of a resumption of violence regardless of the outcome. Similarly, even if tensions remain simmering in Rwanda, at the Rwanda tribunal, the genocide had ended by the time the tribunal opened its doors, and in Sierra Leone, a peace accord seemed to be holding as its Special Court began its operations. However, the ICC's work has proceeded as crimes have continued, and the ICC has become an unwilling, and perhaps unwitting, actor in the conflicts under its examination.

The Uganda situation is an unfortunate case in point. The Ugandan government invited the ICC to investigate LRA abuses, a process that coincidentally started with the continuation of protracted peace negotiations between Kampala and the rebels. In 2005, negotiations were making slow progress in bringing the LRA off the battlefield. Yet, during the discussions, the ICC announced indictments of the LRA leadership. Lead negotiators were stunned by the ICC's decision, and threatened to disband the peace process. Tribal and religious leaders throughout Uganda launched campaigns against the ICC's intervention, "furiously lobbying" the Court to back off.[37]

This reaction should not have been surprising given the Yugoslavia tribunal's experiences—the only modern court established while its conflict was ongoing. The tribunal's indictment of Milosevic in 1999, issued in the midst of negotiations toward peace between Serbia and NATO, similarly "stunned" Serbia and blighted hopes for a quick solution to the impasse.[38]

Interestingly, in Yugoslavia, the debate between peace and justice has often seen unexpected proponents on the side of peace *over* justice. In October 1999, the UN Human Rights *rapporteur* for Yugoslavia, former Czech dissident Jiri Dienstbier, forcefully demanded the lifting of Milosevic's indictment. "We have to ask ourselves whether from a moral point of view the fate of a single dictator is more important than the fate of millions of people in the Balkans," he asked.[39] After the Dayton Treaty had established some measure of stability, former Swedish prime minister Carl Bildt, then the international community's chief representative in Bosnia, moved that all prisoners, even suspected war criminals, be released.[40] This demand followed that of Philippe Morillon, the French general commanding NATO forces in the Balkans who claimed that a general amnesty for accused war criminals was the "only way to calm the [rampant] anguish and mistrust" in the region.[41]

The entire NATO operation, ever since its first deployment in the early 1990s to secure peace in the former Yugoslavia, has often looked askance at the work of international justice. It has been concerned that a focus on justice would be counterproductive to its peacekeeping mission; the alliance went so far as refusing to detain several ICTY indictees, and on several occasions even cooperated with indictees. Far from arresting him, NATO found Ratko Mladic, the military leader of the Bosnian Serbs and the driving force behind the Srebrenica massacre, "extremely useful in keeping things quiet as the peacekeeping force went about its work."[42]

In this vein, an August 2007 editorial detailing a strategy to "solve" Darfur jointly authored by French president Nicolas Sarkozy and British prime minister Gordon Brown struck many, including Justice Goldstone (the first prosecutor at the ICTY and ICTR) and others, as odd. The nine-hundred-word essay, which was titled "We are Pushing and Pushing to Save Darfuris," concluded with the two leaders stating that it "is the combination of a ceasefire, a peacekeeping force, economic reconstruction, and the threat of sanctions that can bring a . . . solution to the region." There was no mention of the ICC investigation, let alone of bringing any of the indictees to justice.[43]

Limited support for international trials was also seen in the Special Panels for East Timor, and also expressed from a seemingly unlikely source. As the Special Panels proceeded, Nobel Peace Prize winner and second president of the country, Jose Ramos Horta, made it clear that political considerations must be taken into account: "The problems of a grindingly poor country can be more pressing than justice for old wounds."[44]

Moreover, in 2003, as a peace agreement was nearing completion regarding the DRC, it was the local community that asked for international trials, and it was members of the international community who questioned its wisdom. In September 2003, DRC president Laurent Kabila asked the UN for a "special criminal tribunal" to prosecute crimes that had occurred through the past decade of violence. However, the international community ignored the plea and some derided the idea. Belgian foreign minister Louis Michel—an otherwise strong advocate for international justice and, at the time, foreign minister of one of the first states to ratify the ICC treaty—admitted that the proposal was a "nice idea." However, he asked: "What is most urgent? To build a state, to give a future to the population, or to hunt down criminals? One cannot always do both. If [trials] run the risk of causing the [peace] process . . . to implode, I say 'no.'"[45]

Even the Ugandan government itself—which had initially invited the ICC's investigation—has had second thoughts, with President Museveni announcing his intentions of "convincing the ICC to drop the indictment if the LRA rebels surrender."[46] Unfortunately, the ICC indictments may have played a role in the continuation of LRA violence; ICC indictees have explicitly said that they will not put down their weapons while indictments are outstanding.

Despite this, supporters of the ICC make much of a December 2007 survey of Ugandans conducted by the Human Rights Center at the University of California, Berkeley. The survey asked locals about their views concerning justice for the LRA. The surveyors found that two-thirds of the respondents said that "justice must be done" for those who committed crimes. Though this has been widely trumpeted by various NGOs and supporters of the ICC,[47] the details of the survey actually suggest that respondents agree with Museveni's (and many other world leaders') flexibility toward justice, especially if peace is at stake. Eighty-six percent of respondents said they would accept amnesties if it were the only means of achieving peace. Moreover, when asked what "justice" means, ICC supporters point to the fact that nearly one-third of the respondents indicated that prosecution by an international court was the best option. A similar number pointed to local courts, and the final third to traditional reconciliation measures. Thus, though two-thirds may claim that "justice must be done," the majority of respondents want that "justice" to happen at home, not in The Hague.[48]

More recently, in June 2008, Prosecutor Ocampo voiced his intention to indict Sudanese president Omar al-Bashir on charges of genocide in relation to the Darfur violence. The activist community applauded the move, but may observers and many of those affected on the ground expressed fear at the impact of such a provocative move in the middle of a war zone. Andrew Natsios, the former administrator of the US Agency for International Development and Presidential Envoy to Sudan, put the question plainly:

> [W] hat are the peaceful options for a way out of the crisis facing the country and what measures are likely to move the country closer to that way out rather than further away? An indictment of Bashir will make it much more difficult for any country or international organization to help negotiate a political settlement with the Sudanese government. Some forms of pressure may force the Sudanese government to negotiate a political settlement, some will only make their leaders more intransigent: an indictment is clearly in the latter category.[49]

The African Union, the former president of frontline NGO *Médecins sans Frontières* (Doctors Without Borders),[50] and others with experience on the ground and in the region concur with Natsios's concerns. Time will tell if their fears are justified.

In the Darfur situation, the UN Security Council could step in; in a concession to the United States (and other permanent Security Council members), the ICC statute allows the Security Council to require the ICC to defer investigations in any case for a renewable period of twelve months, if it finds the investigation a threat to peace and security.[51] This, however, would require passage of a Security Council resolution, which is open to the same political pressures, and potential vetoes, as any such resolution.

For his part, ICC prosecutor Ocampo has claimed that "if a solution to ending the violence was found, and continuing the investigation did not serve the interests of justice, then the ICC would stop the probe."[52] Despite the allowance within the ICC treaty for the prosecutor to withdraw a matter in the "interests of justice," it not clear what this means or how the ICC's supporters and the ICC's judges would view such a withdrawal. It is uncertain how the prosecutor would withdraw given the political, diplomatic, bureaucratic, and legal confines and pressures of the ICC treaty and the ICC institution. Museveni's stated desire to ask the ICC to remove its indictments has angered many who have suggested that the ICC is not a tool that can be employed and removed at the will of member states. Indeed, the ICC in this regard is bulky (and purposefully so) and not nearly as forgiving or flexible as domestic systems often are.

"Solving" Future Bosnias

> There will be other Bosnias in our lives, different in every detail but similar in one overriding manner: they will originate in distant and ill-understood places, explode with little warning, and present the rest of the world with difficult choices—choices between risky involvement and potentially costly neglect.[53]
>
> —Richard Holbrooke, lead US negotiator,
> Dayton Peace Conference.

With both the intractable problems of providing a locally accepted, uniform, international criminal justice, and the confused views of the international community on internationally provided justice in mind, there are serious limitations to The Hague process, whether it be in the Yugoslavia tribunal of 1993 or the International Criminal Court of 2008. It is noteworthy that the world community both promotes internationalized justice via the ICC and yet doubts whether it works, as shown by its move away from pure international justice in its "hybrid" courts and the less-than-universal support given to "justice" when it conflicts with "peace." The shortcomings of The Hague process have not simply been faults of bad management or the teething of a criminal justice system awakened after fifty years, but rather limitations that are inherent in international criminal justice. The ICC was founded with the best of intentions, and the Rome Treaty is as important a convention on human rights as any; however when we examine how the treaty works and likely will work, we can only agree with the aphorism of a long-lost critic: "The road to Hell is paved with good conventions." For those who believe that "justice" and prosecutions of some sort must be done in the wake of serious crimes, a different route must be found. Fortunately, there is another place to look for solutions, a place long thought incapable of producing justice after conflict—the devastated socieites themselves.

Chapter 8

THEY SAY IT CAN'T BE DONE

Ken Roth is a slight, bespectacled New Yorker who still talks like a federal prosecutor, a job he has not held for two decades. He is the executive director of Human Rights Watch, one of the primary supporters of international criminal justice and the ICC. Yet, even he agrees that having domestic trials is better than international trials— "That's common sense," he argues. But, he claims that "we can't possibly" have trials in the countries directly involved in perpetrating or being victimized by war crimes or other mass violations. He asserts that entrusting such trials to those states is a recipe for unfair prosecutions for "former" belligerents and impunity for allies.[1] To borrow from Carl von Clausewitz, much as war is a continuation of politics by other means, postconflict domestic "justice" is simply a continuation of war by other means.

If the past is prelude, Roth's statement has merit. From the murderous "justice" Henry V provided the vanquished French at Agincourt in 1415, to the troubling "self-justice" provided by the Germans and Turks after World War I at Constantinople and Leipzig, to the Soviet show-trials of Nazis in post–World War II Eastern Europe, to the "collaborators'" prosecutions in Bangladesh after its cruel war of 1970–71— in each of these cases and countless more throughout history, neither those states implicated in perpetrating war crimes nor those states that have endured the worst of such crimes seem to have held just trials.

Recent cases appear to reinforce the trend. Immediately following the cessation of hostilities in the Yugoslav civil war in 1995, Croatia began a series of war crimes trials, almost always against Serbs. The cases had conviction rates of over 90 percent and often ended with absurd results: in proceedings against Serb Svetozar Karan, the court found him not only guilty of war crimes, but also of being *personally* responsible for the "500-year history of Serb crimes against Croatia."[2] Meanwhile, despite evidence of Croat misdeeds, Zagreb seemed to refuse to contemplate large-scale trials against Croats in the years immediately after peace. The "typical" post-atrocity dance was at work: Croats would escape and Serbs and others would face the full brunt of "justice."

Yet, all was not as it appeared.

Indeed, Croat Miro Bajramovic might disagree with just how uniform his country was on this score. As a former Croat paramilitary, he was the subject of a September 1997 interview published in the *Feral Tribune*,* a major Croatian publication. Bajramovic provided chilling detail about his wartime actions, stating that he was "directly responsible for the deaths of 86 people . . . personally [killing] 72 people, including 9 women."[3] The Croatian public was horrified, and so too were government leaders. Within *hours* of the interview's publication, a state prosecutor asked for an investigation into Bajramovic's claims and within a few days he was detained. Bajramovic was tried and convicted, and then tried again twice when the Croatian Supreme Court found irregularities in the verdict.[4] At the same time as the Bajramovic affair erupted, Croatia was also working to prosecute former enemies. In far eastern Croatia, five Serbs were put on trial for war crimes perpetrated against Croats, and were convicted under questionable circumstances. Rather than letting the tainted "justice" masquerade for the real thing, the Croatian Supreme court again stepped in and refused to let the verdicts stand; the Court overturned the decision due to unfair process.[5]

---

*This weekly newspaper was originally founded as a satirical magazine; hence its name, which is a play on the "*Herald*" Tribune. However, once the Yugoslav war began, the magazine became a serious, if at times sensationalist, newspaper.

Though these cases were far from perfect, they give a clear indication that at least in postwar Croatia impunity for allies and overprosecution of former belligerents, was not black and white.

Supporters of Roth's thesis may dismiss such countercases as anecdotal, if not apocryphal. Yet while one case may be branded fortuitous, and perhaps two cases coincidental, the argument breaks down once one looks at the broader scope of history and sees hundreds, if not thousands of such cases. A consistent trend can be seen in even the most unlikely of circumstances where real trials have been successfully held—real trials for "us" and for "them." Such fair trials are more than random islands of justice in a sea of inequity.

This does not mean that such cases have not been surprising or even unlikely. In 1420, Henry V—the same monarch who so mercilessly slaughtered the vanquished five years earlier at Agincourt—gave a real hearing to Seigneur de Barbasan. Barbasan appeared before Henry accused of brutally murdering John the Fearless, a putative ally of the king's. Henry gave Barbasan a hearing (instead of simply returning the favor), and sentenced him to death. But Henry actually allowed Barbasan to appeal the ruling and when an international panel of experts on the laws of chivalry overruled the king's verdict, Henry incredibly complied and released Barbasan.[6]

In 1770, an equally surprising case of "fair" trial came to pass in colonial Massachusetts after nine British soldiers were tried for murder. This followed the "Boston Massacre" in which Red Coats killed five unarmed Americans. Despite the sour relations between Britain and her American colonies, along with the public thirst for revenge, the nine British soldiers received due process. And this was before a jury of colonialists embittered by the Stamp Act, the Townshend duties, and Quartering Acts—the combination of which would help propel the Americans to war five years later against the British. The colonialists moved the trial outside of Boston, in order to assure a more dispassionate courtroom, and one of the colony's leading attorneys—John Adams—represented the defense. The British captain was acquitted based on lack of evidence, six others were similarly found not guilty, and only two, both of whom had been proven to have actually fired their weapons, were convicted.[7]

In the 1846–1848 Mexican American War, American general Winfield Scott issued his General Orders 20 and 267, which created "military commissions" to try "any inhabitant of Mexico, sojourner or traveler" who committed ... offenses against US soldiers, and "any individual of the [US] forces, retainer or follower" who committed such crimes against an inhabitant of Mexico or another "individual of the forces."[8] Though there is conflicting evidence whether more Mexicans or Americans were brought before such trials,[9] Mexican defendants were acquitted more readily than Americans.[10]

In the US Civil War (1862–1865), "fair" trials for allies and enemies became regularized (even if not commonplace) thanks to the Lieber Code, the first (and most enduring) modern code of battlefield conduct. The code was used as a basis for the postwar trial of Henry Wirz, the warden of the particularly infamous Confederate prison at Andersonville; though the conviction was undoubtedly correct, it nonetheless stunk of victors' justice and judicial retribution. However, in other trials, the Lieber Code was the basis for thousands of court-martials by the Union Army against Union soldiers.[11] Additionally, there were fair trials against the enemy. For instance, Confederate major John McGee was tried at Raleigh, North Carolina, in 1866, accused of causing the deaths of several Union POWs; despite the flush of the Union's recent victory and the clamor for retribution, McGee was acquitted after a protracted trial.[12]

By the end of the nineteenth century, the legalization of wartime behavior had even reached Asia and Latin America. During the 1894–95 Sino-Japanese War, although the Japanese doubted whether the Chinese would respect modern conventions and customs of international law (in regards to enforceable, legal conduct on the battlefield), they nevertheless decided to abide by them. Tokyo issued regulations in conformity with international law at the beginning of both the Sino-Japanese war (1894)[13] and Russo-Japanese war (1904),[14] and attached "distinguished Japanese ... scholars" of international law to each of their armies in the field to ensure compliance.[15] In the 1894 conflict, Japanese admiral Togo Heihachiro was recognized for his mastery of international law: a British court found that he had been in total conformity with the law when he had ordered the sinking of a British vessel—it had been working for the Chinese navy.[16] The Chileans provide another unlikely case. Prior to the 1879 beginning of its War of the Pacific against Peru and Bolivia, Chile issued regulations similar in form and meaning to the Lieber Code. Chile even bound itself to the Declaration of London, requiring its forces to follow the strict dictates of maritime military law, though it was unlikely that it had to. Moreover, given the nature of the War of the Pacific, doing so was certainly not in its interest.[17]

The proliferation of such rules made the seemingly quixotic exchange between General Hugh Scott and Pancho Villa on the eve of the 1914 US Mexican Border Conflict meaningful: Scott sent Villa a copy of the recently formalized Hague Rules on the limits of wartime behavior. Villa, who was otherwise known for brutal and even random violence, responded in kind and proceeded to limit the style of his guerilla operations and even tried his own men if they killed wantonly.[18]

World War I saw all sides enter the conflict armed with the law as well as weapons. Alongside every attack and counterattack, all sides lodged legal charges. Though the troubling trials in Leipzig and Constantinople after the war rightly garnered attention, there were other fair trials that occurred during the war. For example, at the height of the conflict, the British lodged complaints against a noncommissioned German officer who served as a guard for Allied POWs. He was accused of consistently mistreating POWs; the Germans responded—they removed him from his command, court-martialed him, and sentenced him.[19]

World War II would provide among the most gruesome cases of crimes and absent punishment. However, it would also provide some astonishing instances of not only a commitment to law, but to real, even merciful justice. Such a seemingly inexplicable commitment can be seen in the government of Czechoslovakia. In exile since the

German invasion of the Sudetenland in September 1938, the homeless administration of President Edvard Beneš was based in Paris, then in London. Despite their itinerancy and the fact that they likely had more pressing concerns, the Czechs nonetheless found it in their interest to operate a sophisticated military justice system for the Czech army; this is all the more remarkable because although the exiled government was made up of many of Prague's most senior and experienced politicians, "not a single active, regular officer of military justice had escaped" to London.[20] Permanent military courts were nonetheless established in London, in the USSR, and on the front, once the Allies began closing in on Berlin. Significant and understandable logistical difficulties emerged in running a military justice system while in exile. This included the fact that the appeals for all court-martial were to the Superior Military Field Court, which sat only in London. Nonetheless, the Beneš administration remained committed throughout the war to fielding a "legal" military that held Czech soldiers to account for violations committed against the enemy. Further, when the Beneš government returned to Prague after VE Day, they held trials of collaborators, and others. Here too, rather than following the predictable script of victors' justice, law appeared to triumph despite the indignities of the occupation. Czech judges showed professionalism and even compassion, and handed down several relatively light sentences to these former enemies if cases against them were weak. The seemingly lax nature of some of these sentences led to political and public reproach.[21]

Even more surprising than the Czech commitment to law was that exhibited by the Nazis. That this is peculiar is self-evident; Hitler, after all, was the man who roused his soldiers prior to the invasion of Poland by purportedly ordering his shock troops "to send to death mercilessly and without compassion, men, women, and children."[22] Yet three days after the Blitzkrieg had begun, the Nazi government gave its *Wehrmacht-Untersuchungsstell für Veletzungen des Völkerrechts,* (Bureau for the Investigation of War Crimes), the authority to investigate not only enemy violations of international law but also "such accusations as are raised by foreign countries against the *Wehr-macht*."[23] The War Crimes Bureau, working alongside the German Foreign Office, joined the fray with the foreign ministries of other engaged countries, making and refuting allegations of war crimes and other violations, while, until the very end of the war, actually investigating their own.

In March 1945, with the majority of Germany occupied and the Soviets readying a march on Berlin, the Germans nonetheless issued a formal legal protest concerning various air raids conducted by the Allies in Italy.[24] Similarly, the Germans remained diligent in investigating their own misdeeds. In January 1945, the War Crimes Bureau began an investigation into a massacre of Allied soldiers at Malmédy, Belgium, during which more than seventy POWs had been shot. The office continued its investigation, even after the German commander in Belgium refuted the story, and even when it became clear that the end of the Reich was imminent. The office submitted its official response to the Allied allegations exactly two months before Germany signed the documents of surrender.

Though odd when compared with the mass crimes being committed by the Reich elsewhere, the War Crimes Bureau even conducted trials during the war of both Germans and captured Allies. For example on September 15, 1939, a German court-martial convicted two German soldiers for killing a Polish shopkeeper and raping his wife. Both soldiers were sentenced to death, with the punishment actually carried out in one case and commuted to life imprisonment for the other.[25] During the French campaign in May–June 1940, German army judges systematically prosecuted abuses against the French civilian population perpetrated by members of the *Wehrmacht*. After the collapse of the French army, Hitler issued a decree demanding restraint on behalf of his soldiers. "Every member of the *Wehrmacht* who . . . commits a crime . . . shall be brought to justice and severely punished."[26] Most trials and judgments coming from this decree were based on the testimony of French witnesses. And since French local police assisted the German military courts in establishing the evidence, convictions against German soldiers were obtained in nearly 70 percent of the cases.[27]

Some of the resulting cases are especially striking and manifestly inconsistent with German activities elsewhere. Thus, when two German soldiers intimidated French Jews in Nice and forced them to surrender their money and jewelry, a German court-martial sentenced one of them to death and the other to twelve years' imprisonment. The judgment, dated April 11, 1944, declared: "The fact that the violence . . . was directed against Jews in no way excuses the perpetrators. . . . [T]he German reputation has thereby suffered."[28]

German military courts in other occupied countries prosecuted German soldiers in a similar fashion. In Norway, a German court sentenced a soldier to three years' prison for plundering. On January 5, 1945, a German military court in Denmark sentenced a soldier to five years for theft, and in September 1943, a German military court in Greece sentenced to death a German soldier who had raped a sixteen-year-old Greek girl and assaulted her mother.[29]

In addition to proceedings of its own, there is significant evidence that the War Crimes Bureau also engaged in staging fair trials for captured members of the enemy. This was even the situation on the Eastern Front, where Germans were noticeably more cruel than on the Western Front. That such trials were held, let alone acquittals rendered, again seems incongruous given the viciousness of the battle and the historical reputation of the German army. Yet, in a characteristic case, the War Crimes Bureau raised charges against a Polish lieutenant named Zmudzinski for his alleged killing of a German POW. The judge ordered an investigation, and once the court was unable to confirm the identity of the POW victim, the case was dismissed.[30] In the largest of such trials, a German military court charged Polish captain Jan Drzewiecki and 37 others with their participation in a forced march of German POWs, which had resulted in 230 German deaths. Of the defendants, 21 were condemned to death, and 1 was sentenced to 5 years in jail, while 16 were acquitted.[31] In all, according to an admittedly incomplete list of proceedings, at least 252 cases raised against Polish POWs accused of abusing Germans were investigated, of which more than two-thirds were dismissed.[32]

In occupied France, the Germans were similarly "legal" when trying French POWs, often refusing to convict them. In 1940, 40 French farmers brutally attacked 4 German pilots after a crash landing. Five French defendants were brought before a tribunal, and only 2 were convicted and sentenced to death. The others were acquitted due to insufficient evidence.[33] Over time, even the sentences promulgated for convicted defendants became less draconian. In 1941, a military court in occupied Paris charged 10 French civilians with mistreating and robbing the crew of a downed German airplane. Two were acquitted, and 8 were convicted of assault, rather than the much more serious crime of being *franc-tireurs* (elements of the French resistance). The most severe sentence was three years. Additionally, three of the convicted were released immediately with the judge giving them credit for the time they served while awaiting and undergoing trial.[34]

Even in the Soviet Union, where Hitler's Barbarossa Decree explicitly limited the War Crimes Bureau's jurisdiction, it appears that military courts actually functioned. In many cases, defendants were acquitted and most cases were dismissed due to lack of evidence.[35] Several cases of abuse by German soldiers against hated Soviet POWs were punished.

Moreover, though Hitler attempted to limit the jurisdiction of the bureau, unless he physically went around the body by ordering the SS or other "nonmilitary" units to engage in certain acts, the bureau consistently stymied him. Numerous German commanders in the field, many of whom disdained the "total war" philosophy espoused by the Reich, sided with the bureau. The commanders did so by regularly disobeying orders from Berlin. The most significant example of this regarded the above-mentioned Barbarossa Decree of May 1941. Barbarossa limited the jurisdiction of military courts on the Eastern Front by removing the automatic requirement to prosecute German soldiers in cases where they had committed arbitrary acts of violence against the local civilian population.[36] Many key officers ignored the new rule, issuing their own battlefield regulations, most of which were in line with the prevailing international understanding of the laws of war.

For example, Gotthard Heinrici, commander of the German Fourth Army, ordered that "offenses against the Russian civilian population shall be punished by disciplinary sanctions or by court-martial."[37] He confirmed numerous death sentences for German soldiers who committed such crimes, including three members of the Twenty-Fifth Armored Division for killing five women, two members of the One Hundred and Sixty-Seventh for plundering, and two members of the Two Hundred and Sixtieth for the rape and murder of a woman. The commanders of the German Eighteenth and Fourteenth armies also ignored the decree; the general of the Fourteenth ordered his chief judge to try a German soldier who had killed a Russian woman, and subsequently ordered the judgment and death sentence be brought to the attention of all of his troops, as a deterrent against this kind of behavior.[38]

Field Marshal Erwin Rommel, who waged Germany's war in North Africa, also despised Hitler's excesses. Rommel is said to have "fought a bad war well, not only militarily, but also morally," refusing to heed the Commando Order issued by Hitler on October 28, 1942, which mandated that all enemy soldiers encountered behind German lines be killed at once.[39]

In the years since World War II, examples of failed trials are well known, often obscuring successful trials. In the Korean War, the tragedy of No Gun Ri—from which no trials eventuated—overshadows cases such as that against Airman Kinder in 1953, who complied with an illegal order to shoot a Korean civilian. The American court-martial that was convened found that Kinder was compelled to ignore such an order; Kinder was dishonorably discharged and incarcerated. In the Vietnam conflict, all justice that occurred against both Vietnamese and Americans is seen through the lens of My Lai—the

1968 event in which a company of American servicemen opened fire on unarmed civilians, killing 350. This conflagration that resulted in only one trial with the defendant, Lieutenant Calley, serving barely five years. Though undoubtedly a black eye on military justice, this obscures cases against those like Marine Private John D. Potter for events all too similar to My Lai. In September 1966, Potter and his patrol stormed the Vietnamese hamlet of Xuan-Ngoc, and engaged in a similar bacchanal of violence: slaughtering innocent civilians, and raping and mutilating others. In contrast to My Lai, the commander of Potter's company immediately suspected misdeeds and ordered an investigation. Potter was convicted of five counts of premeditated murder, rape, and the attempted rape of a second Vietnamese woman. In a Marine Corps court-martial that was composed of Marine officers and that sat *in* the combat zone, Potter was convicted and sentenced to confinement at hard labor for life, reduction in rank to private, loss of all pay and allowances, and a dishonorable discharge. Twenty-seven other Marines were also tried for homicide.[40]

In 1979, Equatorial Guinea—the former Spanish colony located on the Gulf of Guinea, Africa—was host to another unlikely trial. Francisco Macias Nguema had ruled the tiny country since independence from Madrid in 1968, proclaiming himself president for life in 1972. Earning for his state the unfortunate moniker, "the Auschwitz of Africa," his decade of rule saw one-third of his population either killed or sent into exile—70 percent of the population had been jailed at some point during the dictatorship.[41] Macias was overthrown in August 1979 and put on trial by the country's new leadership before a mixed military/civilian court. The trial was held in an old theater (in order to accommodate interested spectators), was broadcast on loudspeakers outside the venue and over the radio, and was open to the international media and human rights observers, including the Geneva-based International Commission of Jurists, which deemed it a "competent tribunal."[42] Among other crimes, Macias was convicted of mass murder, a charge that human rights observers concluded was well established by the court.[43]

Five years later, on the other side of the world, the rise of the military juntas in South America would result in another set of domestic proceedings.[44] The military leaders who rose to power in Argentina in 1977 brutally suppressed dissent, resulting in thousands of "disappeared" citizens, torture, and thousands of extrajudicial killings. By 1983, their "movement" had run out of steam, hamstrung under both mounting revelations about their human rights violations and the aftereffects of its disastrous war with Britain over the Falklands. The military opted to organize elections, and even allowed vigorous debate about whether trials would be conducted against those implicated in the Dirty War. The eventual winner of the election, Raul Alfonsín, campaigned explicitly on the promise to investigate abuses and bring to trial military chiefs and officers who committed the worst excesses.[45] True to his platform, he decreed a Presidential Order to begin legal processes against the junta immediately upon assuming power.[46] The armed forces were still intact, and they looked with concern at the proceedings.[47]

The first trials against the former leaders resulted in the conviction of five military commanders for human rights abuses, and the acquittal of four others on all charges.[48] More trials followed in 1985 and 1986. "[I]n all 481 military and police officers were indicted; 16 were tried . . . 11 were convicted."[49] The trials were far from perfect or comprehensive. An amnesty law, *Ley de Punto Final* (the "Full Stop Law"), was promulgated in December 1986, ending investigation and prosecution of those involved in the junta's crimes. And it is an unfortunate postscript that the subsequent Argentine leader Carlos Menem pardoned the criminals. However, the amnesty laws were recently repealed and trials have resumed. There have been some difficulties and some violence,[50] but in September 2006, Miguel Etchecolatz, the former deputy commander of the Buenos Aires Provincial Police, was found guilty of crimes against humanity and incarcerated for life. As of this writing, at least four hundred others are awaiting trial.[51]

In 1987, Africa returned to the forefront with the trial of Jean-Bedel Bokassa, the delusional leader and self-crowned "Emperor" of the Central African Republic (a former French colony southwest of

Sudan). His thirteen-year reign was marked by extremes in profligacy (his 1976 coronation consumed one-third of his country's annual budget and during his dictatorship he purchased three hundred limousines and a dozen European villas) and cruelty (in April 1979 he had as many as sixty children killed when they protested being forced to wear the government-required school uniform). Bokassa was deposed in September 1979 and fled to France; he was convicted in absentia in 1980, but decided to return home in 1987 to exonerate himself. Upon the "Emperor's" return, Bokassa's successor, André Kolingba, decreed that the former leader "will have the right to a public trial, the problem will be settled and we can bury the past."[52] The 1980 verdict against Bokassa was swept aside and starting in late 1986 a nine-member court—three judges and six jurors—heard the case anew. One hundred witnesses appeared, and observers—evidently unfamiliar with the Macias trial a decade earlier—noted that this was the "first time in the history of postcolonial Africa that a former chief of state was put on public trial with full guarantees for his defense."[53] Broadcast on radio and television, his trial proved so "rivet[ing] that government officials fret[ted] that the [work] production of public servants and other workers . . . all but ground to a halt."[54] The trial was imperfect, and many believe that Bokassa would be found guilty of all charges as a matter of course. However, while convicted of treason, murder, and embezzlement, Bokassa was acquitted of several killings for which the court president Edouard Franck said that details were lacking.[55] He was ordered to return $1 million to the state and his "belongings and property in [the country's capital] Bangui were seized."[56]

The Yugoslav wars of the 1990s, the catalyst for the return of international justice, proved another fertile ground for domestic trials: the conflict saw dozens, if not hundreds of trials conducted by combatants against belligerents, and by combatants against their own.

The war, which began with the departure of Croatia and Slovenia from the Yugoslav federation, quickly descended into an ethnic free-for-all with Serbs pitted against Croats pitted against Bosniaks pitted against Serbs. All sides committed crimes. Despite the level of mutual animus, fair, interethnic trials began very early in the war. In July 1992, in Belgrade, a Serb court convicted Croatian guardswoman Ksenija Piplica for extrajudicial killings of Serbs, a trial that saw no complaints from Zagreb or the international community,[57] and one in which the defendant was accorded robust legal protections that allowed Piplica a spirited defense and even an appeal.[58]

In early March 1993, in the midst of the Siege of Sarajevo, a military court was established to try Serb Borislav Herak and his colleagues, who had admitted to various brutalities committed against Bosniaks. That largely Bosniak Sarajevo was under siege and that there were regular attacks from Serbs in the hills was immaterial to the proceedings. On March 13, Serbian troops, who had gotten word of the trial, launched three mortar rounds at the courthouse, with one striking the roof. The trial continued, with the only concession to the surrounding battle coming from the judges' frequent call for testimony to be repeated if it had been drowned out by a nearby exploding shell.[59] Moreover, to forestall concerns about bias, several roles in the trial were assigned to Serbs, including that of the prosecutor and one of the five judges.[60] The trial was also open to reporters and American cable network "Court TV" aired the proceedings.[61]

May 1993 is illustrative of the Yugoslav activity on the war crimes trial front. That it was such an active month is ironic given that this was the month that the international community inaugurated the Yugoslavia tribunal, with one its rationales being the perceived inability and lack of desire of those in the Balkans to legally address war crimes. The facts on the ground suggest a somewhat different reality. In the first week of May, a Montenegrin court (which was thought hand in glove with Serb authorities) convicted four Bosnian Serbs for murdering a Muslim family, a crime the court condemned as a war crime. [62] Though three were in absentia, each was sentenced to twenty years in prison, and Vidoje Golubovic—who had the misfortune of being caught—began his incarceration immediately.[63] On May 8, authorities in Trebinje, in the Republika Srpska (the Serbian part of Bosnia), charged sixty-six people for "war crimes against civilians," with many Serbs among them, and began legal proceedings.[64] The following week saw the Bosnian Serbs insist that Naser Oric, the Muslim commander whom they blamed for massacres in places such as Ratkovici, be handed over to stand trial for war crimes. Shortly thereafter, authorities in Pale and Banja Luka, Bosnia, with the aid of the Belgrade-based Yugoslav Commission for Investigating War Crimes, published a list of two hundred Muslims who had committed war crimes against Serbs in Bosnia and demanded their surrender. [65] Finally, on May 30, in Doboj—a region in northern Bosnia that had been almost entirely stripped of its multiethnic past and was by then home to an almost uniform Serb population—the local war crimes commission forwarded a large number of Croat and Muslim names to local prosecutors for investigation and trial of war crimes committed in the region.[66]

As the wars continued, the pace of trials quickened. In 1994, the two Vuckovic brothers, Vojin and Dusan, members of the Serbian Yellow Wasps—one of the marauding bands of paramilitaries that terrorized the Balkans during the wars—appeared before a Serbian court charged with killing Bosniaks. For the Serb government, which "had stridently denied knowledge of or involvement in war crimes in Bosnia and Croatia, the arrest of the Vuckovic brothers was a stunning policy reversal,"[67] and served as a direct challenge to most Serbs' view of the war.[68] Proceedings began in November 1994. The process was slow, and human rights observers complained about several aspects of the trial: the "forgivingly worded" indictment,[69] the favoritism that guards and judges often showed to the accused, and reports that Milosevic himself had ordered the brothers be exonerated. In short, legal observers were convinced that the outcome was a foregone conclusion—one brother would be acquitted and the other found guilty, but only of lesser charges such as arms dealing.[70]

Yet, in July 1996, before a panel of five judges the court found both brothers guilty.[71] Vojin was indeed found guilty of the lesser charge of illegal possession of arms. Dusan was sentenced to seven years and his brother to one. However, the case was not yet over and both appealed their verdicts and sentences. In 1998, the Supreme Court of Serbia upheld the convictions, and actually lengthened Dusan's sentence to ten years, finding him explicitly guilty of "war crimes against the civilian population and rape." Vojin's verdict was also upheld.[72] Far from hiding either the initial verdict or the Supreme Court's decision, the official Serbian news agency reported on it quickly and extensively.[73]

In October 1997, a Serbian court convicted Bosniak Ferid Halilovic for torturing detainees. The court allowed a real defense, and invited international observers who "carefully followed the trial" and found no "major concerns" regarding its fairness.[74] On the Bosniak side, also in 1997, several Bosnian Muslims began to be prosecuted for war crimes committed during the conflict. Concerned about bias if held in the countryside amidst Bosniak partisans, prosecutors moved some of the trials to Sarajevo.[75]

Two years later in 1999, a Serbian court ruled that three Bosniaks had been wrongfully convicted for the murder of Serbian laborers; a fourth defendant's conviction was upheld but his sentence was reduced. In the same year, a local court in Sarajevo (dominated by Bosniaks) acquitted Serb Miodrag Andric for war crimes and permitted witnesses to testify remotely from a Serb court.[76]

A year later, Ibrahim Djedovic, who had been a senior rebel Bosniak official accused of committing war crimes against civilians and members of the regular, primarily Bosniak, Army of Bosnia and Herzegovina, was brought to trial before a Sarajevo court that observers were convinced was predisposed to convicting him.[77] The international community claimed the trial was a "joke," that it was politicized, and that the judiciary had no independence.[78] The Bosnian courts were sure to convict someone who had been so troublesome to the state. Yet, though there were some procedural problems, Djedovic was acquitted as the judge decried the prosecution's complete lack of evidence that pointed to the defendant's involvement in war crimes.[79]

As the end of 2000 arrived, the crimes that had taken place in Kosovo in 1999 began to take center stage. During the last three months of 2000, Serb courts convicted Serbs of war crimes committed in Kosovo; still more Serb trials of enlisted soldiers and officers were held in 2001 and 2002. In one noteworthy proceedings, Sas Cvjetan, a member of a Serb paramilitary group, was convicted in Belgrade for executing fourteen Albanians, and received a twenty-year sentence. The Serbian Supreme Court overturned the sentence and ordered a retrial; however, on retrial, Cvjetan received the same verdict and same punishment.[80]

Meanwhile, in Sierra Leone, battered by a decade of war and hampered by an already limited judicial infrastructure, the height of civil conflict nonetheless saw a resilient focus on establishing domestic legal accountability. The UN secretary general's special envoy to the country reported in April 1998 that the government was prosecuting fifty-nine persons in the civilian courts, with another twenty defendants detained and set to begin trials within a month. The report stated that "civilian trials have, so far, proceeded in conformity with normal criminal procedure."[81]

To many observers, more recent trials in the Balkans have been even more surprising, both for their existence and their outcome. One such "surprise" occurred in early 2008 in the Serb capital, Belgrade. In February Kosovo declared independence and Serbs were furious, convinced that their historic homeland could not rightfully secede. Shortly thereafter, the Yugoslavia tribunal in The Hague acquitted Ramush Haradinaj, a leader of the Kosovars during the 1999 battle with the Serbs, further enraging the Serb population. Yet a few weeks later, Serbia's domestic war crimes prosecutor, ignoring the seething political class and the public clamor for revenge and desire to close ranks against those who wished to persecute Serbia for its "rightful" protection of its homeland, brought charges against four Serb fighters accused of a massacre against Albanian Kosovars in 1999.[82] The political environment could hardly have been less favorable, but the prosecutors in Belgrade in April 2008, much like similar prosecutors seen throughout history, attempted to pursue justice in the face of mass opposition and long odds.

✳

Despite these broad trends and rich history, Roth's words continue to resonate: war crimes have continued and in many cases the perpetrators have not been punished, or have only been punished when an enemy is the defendant. This is puzzling. If it is possible for states to prosecute their own and to fairly prosecute others—as history, and recent history especially, shows—why have so many states failed to do so? More hopefully, what, if any, criteria link the successful prosecutions? Are these common factors exportable or creatable in other states?

There are specific strategies that have proven successful across regions and time that have enabled successful domestic prosecutions. And, aspects of such strategies, even if nascent, are present in nearly every state. There is reason to believe that a successful approach to addressing war crimes could be concocted in almost *any* state attempting to judicially deal with atrocities.

The states that have successfully addressed war crimes committed both against them and by them have leveraged some combination of five key characteristics:

1. A military leadership animated by fear and pride
2. A media that encourages truth and that taps into a societal sense of shame, disgust, and fairness
3. Lower-level political and opinion leaders providing a base of support for trials even if support is lacking at higher levels
4. Officials involved in trials, such as judges and lawyers, allowing flexibility in all aspects of the proceedings
5. The international community deftly promoting, cajoling, and demanding domestic accountability

1) THE MILITARY HIERARCHY—
A QUESTION OF FEAR AND PRIDE

In September 2006, as the Bush administration was still recoiling from the summer's harsh rebuke from the Supreme Court on the treatment of detainees at Guantanamo Bay, another battle emerged, seemingly surprising the White House. The Supreme Court had held, in strident language, that the administration's handling of detainees—from their arrest, to their interrogation, to their detention—was inappropriate and against both American law and America's international obligations. Trying to follow the letter of the Court's pronouncements but clearly not its spirit, the White House presented a bill to Congress that was designed to overhaul the system for dealing with captives from the "War on Terror." As presented, the legislation limited the application of human rights treaties to detainees and allowed trials against detainees to proceed without many of the protections of the domestic system. It looked like a perfect example of the "overprosecution" of belligerents unfortunate enough to be captured—a basic quality of the pseudo-justice that is the "victors' justice" of which Roth and others complain.

Yet, rather than a strictly partisan debate, what initially emerged was opposition within the president's own party. A common element amongst Republican dissenters was their prior military service. These politician-veterans, some who had been prisoners of war and others who had received numerous decorations, immediately rebelled. Their revolt and the reasons behind it shed light on what animates the military (and those sensitive to the military's concerns), and how that animation can lead to fair (or at least fairer) trials for war criminals.

Arizona senator and 2008 Republican presidential candidate John McCain, who had been a "guest" at the Hanoi Hilton for nearly six years, was among the most vocal opponents of the Bush plan. He argued that the plan risked our moral standing, and it risked the lives of Americans defending their country. Colin Powell, the former chairman of the Joint Chiefs of Staff and Bush's first-term secretary of state, made a similar claim, holding that such legislation would add to the moral doubts of the "War On Terror," and would unquestionably imperil our troops. Active duty personnel and especially military lawyers who testified before Congress on the matter strongly agreed. At the base of these anxieties were two drivers, each of which can both prevent war crimes and can promote the prosecution of war crimes if they occur: fear and pride.

Both during combat and afterward, militaries have long been concerned with reprisals. In almost any war or conflict, this fear has motivated certain behaviors, often surrounding war crimes. In the English Civil War of the seventeenth century, each side was so concerned that the other would stoop to barbarism that they both fought the conflict as a "foreign" war, providing the same respect to each other as they would a bona fide other state. Given that each side denied the validity of the claim to nationhood of the other, this was a substantial concession, but one born of self-interest. During the American Revolutionary War, the threat of reprisals secured respect for the rules of war from both sides. In a sense, the concern of reprisals is a smaller, more concentrated version of the "Mutually Assured Destruction" stalemate that kept the Cold War from heating up—if all sides are fearful about the response of the other, they will refrain from unneeded provocations.

There is evidence that this concern for reprisals is directly invoked in both macrostrategy by senior military leaders and in microdecisions made by individual soldiers on the battlefield. It helps explain why German activities in World War II on the Western Front were comparatively humane as compared with their behavior against the Russians. It also helps in understanding the relatively kind treatment Americans provided enemy prisoners captured during the Korean War. In both cases, states and armies were fearful of what might happen to their own soldiers if such standards of care for treatment of their POWs were not scrupulously upheld. Evidence even suggests that the willingness of a soldier to surrender during battle is directly related to his perceptions of how well he will be treated once detained. A combatant who can look forward to a warm bed and a cigarette, rather than the potential of torture and unending captivity, is less likely to fight to the death.

What is true of battlefield strategy is also true of prosecuting war crimes.

The concerns voiced by the military veterans in Congress that September regarding the Guantanamo Bay detainees were based on this understanding, an understanding that veterans intuitively recognize.

Though the threat of reprisals has often led to strategic decisions on the battlefield and decisions *not* to prosecute detainees—as in the Korean War for POWs held on both sides of the DMZ—this has not always been the case. Fear of reprisals has also led to trials of personnel within one's own army. A key, and perhaps unlikely, example of this can be seen in the Palestinian Authority (PA) prior to the election of Hamas in January 2006. Since the start of the Oslo Peace Process in the early 1990s, Israel increasingly held the PA institutionally responsible for any acts of terror in Israel proper that emanated from any territories under PA control. Israel responded violently to such attacks. To avoid retaliation, the PA tried to preempt the Israelis by regularly bringing charges against whomsoever it (or Israel) deemed to have been involved in an attack. Though it may seem ironic that the charges the PA most often levied against terror cells were the same as those they brought against Palestinians collaborating with the Israelis, this parallelism makes sense from the standpoint of avoiding reprisals. The PA viewed collaborators who worked with Israelis as weakening the PA, and terrorists who worked to weaken Israel as militarily identical because they both resulted in attacks on the PA. That the legal ramifications would be the same followed as a matter of course. The cases were not always fair, and often left much to be desired from the perspective of international standards of justice. Yet, despite the conventional wisdom that suggested such trials would never occur, they in fact did. The fear of reprisals forced the PA to legally challenge and punish acts committed in the name of, and for the ostensible good of, the Palestinian movement.[83]

✳

The second set of concerns that animates militaries relates to pride and the moral authority of a state and its armed forces. In the words of Michigan Democratic senator Carl Levin, a further ardent critic of the Bush detainee legislation in 2006, we should avoid actions that are "abhorrent to American values."[84] Here too, it is not just being American, but rather being a soldier, that brings with it strict limits on behavior. Much as the most effective sanction to ensure compliance with the law of chivalry was the "knight's fear of dishonor and public reprobation,"[85] the modern soldier, in order to be accorded the title "soldier," must exercise discipline, must use power with legitimacy, and must do so with honor. Each characteristic has become directly linked to war crimes prosecutions.

Discipline

At one time, the only clear reason to prosecute war crimes was to ensure discipline. A fighting force is only effective as long as it is able to control its troops, and if a soldier steps out of line—whether or not his actions help the military campaign—it does injury to the overall operational ability of the army.

This concern for discipline can be seen across time and place, with military regulations throughout the world upholding its importance. Early codes of military conduct, such as the Lieber Code of the American Civil War and the Code of Gustavus Adolphus promulgated preceding the Thirty Years' War in 1618, were explicitly motivated by concerns for discipline, rather than fear of reprisals, let alone humanitarianism. This focus on discipline led to substantial numbers of court-martials. There are many examples of this. In the American Revolutionary War, on the US side, three thousand court-martials were conducted of American forces,[86] and the American Congress was said to have shown "great solicitude to maintain inviolate the obligations of the law of nations, and to have infractions of it punished."[87] During the Civil War, the Union held more than one hundred thousand court-martials of its own troops.[88] In World War II, the US government conducted more than two million court-martials of its own soldiers, airmen, and seamen.[89] This is an astonishing number when one considers that the United States only had sixteen million men under arms during the war. In Europe alone, during the period from June 6, 1944 (D-Day) to the conclusion of hostilities in May 1945, the US Army court-martialed and executed ninety-five American soldiers for violating laws of war.[90] And in Vietnam, from 1965–1973, one hundred sixty US military personnel were convicted in court-martial for a variety of war crimes, ranging from the killing of POWs,[91] to the disrespectful treatment of dead enemy soldiers,[92] to the murder of Vietnamese soldiers.[93] The conviction rates during the Vietnam War were quite high: more than 50 percent of cases brought before court-martial resulted in guilty verdicts.[94]

Despite the initial, one-dimensional concern for military discipline, in today's world the concern for discipline leads increasingly to prosecutions. To be disciplined *means* punishing war crimes. This is especially clear in the growing number of countries coming to legally enshrine binding "universal principles"—such as the Rome Treaty on the International Criminal Court, which defines and penalizes specific war crimes—into enforceable domestic law. Such domestic law was the basis for Britain's first-ever domestic war crimes charge in September 2006, when a court-martial found Corporal David Payne and two others guilty of war crimes committed against Iraqi POWs in the opening days of the 2003 invasion of Iraq.[95] This was also the basis for the court-martial of several high-ranking Serb officers during the Yugoslav wars, such as those commanders who violated a brokered ceasefire.[96]

Legitimacy

Colin Powell's concerns regarding the Bush administration's legislation centered on the moral force of American actions, a corollary to the duties of soldiering, and one that has been present in soldiering for centuries. War crimes directly impinge on the legitimacy of soldiers' behavior. Though perhaps especially clear in the American case, such concerns are often equally resonant for rebel forces, and among many of those one might think would be least likely to follow such rules. For instance, in the seventeenth century both the Royalists and the Parliament in the English Civil War adopted official Articles of War that limited their forces' discretion on the battlefield. "Real" armies needed real legal limits.[97] By the time of the American Revolution a century later, it was manifestly advantageous to the rebellious United States to follow the rules of war scrupulously, "for by so doing it extended its credibility as a sovereign."[98]

Though this striving for credibility by militaries has happened throughout history, its ubiquity is a post–World War II phenomenon and the near uniformity by which forces pursue such credibility is remarkable and appears across a diversity of actors. Thus, the Biafran Army (the forces of Biafra, a region in Nigeria that attempted to secede in 1967, sparking the Nigerian Civil War) quickly developed a legal code after its founding. The Biafran force only *existed* for three years (1967–1970);[99] and yet it felt necessary to promulgate and enforce such a code. This trend also explains why the Palestinian Liberation Organization (PLO), sought to "sign" the Geneva Conventions, and agreed to be bound by them. Signing (and living up to its conditions) is what states do, and any entity that aspires to statehood consequently feels that it must do so.

Honor

While the days of chivalric courts have passed, there is much in even the most modern of militaries that harkens back to those times. "Honor" for both unit and country is often promoted both to prevent the commissioning of war crimes and to justify their punishment. A recent case is instructive. British lieutenant colonel Tim Collins, the commander of the six hundred troops of the First Battalion of the Irish Regiment, led the initial British troops into Iraq in March 2003. On the eve of the invasion, he provided what would become a famous admonishment to his troops. He implored his troops to be "ferocious in battle and magnanimous in victory. . . . You will be shunned unless your conduct is of the highest, for your deeds will follow you down through history."[100] Despite Collins's rank and fame—Prince Charles wrote to Collins to praise his speech and President Bush was said to have a framed copy hung in his private office—even Collins could not escape the duty of honor. Following allegations of mistreatment of POWs and civilians in the south of Iraq, which had allegedly occurred on his watch, Collins was investigated diligently by the Special Investigation Branch of the Royal Military Police. The honor of the military was at stake. And it was only after in-depth examination that Collins was acquitted.[101]

A similar sense of honor in fighting can be seen in the early 1980s during the Falklands campaign waged between Argentina and Britain. The Argentines displayed a clear devotion to honor. This led them to refrain from improper behavior, often to their detriment. When the British forces entered the Falkland capital of Stanley after breaking the Argentine siege on the city, they were surprised to find that civilians—*British* residents of the archipelago—had adequate stocks of food and even alcohol. The occupying Argentine army had neither robbed nor attacked the civilians. This was all the more surprising because many of the Argentine soldiers were themselves going hungry, and despite their military firepower they had refrained from delving into civilian stocks. This evidently hampered the Argentines' ability to repel the British advance.[102]

Second, when it became obvious that his forces would be defeated, Argentine leader Leopoldo Galtieri told his Falklands commander, General Mario Menendez, to counterattack with as much force as he could muster and without respect for any legal niceties. Menendez ignored his orders, at great personal loss. As soon as he returned from the war, he was stripped of his rank and cashiered from the army. One of Menendez's battlefield commanders, Brigadier General Oscar Jofre, later admitted that the end of the ground war was hastened due to his desire to limit even the *potential* for the commission of war crimes.[103]

The issue of honor can even be seen in the disdain expressed by "regular" military forces for the paramilitaries that have often fought alongside them—from the SS in World War II to various groups in the former Yugoslavia. The SS, and other "special" troops, operated outside military justice during World War II. The *Wehrmacht's* War Crimes Bureau had limited jurisdiction over these forces. Yet, there were numerous commanders who expressed disquiet about some of the brutality of these German "irregulars." In October 1939, German general Johannes Blaskowitz, who led part of the attack into Poland, demanded that two SS colonels be court-martialed. He protested directly to Hitler, bemoaning the "blood lust"[104] of the SS in Poland and argued that "every soldier feels offended and repulsed by the crimes being committed in Poland by citizens of the Reich. . . . A soldier cannot understand how such crimes can remain unpunished, crimes that occur in a sense under the army's protection."[105] Hitler dismissed the request, reportedly saying that: "You can't fight a war with the Salvation Army." Blaskowitz maintained his revulsion for the SS, moving to press charges against Josef Dietrich—one of Hitler's inner circle—and court-martialed any of his own men discovered cooperating with the SS. Berlin tired of his complaints and finally relieved him of his command in Poland in 1940.[106]

Among Bosnian Croats, there was similarly great sensitivity to the activities of paramilitaries and pledges to remove and try offenders. In May 1993, in response to a request by the UN's War Crimes Commission, Jozo Leutar, a commander of the Bosnian Croat regular forces, expressed his army's and government's shock at what was found at Ahmici, the site of savage massacre by Croat irregulars in April of that year: "None of our brigade members as well as nobody in the entire [army] will ever make excuses for criminals within us." [107]

Both types of behavior—one motivated by fear of reprisal, the other by desire to maintain honor and justice—can be instituted in states, often with the assistance of actors mentioned below (in the media, for example). Both the fear of reprisal and the devotion to honor are present in almost every military and state, and it is often simply a matter of uncovering them, by making threats of reprisal real or reducing the esteem in which a society and the wider international community holds a state's armed forces.

2) MEDIA—SOURCE OF INFORMATION AND TAPPING A SOCIETAL SENSE OF FAIRNESS AND DISGUST

> *The power of the media to create and destroy human values comes with great responsibility.*
> —International Criminal Tribunal for Rwanda, Verdict in "The Media Trial," December 9, 2003.[108]

The two-year-old girl was dying. After a life too short and too hard, a *Médecins sans Frontières* nurse held the child, looking at her bulging eyes, patting her distended belly. Flies were everywhere. Then, it was over; the nurse moved her hands over the girl's face, closing her eyes for the last time. Flies continued to swarm, landing on the now lifeless figure in the refugee tent.

This scene, broadcast on television and in the press throughout the world, was most people's introduction to 1992 Somalia; the famine and civil war in the Horn of Africa would cost millions of lives.

This fleeting image of a dying child—lasting only a moment when broadcast—engendered enough sadness and guilt in the United States to force the first Bush administration's hand: the White House ordered Marines into Somalia to deliver food and supplies to the most distressed regions in the country. Yet within a year, similarly emotive images would force the new Clinton administration to change tack: a single 2.5-second shot of a dead American soldier being dragged through the streets of Mogadishu caused Clinton to order an immediate withdrawal.

The Somali case is one of the clearest instances of the media's power not only to construct a narrative but also to force a response.

Such images and reporting can also influence both the prevention of war crimes and their punishment. Compare the Korean War with the Vietnam conflict: the similarities between two of the more appalling acts in each, the events at No Gun Ri in July 1950, and the massacre at My Lai in March 1968, are startling. In each, groups of soldiers, clearly unaffected by pride or the fear of reprisals, set upon innocent civilians, slaughtering dozens. However, the outcomes of the two events were radically different. My Lai came to light within a year of its occurrence, the result of leaked letters to the press and the diligence of reporters on the ground in Vietnam and in America. And, in an unprecedented move, the media even published pictures of the dead. No Gun Ri, however, was committed in an age before embedded reporters, and was consequently a far more anonymous event. The entire affair only came to light fifty years after it occurred. Consequently, that My Lai resulted in prosecutions—even if imperfect—and No Gun Ri did not is not surprising. The media forced the government's hand after My Lai.

Media influence on war crimes derives from the importance of public opinion in times of conflict. The necessity for modern war to be more "total" even as it has become more limited, has meant that in almost any state, the majority of populations are called—in one way or another—to serve or support their nation in a time of crisis. Such support is usually expressed, aided, or hindered via the media. Broadcasting war crimes can, in the words of Mao Tse Tung, "make a soldier's job . . . impossible. The bitterness created by war crimes can cause the defeat of the greatest armies,"[109] by making the citizens of a belligerent state unified in their opposition and citizens at home unsure of their support. The United States learned this to its detriment in 1901 when revelations of US abuses in its attempt to put down an insurrection in the Philippines caused such an uproar that it threatened to derail President Theodore Roosevelt's foreign policy.[110]

Ninety years later, Mao's adage was at play during the First Gulf War when the media directly influenced military strategy. United States and coalition commanders decided very early that regardless of military benefit, indiscriminate bombing of Iraqi targets was infeasible because such attacks would provide Saddam with propaganda against the coalition. The fear of the use of the media led directly to an increased concern for lawful military strategies. It has been argued that in the First Gulf War, even the perception of a violation of the rules of war—when the rules had, in fact, been adhered to—was enough to move military decision makers and strategists to engage in even more seemingly law-abiding behavior.[111]

Modern technology and the immediacy and ubiquity of the media have made Mao's statement even more prescient. While the advent of the telegraph allowed William Howard Russell to laboriously tap out in Morse code his dispatches about the Crimean War, cementing English public opinion against the conflict, the prevalence of digital cameras and instantaneous communication has only increased the power of the media. The ubiquity of technology meant that as soon as photos of the Abu Ghraib abuse surfaced, the entire world saw them within hours. This did untold damage to the ability of US forces in Iraq and Afghanistan to both secure multinational assistance and maintain support at home.

The heart of the media's power to promote an accounting of war crimes comes from its ability to inculcate specific feelings in viewers and readers: shame, disgust, and a sense of fairness.

"Shame" experienced by a population, much like dishonor experienced by the military, can move even the most reluctant societies toward trials and even real remorse. Shame regarding the Guantanamo Bay detention facility led to many Americans wishing that it would be closed. Shame regarding Japanese excesses during World War II has led to a strong movement among progressive Japanese citizens to directly confront Tokyo's crimes. Shame for Serbs has led to war crimes committed by Serbs to be increasingly investigated. Until such crimes are punished, "there will be dirt on the name of our nation," said Captain Dragan Karleusa, a former deputy chief of the Interior Ministry.[112] And, especially since 2001, the Serbian government has been aggressive in pursuing Serb perpetrated war crimes for reasons, at least in part, of state pride.

Meanwhile, if the populace, government, and others can be disgusted by war crimes reports, the likelihood of action—both regarding punishment and deterrence—is very high. Nuremberg itself was in large measure instigated by this feeling. Widespread press reports not just about German war crimes, but about crimes concurrently committed around the world, in the Spanish Civil War, in the Japanese invasion and subsequent Rape of Nanjing, and in Italian bombings of Ethiopia (in which Mussolini resorted to chemical weapons), eased some Germans' initial acceptance of the trials.

Disgust has played a similar role in more recent cases: the American public's reaction to My Lai; Israeli feelings regarding the "Meir" case (a January 1988 case in which Israeli colonel Yehuda Meir ordered his troops to "break the bones" of detained Palestinians)[113]; public "scandals" in Germany that led to renewed ardor in postwar prosecutions of Nazis during the 1960s and 1970s; the graphic "dead babies" testimony against Milosevic at the ICTY, which instilled "guilt and contrition" on the part of even the most recalcitrant of Serbs;[114] and the British and American publics' reactions following the abuse scandals in Iraq and Afghanistan. All were all critical components in promoting prosecutions and were motivated largely by a profound sense of societal disgust at what was reported by the media.

Though disgust or shame may be more sensational, a public perception of "unfairness" is no less visceral, and can be determinative for the provision of fair trials for former (or current) belligerents. Concerns for unfairness are at the heart of Rwandan and Balkan anxieties regarding the justice being provided to them by their respective UN tribunals. The "unfairness factor" was noted very early in modern international criminal justice. Justice Radha Binod Pal, the lone Indian judge hearing the Tokyo Trials after World War II, cast the sole dissenting vote at the trials. He argued not that the defendants were innocent; in fact, he claimed that the evidence that the defendants had committed the charged atrocities was "overwhelming." His concern was with the fairness, and in particular the *perception* of unfairness that the media had inculcated of the trials. Justice Pal lamented that proceedings that appear unfair not only likely violated the rights of the accused, but would contribute to loss of respect for the rule of law—and consequently reduce the likelihood of future trials.[115]

3) LOWER-LEVEL POLITICAL LEADERS AND OPINION LEADERS— PROVIDING SUPPORT FOR TRIALS

Along with wreaking havoc on the treasures from the national museum, office machines from ministries, and weapons from police stations, the lawlessness of postinvasion Iraq did not spare the justice system. Looters gutted nearly every court in the land, effectively stripping "justice" of any home it might have had. Making matters worse was the aftertaste of three decades of Saddam's regime, during which he had perverted a once proud justice system that traced its lineage to Hammurabi, cowed creative legal thinking and bullied judicial independence. Senior judges and legal academics—who were compelled to align with the Ba'athists in order to maintain their positions—were particularly affected. Consequently, once the occupying forces began to think about rebuilding domestic rule of law and mounting trials for war crimes, they were faced with a judicial infrastructure and leadership unfit for the task.

Yet, instead of decamping justice to a location out of the country—as was done in Yugoslavia and Rwanda when the international community was faced with similar circumstances—clear-eyed observers like Jamal Benomar, a UN expert who had been involved in rebuilding the rule of law in many postconflict zones, recognized that physically removing the process of justice outside Iraq would alienate any progressive jurists who were left.[116] And, indeed, once the immediate post-invasion dust had settled, and the Coalition Provisional Authority (CPA) began to investigate the situation, it soon realized that outside the senior leadership there were judges and lawyers inside Iraq, and numerous legal thinkers and activists in exile, who were free of corruption and the taint of Ba'athism.

The State Department developed a committee of exiled Iraqi attorneys, many of whom wished to return or at least assist in the redevelopment of the Iraqi legal system. The CPA established a Judicial Review Commission to vet sitting Iraqi judges; of the 869 judges the CPA reviewed, it removed only 135 of them due to concerns about their professionalism and Ba'athist sympathies.[117] The result has been that Iraqi justice was reinvigorated using primarily indigenous talent to do so. Judges and the wider system have been hampered by financial shortfalls and continued violence. But it is evident that there existed a large number of Iraqi jurists who were ready, willing, and capable to help rebuild the rule of law. This has been as true at the local, provincial levels as it has at the highest reaches of the system, including the Iraqi Special Tribunal that has tried senior leaders of the Saddam regime.

Though the CPA-vetting process was comprehensive, it failed to catch everybody. And, even more importantly, it failed to silence some of the political criticism from outside the justice system by powerful local leaders who resented the end of Ba'athist Iraq. In short, justice in post-Saddam Iraq, much like in post-Milosevic and post-Tudjman Yugoslavia, has been tested by the continued presence of challengers inside and outside the judicial system who have been linked with their regime's war crimes past and who have been unwilling to see trials. Yet, though the acts of senior political figures, military leaders, and even judges who may wish to stymie trials are important, history suggests that they are not determinative. While a modicum of social stability, state political will, and judicial capacity are required to pursue trials, the amount needed is not only more modest than most contend, but also regularly present in the lower levels of the state, even if absent in the upper echelons.

What is needed for domestic war crimes proceedings is a core of professionals—judges, lawyers, soldiers, and others—who have sufficient respect for their own professional identity and integrity to divorce themselves from what might be overwhelming political pressure to either commit crimes or ignore them. In many cases, even if senior leaders militate against international law and trials in particular, such trials can still take place.

Trials that occurred in the wake of the violence of East Timor's break from Indonesia are a powerful example of the resilience of junior officials committed to justice. Proceedings were begun in both the Timorese capital Dili and the Indonesian capital Jakarta. Though each set of trials was imperfect, human rights observers were especially critical of those in Indonesia, noting with derision that the conviction of any defendants was "due to the notable bravery of a few individual judges rather than to a credible system of justice."[118] Though reported pejoratively, this fact could be viewed positively insofar as it shows that justice can be served by the will of a few brave people. The entire state was not needed in order for prosecutions to occur, for the guilty to be convicted, and the innocent acquitted. Few states are monolithic and even fewer are completely bereft of voices demanding accountability for all violators.

In Serbia, at the height of Milosevic's dictatorship, most thought that the leadership completely subjugated the justice system. Not so; hundreds of judges critical of the president remained, some of whom eventually resigned,[119] and yet some of whom stayed in office and questioned Milosevic's hegemony. Importantly, once Milosevic had been overthrown these judges were ready to resume their roles.[120]

The same was true of the *Wehrmacht* War Crimes Bureau in World War II. One might ask how, in an environment of death camps and medical experimentation, was it possible for a harbor of legality to survive? It was brave individuals who managed to maintain a semblance of legal order amidst the immorality of National Socialism. Throughout the war, at the top of the *Wehrmacht* legal office there were no National Socialist Party members. Though over the course of the war some judges became torn between their legal judgment and the state's National Socialist desires,[121] many judges came to see the legal department as a refuge from the oppression of domestic Nazi politics. The bureau's long time chief, Johannes Goldsche, was a veteran of the Prussian War Crimes bureau, and had little sympathy and less patience for the Nazis or their methods.[122] Further, far from being comprised of Nazi sympathizers, the Bureau's personnel records reveal that the legal department was actually home to a number of opponents of National Socialism. Helmuth James Graf von Moltke, a one-time bureau senior lawyer, was the founder of *Kreisauer Kreis*, one of the major anti-Hitler groups; he had argued during the war for the Germans to abide by both the Geneva and Hague conventions (setting out rules for legal war fighting), even though Berlin was party to neither. His views won him enemies in the regime and he was arrested, tried for treason, and executed shortly before the end of the war. Other senior officials, including Karl Sack and Rudolf Schleicher, were actually involved in the conspiracy to assassinate Hitler.[123]

Further, officers in the bureau who became too enamored with National Socialism were quickly identified and marginalized. Judge Otto Schweinsberger, for instance, refused to prosecute a German civil administrator in Russia who had murdered seventy-five Jews in the village of Balabanovka. He explained that he felt himself equally responsible as a National Socialist and as a judge, choosing to err on the side of his Nazi conscience. His attitude was highly disapproved of by his superiors, and he was removed from the case. Following the war, criminal proceedings were launched against Schweinsberger for his failure to prosecute the case, resulting in a two-year prison sentence.[124]

4) Trial Participants—A Commitment to Flexibility

You cannot miss the sky-blue, starched-stiff shirts worn by the stern-looking UN guards at the international courts in The Hague, Sierra Leone, and Tanzania. You can't but notice the polished, heavy wood defense and prosecution stands placed at a particular angle in each court, not to mention the sharp lines of the silk robes cloaking the unforgiving judges. It all seems so thought-through, so tradition-laden, so permanent. The gravitas is purposeful and impressive; however, it is troubling and has led to one of international criminal justice's most serious shortcomings: the self-developed perception of tradition and "correct" practice in the system when, in reality, very little settled precedent exists.

Successful war crimes trials in the domestic arena have almost invariably proceeded with an acknowledgment of this lack of tradition. Rather than showing a weakness or thinness of judicial procedure or legal thinking, such flexibility, in almost all aspects of war crimes trials, has proven beneficial. This flexibility can be illustrated by several specific questions, ranging from whom prosecutors choose to indict, to the timing of such an indictment, to the law used in a prosecution, to the end goal of such trials. While many in the international criminal justice field may believe that each query has a definitively correct answer, practitioners of successful war crimes trials know that allowing flexibility in their responses has been the only effective way forward.

Who Is Indicted?

John Cooke's place in history was confirmed in January 1649. The English Civil War was over, the Royalists had been soundly beaten, and the Republicans under Oliver Cromwell had taken control. As the solicitor general of England, Cooke was called upon by the House of Commons to file criminal charges against Charles I, who had been removed from office during the conflict and imprisoned in Windsor Castle. Before Westminster's decision to try Charles I, several kings had been deposed, and some kings had been executed, but until John Cooke stood before the 135 commissioners appointed as judges and jurors in Windsor Castle, the idea of actually bringing a monarch to trial for his crimes was novel, if not heretical. Many thought that the monarch was divinely appointed and hence immune to the whims of mere mortal justice. Cooke was unmoved by the unprecedented nature of his role and charged the king with being "a tyrant, traitor, murderer, and public and implacable enemy to the Commonwealth of England."[125] The proceedings began on January 2, and concluded by January 29, with the former monarch tried and convicted of treason and "high crimes." He was beheaded on January 30.

A century later, French king Louis XVI would meet a similar fate. Following the French Revolution, the French Republican parliament tried the deposed monarch. After a month-long trial for "high treason," Louis was sentenced to death on January 21, 1793.

Slobodan Milosevic, Charles Taylor, Augusto Pinochet, and Saddam Hussein have followed the lead of Charles I and Louis XVI, as deposed heads of state indicted for acts they committed against their own people and others. In each case there was real meaning to the fact that it was not just the foot soldier who wound up in the dock, but the tyrannical leaders who were called to account for crimes stemming, in the words of the Milosevic indictment, from "the natural and probable consequences of their commands."

Comparing the prosecutions of Charles I, Milosevic, and other leaders to those following a particularly distasteful spate of abuses committed by US servicemen in Iraq is jarring. In March 2003, Lynndie Rana England, a twenty-three-year-old reservist in the US Army, was serving in the 372nd Military Police company in Iraq. She was assigned to the Abu Ghraib prison complex in Iraq, a facility once favored by Saddam Hussein's regime and adopted by the occupying forces. Acting in a way that she would quickly come to regret, England and other military staff engaged in a series of sexually, physically, and psychologically degrading acts against her Iraqi charges. She was shortsighted enough to allow her colleagues to photograph her participating in many of the acts, including most infamously a picture of her holding a dog leash attached to a naked Iraqi prisoner's neck.

When the pictures came to light and a court-martial was ordered, England was one of the first to be charged. She was an easy target, a specialist (just above the rank of private), with reams of incontrovertible evidence allayed against her. She was found guilty, along with nearly a dozen other low-ranking soldiers, and only a few higher-ranking members, including Brigadier General Janis Karpinski.

The dichotomy between the leadership trial orchestrated by John Cooke and the largely low-ranking trials that marked the legal outcome of the Iraqi prison abuses raises the troubling question of who should be prosecuted. The purist might hope to bring all perpetrators to justice—"They always said: 'Hang all the people who committed crimes'"[126]—yet, given that many war crimes have thousands, if not tens of thousands of suspected perpetrators (as in Rwanda), some selectivity is evidently required. And indeed, in Rwanda there was a quick "realization that there might be too many." [127] The current canon of international criminal law recognizes this pragmatic necessity and has opted to try those "most responsible for the crimes," defining that enigmatic phrase to mean the highest political and military leaders who can be brought to the dock.

However, in so doing, supporters of international criminal justice have overlooked the fact that successful war crimes trials on the domestic level have usually fit somewhere between the head of state prosecutions of Charles I and the low-level soldiers charged with the Abu Ghraib abuses. Successful domestic war crimes trials have recognized that despite the majesty of literally putting *the* majesty on trial, there are risks to doing so and benefits of looking lower down the chain. The primary problem with prosecuting very senior individuals is not just that their power—or remnants thereof—may defeat such trials. Rather, for these individuals to be found guilty, a level of evidence is needed that may not exist. Whereas the crimes of Lynndie England were plain for all to see, the orders of her higher ups—and especially if intermediated by several ranks—are much more difficult to find, let alone authenticate. This is one reason that the trials against heads of state have been so complex, so expensive, and, in the end, often so unsatisfying. At the time of Milosevic's death, his trial had spread out over four years, had heard from more than three hundred witnesses, collected thousands of pieces of evidence, and cost more than $200 million—and was not yet finished when he died.

In each case of successful domestic war crimes prosecutions, the convening authorities have weighed the needs for justice against the desires of victims—many of whom may prefer to see lower-level perpetrators, not leaders, being tried—and the critical political issues of the impact of high-level prosecutions. This latter consideration is critical. Though historic, the early monarch trials led to serious backlash. The Charles I case created a martyrdom cult around the leader eventually allowing for the return of the monarchy. The death of Louis XVI set the stage for the rise of Napoleon and his own brand of absolutist tyranny. The line between effective punishment that teaches and deters and that which belittles and enrages is very hard to discern. With modern day war crimes in Africa, Asia, and Europe often implicating thousands of potential defendants, not everyone can be prosecuted. Successful war crimes prosecutors know that not everyone ought to be, and the decision as to whom to charge needs to result from careful analysis of the political and legal realities combined with the needs of victims and the larger society. The reflexive choice to charge the "most senior" might not always be the right option.

When Are Defendants Indicted?

"Justice delayed is justice denied," is a common maxim usually credited to nineteenth-century British prime minister William Gladstone. The phrase actually finds its roots much earlier, in the 1215 Magna Carta. In the United States, the framers of the Constitution adopted their own version, enshrining the right to a speedy trial in the Sixth Amendment. More than one hundred countries have since come to subscribe to an international treaty mandating that anyone arrested be "promptly" brought before a judge. While the necessity for quick justice seems intuitively satisfying, success in war crimes prosecutions has often relied on recognizing the countervailing concern of a "rush to justice."

In the war crimes context, domestic prosecutors have regularly been more apprehensive about justice being provided too quickly rather than too slowly. Once trials begin, haste is important, and delay—as seen in the UN courts—is very troubling. However, there is some doubt whether the international community's push to quickly pursue trials is always the best course.

Germany waited thirteen years after Nuremberg to start its domestic proceedings; South American states waited twenty years, or more, since the days of the juntas to begin proceedings against Augusto Pinochet, Guillermo Laborda, and others. France has only recently begun to address the crimes that occurred in Algeria during the conflict from 1954–1962. In November 2001, a trial began against General Paul Aussaresses for crimes the French general committed during the Algerian war.

While time may make some aspects of prosecution more difficult—as witnesses die and memories fade—in general, the longer one waits, the easier prosecutions will be. Moreover, it is not entirely evident how to measure the harm in waiting. Were the trials of Adolf Eichmann (twenty years after his crimes) or Maurice Papon (fifty years after his infractions) any less effective, important, or successful because they occurred so much after their crimes? This is hard to say and goes to the heart of what "success" means and what the goals of the process are. No universal answers exist to these questions. However, legally speaking, as there are no statutes of limitations for war crimes, there is no legal pressure to mount trials as soon as possible. And, more importantly, a rush to trial might actually provoke wider injustice.

In South America, prosecutions against the junta that ran Chile three decades ago are only commencing now—a travesty according to some. Yet, at the time of the junta's departure, Chilean society was too split and the military too strong to contemplate trials. It is widely agreed that had prosecutions been attempted immediately upon the fall of the generals, today's Chile—democratic, prosperous, and stable—would have emerged much more slowly, if at all. In the Argentine case, in which the generals were prosecuted immediately upon their departure from the political sphere, perhaps the pardons granted by President Menem would not have been needed had the trials been staged after the postjunta society had solidified. Similarly, that the Taylor trial in Sierra Leone had to be moved from West Africa for fear of instability suggests that timing might not be ripe. Interestingly, local West African leaders showed little interest in pursuing Taylor at the time. Liberian president Ellen Johnson-Sirleaf, whom one might think would have been especially keen to see Taylor prosecuted given the destruction he wrought as her predecessor, was concerned that a trial would make it more difficult to rebuild her state. It was only after she was pushed by the United States did she come to support the proceedings. And, even then she demanded that the trial not be held in her backyard.[128]

Once timing is decided upon, the next fundamental question relates to the legal basis for the trials. Are war crimes truly "international" crimes and thus only answerable under international law or are there appropriate and effective domestic analogs to international code that might prove more effective and more resonant?

What Law Is Used as the Basis for the Trials? Domestic or International?

In places, the "Wall"—alternately known as the "Apartheid Fence" or the "Security Barrier"—is a massive, ten-foot-high concrete structure, replete with guard towers, electronic monitoring devices, and a veritable moat on either side. The Israeli government began its construction in 2002 following a spate of particularly deadly terrorist attacks on Jewish civilians from terrorists who had traveled into Israel proper from the West Bank. The wall was designed to stop such incursions. As it winds back and forth over the demarcation line between Israel and the West Bank, the structure encircles Jewish settlements while limiting Palestinian access to thousands of acres of cropland, and makes some irrigation waters completely inaccessible to Palestinian farmers. For many Palestinians and Israelis, the imposition that the wall places on the average Palestinian is a war crime, a form of collective punishment explicitly condemned by the Geneva Conventions. With the aid of the Israeli advocacy group *B'Tselem* ("Human Dignity"), aggrieved parties in 2003 filed suit in an Israeli court asking that the wall be found illegal. Simultaneously, beginning a complex dance between international and domestic law, the UN General Assembly asked the International Court of Justice to rule on the wall's legality. What resulted was a clear indication of what sort of law has the most teeth.

By July 2004, the cases had wound their way through both the domestic and international systems. The Israeli and international courts, each relying heavily on international human rights law, ruled only days apart and arrived at the same verdict: at least some parts of the barrier were illegal and such segments needed to be altered if Israel was to act consistently with international norms. The immediate reaction to this accordance was not an agreement by the Israelis to follow the international decision. Rather, the government completely and explicitly repudiated it, and manifestly took to following the guidance of its own court, not the "foreign" laws of the ICJ. This was despite the fact that the requirements imposed by the decisions were actually more alike than different.[129]

The same sort of national protectionism also occurs in more explicit war crime prosecutions. Though the crimes of "genocide" or "crimes against humanity" have rhetorical bite, they arguably have less impact than domestic charges, which allege the same infractions but define the crime under domestic law. International criminal courts that have emerged since the Yugoslavia and Rwanda tribunals have invariably brought domestic law into the mix, with many explicitly designed to give domestic law, rather than international law, primacy. Domestic law has been included in international tribunals established to address Cambodia, Iraq, Sierra Leone, Lebanon, and East Timor. In the latter case, the Special Panels for East Timor invoked domestic law much to the chagrin of international observers, especially when trying individuals of various abuses that had clear correlates in international law. Yet, in so doing, the East Timorese asserted a measure of ownership over the crimes that were committed.

This reality makes one further doubt Antonio Cassese's argument that international courts are the best place to adjudge crimes such as genocide because they are "international crimes." They may be "international" crimes, but, as Eleanor Roosevelt said of "universal" human rights, they were committed "at home" and gain their meaning there.

Are "Criminal" or "Civil" Charges Filed?

On February 16, 1987, John Demjanjuk sat silently before the Israeli Supreme Court, looking uncomfortable in his brown prison jumpsuit. One year earlier, the retired Cleveland autoworker had had his US citizenship revoked and was extradited to Israel on charges that he was "Ivan the Terrible," a brutal SS concentration camp guard during World War II. To many observers the scene of Demjanjuk awaiting judgment before the court and in front of a nation of rapt viewers bore an uncanny resemblance to the war crimes trial of Adolf Eichmann who was brought before a Jerusalem court twenty-six years earlier. Both men sat ashen-faced before the court, their eyes hidden behind seemingly identical heavy, black-framed glasses. Despite their similarities, the two trials would have drastically different results: Eichmann was convicted of crimes against humanity and sentenced to death. Demjanjuk, however, despite being positively identified by nearly a dozen Holocaust survivors and being found guilty of committing extraordinarily savage acts of violence during the war, was released by the Israelis and returned to the United States.

Though Demjanjuk clearly deserved the harshest of criminal punishments, his case brings to light the limits, and problems, of charging someone with "criminal" wrongdoing.

While it may seem self-evident that war *criminals* ought to face criminal charges, there are risks to pursuing criminal prosecutions, which seek to incarcerate or execute offenders, and there may be benefits to filing civil charges, which usually seek to impose financial penalties on offenders. The principal hazard is that if a criminal case is to be fair the prosecutors have to face a greater risk of acquittal. In most systems the standard of proof required for criminal cases is much higher than for civil cases—in the United States and many other countries it is the difference between the onerous "beyond a reasonable doubt" that is needed to lock someone away, and the much less searching "preponderance of the evidence" that is usually needed to secure a civil conviction.

This proved the prosecutors' undoing in the Demjanjuk case. Assiduously following the strictures of criminal law, the Israeli Supreme Court acquitted Demjanjuk, despite the fact that the prosecution demonstrated that he was a Nazi death camp guard. The shortcoming in the prosecutor's case was his inability to show beyond a reasonable doubt that Demjanjuk was a *specific* guard. At the end of the trial, "the court retained doubt as to whether Demjanjuk was 'Ivan the Terrible' who held murderous sway at Treblinka from 1942–43, or another guard who served with equal violence during a similar period at Sobibor, Majdanek, and Flossenberg."[130]

A civil case against Demjanjuk, while also resulting in his release and likely not providing any financial windfall to victims (as he had little money), would at least have allowed his victims to legally brand him the perpetrator that he is. International criminal justice is solely a criminal system; there is no provision for civil crimes or punishments.

The Promise of Civil Prosecutions

In addition to the risks of acquittal in criminal cases, history demonstrates four decisive benefits of civil cases. Civil cases can be more effective in the search for truth, in the maintenance of peace, in the empowerment of victims, and in setting the stage for society's acceptance of more serious criminal charges.

For many supporters of international justice, the supposed ability for a trial to create an agreed-upon version of history, a true account of what happened, is one of the primary reasons such trials need to occur. However, in as much as trials are designed to provide societies and victims a fuller understanding of what happened, civil suits are almost always superior to criminal. As mentioned in chapter 7, the confrontational component of a criminal case is not conducive to full truth telling. Instead, if a criminal case is organized fairly, with the accused's rights accorded full respect, a wily defendant may be able to use the very procedures in place to protect his rights to delay and obfuscate, using the trial as a political soapbox while providing little to no information to victims. Civil cases, with lower stakes and more liberal allowance for admission of evidence, are much more effective in providing a full accounting of events.

The lower stakes of a civil case provide an additional benefit of civil prosecutions—they rarely imperil peace. War crimes most often occur during wider clashes. Peace treaties are regularly delicate and impermanent, often buttressed solely by mutual assurances of amnesties. Amnesties have long been a part of truce provisions for international conflicts (the 1783 Treaty of Paris that ended the Revolutionary War between the United States and Britain included one). They have been even more critical in securing the end to civil wars, which coincidentally are the types of conflicts in which a majority of the most gruesome war crimes have taken place. The English Indemnity and Oblivion Act in 1660, which saw the end of the English Civil War, provided amnesty to opponents of the monarchy for acts committed during the Interregnum. Moreover, both during and after the American Civil War, the Union provided an extensive amnesty to Confederate soldiers. Following the Finnish Civil War of 1916, both sides amnestied each other, forgiving those "who had behaved too severely." And, more recently, Angola, Algeria, Guatemala, Tajikistan, and Mozambique have all opted for similar official forgiveness following civil strife.

Criminal cases that strive to strip hard-negotiated amnesties may not only prolong the conflict, but may serve to break down any tenuous stability that might have been attained. For example, the investigations of the ICTY complicated a peace settlement between the Macedonian government and former Albanian guerrillas accused of committing atrocities. The settlement agreement paid heed to The Hague and granted the rebels an amnesty except for crimes indictable by the ICTY. The tribunal's subsequent decision to investigate rebel atrocities led the guerrillas to destroy evidence of mass graves, creating a pretext for hard-line Slavic Macedonian nationalists to renew fighting in late November 2001 and to occupy Albanian-held terrain. The same sort of reactions can be seen in ICC cases in which indictees have been unwilling to relinquish their arms so long as the international charges hang over their heads.

While potential criminal liability may provide renewed impetus for conflict, and even the commissioning of further war crimes, civil liability has proven less inflammatory. For instance, in Argentina, throughout the 1980s, prosecution of any members of the junta was impossible. However, civil lawsuits were allowed. In 1987, for example, Daniel Tarnopolsky sued Emilio Massera—one of the first leaders of the Argentine dictatorship—for damages resulting from the disappearance of his family in 1976.[131] The state consented to such efforts, with the view that they would not upset the fragile social and political balance established by the "Full Stop Law."

Further, civil cases have the added benefit that they can empower victims. By definition, civil cases against perpetrators are victim-instigated, rather than state controlled. This permits victims to determine the appropriate scope of legal culpability and to reach perpetrators that the state would otherwise prove unwilling to bring before a court. Such empowerment extends to the outcome of civil proceedings, which have often provided victims with things that criminal proceedings never could: admission, apology, and compensation. This is evident in Japan where despite Tokyo's continued refusal to hold criminal trials for World War II atrocities, since 2000 victims have filed civil suits against the state, officers of the Imperial Army, and Japanese corporations active during the war. One of the first targets was Kajima, a large Japanese construction firm that was an unabashed supporter of the Empire's expansionism during the 1930s and 1940s. In November 2000, defending against a victim's lawsuit, the company was forced to officially acknowledge that Chinese laborers were worked and tortured to death in slave-like conditions in its factories during the war. In an out-of-court settlement encouraged by the judge, the company offered $4.6 million to the victims' relatives. Other Japanese corporations have since been similarly compelled to acknowledge their wartime wrongdoing, many admitting to committing still politically sensitive atrocities during the Japanese occupation of Korea and northern China. While criminal trials have not been possible, the Japanese state and public have come to accept, and in some cases even applaud, the civil suits.[132]

A final benefit of civil lawsuits is the potential of such suits leading to the acceptance of more serious charges in the future. A common refrain heard in many states facing "international" criminal justice is that if only the international community had allowed or promoted the civil prosecution of war criminals first, the task of international criminal prosecutors would be greatly eased.

Those overseeing domestic war crimes proceedings have intuitively realized the power of civil trials to ease broader acceptance of trials, and the charges allayed in domestic prosecutions almost always include some financial crimes or other civil wrongdoings. For instance, the trial of Equatorial Guinea leader Macias is most well known for its inclusion of genocide and murder, but a crime that prosecutors focused equal attention on was that of embezzlement. In Mali, West Africa, former president Moussa Traore faced the courts twice—for crimes against humanity *and* embezzlement, with the latter proving more captivating for the domestic audience.

Some citizens of regimes that commit atrocities are even willing to overlook war crimes under the assumption that during war horrific acts will occur and all sides will be guilty of some violations. Yet, as Alex Boraine, a head of South Africa's Truth and Reconciliation Commission noted, "the same people will be far less patient with a leader who is charged with corruption and fraud."[133] This is even more the case for residents of postconflict countries, where an understandable self-interest can help turn the tide toward trials. The "average Serb citizen [was] interested in what Milosevic did to [them], not to others."[134] Milosevic stole billions,[135] and his government's chronic mismanagement and corruption halved Yugoslavia GDP during the 1990s and caused unemployment to explode to 40 percent.[136] At the time of his extradition many observers noted that more complete "revelations of his financial swindles and other abuses of power," with the backdrop of the economic basket case Milosevic had rendered once-robust Yugoslavia, would likely have "extinguished what[ever] remain[ed] of his popular following."[137] Had the Serb people come to understand the scope of Milosevic's theft—a likely result of the prosecution he would have faced at home if his Serb trial had been permitted to commence—war crimes "would no longer seem an affront to Serb nationalism." [138]

In addition to recognizing that the local community may have different interests than the international community in pursuing war criminals, domestic trials also have the flexibility to admit that "justice" is not the only goal of prosecution.

Is the Search for Justice the Only Goal of a Prosecution?

In July 2005, Ali Mohamed Osman Yassin, the Sudanese justice minister, told the British Broadcasting Corporation that his government had begun war crimes trials against nearly a dozen suspects accused of rape and genocide in Darfur. The timing of the announcement, coming just three weeks after the International Criminal Court began its own investigation into the events in Darfur, was, at best, suspicious.

Five years earlier, in 2000, the Croatian government announced that it was turning over a new leaf, no longer ignoring the war crimes committed during the Yugoslav conflict by Croats; within weeks dozens of trials went into preparation. The quick change in tactics, coming on the heels of a report by the EU that domestic trials against Croats were required before admission into the EU would even be considered, made the timing of the decision, as it was in Sudan, interesting.

Regarding the wider Balkan conflict, critics have complained vociferously about such "questionable" exercises of war crimes justice: the little that was reported on Bosnian Serb prosecution of Serb war crimes during and after the Yugoslav wars has almost always been qualified by the claim that the "only reason" Bosnian Serbs were pursuing trials was so that they "would give the impression" that they were "cracking down on war crimes."[139] Miroslav Panic, who campaigned unsuccessfully in a 1992 Presidential election against Milosevic, expressed full throated support for war crimes trials, but was pilloried by many ICTY supporters, angry that Panic was using the potential for trials as a weapon against the regime, rather than as a tool for attaining justice.[140]

In the eyes of judicial purists, each of these cases is troubling since in each, war crimes trials, and support for such trials, appear based at least partly on reasons other than the search for "true" justice. While it may be better if postconflict states were committed solely to justice in their pursuit of trials, it would be shortsighted to contend that domestic trials based on anything but the pure desire for justice are a sham. Clearly, some of the benefits of prosecutions nonetheless eventuate, even if justice is not the "goal" of the exercise. Moreover, demanding total devotion to justice in the execution of domestic war crimes trials by states is to demand more of such states than even the most consolidated, "rule of law" states demand of themselves.

In many contexts, it is viewed as a testament to the strength of a system of law if judges, lawyers, and law enforcement officials who do not agree with a law nonetheless enforce it. After all that is what the "rule of law" is. A nation of laws is one governed by edicts above individuals, and it is the following of laws, rather than the specific rationales for doing so, that makes a nation law-abiding. In domestic systems throughout the world, even laws that are widely disliked are not disregarded. And it is viewed as a triumph for law that institutions and citizens enforce such laws, even while endeavoring to have the law changed.

The good that can be accomplished by even a half-hearted devotion to following the rule of law is significant. That a dozen Indonesian soldiers were convicted during the Jakarta Trials, that the Leipzig and

Constantinople trials following World War I managed to prosecute—even if imperfectly—scores, and that the Palestinian Authority's "Security Courts" tried dozens of terrorists (for fear of Israeli reprisals), were all positive. In all these cases, undoubtedly guilty people were convicted, even if the underlying rationale for doing so was more politically motivated than judicially so.

Further, an orthodox view mandating the sole goal of "justice" for domestic war crimes prosecutions neglects the fact that international war crimes prosecutions have rarely been so pure. At the Tokyo Trials, the US occupiers chose not to prosecute Emperor Hirohito and the imperial family; this was not for reasons of justice. Several judges at the trials noted that the emperor was clearly guilty of war crimes.[141] Rather than justice, the Americans were concerned about their ability to occupy Japan and capture the Japanese people's hearts and minds. It was thought that this would be more difficult if their spiritual leader were facing charges.

Such mixed goals have been present not just in the actual process of international trials, but also in their pursuit. That is, in the international community's quest for "pure" war crimes justice, it has often resorted to means that have made justice subsidiary to other goals. For instance, once again in Serbia, it is evident that Belgrade's eventual transfer of Milosevic to The Hague had little to do with his, or wider Serb guilt. Instead, it was the product of Western pressure, domestic political calculation, and money—$1 billion in funds and loan guarantees.[142] Though The Hague was pursuing Milosevic for war crimes, the Serbian people, at least initially, were not focused on justice for justice's sake. They were focused on the ICTY's "justice" as a means to secure economic support for their devastated economy. Similarly, in Liberia, Washington threatened to "withhold economic life support" unless the government immediately pushed for a war crimes trial of Charles Taylor. Again it was not "justice," but self-interest that forced the Liberian leadership down the path toward a Taylor trial. The Liberian government had wanted to wait until the country was more stable before pursuing a trial but could not afford to do so.[143]

5) INTERNATIONAL ACTORS—ACTIVE, NUANCED PRESSURE

In the late 1950s, as the West German state was slowly coming to terms with German actions during World War II, domestic war crimes trials began. At first, there were few prosecutions, but very quickly they gathered steam. Five years later hundreds of trials were starting. Yet, as quickly as they started, domestic German debates erupted, regarding the wisdom of trying Nazi crimes. At the time, there was a legal limitation on prosecuting crimes more than twenty years after their commission. Many in West Germany, eager for the country to move on, wished to end trials as soon as the time had run out. Initially the *Bundestag* agreed and in November 1964, Parliament passed legislation ending the prosecution of Nazis as of May 1965—the twentieth anniversary of the end of World War II in Europe. Global reaction was swift, united, and intense, with states and international organizations explicitly condemning any enforcement of the new law. The international community was resolute that prosecutions needed to continue regardless the statute of limitations. Arguing that the statute needed to be rescinded, Morris Amchan, a deputy prosecutor at Nuremberg, set out the risks that West Germany faced if it decided to limit prosecutions through this "legal loophole":

> [The] recognition of [its] . . . moral obligation . . . has in large measure contributed to the acceptance of the West German Government in the community of nations. There is a real danger that this favorable image, so painstakingly created, may be wiped out by the termination . . . of the trials.[144]

The direct result of this fear of ostracism was that the West German parliament extended the statute of limitations until 1970. And when faced with another round of reprobation, extended the statute until 1979, when, under an onslaught of nearly one million postcards from around the world (a political campaign supported by diverse political figures from the United States and Europe) it finally scrapped all statutes of limitations for the Nazi crimes.

The German case represents one of the enduring truths about domestic prosecutions. While completely internationalizing criminal justice may produce problems, there remains an important role for effective, strategic use of international power in promoting *domestic* accountability for war crimes. If it had not been for the international community's pressure, Bonn may have ceased its trials shortly after they had begun.

More recent examples can be seen from the 1990s. In December 1991, when the first Croat "rebels" were captured in the Yugoslav civil war, Serbian military courts began proceedings against *both* Croatian POWs and a large number of Serbian irregulars accused of crimes against civilians. Many suggested that the "prosecution of Serbian irregulars was spurred by the contemporaneous arrival in Belgrade of a team from . . . [the international organization] Helsinki Watch, which [was] due to spend a month investigating allegations of massacres of Croats and Serbs."[145] Already the Serbs were concerned about their international image and the treatment of their own POWs, and adjusted their prosecutions accordingly.

Though it is a balancing act between needed aid and overbearing support, such helpful acts of internationals—both individual countries and/or groups of countries—have been important of their own accord and even more so in their instrumental effect in exerting pressure on some of the actors in the military, media, and others previously mentioned. Israeli actions created the fear of reprisals that led to Palestinian trials for terrorists; the threat of UN sanctions led to trials for Indonesian officers in Jakarta; the United States' Voice of America (and in particular its Radio Free Europe), BBC World Service, and Radio France Internationale have also proven critical in providing media coverage in many countries, resulting in internal pressuring for trials and proceedings to address war crimes.

Two means exist through which international actions have proven effective in fomenting domestic attention to war crimes. First, though it may be diminishing, at least historically, the prestige and gravitas provided with the "international" ensured a base level of civility in international dealings. Though wars break down this respect, it is interesting that what states may enthusiastically do in the domestic sphere, they often will not in the international.

For instance, during the Falklands engagement the Argentine army sought to largely fight a "clean war" against the British, and refused to stoop to war crimes. Yet, this was the same army that was simultaneously conducting a "Dirty War" (*Guerra Sucia*) at home throughout Argentina, against Argentines suspected of subversion.

The threat of reprisals is a part of this double standard, but there is something more to this policy than self-interested duplicity. Historically, the insertion of international actors into domestic relations has often led to gains for peace and stability, even if not justice. Peace negotiations and peacekeeping have often worked, in measure, because of the cachet of international involvement. The defusing of a likely war between Cameroon and Nigeria in 2004 over the disputed oil-rich Bakassi region would not have been possible without the insertion of the international community's good offices. This desire to curry favor with the international community is even more pronounced among weak states and new states, those most likely to be emerging from periods of mass violence and thus most likely to be involved in prosecutions.

The other way international actions have contributed to the occurrence of trials is by exerting pressure. This is directly linked with the threat of reprisals mentioned above, which has proven so effective in promoting trials and limiting the commission of war crimes. Of course the pressure of the international community is only as powerful as states fear the underlying threats. The kind of pressure chosen has proven determinative in eliciting the desired outcome. This can range in severity from ostracism to sanctions to physical threats; the past twenty years have seen the international community resort to each of these threats in order to pressure a state to deal with war crimes. It seems that ostracism, as was threatened in the German case above, has been amongst the most powerful of these tools, most often leading to the judicial response sought by the international community. Ostracism also appeared to work in Libya, as Gaddafi's pariah status only changed once he agreed to foreswear nuclear weapons and submit Libyans accused of the Lockerbie bombing to trial (though not in Libya). That ostracism is so effective is because it is so open to nuance and targeting. Physical threats and even "smart" sanctions, in contrast, have proven blunt tools that have provoked confrontation but rarely a change in policy that would bring about any trials.

The second instrument, that of sanctions, became a favored tool of the late twentieth century, but the evidence of sanctions leading to any effective changes in domestic policies—let alone domestic trials for war crimes—has been limited. Analysis of sanctions conducted in the late 1990s revealed that of the 115 cases of sanctions that had been imposed since 1945, only five could be considered "successful," in that they achieved the goals of the international community.[146] While sanctions against regimes have been instigated in order to push for a broader respect for human rights, there are no cases of sanctions actually being imposed and targeted in order to push for domestic trials. History suggests that sanctions are too unwieldy an instrument to compel meaningful trials. Moreover, as the UN "Oil for Food" scandal showed clearly, sanctions are often not an effective tool to diminish political leaders; rather they tend to strengthen their resolve while injuring the populace. Sanctions have been used prior to domestic war crimes trials—such as in Sudan and the Balkans—but not only were domestic trials not the stated goal of such sanctions, but it seems that it was the target states' concern for ostracism or violence (rather than the forced deprivations caused by sanctions), that was at the heart of their decisions to actually proceed with trials.

The final threat, physical harm to a country if such trials were not conducted, has historically led to no trials or to trials that are questionable. The former can clearly be seen in the unfortunate episode of the UN's attempted incursion into Somalia.[147] Operating under Security Council orders that "authorized the arrest, detention . . . trial, and punishment"[148] of armed factions plaguing the country, the UN launched a raid in October 1993 on the Olympia Hotel in Mogadishu. The result of the operation was not only a military failure, resulting in the deaths of many UN soldiers, but also a legal and humanitarian debacle. No trials ever eventuated, and the "declaration of war" by the UN obviated any trust that the factions had in the UN, which subsequently made the execution of the UN humanitarian mission all but impossible. The Somali case is a powerful example of the international community overstepping its bounds in the pursuit of "justice," without weighing the dangers of doing so.

As the Somalia case hinted, if the international community operates with too heavy a hand, there may be no justice, or a very troubled justice. The post–World War I trials in Leipzig and Constantinople, conducted by the losing powers at the insistence of the victors, are a powerful illustration of these concerns. Here, the victorious powers ratcheted up pressure on the Germans and Turks until prosecutions eventuated: the British occupied Istanbul with one million men and the French retook parts of the Ruhr Valley in retaliation for German intransigence in putting together the legal proceedings. Yet, the impact of such threats on justice were not necessarily positive. When operating under an explicit physical threat, it is difficult for domestic authorities to amass even the arguably minimal requisite local support needed to embark on the politically trying process of domestic trials.

A key problem with the World War I trials was that though they were officially "domestic" proceedings, the involvement of the international community was so direct and so overwhelming that they all but lost their domestic character. International needs were demonstrably more important than domestic ones.

This other problem of over involvement of the international community is apparent in the Nuremberg/Tokyo process and the Special Panels for East Timor. In both cases, international actors were so enmeshed in the trials that international political requirements trumped domestic prerogatives. In the post–World War II trials, this led to a mass release of convicted Germans and Japanese, due to political concerns. "The importance to the West of securing . . . German [and Japanese] support in the Cold War trumped the requirements of justice."[149] This history of politically driven commutation and amnesty made domestic trials in Germany a decade later much harder to stage and added to the difficulties of obtaining any admission from the Japanese state as to its wrongdoing.

In Indonesia, international involvement was significant but oscillated; various international actors, such as the UN and the United States, were explicitly committed to supporting the domestic proceedings but, at critical junctures, ignored requests for assistance. For example, in February 2003, the Special Panels issued an indictment against the former Indonesian minister of defense, General Wiranto. While the UN had taken credit for prior indictments, the organization distanced itself from this one. Unlike the other indictments, which had been largely against junior officials and members of local militias, Wiranto was a major figure in Indonesian politics and at the time of the indictment was gearing up to announce his candidacy for the Indonesian presidency.

Upon closer examination, it became evident that it was not the local prosecutors who spearheaded this indictment. Despite the fact that the prosecution office at the time was staffed by both East Timorese and UN internationals, the former were involved in prosecuting ordinary crimes while the latter were charged with addressing war crimes and other more serious infractions. As such it was almost certainly the work of the UN staff who opted to indict Wiranto. Thus it is not surprising that the East Timorese president distanced himself publicly by stating that he regretted the fact that the prosecution did not confer with senior government leaders prior to the issuance of the charges. The president further repudiated the indictment arguing that "it was not in the national interest to hold a legal process such as this one in East Timor."[150] The UN itself, realizing that it may have crossed a line, also stepped back and refused to support the charges, leaving the East Timorese prosecutors in a very awkward position. This combination of domestic and international derision led not only to a failure to bring Wiranto before the court, but also reduced the overall legitimacy of the enterprise. The overwhelming international aspect of the trials, while perhaps needed in part due to the state of the East Timorese justice system at the time, proved in the end one of the Special Panels' fundamental weaknesses.

As evidenced by trials in East Timor, in Leipzig, and in Constantinople, the international community must be clear and nuanced in its assistance; too little involvement, and there may be not enough pressure brought to bear to compel prosecution; too much involvement, and domestic resentment could make any real prosecutions all but impossible.

CONCLUSION—*PUTTING IT ALL TOGETHER*

No single approach is available that will encourage local war crimes trials in every instance. However certain facts suggest that formulas that would result in domestic war crimes proceedings could be fabricated nearly everywhere that war crimes have occurred and continue to be committed.

Of all the factors, the linchpin is the role of the international community, which can act irrespective of conditions on the ground. International actors are uniquely positioned and if their resources are used judiciously and strategically their power to promote meaningful trials is significant. The international community can remind offending militaries of the importance of pride and the threat of reprisals; it can aid the media in disseminating information by providing access to satellite feeds, radio broadcasts, and other tools; it can identify lower-level players who can run trials and protect them; it can promote the needed flexibility of trials by sharing best practices; and it can threaten ostracism to leaders who may remain obstinate.

Using the Toolbox

Very few states are completely bereft of the five characteristics described above; as such there is a potential for domestic war crimes trials in each. For example, in the Democratic Republic of the Congo—the source of one of the ICC's initial cases—there is instability and a weak justice system. But its president proposed establishing an international court to address the crimes in his country and the ICC has suggested that it could hold hearings in the country. And, indeed, some limited local trials have occurred. Together, these facts suggest that the idea of postconflict justice is neither anathema to the political and judicial leadership of the country nor is the security situation so fragile as to make more extensive trials impossible. In Sudan, where Khartoum's involvement in the Darfur genocide makes for a recalcitrant state regarding trials, it has been evident that when the international community has worked as one, the regime has quickly folded; its own "war crimes" trials, and the risk of economic sanctions given Khartoum's reliance on revenue from its petroleum, both provide openings for encouraging domestic justice. And, in Iraq, though the US-established Iraqi Special Tribunal (IST) is certainly a flawed entity, it has achieved a measure of support in the country. Many have concluded that the IST passes the "fairness" test,[151] with the real concern being security on the outside, rather than the structure of the tribunal on the inside. Regardless, the support for the idea that Saddam's henchmen should face justice provides once again an opening to have domestic proceedings, even if the IST would need reform in order to more effectively take on this task.

Potential is present in each of these cases. In order to more clearly see the survival of the possibility for domestic war crimes trials amidst unpromising surroundings, we need to look at a state that has been the target of international judicial institutions, but arguably did not need to be. It could have largely managed domestic trials on its own. Recognizing that all cases are unique, one can nonetheless establish a spectrum of states: on one side are those states totally decimated or occupied by protrial forces; on the other side are states that have remained intact after the violence and are reluctant to pursue trials. History provides several examples of each.

Postwar Germany and Japan were occupied by protrial forces (primarily the United States). Bosnia also fits into this category as it was "occupied" by the UN, backed by thousands of NATO, and more recently EU forces since 1995. A domestic war crimes court opened in Sarajevo in March 2004, the "State Court." Given the circumstances, the State Court's first director argued to me that his court could have been functional shortly after the bullets stopped flying. The UN could have provided the legal overlay, and the NATO troops could have provided aid in keeping the peace, and assisted in investigations and apprehensions. True domestic trials could have been started much earlier than they did.

There would have been difficulties if trials started in Bosnia in the immediate wake of the Dayton agreements. Supporters of moving trials to The Hague point to the recalcitrant Serb "entity" within Bosnia that proved so unwilling to give up the Yugoslavia tribunal's senior indictees: Ratko Mladic and Radovan Karadzic. But this obstacle to trials was clearly one of international will, not ability; NATO forces have been largely unwilling to aid in the capture of indicted war criminals, in the early days actually impeding the ICTY's efforts in the region. In one case, NATO personnel

> went as far as modifying a poster printed on the behalf of the ICTY. . . . The original poster identified all publicly indicted war criminals with their last known addresses. After journalists challenged the US military's claim that it had insufficient intelligence to arrest the war criminals by pointing to the addresses on the poster . . . [NATO] reprinted the poster without the addresses. The decision outraged the ICTY who asked that its logo be removed from the poster. At the end of this controversy, [NATO] [refused . . . even] to distribute the posters.[152]

In other cases, NATO soldiers subverted the ICTY by ignoring war criminals. According to William Stuebner, a former long-time Bosnia scholar at the US Institute for Peace,

> one indicted war criminal was living within one hundred meters of the British garrison in the town of Banja Luca, in Bosnia-Herze-

govina [but was not arrested]. Another got drunk over a bad conscience and tried to turn himself in at a Dutch checkpoint but was turned away because his picture didn't appear on the tribunal's 'wanted poster.' Still another reportedly thought it a big joke that he passed through an American checkpoint every day with a military ID card that clearly named him. . . . Italian peacekeepers literally [turned] their backs as a convoy carrying Radovan Karadzic came by with lights flashing, just so they wouldn't 'encounter' him. . . . Meanwhile, both Karadzic and Mladic—the two most wanted war criminals—were seen every day on the streets of the cities of Pale and Han Pijesek, in the French and American sectors respectively. [Neither were apprehended].[153]

The importance of whether the troops "encountered" Karadzic or Mladic came from the "bizarre operating procedures" under which NATO forces were permitted to detain war criminals they "encountered" but were not permitted to purposefully look for them.[154]

Evidently, political will has not been merged with military capacity in Bosnia, but it clearly could have been, and domestic trials of even senior leadership could likely have taken place.

Rwanda fits into the "decimated" category, and supporters of international justice ask how a destroyed state could possibly host such complicated and politically wrought trials. But here there was a missed opportunity by the international community. In the wake of the conflict, Rwanda explicitly asked for assistance to reestablish its justice system. It allowed international human rights experts into the country, worked with international legal experts to pass laws to proceed with trials, and balked at the notion of moving its justice outside the country. For Rwanda, it was an issue of capacity rather than ability or desire; and the international community chose to provide such capacity to the UN tribunal as opposed to domestic proceedings. The alternate path could have been chosen.

Even if a state, including a "failed" state or an occupied state, presents difficulties for promoting domestic war crimes trials, the most challenging case for promoting such trials is in a state undergoing or emerging from mass crimes that has nonetheless survived the tumult of violence intact. Such a state is less malleable, and if the state's citizens oppose trials, and if the state's political hierarchy could be damaged by such proceedings, pursuing prosecutions can not only be difficult, but dangerous. Yet, this was the case in Argentina, which had trials in the early 1980s. There, the largest obstacle to trials stemmed from the fact that the same military that was implicated in violations remained a force in the country. Those trials were successful and even if the convicted were subsequently pardoned, there was little doubt that the trials that were held provided a measure of real justice.

In more recent times, the state that is among the best examples of such a "challenging state" in which to promote domestic war crimes is the former Yugoslav state of Croatia. Croatia emerged from the Yugoslav wars as the only "winner" in the contest, with its president Franjo Tudjman the only leader during the Dayton negotiations able to consolidate the territorial gains he had amassed during the conflict (and during the commission of awful crimes). He returned from Dayton resolutely defending the "Homeland War" and all but refused to launch real prosecutions at home or to cooperate with The Hague. The populace appeared to support him, as did the still powerful military. Yet, all was not as it seemed, and the longing for justice was there. And, if the desire was not only manifest, but also acted upon in postwar Croatia, it is hard to see how such a desire or ability to provide local justice could be completely absent anywhere.

Chapter 9

CROATIA
Justice in the Shadow of
The Hague

The reincarnation of a Nazi-inspired state; a population awash in its own victimhood; a media muzzled; an army committing appalling war crimes; and a delusional, if not megalomaniacal, leader "advised" by a coterie of "yes-men"—these are hardly ideal building blocks for a state to justly and dispassionately host trials for both its citizen wrong-doers and those of the former enemy. Yet, in modern Croatia, which at its birth in 1991 was burdened by each of these handicaps, there have been real, fair trials, both during the Yugoslav civil war—which it so savagely contested—and ever since.

This shouldn't be surprising. A closer look at the state from 1991 reveals the continued presence of a military concerned about honor and reprisals. It also shows a media that, while hampered, refused to be fully cowed and remained committed to its professional role as a counterbalance to political power. Moreover, it also reveals a population increasingly tired of political grandstanding and mass corruption. In short, the ground was ripe for domestic trials. And, had the international community more closely examined the situation and helped to provide the needed catalysts, more trials would likely have occurred. The story of Croatian war crimes trials since 1991 is one of missed opportunities in forcing Zagreb's hand, and in the counterproductive mixed messages the international community has sent about Croatia's pursuit of local trials.

�֍

It was an unlikely invasion. In June 1972, a small group of young Croat émigrés—none older than thirty—then living in Australia, Sweden, and West Germany decided to foment a rebellion in Yugoslavia. With funds supplied from sympathetic Croats abroad, they amassed a small arsenal of rifles and machine guns. Fifty strong, they crossed the Yugoslav border from Austria undetected, and drove south to the forests near the town of Bugojno. Hoisting the independent Croat flag—the red-and-white checkerboard—they launched their attack.

Though Belgrade was startled by the attack, the revolutionaries were no match for the Yugoslav National Army, which quickly quashed the "invasion," killing as many as a dozen and wounding a dozen more.[1]

The goal of this quixotic enterprise was to wrest Croatia away from Belgrade's grip and reclaim Croatia's rightful place as an independent state. The invading men were the new generation of Ustasha, the Croatian nationalists who briefly ran an independent Croatia from 1941–1945. The young fighters thought it was worth sacrificing their lives to try to return Croatia to this glory.

Even from the standpoint of the 1970s, let alone from that of today, the "independent" Croatia for which these young men strived was a bizarre state to champion, let alone to die for. It was independent only in name—quite literally it was called the "Independent State of Croatia"—the kind of self-referential, self-description that remains the province of uncertain polities. It would be a stretch to call it independent at all, as it was run as a wing of the wider European fascist experiment, owing economic support to the Italian fascists and intellectual support and political allegiance to the Nazis. It is not coincidental that the term *puppet government* made its first appearance during this period. The leader of "Greater Croatia" was the quisling Ante Pavelic, a man who gladly did Hitler's bidding, and whose only visible concession to Croatian autonomy was to insist that his followers intone *Za dom!* ("For Homeland") and *Spremni!* ("We are ready"), instead of the German *Sieg Heil.*[2]

On top of its faux independence, "independent" Croatia was a certifiably genocidal state: it had the largest network of concentration camps outside Axis-occupied Europe, including the immense Jasenovac concentration camp, a complex of eight camps spread out over ninety-three square miles. Hundreds of thousands of Serbs, Jews, Romani, and others were enslaved, tortured, and slaughtered at the camp. Though as deadly as Auschwitz, Jasenovac was less mechanized; there were no ovens or gas chambers. The killings were accomplished by other various and brutal, barehanded methods including throat slitting, skull smashing, and mass hangings. So vile were some of the Ustasha's activities that Croatian Gestapo leaders even complained to Berlin about their "bestial manner."[3] On several occasions during World War II, the Nazis actually arrested and detained particularly infamous members of the Ustasha.

This was the state that the young invaders wished to resurrect.

Though the 1972 seccession attempt failed, the young Croat émigrés killed in the Bogojno woods in June 1972 did not die in vain. When Croatian independence finally did come in 1991, it came under the Ustasha banner. The leader of the successful independence movement was Franjo Tudjman, a historian by profession, who had fought against the Ustasha during World War II, but had become an ardent (if politically opportunistic) convert to the Ustasha movement later in life.

A Croatian nationalist who bridled at Belgrade's control, Tudjman had been jailed as a young man for questioning Tito's hegemony. Tito, who was Croatian born, deflated suggestions of autonomy for his birthplace partly by equating any "independent" Croatia that might emerge with Ustasha terror. Tudjman began to question how bad the Ustasha had been, becoming increasingly convinced that Serb ideology and Serb memory, and Tito's Yugoslav ideal, had perverted the truth. Tudjman's 1989 book, *Bespuća Povijesne Zbiljnosti* (*The Horrors of War*), was a culmination of this thinking, setting out a long (and to many Croatians, convincing) argument that the reported casualties of Serbs, Jews, and others during World War II in the Independent State had been grossly inflated. Tudjman doubted the wholesale slaughter that had occurred under Croatia's watch, and in particular doubted the scope of devastation that had occurred at the Jasenovac camp. Far from the camp's being a part of the Croatian death machine, he claimed that Jasenovac was a simple detention facility actually run by a clique of Jewish prisoners and it was they who had murdered fellow Serb and Romani inmates. He wrote that "[a] Jew is still a Jew. Even in the camps they retained their bad characteristics: selfishness, perfidy, meanness, slyness, and treachery."[4]

Not all Croatians during World War II were Ustasha and there were a sizeable number of partisans, including Tudjman, who had fought against the Nazis. Yet, in a feat of impressive political engineering, Tudjman was able to leverage the Ustasha philosophy, recast it as uni-fyingly Croatian and Catholic, in contrast to the predominantly Serb and Orthodox that prevailed in other parts of Yugoslavia, to bring Croatia together. He spouted that all Croats were equal victims, not of the Nazis, but of the Yugoslav state and especially of the Serbs. He con-tended that the independence Croatia enjoyed all too briefly in the 1940s needed to be reclaimed in order to avenge this suffering. These arguments resonated with a large proportion of the populace. Resur-recting the symbols of the Ustasha period—including the formerly shunned red-and-white checkerboard flag, Tudjman rallied the Croat-ians to reclaim not just Croatian independence but also all of the lands that had historically been Croatian. One of the results of this strategy were the 1995 military operations, "Lightning" and "Storm." The two operations, the first occurring in May and the latter in August, suc-ceeded in pushing Serbs from the crescent-shaped country, making formerly pluralist Croatia more than 90 percent "pure."[5]

Once independence had been won, Tudjman continued his re-habilitation of the Ustasha, now with the full machinery of government behind him. The Yugoslav *dinar* was replaced with the *kuna*, the cur-rency the Fascists had introduced in the 1940s.[6] Tudjman's government "granted Fascist veterans lavish benefits, invited them to military cele-brations and glorified [their] . . . fighting prowess."[7] The new regime filled leadership posts with former Ustasha and their sympathizers.

"Vinko Nikolic [a leading Ustasha ideologue] was given a seat in Parliament. . . . Mate Sarlija [a senior Ustasha officer] was made a general. . . . And former Ustasha commander in Dubrovnik, Ivo Rojnica" was appointed an ambassador.[8] Not surprisingly, members of parliament and cabinet ministers publicly defended and praised the Ustasha.

Tudjman went further. He saw to it that history books "were rewritten, the name of the Square of the Victims of Fascism in Zagreb . . . changed . . . 3,000 anti-Fascist monuments were destroyed,"[9] and the president "defiantly named streets in Zagreb after officials of the pro-Nazi regime that ruled Croatia as Hitler's handmaiden."[10] Of note, Tudjman was particularly keen on renaming streets and buildings after Mile Budak, who had written the Ustasha's anti-Semitic codes.[11] In ways almost too numerous to count, the Croatian Fascist state of World War II was recreated, and became "the foundation on which today's Croatia was built."[12]

All the while, Tudjman built up an increasing cult of personality, often ostentatiously adopting the image, and even the persona, of Tito—of whom he modestly said was the "greatest Croatian politician ever . . . until Tudjman, that is."[13] Simultaneously, Tudjman set about the continued eradication of Tito's multiethnic Yugoslavia. Tudjman moved into Tito's villa on the Croatian island of Brioni; he was "fond of going to the wine cellar and getting a vintage bottle from the year of his guest's birth"—which Tito had been known to do—and took to wearing white military dress uniforms (Tito's trademark).[14] Tudjman's accouterments were so heavily festooned with gold braid, ribbons, self-awarded medals (nine of them), and sashes that Franz Vranitzky, the former Austrian chancellor, once remarked that he "pranced around in the sort of fantasy uniform not even seen in the Vienna opera."[15] Added to his own sartorial style, he dressed his personal guards in red and gold tunics—"mock historical garb"[16]—to watch over the Zagorje Villa, his official Zagreb residence (a mammoth home overlooking the capital that had been owned by a Jewish family prior to World War II and which he renamed the "Presidential Palace"). He dipped into state coffers to purchase a $14 million Learjet and a fleet of two hundred

BMWs for official use—"you need something comfortable," explained Branimir Jaksic, Tudjman's deputy chief of staff. A large entourage accompanied him while he traveled, with red-carpet treatment mandated for his arrivals.[17]

State media were fawning. Official sycophants replaced many journalists, and Tudjman's hangers-on consistently threatened those who dared question the government. July 1991 saw Ante Beljo, the party secretary, lash out at media outlets that did not toe the party line, warning that "some newspapers and journalists do not respect the sovereignty" of the republic and that "the people are dissatisfied" with the reporting of some dailies.[18]

When some in the media refused to back down, Tudjman raised the stakes. His stratagems were novel, even if clumsy: in one case, to combat one independent-minded paper—the city of Osijek's *Glas Slavonije*—the Tudjman-allied local government counterproductively bought up a full page ad in the newspaper itself calling for readers to boycott the newspaper.[19] When such ham-handedness failed to either reign in the paper or to scare off its readers, Tudjman arranged to remove editors of major papers under the guise of patriotism—he tried to conscript troublesome journalists into the Croatian army.[20] Though similarly practiced by some of his Balkan adversaries,[21] this move was also so bald-faced that he was forced to step back. However, he did pursue a "privatization" program that managed to either force media to fold—as occurred with *Danas*—or to relinquish control over a paper to a government-appointed "administrative council" putatively in preparation for full privatization.

He branded the *Feral Tribune*, a particularly critical publication, "pornography," thereby burdening it with a 50 percent excise tax. Tudjman also decreed a draconian press "freedom" law that threatened to incarcerate perpetrators for up to three years for libel or insult. Tudjman then began to sue journalists and publishers. At one point, the *Feral Tribune* was forced to defend thirty suits. Other papers were also sued, such that within a year of the law's passage there were almost "500 cases against Croatian journalists . . . pending[, including] . . .

140 criminal libel cases. The total damages . . . sought [were] over $13 million."[22]

Yet, at each stage of Tudjman's crackdown on the media, he met with dissent. Despite his attacks, the media remained, and the potential for domestic war crimes trials—which Tudjman vociferously regaled against—grew.

Under the onslaught, the media actually increased their attacks on the regime, often exposing war crimes and agitating for trials. *Danas* and *Slobodna Dalmacija* were particularly known for "their biting criticism and satire . . . aimed personally at Tudjman and his administration."[23] The *Feral Tribune*, however, was in a class by itself and through the wonders of Photoshop was perhaps the most skilled at skewering Tudjman's views of himself and history. Thus, recalling the less than heroic history of Ustasha Croatia, and the growing dictatorial tendencies of their current president, the *Tribune* published actual elementary school class pictures of Tudjman, Hitler, and Stalin—each coincidentally occupying the same position in their respective photos. Above the three, the paper ran the headline: "Great Leader, Top Row, Center." And, Tudjman's "peripatetic political love life"—in which he moved allegiances between Serbian Slobodan Milosevic and Bosnian leader Alia Izetbegovic and then back again depending upon his mood and fortunes on the battlefield, invited front page spreads of Tudjman and his current "love" in bed together naked, with a headline asking "Is This What We Fought For?" The print media was not alone; broadcast media was also strident in its opposition: satellite television was out of the government's reach and even terrestrial radio remained. Radio 101 stayed on the air and Tudjman's primary adversary, Vladimir Gotovac, often claimed on the air that the media, army, and police had become politicized and undemocratic.[24]

The wider citizenry also found Tudjman's excesses objectionable, and many ridiculed the press freedom rule. One prominent Zagreb lawyer said publicly that the law "would only be valid . . . in 1936, in the Soviet Union." And cognizant of the financial pressures that Tudjman placed on the media, many readers began to regularly buy multiple copies of their favorite publication.[25]

The art scene also remained an opposition force, satirizing the regime as often as it could. *Spikom na Spiku*, a play lampooning Tudjman, was staged in Zagreb and in one memorable scene had Tudjman worshipping at Tito's feet—it became one of the longest lasting and popular productions of the early 1990s.

The judiciary, both in lower and higher courts, also refused to break. The Supreme Court overturned Tudjman's designation of the *Feral Tribune* as pornographic. Judges also made sure that no libel/insult case succeeded. The government won no significant cases brought under the "freedom" act directed at the media.

Finally, the Croatian military remained an independent force, angered by Tudjman's refusal to recognize the violations committed in Croatia's name by allied "paramilitary groups." Such paramilitaries were the instigators of the Ahmici massacre in April 1993, in which nearly one hundred twenty Muslims were slaughtered by a Croat force, destroying all homes and the village's two mosques. Many commanders in the regular forces were appalled at the wanton destruction. They urged Tudjman to allow a war crimes enquiry, saying that the Croatian army would never "make excuses for criminals within us."[26] The importance of "honor," especially for a new military such as Croatia's, was critical.

These pressures were present during the war and increasingly so after the war. War crimes trials have been held during both periods. At times Tudjman evidently viewed the trials through the lens of political opportunism rather than justice, but real trials nonetheless took place.

DURING THE CONFLICT

Two months prior to declaring independence in June 1991, Tudjman had already begun his assault on Yugoslavia and especially the Serbs, using law and the threat of war crimes prosecutions as instruments of attack. In April, before an attack on a Serb position in Plitvice National Park, Tudjman launched a distinctly legal volley. He forwarded eighteen Serb names to the local Croatian prosecutor in Karlovac, charging the Serbs with the violation of armed rebellion and the war crime of "waging an illegal war."[27] In September 1991, Croats also attempted to use the law to evict the remaining Yugoslav soldiers from their territory. This resulted in several Serbs being court-martialed as Zagreb claimed that their uninvited presence on "sovereign Croatian land" was a violation of the laws of war.

By 1992, more explicit charges of war crimes were being lodged and not just against Serbs. In October 1992, Zagreb issued arrest warrants for four leaders of a Croatian paramilitary group, charging them with war crimes violations for activities in Bosnia.[28] The law was also abused in this early process. This is best exemplified by Zagreb's mid-1992 claim that the government was planning to prosecute twenty thousand Serbs in Croatia for war crimes. Not only was there scant evidence of any crimes committed by the vast majority of these Serbs, but it was obvious to all observers that the real goal of Tudjman's mass trials would be to limit the movements of Serbs out of the Serb "zones" within Croatia for fear of arrest and prosecution.[29]

Yet some focus on law was bona fide. It may seem incongruous, but during this early period, Tudjman took real steps to investigate and prosecute war crimes. Nineteen-ninety three was a banner year in this regard. Following the formation of the political opposition's human rights committee,[30] Croatia seemed more amenable to the necessities of human rights law and even allowed the UN into the country to investigate war crimes committed by Croats.[31] The nongovernmental Croatian Helsinki Committee—which was established to monitor such abuses—was also active during this time, and released scathing reports about war crimes committed by Croats as well as the government's failure to adequately intervene to bring an end to Serb suffering in the country.[32]

In April 1993, Croatia adopted a new criminal code that specifically targeted war crimes. In its list of offences the code included "most parts of the major crimes against international humanitarian law."[33] The final "human rights" event of 1993 was the December publication by the

Croatian Supreme Court of data on war crimes trials held between January 1991 and November 1993. Interestingly, for a judiciary that many believed had been browbeaten by Tudjman's cronies, the report was frank and did not show the government in the best light. It even provided a refreshingly honest rationale for why the report was being published: apparently Tudjman's government was extremely sensitive to "sensationalist reports in the media of alleged deliberate persecution in trials of Croatian citizens of Serb nationality."[34]

The Court reported that 14 cases, covering 38 people, had been completed that were based on violations of "humanity and international law."[35] Only 20 of the people were definitively of Serb nationality. However, 37 of the 38 were not in custody, and the trials were conducted in absentia. The one trial that was conducted with a defendant present was against a Croat, and he was convicted for committing crimes against prisoners of war and sentenced to 14 years. The Court acknowledged a heavy emphasis on Serb defendants, admitting that even if only 20 were definitively Serb, most of the "unknowns" were likely Serb as well. However, Croatia attempted to mitigate this seeming bias in a persuasive manner. Shortly thereafter, Croatia passed an amnesty law that dealt with criminal acts committed in armed clashes—these acts, though illegal, did not rise to the level of war crimes. Nevertheless, the amnesty law resulted in the suspension of nearly four thousand trials, with the vast majority of beneficiary defendants being Serb.[36]

In the lead up to the Dayton Agreements in November 1995, however, the situation regarding war crimes and the rule of law deteriorated. Authorities stepped up prosecutions, both against those "taking part in the armed rebellion against the Republic of Croatia" and those engaging in war crimes against Croats, which almost always were Serbs. Tudjman used the law to harass Serbs, for the sole purpose, said Veljko Dzakula, the head of the Serb Democratic Forum in Croatia, of purging them from the country.[37] Thus, the increasingly frequent war crimes charges were a key component of this strategy, leading to many cases, including one mass case in the seaside town of Zadar where 18 rebel Serbs, 17 in absentia, were sentenced to prison terms ranging from 10 to 20 years for killing 43 Croatian villagers in 1991.[38] The Serbs, now convicted, would not dare return.

The situation was not all negative for the Serbs in Croatia. Many Serbs, including Dzakula, were granted Croatian citizenship,[39] and during the 1995 election, Serb candidates for the Croatian parliament vigorously and openly campaigned with few reported imposed limits.[40] The 1995 elections were also noteworthy for their manifestation of just how weak Tudjman's base of support really was. Despite controlling most news media, his party only barely held its parliamentary majority, and lost in almost all major urban centers, including Zagreb. An opposition politician was appointed mayor of the capital, but Tudjman, for months, refused to let him take his post.[41]

During the war, there was dissent, there were cases of fair trials, and there was clear evidence that Tudjman and his regime could be pressured via concerted international effort. There were many parts of the Croatian state—including parts of the judiciary—that were, however, unwilling yet to take on war crimes. In June 1994, Milan Vukovic, then president of the Croatian Supreme Court and head of the state commission on war crimes, contended that "war crimes did not happen on the Croatian side."[42] However, for each Vukovic, there were others, perhaps lower in the judiciary and political establishment, who did not see the world so simply, and who knew that some of what happened in the war had been perpetrated by Croats. They wanted to act, and given Tudjman's weaknesses and the presence of elements in Croatian society who similarly wished trial to occur, the ground was thus sufficiently fertile to enable domestic judicial efforts once the bullets stopped flying.

TRIALS POST-DAYTON—WHO WAS DOING WHAT? (1996–2000)

Of the three leaders who were sequestered at Wright Patterson Air Force Base outside Dayton, Ohio, during November 1995, it was only Franjo

Tudjman who would emerge truly "victorious" after the Peace Agreements were negotiated. For Milosevic, Dayton was a bitter pill, forcing him to concede the break up of Yugoslavia and the massive decline of Serb power and esteem. For Bosnian leader Izetbegovic, he may have legally secured a "sovereign" Bosnia, but he knew that his borders were porous and his nominally triethnic government was irreconcilably divided; more than a decade later the country remains a ward of the West and faces the chronic potential of violent dissolution.[43] However, for Tudjman, Dayton was a solidification of the territorial and national goals that he had sought since his youth—the 1972 "invaders" were finally avenged. Dayton cemented Croatia's "historical borders" and officially welcomed the state into the community of nations.

Tudjman returned to Zagreb a conquering hero with renewed political power. He immediately began to use some of that political capital to erect obstacles to war crimes prosecutions. Consequently, this period, from post-Dayton until Tudjman's death nearly four years later, is usually regarded as the most unlikely time to have forced Croatia's hand to investigate and prosecute her own crimes. It was during this period that Croatia became more assertive as an independent state, more sophisticated in its arguments denying that Croatians perpetrated war crimes, and more devious in its relations with the Yugoslavia tribunal in The Hague. Through a combination of legal and political chicanery, and, according to some at the ICTY, significant actions by official government and intelligence officials, Tudjman guided his state such that it would avoid accepting culpability for war crimes, while deftly shifting all the blame to the "clear" perpetrators of the misdeeds: the Serbs.

Yet, much like in the early period, the situation was significantly more nuanced than it may have appeared. Tudjman's "unassailable" position was far less secure than his bluster suggested. He and his top advisors were buffeted by increasing dissent and dissatisfaction at home—regarding war crimes and other issues—and, perhaps most violently, by outside forces that time and again forced a weak and still-ostracized Croatia to do their bidding. At times, this included cajoling

Croatia to hold war crimes trials. Thus, it might appear counterintuitive for Tudjman to make one of his first post-Dayton acts the passage of a further amnesty law[44] that again primarily benefited Serbs. Tudjman even arranged for the "voluntary" surrender of some of his generals to the ICTY. Yet, both of these acts made a great deal of sense in light of the "real" position and harsh realities that Croatia faced.

Though external pressure was critical, it was those inside the country who truly realized the weakest links in Tudjman's leadership. Again the media was critical, and it is enlightening that the vast majority of stories and articles in the still-independent press that rankled the leadership were those that questioned the "glories" of Croatia's past. Tudjman was a professional historian, and he knew the political value of history—and in particular, a carefully crafted historical narrative of Croatian struggle and victory—to his pan-Croatian cause. Ironically, it was history—both the recent war and the more distant activities of the Ustasha—that provided ready fodder for the press to attack. Tudjman was fast losing ownership of *the* history that served as the basis for his Croatia. It would soon become even more tenuous, and domestic trials legally impugning this history would soon become a reality to Tudjman's evident chagrin.

A Croatian Nazi in Argentina

With the celebration of Ustasha history so central to the emergence of modern Croatia, the emergence of the Dinko Sakic affair in 1998 stunned many observers. Sakic was a Croatian who had emigrated to Argentina in 1947 and had lived anonymously among the thousands of Central and Eastern European immigrants who flooded the country in the wake of World War II. It is unclear why he broke his silence after five decades of Argentine life, but in April 1998, he gave an interview to a Buenos Aires television station in which he detailed his Ustasha past and, more importantly, revealed that he had been a commandant of the Jasenovac camp. He was unrepentant, telling his interviewers that he "[slept] like a baby, [and if he] were offered the same post today, [he] would accept it."[45]

That the Argentines were quick to act against Sakic is not surprising—the state was eager to shed its image as a haven for Nazis. However, the speed with which the Croatian government demanded his extradition was striking. By April 10, *four days* after Sakic's interview was broadcast, the Croatian ambassador to Argentina announced that his government "will solicit the extradition of Dinko Sakic so that he can be tried" in Zagreb.[46] The Argentines were only too willing to hand their émigré over, and both Sakic and his wife (also implicated in Jasenovac crimes) were quickly transferred to Croatian authorities. The trial began in May and concluded in October with a resounding conviction and a twenty-year sentence.[47] With a clear eye on the Yugoslav wars, Chief Judge Drazen Tripalo said that the court "hope[s] that the sentence—made fifty-five years after the events—will be a warning that all those who committed crimes in the near or distant past will not escape justice."[48] Upon appeal, the Croatian Supreme Court upheld the verdict in October 2000.[49]

The story of how the Sakic case arose so quickly and forcefully, despite its clear impact on Tudjman's nationalist philosophies, says much about how domestic courts may have been ready to handle 1990s Yugoslav war crimes cases earlier than anyone believed. Tudjman knew Sakic; the president had made a state visit to Argentina in 1994 and the two had enjoyed a "friendly meeting."[50] Noting his warm relationship with the president, Sakic was interviewed by a Croatian magazine shortly after Tudjman's visit. In the interview, Sakic expressed pride in his wartime record and regret that more Serbs had not been killed at Jasenovac. Tellingly, that interview was published in Croatia but passed with little notice; however it did pique the interest of Nazi hunters from the Simon Wiesenthal Center, which began putting pressure on Croatia to address its Ustasha past. Nothing happened until the Argentine television interview three years later. Following the broadcast of this interview, immense pressure from European and other Western states rained down on Tudjman. The Croatian president openly admitted that he indicted Sakic solely to placate his Western backers.[51]

Yet, even when Sakic arrived in Croatia, his trial and conviction were not a foregone conclusion. Nationalist support for him was strong, and there were acts of violence (and many more threats of such violence) against people who wanted to testify against him. As Croatian writer Slavenka Drakulic put it:

> many of the witnesses who originally said they remembered seeing Mr. Sakic supervise killings and torture . . . suffered a sudden lapse of memory. All that they [recalled] . . . is that he had an impeccable uniform and shiny boots. Several of them [admitted] . . . that they changed their testimony after they received . . . death threats.[52]

During each day of the trial, the courtroom was filled with nationalist supporters, and defendant Sakic would often lead them in threatening jeers at those witnesses who claimed to have seen Commandant Sakic's handiwork. Despite these difficulties, the Zagreb County Court, and in particular presiding judge Drazen Tripalo, ran what is widely believed (even in Croatia) to be a fair trial. The court took pains to assure the health of the elderly defendant, giving him any needed medical treatment and assuring his fitness to stand trial.[53] Sakic's wife, Nada, who had also been indicted and against whom there were very plausible accusations of participation in some of Sakic's acts, was acquitted due to scant evidence.[54] Further, the court admitted that the quality of some witness testimony was low (perhaps due to the threats) and thus the exact scope of the crimes committed at Jasenovac on Sakic's watch was not known—"several thousand" deaths were all that the court could definitively account for.[55] Moreover, Sakic was allowed to appeal to the Supreme Court, and it appears that he had as fair a hearing at the appellate level as he had received below. Tudjman was intent on making sure that the international community believed the trial was fair, and even invited observers who could hardly be considered unbiased toward Sakic. For example, Tommy Baer, the honorary chairman of B'nai B'rith

International (one of the world's largest Jewish welfare organizations), was present through much of the proceedings, and stayed in Zagreb as a personal guest of the Croatian president.

An enlightening postscript to the trial is what happened to the participants in the proceedings. It is often thought that even if brave government officials (be they lawyers, judges, or army officers) have been able to stand up to states unwilling to address their war crimes past, such officials do so at their own risk and regularly suffer severe consequences. Historically, officials in such circumstances have often felt negative repercussions. Many Argentine officers stationed in the Falklands refused to follow their illegal orders to commit war crimes; yet, once they returned to Argentina they were punished and removed from the army. However, the opposite seems to have been true in Croatia. No matter how devastating the proceedings were for the Tudjman government, the Sakic trial did not mark the end of Chief Judge Tripalo's career; rather, he kept his post as the president of the Zagreb County Court and in 2004 was even appointed to the Croatian Supreme Court.[56] He was celebrated for having both managed the trial despite pressure exerted on him and for issuing an appropriately severe sentence. Tripalo's outcome is no different from that of many of the judges who repeatedly ruled against Tudjman's excesses. Marin Mrcela, for instance, who ruled against Tudjman in several of the leading libel cases against media outlets, also remained in office. He became a champion of a free press and, in endeavoring to help members of the media who were sued by the state, he authored the *Journalist's Guide to Criminal Court Proceedings*. He too remained a judge at the Zagreb County Courthouse—the most prestigious and important of the district courts in the country—which is where he worked when I met him in the summer of 2005.

Given the sensitivity of the topic—directly questioning the Ustasha past—several factors had to come together to make the Sakic trial possible. First, as is evident by Tudjman's weak support for the legal process, the number and seniority of officials actually needed to prosecute Sakic was rather low. What the state did not provide was compensated for by what was provided by concerned members of the international community: pressure to hold the trial and oversight to ensure its fairness. Acting in difficult conditions and directly against the wishes of senior politicians and military leaders, diligent members of the judiciary nonetheless staged a trial—often under threats to their safety, and with only scant resources—that rivaled the complexity of some war crimes cases held at The Hague.

Second, Tudjman was honest in his assessment that even though he would have rather let Sakic live out his life in Argentina, he was compelled to indict him due to international pressure. At the time, Croatia was in a very weak position and thus highly susceptible to such pressure. The Croatian economy had been devastated by war and Zagreb was eager for private sector investment as well as loans from the International Monetary Fund, the World Bank, and the European Bank for Reconstruction and Development. It desperately wanted to solidify its long-held belief that it was a Central European state, rather than a Balkan one, and so it looked hopefully at Brussels and the potential of EU membership. Brussels was also in Zagreb's gaze due to NATO: membership in NATO would help to cement the new Croatia, definitively turning its back on its Slavic, Communist past. Croatia was also especially solicitous of Germany. Berlin had, after all, been the first state to recognize Croat independence and had dragged the remainder of Western Europe and then the United States into accepting Croat sovereignty. What the Sakic case reveals most clearly, is that a firm and consistent message from the international community—in any of its guises—was an effective tool in compelling Croatia to legally address a past that it wished to forget.

The international community would consistently play a role from 1991 until today, regularly impacting trials through a heady combination of financial inducements and the carrot of international acceptance. For instance, in May 1997, Croatia agreed to extradite another indictee to The Hague, but only after "Washington had made clear its displeasure at Croatian foot-dragging by instructing US representatives at the IMF to abstain on the vote which approved a $500 million

. . . loan."[57] The Americans were forceful and direct in communicating the fact of the quid pro quo between war crimes prosecution and greater integration into the West's political, economic, and security establishments.

In October 1997, when ten Bosnian Croats "surrendered themselves" to The Hague—including Dario Kordic, who was one of the highest-ranked Bosnian Croats to be indicted—there was again clear evidence that Croatia's hand had again been forced by economic and diplomatic pressure which had emanated from Brussels and Washington.[58] The surrender followed directly from the increased explicit pressure international actors placed on Croatia to live up to its Dayton commitments,[59] and lower-key nondiplomatic threats made by senior American officials—including Ambassador-at-Large for War Crimes David Scheffer and others—that noncooperation could lead to sanctions.[60]

Most notably, EU accession negotiations were stalled while Croatia appeared to be actively assisting General Ante Gotovina—a senior ICTY indictee—in his continued evasion of The Hague. Accession negotiations finally resumed in late 2005, not coincidentally nearly simultaneous with Gotovina's capture in the Canary Islands, which was made with the assistance of Croatian intelligence.[61]

Apart from Croatia bending to the will of the international community, there were more developments within the country that also promoted the possibility of fair trials. The Bajramovic case (discussed in the previous chapter) was a marker both of Croatia attempting to more honestly deal with its war crime past, but also of the uniquely nonlegal issues that drove public support for trials. Bajramovic was the Croat who admitted to directly killing seventy-two people during the war and whose unit was involved in an ethnic cleansing program that executed four hundred Serbs. Bajramovic's arrest and subsequent trial were widely celebrated through Croatia. On closer analysis, it appears that the rationale for Bajramovic's admission coincides with another potential inroad that could have encouraged prosecutions.

When asked why he agreed to the interview with the *Feral Tribune*, Bajramovic admitted that he did not have any money and was upset about the corruption that had enriched so many of Tudjman's associates, who themselves had been involved in war time violence. "I was silent about this for a long time, expecting that someone in this country would remember that I exist. . . . [Yet,] my children eat just like [member of parliament Tomislav] Mercep's do, yet he has two houses in Zagreb, two apartments and a house on [the Adriatic resort island of] Brac, and he came from Vukovar without a kuna in his pocket."[62]

The unity created by independence was fraying under the realities of Croatia's stagnant economy and the clear, ever-enriching kleptocracy that was running the country. Much as with the lack of tolerance for the gangsterism and corruption during the war, anger about the inequality of independent, free Croatia, began to loosen war-forged bonds in the years after Dayton. Bajramovic's invective directed at Mercep was only one of several public and official moves against the robber barons who had become enriched during the war at the expense of the greater public. The arrest of Croats Mladen Naletilic and Vinko Martinovic was as much related to their war crimes as it was their clearly ill-gained ostentatious lifestyles. Naletilic, whose body guards were "easily recognized with their designer sunglasses" lived in a "heavily guarded castle," while Martinovic enjoyed riding around Mostar "in the city's only Jaguar, followed by his body guards, all of whom openly def[ied] the injunction against carrying weapons."[63] As Croatia's economic and employment situation deteriorated and the "war-bred underworld" began to clearly threaten peace, Croats increasingly demanded that the gangsters *qua* war criminals be brought into line.[64]

A Dash of the International, But Not Too Much

In a recipe, certain ingredients, if not dispensed judiciously, can come to overpower the dish. The same can be said regarding the elements that can lead to domestic war crimes trials. And, the ingredient that must be most carefully employed is the pressure of the international community, and this is especially true if its message is unclear. This was seen in Croatia in the years after the 1995 Dayton Treaty, where even if the Croats wished to follow the dictates of the international community, the community was at times so divided that it was unclear exactly what it wanted. Reports issued by international organizations, throughout the immediate post-Dayton period, were often contradictory, making it that much more difficult to establish a coherent international policy toward Croatia. Thus, in response to the US State Department's 1997 Human Rights report, which questioned the country's human rights record and claimed Croatia was only "nominally democratic," senior Croat politicians were understandably flummoxed as that description "overlook[ed recent] positive assessments about the situation of human rights in the Republic of Croatia by other international sources: the Council of Europe, [a] report by [a] UN special rapporteur, the OSCE and others"[65]—all three of which had been more positive about the state. The State Department report also neglected Croatia's recently announced support for the establishment of military special forces operations to track down war criminals in Bosnia, regardless of the ethnicity of the indictee.[66]

And, in March 1999, the OSCE issued a scathing report on Croatia, primarily dealing with its cooperation with The Hague tribunal,[67] but a few months later—after little had actually changed on the ground—a visit by an envoy from the United States concluded that the US government was now satisfied with the level of cooperation.[68]

One of the more counterproductive international activities during this period was the actual shifting of war crimes proceedings already underway in Croatia from Croatian courts to The Hague. In each instance, the defendant in the proceedings was a Croat. That is, once the Croatian state had stepped up to actually investigate, prosecute, and convict some of its most powerful and well-connected citizens for malfeasance during the war (or at least related to the war), the international community nonetheless insisted that the detainees and their cases be transferred to the ICTY. This was even after Zagreb offered to allow international monitors to observe the domestic trials and even agreed to accept assistance from other states in order to assure fair trials.[69]

Two cases are of note: Vinko Martinovic (alias Stela) and Mladen Naletilic (alias Tuta), mentioned above, were both powerful Croatian gangster war criminals indicted by The Hague and transferred to the tribunal in 1999. However, their Hague trials were the culmination of a domestic legal odyssey that had begun several years earlier. These cases are illustrative of the growth and maturation of the Croatian judicial system. Both Tuta and Stela were arrested in early 1997. This in itself was somewhat remarkable given their strength. Only a few months earlier in their powerbase city, Mostar (a half-Croat city in Bosnia), a local policeman, Zdravko Culjak, was almost killed after he had arrested a comparatively minor local criminal, compelling the authorities to release the criminal two hours later.[70] That Tuta and Stela, who were senior figures in the Croatian gangster establishment, were subsequently arrested and remained in detention marked a significant change. Moreover, that any trials occurred at all is noteworthy since at the time of their arrests conventional wisdom suggested that they had been detained solely "for show." Regarding Tuta in particular, any trial was thought unlikely, given his friendship with Croatia's hardline nationalist defense minister.[71]

Nonetheless, Tuta was put on trial in Zagreb in November 1997, charged with kidnapping and incitement to murder.[72] And, though some difficulties arose with his trial—including the lack of cooperation of some witnesses[73]—there is no evidence that the trial was being conducted unjustly when it was stopped by the ICTY in December 1998. Stela, meanwhile, was also put on trial in Croatia and his domestic trial concluded in early December 1998 with the court finding him guilty of murder. He was sentenced to eight years in prison.[74]

The ICTY, meanwhile, issued an indictment for both men in late December 1998,[75] and demanded that the men be transferred to The Hague. It is true that the domestic charges Tuta and Stela faced did not explicitly deal with the war crimes covered in the ICTY indictments. Despite this, it is far from clear that demanding their removal to The Hague was the best option. Instead of removing the cases, the Croatian prime minister proposed asking Croatian prosecutors to add war crimes charges to those already allayed against the men.[76] It was even suggested that international observers could monitor the resulting trials.

Not only was there very likely a way to prosecute the two for war crimes in Croatia, but also extraditing Tuta—whose Croatian trial was ongoing—raised a serious constitutional issue. His counsel argued (probably correctly) both that the Croatian constitution did "not envisage the possibility of interrupting a trial,"[77] and that the law on cooperation with the ICTY was in opposition to the Croatian Law on Criminal Procedure.[78] Tuta's lawyer maintained that it was not in response to law, but rather to the international community's pressure—with implicit threats of sanctions,[79] and an explicit straining of relations with the EU[80]—that finally led to Zagreb's agreement to extradite his client. The order of events surrounding his extradition provides some support to this claim. In August 1999, the ICTY filed a letter with the UN Security Council complaining of Croatia's refusal to extradite Tuta.[81] This followed several months of attacks on Croatia's lack of cooperation and claims by the UN and others who posited that Zagreb orchestrated an official campaign aimed to "encourage distrust and hostility" toward the tribunal among the Croatian populace.[82] Less than one month after the ICTY official complaint, Tudjman finally relented,[83] as did his judges.[84] Tuta appealed the decision to the Croatian Supreme Court, which rejected his petition,[85] and he was subsequently removed to The Hague.

In Stela's case, it seems that war crimes charges would have been even more easily added to his domestic trial. Stela had lost considerable support among Croats, and at his sentencing for the murder charges, he yelled at the judge, calling him "a heap of garbage" and lamented what a sorry state Croatia had become.[86] Stela also provides an interesting comparison between what might have occurred had the cases remained in Croatia, compared with the result at the ICTY. Stela was sentenced to eight years in Croatia for murder,[87] while he received eighteen years at the ICTY for his involvement in the ethnic cleansing.[88] Croatia was evidently not shy about incarcerating its convicted citizens for significant periods of time. Consequently, it is plausible that had the ICTY charges been appended to the charges he faced in his domestic trial, he may have received as severe, if not a more severe, sentence than the one he received in The Hague.

Conducting trials in Croatia would have both avoided a constitutional problem and demonstrated respect for Croatia's movement toward rule of law. Doing so would have also provided needed support to the ongoing efforts to reform and strengthen the country's justice system.

DOMESTIC TRIALS AND HAGUE OBSTRUCTION IN CROATIA (2000–PRESENT)

Though Tudjman stated otherwise until the very end, it was clear to Croatians and observers that his health was failing throughout 1999. In fact, for the last six weeks of his life, as he lay incommunicado in a local hospital, his authority had already been officially transferred to Vlatko Pavletic, the speaker of the parliament. Tudjman died on December 11, and his anachronistic, "Croatia über-alles" nationalism became unsupportable. His death further revealed the fragility of the support he had while alive, and the Croatian desire to move forward while accepting and addressing the past. Questioning the state's Ustasha past and the less-than-heroic actions undertaken in Croatia's name during the Yugoslav wars became government policy, which was then echoed amongst the population at large in the coffee houses of Zagreb. Croatia turned over a new leaf with The Hague and began to assist prosecutors, often without question, and relinquished thousands of state archive documents that Tudjman had kept hidden "for reasons of national security." Yet, though this most recent period has been most marked by Croatia's Hague cooperation, it also deserves recognition for Croatia's own legal activities to address the past. There have been some difficulties, hiccups, and mistakes in this domestic process, and there remain loud—though increasingly peripheral—forces that are committed to obstructing the country's war crimes judicial activities. Despite Croatia's efforts at home, and though there have been dozens of trials, the contemporary era could also be known for the international community's frequent rebuffing or even obstructing of Croatia's domestic war crimes proceedings.

Tudjman died in December 1999, laid to rest in an honored place in Mirogoj Cemetery, which for Croatia is a combination of Arlington National Cemetery and Westminster Abbey; it is the burial site of Croatia's great and good. His tomb, which also serves as a virtual cenotaph for Croatia's war dead from World War II and the Yugoslav wars, is a huge, multi-ton marble slab near the entrance to the burial grounds. To this day, cemetery keepers are given the task of keeping fresh-cut flowers strewn about the stone.

The outpouring of grief on the streets of Zagreb and the ruling party's exploitation of Tudjman's demise for political gain, made some believe that the nationalists would maintain their powers and war crimes prosecutions would now be even more difficult to stage without Tudjman. Yet, within a few months, Croatia was under a new, reformist president, Stjepan Mesic, who quickly moved toward more domestic war crimes prosecutions. Mesic destroyed the sacred cow of Croatia's unadulterated victimhood, intoning that "*all* sides were guilty in the 1990s conflict."[89] He convinced several veterans groups, who had been vocal opponents of war crimes prosecutions, of the necessity of war crimes trials against Croats.[90]

In April 2000, the Croatian government allowed ICTY investigators into the country to investigate the Gospic massacre, an event in October 1991 in which hundreds of Serbs were killed by Croatian forces.[91] In September 2000, the government planned to conduct still more domestic war crimes trials and provided further evidence to The Hague. A few months later, President Mesic also stood up to any remnants of the military's nationalism, citing the need for a depoliticized military as he removed seven senior generals who had proclaimed that Croatia was insulting the country's history by prosecuting Croatians for crimes against Serbs during the conflict.[92] In the fall, Croatian authorities arrested a number of war crimes suspects, including General Ivan Andabak,[93] a Bosnian Croat wanted by Sarajevo. Mesic quickly agreed to extradite him to Bosnia for trial. It appeared that Croatia was now eager to prosecute its own and even help others do the same. December saw the president once again acknowledge the existence of Croatian-committed atrocities during the war, and urge domestic courts to move swiftly on those cases.[94] Meanwhile the Croatian prime minister Ivica Racan used his end-of-year address to reiterate Croatia's willingness to investigate and prosecute war crimes perpetrators.[95]

The government's policy would be expanded in 2001, as it repeatedly stated, that "the uncovering, investigating, and processing of war crimes . . . [had been] unsatisfactory."[96] Even as the government's policy on war crimes trials came under greater attack, it remained resolute. Mesic overturned a law that exempted war veterans from prosecution[97] and publicly stated his regret that local war crimes trials were not held in greater numbers earlier.[98]

Domestic war crimes trials were conducted in large numbers and Zagreb even attempted to reverse some of the bias that had been seen in earlier cases. In 2002, the state prosecutor officially asked his deputies to review close to two thousand war crimes cases because they had been "insufficiently verified," often "dubious," and were the result of "investigations conducted in an inferior manner."[99] Charges against many Serbs were dropped as a result of this review.

Present, but Not Insurmountable, Problems with Domestic Proceedings

Even in light of these developments, many in the international community refused to recognize the validity of domestic trials. Their argument was that there were serious irregularities in many proceedings, and a seeming bias against Serb defendants. An OSCE report concerning the war crimes trials it observed throughout 2002 lays out the case in its most persuasive form, focusing on three primary areas of injustice:

1. The vast majority of war crime proceedings monitored in 2002 involved Serbs alleged to have committed war crimes against

Croats. At all stages of proceedings, except for acquittals, Serbs constituted the bulk of the defendants, 28 of 35 arrests; 29 of 51 releases; 114 of 131 persons under judicial investigation; 19 of 32 persons indicted; 90 of 115 persons on trial; 47 of 52 persons convicted.

2. Verdicts issued in 2002 demonstrated a significantly different rate of conviction and acquittal depending upon the national origin of the defendant. While 83 percent of all Serbs were found guilty, only 18 percent of Croats . . . were convicted.

3. In absentia proceedings continued in 2002, ranging from a low of 1 to a high of more than 50 in absentia defendants in a given case. In absentia proceedings were brought almost exclusively against Serbs.[100]

Amnesty International and Human Rights Watch confirmed these findings.[101] Other serious problems existed, including a concern for witness security, made evident with the murder of Milan Levar, who was set to testify against fellow Croats about crimes he had witnessed during the war.[102]

While Levar's death was tragic, it was noteworthy for its rarity. Moreover, though any ethnic bias in prosecutions is troubling, it is easy to extrapolate too broadly from specific instances to impugn the entirety of the Croatian justice system. There was much in the political and judicial environment that served to mitigate these shortcomings. Also, Croatia's leadership long acknowledged such problems. President Mesic himself publicly stated his concern with the "lower courts passing 'unacceptable verdicts' that made it 'obvious that the length of sentence depended on the ethnicity of the indictees.'"[103] Further, the Croatian Supreme Court was busily overturning and otherwise resentencing many of those unjustly dealt with. Moreover, some of the problems the OSCE and others identified were geographically constrained. The *Lora* Case, which has become infamous and a prime example for those asserting Croatia's unfair justice system, powerfully illustrates this contention.

The "Botched" Lora Case

The *Lora* case dealt with war crimes committed at a former military prison at the Lora naval base in Split in 1992. Two Serb civilians and two prisoners of war were killed after significant torture. Several detainees at the facility came forward after a brief investigation. All eight of the defendants were arrested in September 2001.[104] All were former Croatian military policemen and their detainment led to loud protests, and even a physical attack on one of the witnesses *inside* the courthouse (as he was waiting to give testimony to the investigative judge). Repeated threats were also made against the prosecutor, and some witnesses would prove too fearful to actually come forward.[105]

After several months of investigation, the trial began in June 2002. Sixty-six witnesses were to present evidence, including fourteen subpoenaed from Serbia (taking advantage of the bilateral agreement between Zagreb and Belgrade on war crimes cooperation).[106] Croatians immediately recognized the trial as critical and emblematic of "the fate of all other future war crimes trials in Croatia." It was said that "[it] will be an indication of the government's readiness to face . . . the more gruesome episodes of our recent past."[107]

However, the proceedings were also promptly deemed a farce in the making. The atmosphere in the courtroom was enough to make one doubt that justice could be possible. Supporters of the defendants outnumbered those of the victims, often filling more than 90 percent of the public gallery. Included among them were Luka Podrug, Split's deputy mayor, and Igor Stimac, the Croatian football star who not only paid for the defense but was often addressed directly by the judge during the trial.[108] Semina Loncar, of the local NGO Coalition for Human Rights, observed the trial and described the boisterousness of the defendants' several dozen supporters as "creating a very tense atmosphere that threaten[ed] to cause incidents. They applau[ded] frenetically when the defendants [arrived] in the courtroom."[109]

Though the spectators were troubling, the key weakness in the proceedings was the judge, Slavko Lozina, who "los[t] crucial pieces of evidence . . . and obviously [had] no control over the proceedings."[110] He was so biased in favor of the defense that he even honored the request of one of the defendants to be granted furlough in order "to have his hair cut in his favorite hairdressing salon."[111] Further, Judge Lozina often did not

> even try to be in charge of the proceedings . . . [allowing defense witnesses] to make observations which [had] nothing to do with the trial and . . . [inappropriately to] discredit witnesses.[112]

There were requests to move the trial to surroundings that were less volatile,[113] and though Croatia's chief state prosecutor approved the move,[114] the Croatian Supreme Court rejected a transfer, holding that such a relocation was not in line with criminal procedure, and that the problems the prosecution noted in the trial would not be improved by a move.[115] The case continued, as did the questionable behavior of spectators and jurists. Nearly sixty witnesses presented testimony, but none from Serbia, as they failed to appear in court even though they had been subpoenaed.[116]

All eight defendants were acquitted in November 2002. And, though there was celebration on the part of defendants and their supporters, an indicator of the metamorphosis in the country was the level and severity of criticism that befell the court from *within* Croatia. Representatives of a coalition of Split NGOs produced a detailed report on the many breaches of legal procedure that had occurred.[117] Well-known Zagreb lawyer Ante Nobilo said the verdict was shameful and based on a "fundamental" legal error: the court never heard from the main witnesses, the former Lora inmates. Nobilo predicted that the Supreme Court would have no choice but to quash the verdict. And others, more provocatively, asserted that the nationalists were somehow behind the trial and verdict, claiming that on the day of the decision, "Croatia gained another hero of the Homeland War—Judge Slavko Lozina."[118]

It is at this point that most critics of Croatia's domestic legal system stop. But the trial itself had a much longer life after the November verdict. Though no official political reaction was released following the verdict, the state prosecutor immediately lodged an appeal. In August 2004, the Supreme Court overturned the acquittal and ordered a retrial. The Court found the first proceedings "fraught with serious flaws in criminal procedure as well as erroneous and incomplete facts."[119] Political reaction to the Supreme Court's decision was loud and positive. President Mesic's cabinet, both due to its view that prosecution was the right course, and no doubt to curry favor with NATO and the EU who were now displaying interest in the trial, expressed strong support for the Supreme Court's order.[120] It would be almost a year before the retrial began, but the defendants were immediately rearrested, an order that the Supreme Court approved[121] even when the local court refused.[122] The retrial began in September 2005,[123] and all eight were convicted in March 2006 and sentenced to multiyear periods of detention.[124] A year later, the Croatian Supreme Court confirmed the sentences.

This postscript to the *Lora* case makes one look at the proceedings in a different light and perhaps question not the Croatian justice system at large, but a particular courtroom in Split. Split, after all, had long been the center of nationalist Croatia, and a hotbed of Tudjman loyalists. Consequently, it makes one question why the case transfer to another, less emotively located court was not approved; after all, many other courts had developed significant experience in successfully staging emotionally and politically charged trials.[125] Also lost in a more simplistic take on *Lora*, and admittedly dampened by the length of time needed for appeals, was the brevity of the trial, especially in comparison to ICTY proceedings. The initial trial was launched very briskly, with the prosecutor and investigative judge going from allegation, to investigation, to indictment, to trial in the space of a few months. Further, it is evident that despite the mood in the courtroom, the majority of Croats did not necessarily support the initial "not guilty" verdict. For instance, shortly after the initial verdict, a film on the *Lora* "military-investigative" detention center, *Lora—Testimonies*, a graphic, Serb-sympathetic account of the wartime conditions in Lora, was premiered at the Zagreb film festival to the consternation of some veterans' groups, but to the praise of almost everyone else who viewed the piece or heard about it.[126]

The System's Operational Safety Valves

The Supreme Court's role, both in *Lora* and other war crimes cases, is also often obscured by critics of the Croatian system. But here, as in so many war crimes cases, the Supreme Court operated as it was designed, as a fundamental check on injustice. Another high-profile case where the Court was active was the 2002 trial of Fikret Abdic, a man who personified the ethnic and religious melting pot that pre-civil war Yugoslavia had been. He was a Bosnian Muslim, but a Croatian citizen; Bosnian authorities wanted him for war crimes committed against fellow Muslims. In 1993, along with twenty thousand others, he had declared the independence of the "Autonomous Province of Western Bosnia." In an attempt to secede from the rest of Bosnia-Herzegovina, they began to wage war against Muslims supporting Bosnia-proper. Abdic, who moved to Croatia after the war, was eventually indicted for war crimes by Bosnia. However, Croatia's constitution did not allow his extradition of Croatian citizens. Consequently, in line with the war crimes cooperation agreement between Bosnia and Croatia, the Croats tried him in Karlovac County Court, southwest of Zagreb. Abdic was convicted, in a trial widely thought to be free and fair, and sentenced to twenty years in jail.[127] The Croatian Supreme Court, however, disagreed with the severity of the judgment, and reduced the sentence to fifteen years.[128]

The Supreme Court's mitigating effect has not, as illustrated by Abdic's case, been limited to ethnic Croatians. Indeed, if anything, it has been more biased toward minorities in the country. For instance, as the OSCE reported in 2002, the Supreme Court granted 18 or 19 defendants' appeals, a reversal rate of 95 percent. Nearly 70 percent of the decided appeals involved Serbs convicted in absentia trials and 90 percent of all granted appeals involved Serbs.[129]

Supreme Court-ordered retrials also demonstrated a seeming bias for Serbs. In 2002, they "resulted in the exoneration of more than half of previously convicted Serb defendants."[130]

INCONSISTENCY OF INTERNATIONAL COMMUNITY SUPPORT

Since 2000, there has been a marked inconsistency in the treatment by the international community of Croatian attempts to domestically prosecute war crimes. This changed somewhat in July 2002 once the UN Security Council ordered the ICTY to begin implementing its "Completion Strategy"—under which the ICTY was directed to complete all trials by 2008 and all appeals by 2010. Until then, The Hague expressed limited interest in assisting Croatia in building up its domestic system, or even recognizing the progress made. The case involving General Mirko Norac, and the odd, counterproductive uncertainty with which the ICTY dealt with him and Croatia's judiciary, is the best example of this troubling trend. It seems to implicate political and economic requirements as the baseline of the ICTY's purportedly *judicial* concerns.

The Norac Case: Now You See Him, Now You Don't

Shortly after Mesic became president in 2000, the Rijeka Cantonal Court in western Croatia had taken up investigation of the 1991 Gospic massacre, during which Croatian forces murdered as many as one hundred Serb civilians. Based upon evidence and testimony collected, the judges in February 2001 decided to broaden their investigation to include Norac and eventually issued a warrant for his arrest.[131]

What did or did not happen at Gospic, and whether or not Croatians were involved, was an explosive political issue, and news of the warrant sent thousands into the streets. Protests were held throughout the country, with many shouting that Norac would only be arrested, let alone tried, "over our dead bodies."[132] One particularly boisterous demonstration of nearly one hundred thousand people was held in Split on February 11, 2001. There, demonstrators demanded early federal elections and an end to war crimes investigations.[133]

After a two-week manhunt, Norac was detained. The Hague's first intervention preceded his capture and according to many, actually catalyzed Norac's eventual arrest. ICTY prosecutor Carla Del Ponte stated that the Croatian courts were granted the right to carry out "all possible proceedings against retired Croatian General Mirko Norac."[134] She announced that The Hague stood ready to assist the Croatian courts in providing evidence. Though never proven definitively, the fact that Norac was arrested a day after Del Ponte's announcement gives some credence to the claim that Norac's capture was actually the result of an agreement he brokered that he would not be extradited to The Hague.[135]

Norac was charged in March 2001, accused of orchestrating the murder of some forty Serb civilians during the 1991 war. The trial began slowly, due largely to procedural maneuvering from the defense, which questioned the impartiality of the judges,[136] and then similar maneuvering by the prosecutors.[137] After the fifth such procedural postponement, some international observers began to ask whether Croatia was "dragging its heels" on the prosecution.[138] In retrospect, given the rights that the postponements were protecting, and the fact that ICTY trials have often been far more delayed by similar activity, the criticism seems somewhat unfair.

Still, there may have been good reason for observers to question Croatia's resolve to handle Norac. The strength of emotions evoked by Norac's arrest surprised and concerned authorities in Zagreb. Over the course of 2001, protests had died down significantly, though there remained some isolated pockets of staunch supporters who manifested their views in somewhat interesting ways: the small town of Sinj, for instance, publicly named Norac an honorary citizen in August 2001, expressing support for his plight.[139] Still, there remained anxiety in official circles about Croatia's ability to weather whatever public storm would emerge from the case.

The trial began in earnest in January 2002,[140] with the state proceeding against Norac and four codefendants similarly accused of participating in the massacre. The entire event was marked by an exacting, dogmatic following of the law, and the implementation of creative solutions to some of the problems that had dogged *Lora* and other trials. Closely held government reports about the Gospic events were made available[141]—a function directly of a government that wished to be more open with its wartime archives than Tudjman's had been. The proceedings used comparatively modern technology—for example, a tape recording given to the court of Norac allegedly ordering killings was provided with a transcription on an accompanying video.[142] Once the judge learned that Serb witnesses were too concerned for their safety to travel to Croatia, the judge agreed to travel to Belgrade, and exploit the now even more robust Serb-Croat war crimes cooperation agreement.[143] The judge "borrowed" a Belgrade courtroom, and, in line with the agreement, asked a Serb magistrate to interrogate more than a dozen witnesses with a list of provided questions.[144] Some Serbs, however, did travel to the Rijeka court, including a former Yugoslav army pathologist who appeared in October 2002.[145]

The defense, quite predictably, claimed bias, but a closer analysis of the case suggested that the defendants' rights were protected. In fact, an overly close reading of the law in the defendants' interests forced the court to release two of the indictees because the duration of their detention prior to conviction had exceeded legal limits.[146] Though there were some difficulties with securing defense witnesses, and some subpoenaed witnesses did not appear,[147] the court heard persuasive testimony from both Serbs and Croats.[148] The defense case was sophisticated and, in light of the evidence, rather strong.

Norac was found guilty in early March 2003, which occasioned further protests, though much weaker and markedly less enthusiastic than the ones held around the time of his arrest.[149] Serbs, by-and-large, were pleased with the decision.[150] Norac, the highest-ranking Croat to be convicted of war crimes in a Croatian court, was convicted of overseeing the killing of nearly fifty Serb civilians in Gospic and was sentenced to twelve years. Two other defendants, Tihomir Oreskovic and Stjepan Granic, were sentenced to fifteen years and ten years respectively.

It was at this stage that the proceedings against Norac took a strange turn. Norac appealed his conviction, but while his appeal was still pending, in May 2004, in a move that struck some as close to subjecting the defendant to "double jeopardy," the ICTY decided to indict him—for activities that took place in 1993 during "Operation Medak Pocket," which the Croatian army had launched to expel Serb forces from their territory.[151] With the ICTY's announcement, it appeared that Prosecutor Del Ponte had reneged on her promise to allow Croatian courts to carry out "*all possible proceedings*" against Norac. In June, the Croatian Supreme Court confirmed the first Norac verdict (found by the Croatian court),[152] and two weeks later Norac arrived in The Hague to plead innocent to the new charges.[153] A day later, on July 9, Norac was back in his Croatian prison cell,[154] and in September 2004, the ICTY went back on itself again, and officially granted Croatia the right to prosecute Norac.[155] No acknowledgment was made of the fact that Croatia had indeed recently just done that.

Of the many things odd about the ICTY's involvement with Norac, the most striking is that it is not clear why The Hague insisted on indicting him and bringing him to the Netherlands, rather than asking Croatia to add the indictment to his existing charge sheet. What was going on here? Alas, it seems that politics and economics, rather than justice (let alone the rebuilding of Croatia's judicial system) seemed to be at play. By summer 2004, the Yugoslavia tribunal was under immense pressure to begin implementing its "Completion Strategy." The Security Council had been very active on the ICTY issue throughout the summer of 2004, and the timing of The Hague's decision to send the Norac case back to Croatia closely comports with the end of the Security Council's meetings on the subject. In short, Norac would have added to The Hague's bloated docket and made closure in 2010, already unlikely, that much more difficult to accomplish. It seems most probable that the ICTY wanted Norac for itself, in order to further burnish its status as the prime source of postwar justice, but once Norac seemed a liability, they no longer wanted the case. None of the issues that are meant to have been taken into account regarding such transfers appeared in any substantial way during the entire process. That The Hague had wasted significant money bringing Norac to the Netherlands, only to ship him back, was not mentioned, nor was the fact that Croatia's recent trial of Norac indicated Zagreb's clear ability and will to try even its most prominent war criminals.

CONCLUSION

Croatia's road to recognizing and addressing its crimes of the 1990s has not been smooth or direct. The continued belief by some in the "purity" of Croatia's actions during the wars—such as that manifest in speeches at the tenth anniversary celebrations of Operation Storm in 2005—is indicative that some parts of society remain wedded to a "Tudjman" view of the past. Though troubling, such views are increasingly on the fringes and especially since 2000 the state has frequently prosecuted Croatians for actions during the war and called for international assistance in order to bring about even more war crimes prosecutions. Unfortunately, its calls have often gone unheeded and Croatia's attempts to prosecute its own have been largely ignored or belittled—even in the face of some remarkable successes. Some of Croatia's requests for aid have been direct: in March 2000, Foreign Minister Tonino Picula addressed an OSCE gathering in Vienna and provided his honest assessment of Croatia's attempts to reform its justice system and pursue war criminals. He said that significant strides in this area had been made and the government was committed to continuing, but Zagreb urgently needed international community assistance.[156] That request went essentially unmet.

Six months later, in September 2000, Croatia arrested a large number of war crime indictees and again made it clear that, with requisite help, it wished to prosecute the defendants in Croatia, rather than in the Netherlands.[157] However, in that case, the ICTY explicitly rejected domestic Croatian trials.[158]

The message from the international community about Croatia's capabilities and desires to prosecute war crimes continued to be inconsistent. Such contradictions reached a crescendo in 2004, around the time of the Norac affair. In April 2004, the EU issued an assessment saying that Croatia was ill-prepared for war crimes trials of any sort, while in June 2004 the OSCE chief of mission in Croatia stated that he could "not see why the Croatian judiciary could not take over a limited number of war crimes trials from The Hague"—theoretically the most difficult and politically charged of the war crimes cases.[159]

Various international organizations also made significant claims of bias. The timing of these accusations was often odd; they were regularly made nearly simultaneous with powerful examples of nonbias. For instance, in November 2004, the American NGO Human Rights Watch published a caustic report of the Croatian war crimes trials, claiming that they were utterly biased against Serbs.[160] Yet, two weeks prior, the Croatian Supreme Court had acquitted several Serbs of war crimes charges due to insufficiency of evidence.[161]

Exacerbating the contradictory reports of many international observers was the fact that though they often called for action and reforms that would cost money, the international community, until very recently, was unwilling to provide such funds for Croatia to do so. Reports on what needed to be done in the Croatian system were coming from more sources than just the NGOs on the ground. The European Court of Human Rights, and its cases that dealt with Croatia, provided an indication of where the weaknesses existed in the system.[162] A great majority of the complaints lodged by Croatian citizens with the Strasbourg court have dealt with the slowness of court proceedings. The cause of this inefficiency was also clear: the Tudjman legacy had depleted the judicial corps,[163] and combined with rising caseloads and a slow civil law system, the courts could not keep up. Urgent investment in modernization, automation, and the development of "fast track" trials were needed. Yet, despite the clarity of the system's shortcomings, it took years for any substantial assistance to start flowing. For instance, it was only in January 2005 that a video link was finally donated to the Zagreb County Court.[164]

The international community at large may not have deliberately obstructed the development of Croatia's justice system. However, for many Croats the same cannot be said for the ICTY, which often has seemed to practice the most malevolent type of neglect when it came to assisting Croatian domestic trials. In November 2002, still reeling from the *Lora* verdict and the refusal of the ICTY to assist Zagreb in that trial, Croatian commentator Vlado Rajic of the daily *Zagreb Vjesnik* made the following charges against The Hague:

It would be inaccurate to say that the [disappointing verdict in] . . . *Lora* was . . . simply because someone in The Hague failed to keep his . promise. However, that could indeed be one of the key factors.

When a Croatian delegation visited The Hague in June of this year, among the topics discussed was legal assistance from . . . [Prosecutor] Del Ponte's office for judicial bodies in Croatia. . . . [Officials] in The Hague promised to provide documentation on events in . . . *Lora* . . . to the Croatian judiciary.

This arrangement was agreed to and then forgotten. . . . [Not] one shred of paper from The Hague has been provided to the County Court in Split or to the State Prosecutor's Office.

Then, in September of this year, the Croatian judiciary sent a request to judges and prosecutors in The Hague, asking them to allow the examination of documentation in connection with war crimes committed in Paulin Dvor, especially the one connected with the transport of citizens killed there from northern to southern Croatia. . . . [That] promised material has [also] not been provided.

[What are we to assume based on this noncooperation?] [First, it is clear] that The Hague does not want to help the judiciary or the Croatian state in prosecuting war crimes, instead consigning them to the status of service providers for The Hague's judicial needs. And . . . second . . . [the] local judicial and state bodies are being put on notice that The Hague does not regard them as equal partners.[165]

Rajic could have added to his comments that the demands the ICTY has made of Croatia have often not served the ends of justice. For instance, the trial of former General Ante Gotovina was delayed for years by the indictee's refusal to go to The Hague. However, the former general "made it clear before he fled that he would [willingly] face trial in Croatia."[166] Gotovina had many supporters in the country, and there is evidence of official assistance that was provided to aid his life as a fugitive. Yet, it is also true that Croatia had encountered popular support for war criminals before and had prosecuted them. Further, as is evidenced by Croatia's involvement in Gotovina's capture in December 2005, the senior Croatian leadership was ready for the general to be tried. Given this, it seems likely that Gotovina, like Norac, could have been prosecuted at home. Uniform, universal support for the prosecution of war criminals was not, and is not, a prerequisite for justice to take place at the domestic level in Croatia.

The Hague's "Rules of the Road" program has been another example of the international community's often counterproductive role in providing justice. This program asked that local prosecutors in the Balkans submit their proposed domestic war crimes cases to the Yugoslav tribunal for approval. The idea was that the tribunal would weed out inappropriate cases and then allow proper prosecutions to proceed throughout the former Yugoslavia. While a promising idea, in practice, the program has arguably hindered more than helped provide justice.

The primary difficulty with the Rules of the Road procedures was that it "considerably slowed down or even halted . . . domestic war crimes cases."[167] Prosecutors complained of waiting up to two years for The Hague to provide them with a determination of whether a case could go forward. Lost momentum in investigation and prosecution became endemic. "It is evident," reported the OSCE in 2005, "that relatively few domestic trials have proceeded to completion and suspects have remained at large whilst case files were being reviewed by the ICTY [due to the Rules of the Road]."[168]

It was never made clear in the Balkans why the ICTY was given jurisdiction over the determination of whether domestic cases should proceed. To many it would have made much more sense had such cases been vetted by a local oversight body (such as the OSCE) which would have been able to act more quickly and with more focus. Local prosecutors in the Balkans were bewildered and frustrated by the system, further sapping energies that ought to have been—and clearly could have been—devoted to prosecutions.

The case of Croatia and its attempts at domestic justice brings to light not just what could be done on the ground, but also a more basic question as to what the ICTY's goals really are. Though the Croatian case does not definitively provide an answer, it does help narrow the list of possible aims. Even if the full scope of Vlado Rajic's indictment of The Hague is not accurate, given The Hague's obstructions, it seems clear that building the domestic justice system such that war criminals can be dealt with at home has not been among the aims of the ICTY. With this, the international community would likely agree. Yet, unfortunately, like the quickly scuppered plans for truth and reconciliation commissions—viewed incompatible with establishing the ICTY and wider international criminal justice—Croatia's trials have been viewed —again until very recently—as the product of a second-class system that could be overruled at any time. This has not been helpful in achieving the institutional and legal growth and development needed in Croatia. It is the growth and solidification of the rule of law in Croatia and the wider region that will in the end be the only true buffer between peace and more conflict. The international community has finally come to realize this and, as the ICTY prepares to close, it is only now rushing to provide the assistance and training that Croatia has long wanted, and for which Croats, in the form of a robust media, aware citizenry, and professional army, have long been ready to receive.

Chapter 10

CONCLUSION
Is it Too Late to Listen to the Canary in the Mine?

With more than one hundred fifty countries signed onto the International Criminal Court and an army of nongovernmental organizations pushing the remaining few toward ratification, it might seem that the warnings and realities described in the previous chapters are given too late. The train has already left the station.

Despite the difficulties of international justice, an aspect of the movement toward the ICC is unquestionably inspiring: that so many of the world's states have come together to declare certain acts categorically unacceptable is a hopeful sign of accord in a century that has so far been lacking such togetherness. Further, while it is true that the forces for international justice are amassed, this does not necessarily mean that international justice in the future—even with the International Criminal Court—must suffer from the same difficulties earlier iterations endured. The key to this optimism is that, in the end, it will be in the ICC's interest, and in the interest of supporters of international justice, to focus more directly on justice at home, rather than justice in The Hague. Quite simply, not only can domestic justice be relied upon, in most instances it must be.

The Paradox

A primary reason for optimism derives from a point of agreement between supporters and critics of international justice: when it comes to war crimes trials, domestic proceedings are inherently preferable. Though some supporters of international proceedings, such as former ICTY judge Antonio Cassese, are less flexible, stating that "international" crimes necessarily merit "international" justice, the mainstream position is more nuanced. However, even for more differentiated supporters of international justice, it seems that the "preference for domestic trials" threatens to become a platitude, a hollow mantra. This is because of the flawed logic in the claim that domestic trials are preferable "if only they could work."

As we have seen, supporters contend it is all but impossible to have effective trials in countries where crimes have occurred or are still occurring—the situation is too perilous, the emotions are too raw. The only place where real justice can be dispensed in these circumstances is on the international plane. The problem with this claim is that not only is it overstated—in that there are hundreds, if not thousands, of cases in which real justice has been served in dangerous, emotionally wrought states—but also that its conclusion, that international trials are consequently the only option, does not follow from its premise. It may be true that trials are difficult to hold in the countries affected, but as history has shown, the difficulties on the ground make international trials every bit as difficult to hold as domestic trials. This is the key irony of international criminal justice: to work at all, international justice relies on the same stability and acceptance by target states that, if nurtured directly, would allow for *domestic* trials to occur successfully.

International courts' lack of power to either police regions in conflict or to forcefully enter postconflict states to investigate, indict, and arrest, means that there is a critical need for domestic cooperation in order for international courts to operate. Indeed, some international courts—such as the Rwanda tribunal—would have ceased to function without it. As long as such cooperation is lacking, and in the absence of either a military occupation as in post–World War II Germany or Japan or a domestic justice system willing to mount trials, neither international nor domestic courts will be able to address war crimes effectively.

This paradox has clearly manifested throughout the Balkans, where there has been a close correlation between the number of war crimes trials underway at the Yugoslavia tribunal and the number being held in the former Yugoslav states. Before 2001, the ICTY was comparatively inactive. This changed during 2001, as its case load jumped 80 percent (the largest single percentage jump since its first trials), and its funding increased by more than 130 percent (when it had increased only an average of 1.25 percent for each of the two prior years). In short, the ICTY "hit its stride," and though the arrival of Slobodan Milosevic in June 2001 certainly played a role, he was not the sole cause of this renaissance. His case accounted for only one of the twenty-four new cases at the tribunal. Rather, the extradition of Milosevic and the increase in other cases at the tribunal was an indication of a broader readiness and willingness in Serbia, and throughout the Balkans, to conduct domestic war crimes trials.

Indeed, Milosevic was arrested, indicted, and set for trial in Serbia before his extradition; that supporters of international justice nonetheless celebrated his arrival in The Hague leads one to question their strength of commitment to domestic trials. Moreover, in line with the paradox, it is not surprising that even before the Milosevic transfer, Serbs had begun a much wider bout of soul searching. This was demonstrated by several domestic war crimes cases. Belgrade successfully prosecuted dozens of soldiers for war crimes, launched politically sensitive investigations of Serb police officers accused of violations against Kosovars and Bosniaks, and "vigorously . . . tr[ied] to uncover crimes committed by Serbs against their neighbors."[1] That is, as the Serbs grew ready to assist the ICTY, they were also becoming ready to run their own trials.

This was even more the case by the time Radovan Karadzic was arrested in July 2008. The circumstances of his arrest further demonstrate how ready the Serbian state was to begin trials itself. He was arrested by the Serbian secret police, long thought a hotbed of Karadzic sympathizers, but which had recently been taken over by a new, reformist security chief. Vladimir Vuckovic, the domestic Serbian war crimes prosecutor, announced Karadzic's arrest and detention. Serbian authorities took him in for questioning and arraigned him before the special domestic Serbian War Crimes Court in Belgrade. The War Crimes Court had been established in 2003, a key component of Serbia's far-reaching domestic war crimes legislation. Indeed, by July 2008, Serbia had already successfully prosecuted several war criminals and at the time of Karadzic's arrest was hearing cases against still more accused. Serbia's efforts were far from perfect, but evidently, the infrastructure, laws, and political will to prosecute war criminals were present. Moreover, unlike in the February 2008 protests over Kosovo's declaration of independence, during which one hundred fifty thousand nationalist protesters marched in Belgrade, with some proceeding to firebomb the American embassy, there was only scant and ephemeral unrest following Karadzic's arrest. This suggests that there were perhaps limited, or at least manageable, risks in holding proceedings against the former Bosnian Serb leader in Serbia.

The situation in Croatia is even clearer; in several cases, the Croatian government was trying the same war crimes suspects wanted by the ICTY, and it could have prosecuted even more had the international community allowed it.

As evident in the two varieties of cases underway at the ICC, the paradox is also emerging in the operations of the nascent ICC. On one side are those matters requested by a state (such as in Uganda, where Kampala invited the Court to investigate and prosecute the Lord's Resistance Army rebel group). On the other side are those matters imposed by the world community through the ICC and disdained by a state (such as Darfur, where the UN Security Council referred the matter to the ICC and the Sudanese government has challenged the Court's imposition). In both situations, supporters of international justice, who hold fast to the paradigm that domestic trials are preferable—if only they could work—face some uncomfortable contradictions. In the case of Uganda, there is little question that domestic justice could work. The Ugandan courts are functioning and the parties have even accepted domestic jurisdiction over their alleged crimes. It would be difficult, and Uganda may well need assistance, but there is little question that trials *could* be held locally. Meanwhile, in Sudan, a recalcitrant government has stymied both the ICC's investigation as well as its issuing of indictments and detainment of perpetrators. Unless the Khartoum government decides to change its mind, by its own volition or through inducements it cannot afford to ignore, the prospects for international justice regarding Darfur are dim. Yet, as soon as the Sudanese do alter their views, the situation would morph into one mirroring that of Uganda. And Sudan would arguably become the preferred location for such trials.

This raises a second component of the paradox. Not only do domestic and international trials rely on the same base state-level requirements, but domestic trials are often the easier of the two in which to obtain the needed cooperation. As history demonstrates, it is often a much bigger step for a country to agree to remove cases to an international body than it is for a country to recognize that justice must be done at home.

The paradox has real effects on the ground, where its presence has arguably led to questionable outcomes if not perverted justice. In the Milosevic case for instance, both outside observers and Serbs decried the unfairness in forcing Serbia to extradite its former president. They claimed that the "Serbian authorities earned the right to put him in the dock by taking the risk" of arresting Milosevic and removing him from the political stage.[2] The Serbs were ready to prosecute, and the international community forced them to do otherwise.

And, in the ultimate of ironies, Milosevic's swift transfer likely had the unwitting effect of forestalling the needed moral reckoning within Serb society. This was because in all too many cases, cajoling a state to give up its citizens for trial involves a hefty quid pro quo that has little to do with justice. In the Milosevic case, the quid pro quo was more than $1 billion in US aid. And thus, the Serbian government's dash to deliver its former leader in time to procure international aid made the case a matter of economic self-interest, rather than the pursuit of justice or recognition of societal remorse. "The war-crimes issue . . . [was] turned into a financial issue" said Latinka Perovic, a Belgrade Serb. She complained that Serbs had a moral duty to address their crimes, but she heard "precious little" about moral duty in the weeks leading up to Milosevic's extradition.[3]

The same dance was seen in the events surrounding Belgrade's July 2008 capture of Radovan Karadzic. That the arrest was an explicit condition of continued discussions towards EU accession, and helped the otherwise battered Serbian president Boris Tadic to buttress his pro-Western credentials, suggested a similar quid pro quo. Again, the only significant talk of "justice" came from outside Serbia, with official pronouncements from Belgrade focusing more on the benefits Serbia could extract from the move than on any indication that Karadzic's arrest demonstrated a national willingness to face up to the terror of the 1990s. The Serbian foreign minister, Vuk Jeremic, was explicit in this regard, stating that "Serbia's new government has a rather ambitious European agenda. We are very serious about our future in the EU and [Karadzic's arrest] demonstrated it."[4]

There was another irony in the Milosevic case that may yet play out in the Karadzic's trial. Though Serbian disdain for Milosevic was growing while a Belgrade trial date approached, Milosevic's arrival in The Hague largely rehabilitated him in Serbian eyes. He became a victim and his trial became seen as a proxy for the prosecution (and persecution) of the entire Serb nation. Karadzic's Hague trial poses the same risks.

In order to avoid such pernicious side effects, and in order to give meaning to the claim that "domestic trials are preferable," the international community should commend local attempts to prosecute senior officials like Milosevic. The ICC can help in this regard, especially if we take ICC prosecutor Ocampo at his word. He has stated that his wish is to have no trials in The Hague; he wants domestic proceedings to render ICC trials unnecessary. Though Ocampo's stated desire is perhaps hyperbole, given the difficulties of international justice, the limitations of the ICC, and the singular benefits of local trials, the Court will hopefully give the as-yet-undefined concept of what counts as "domestic willingness" a broad, inclusive meaning.

Survivability and Domestic Buy-In

The second set of reasons that the ICC and supporters of international justice will be forced to focus on domestic solutions is that regardless of the exact role assigned to international justice, most would agree with the importance of the survivability and sustainability of any good that justice provides. "Justice" that is provided only to be undone or (even worse) gives birth to a new round of violence is not true justice at all. In order to avoid this, a focus on domestic institution building is critical.

The error of doing otherwise can be seen in the Japanese case following World War II. At the Tokyo Trials, twenty-eight "Class A" war criminal defendants were brought before the tribunal.[5] Yet, despite weeks of often-gruesome testimony, recounted in excruciating detail in the media and then in the thousand-page decision of the judges, the trials did not instigate a bout of soul searching on behalf of Japanese citizens. Many of those convicted and executed remained national heroes, evidence of their wrongs ignored or disbelieved.

More troubling than the social exoneration of criminals was that Imperial Japan's cruel wartime history failed to resonate in the country, despite vivid reports of atrocities presented during the trials. The most well-documented, ghastly acts undertaken by the empire were not accepted as fact by the majority of Japanese people. The Nanjing massacre—aka the Rape of Nanjing—is a leading example. The massacre was a bout of unremitting brutality perpetrated between December 1937 and February 1938 by the Japanese army against a civilian population in occupied Nanjing, China. The event was the basis for many charges at the Tokyo Trials, which concluded that during that three-month period at least two hundred thousand Chinese people were killed, and at least twenty-thousand Chinese people (from baby girls to elderly women) were raped.[6] The court spoke of still further "abnormal and sadistic" behaviors undertaken by the occupiers including mutilations, live burials, and torture.

The testimony, accusations, and findings of guilt by the trials were all well known throughout Japan. For decades, however, Japanese "considered the verdicts to have been little more than the products of 'victor's justice,' rather than an accurate legal or ethical assessment of the Imperial army's perpetration of an extremely inhumane massacre."[7] It was not until nearly thirty years had passed and Japanese journalist Honda Katsuichi began investigating and writing about the event that public conscience seemed to shift. Katsuichi's numerous articles in the *Asahi Shinbun* newspaper, followed by his book, *Journey into China*, were the first exposure most Japanese received to one of their own examining and judging the events of the 1930s and 1940s. It was only then that most Japanese began to accept the wrongdoings of their fathers and grandfathers.

The reason for this slow recognition of wrongs was that there had been limited buy-in from Japanese society into the Tokyo Trials. International justice had been grafted on top of a dysfunctional society without any concern for institutional or cultural support that was necessary to nurture and sustain the lessons the trials rendered. The trials did little to impact feelings of imperial glory that still permeated society. To this day, Japan has refused to issue an official mea culpa and relations with many of its Asian neighbors remain stunted because of Tokyo's continued lack of remorse.

Tokyo, Nuremberg, and the more recent cases of international justice have all been Band-Aids for much more serious social problems, problems that allowed violations to occur in the first place. Putting courts on top of broken societies and assuming that they will fix the societies is akin to pursuing democracy solely by promoting elections. Merely having a leadership elected by the people does not result in a sustainable liberal democracy. Similarly, simply having some trials of senior leadership does not necessarily result in either a society that respects the fact that such crimes even occurred or a society that is truly chastened so that such crimes are unlikely to recur.

It is true that even having real, domestic trials is no guarantee that their message will take hold for everyone. For instance, when convicted Croatian war criminal Dinko Sakic died in prison in July 2008, his funeral, which included burial in a full-dress Ustasha uniform and his priest intoning that Sakic was a "model for all Croatians," was condemned by some groups for its "outrageous display of unrepentant racism, anti-Semitism and xenophobia."[8] However, the funeral was a private affair, with official state organs using Sakic's death as an occasion to once again condemn Nazi and Ustasha crimes.

Naturally it is difficult to conclude that it was because of Sakic's domestic trial and its aftermath that the majority of Croatians seem to have taken on board the Ustasha horrors. However, following from the Japanese case, it is doubtful that an international trial conducted by non-Croatians would have had the same resonance.

There are clear limits to the impact of a primarily top-down approach to justice. Sooner or later, supporters of international justice will have to concede that it is only by addressing the societies where crimes actually occur that lessons of punishment, deterrence, or reconciliation have any hope of being heard, let alone heeded.

Peace vs. Justice—A Way Out

A further basis for optimism in spite of the ICC juggernaut comes from the fact that the ICC has become a player in ongoing conflicts. Unlike Nuremberg, Tokyo, or the Rwanda tribunal, violations have continued in the four situations in which the ICC has become involved: Uganda, Democratic Republic of the Congo, the Central African Republic, and Sudan. As of 2008, in Uganda, the violence between the Lord's Resistance Army and the government continues unabated, despite ICC investigations. In the Democratic Republic of the Congo, the ICC announced its investigation in June 2004, and the violence of the underlying conflict escalated toward the end of 2004: observers estimated that thirty-one thousand conflict-related deaths occurred each month, along with increasing abuses. The crisis and killings have continued ever since, despite the ICC's investigation and the presence of seventeen thousand UN peacekeepers, the world's largest detachment of blue helmets. The ICC's investigation into the Central African Republic is unique because it is the first time that the Court is looking at allegations where sexual crimes far outnumber actual killings. Unfortunately, the ICC's announcement of its investigation in May 2007 has been followed by a disturbing increase in sexual violence; according to a UN report in early 2008, 15 percent of women and girls in the country's north have become victims, and in the six months since the announcement of the ICC investigation, aid groups provided care to one thousand recent rape survivors. Since the June 2005 opening of the ICC investigation, violence in Darfur has continued.

While these disturbing facts do not necessarily suggest any causation between the ICC's involvement and continuing violations, they do show that the ICC does not appear to deter continuing violence. This is a limitation that has been shared by the Yugoslavia tribunal, which also began its operations while conflict was ongoing. Inasmuch as the ICC's investigations have been connected to continued violence, this linkage has again raised the difficult question of peace versus justice. As discussed, many see this debate as involving a false choice. However, it is clear that in many cases fighters have explicitly refused to lay down their weapons as long as there remains the threat of an international indictment.

For instance, in the former Yugoslavia, the war-crime-laden conflict in Macedonia between Slavs and ethnic Albanians was finally put to rest once an implicit amnesty was included in the negotiations. Similarly, in Kosovo, throughout the tense early days after Milosevic pulled Serb forces out of the province, the international community purposefully turned a blind eye to atrocities when doing so seemed necessary for stability.[9]

Seen in stark terms, the peace versus justice debate is a zero-sum game, and one for which champions of international justice are finding it difficult to gain support for the side of "justice," at least from among those on the ground who have the most to win or lose. The surveys of affected populations in northern Uganda reveal as much: nearly 90 percent would be willing to forsake "justice" if peace could be secured.[10] Despite this, the calculus changes if we add domestic justice to the mix. Judicial solutions begin to appear. For instance, in Uganda, the Lord's Resistance Army has become much less resolute in its opposition to trials if there is no risk that leaders will be extradited to The Hague. The Djuba negotiations between the rebels and Kampala made this an explicit prerequisite of an agreement; negotiations sadly broke down at least partly due to the issuance of ICC indictments.

The complexities of the situations under investigation necessitate that the ICC be flexible in ways uncontemplated by the states that negotiated the ICC treaty in 1998. Prosecutor Ocampo has stated that if he believed the ICC to be impeding peace, he would pull back. The problem, however, is that it is unclear how he can do this. The ICC is designed to be a relatively inflexible entity, and many have criticized Ugandan president Museveni for "using the ICC" in offering the revocation of the ICC indictments as a sweetener in LRA negotiations. Legally speaking, it is not clear how such a revocation would work; under the ICC's rules Museveni clearly does not have the power to withdraw the indictments unilaterally. An indictment could be revoked by ICC judges, but presumably that would only happen if the judges found that the facts alleged in the indictment were not supported. In this case, there is little doubt that the facts alleged are true. Similarly, the prosecutor can put investigations on hold "in the interests of justice," but no one knows quite what that means, and it might be a politically and bureaucratically untenable option. And, under Article 16 of the ICC Statute, the UN Security Council could also request that an investigation be "deferred" for a year. Given the politics of the Security Council, however, this too seems unlikely, as there is no tool by which the Security Council can direct the ICC to withdraw already-issued indictments.

Though the ICC may be legally trapped in the case of Uganda, in the future the Court and the international community should become more flexible in their interpretation of both the ICC's operations and its goals. Other than helping secure an end to conflict, it is possible that there would be other benefits to domestic prosecution, especially if closely monitored by the international community. Key among these benefits is that due to the necessity of state cooperation, there is a greater chance that all sides will be prosecuted at home than abroad.

In Uganda, such evenhandedness is important. Human Rights Watch has documented substantial violations on the part of the government soldiers fighting the LRA. But due primarily to political realities, and the fact that the Ugandan state would likely evict the ICC if it turned its attention on the national troops (in addition to the LRA), it seems unlikely that the ICC will be able to prosecute government soldiers. It is important to note that not all domestic trials have succeeded in focusing judicial scrutiny on all violators; in Rwanda any domestic trials that have occurred have been as devoid of Tutsi defendants as the international trials in Arusha have been. But, given political constraints, and evidence from the Balkans, Germany, and South America, it seems more likely that over time, domestic trials could bring a more representative group of violators to the dock than international courts could.

A LIMITED INSTITUTION— INTERNATIONAL JUSTICE AS FOREIGN AID

The ICC's budget is set to increase every year for the foreseeable future, as the organization grows to its full size and more cases begin to be processed. Yet, no matter how large the Court becomes, internal capacity and the limits of "judicial assistance" will constrain it. This too necessitates that advocates for real war crimes justice support domestic judicial solutions.

Most crimes in most states will fall below the ICC's radar. The ICC does not, and will not, have the capacity to process all the crimes that

deserve attention, forcing the international community to make difficult decisions. Additionally, once finances enter the equation, the
number of situations deserving of ICC action that the international
community may choose to "overlook" will likely grow, depressing the
number of ICC cases further. Quite simply, the ICC's funders may
want more for their money. International justice is extremely expensive, and domestic justice can be remarkably cheap in comparison. In
Bosnia, for example, an international grant of $16 million was suffi-
cient to cover both the provision of a special war crimes courthouse in
Sarajevo and its operations for two years. At the Yugoslavia tribunal's
current budget level (in fiscal 2008), this amount is less than *one month*
of work in The Hague. With a financially strapped international community, this form of economical justice should be attractive.

For the cases in which the ICC will not appear, the only hope for
justice will rest at the domestic level. Consequently, current supporters
of international justice would be well served in keeping their eyes on
the global situation, pinpointing problems and violations, and helping
those involved to arrive at a solution (prosecutorial or otherwise). The
absence of the ICC in the vast majority of situations in which violations will occur provides no other option.

However, even in those situations that receive ICC attention, there
will inevitably be a relative lack of *international* support to provide justice. This will be because of the nature of support the ICC can provide.
As in the larger debate regarding international justice, the promise and
peril associated with foreign aid provides a telling warning. Aid is a
$100 billion annual enterprise and though much benefit has been
derived from official aid, most observers find that the good of foreign
aid is highly concentrated on addressing "short-term, gap-filling"
needs, with aid falling short when attempting to find sustainable outcomes.[11] Consequently, all too often the more aid provided, the more
aid is needed. "Aid dependency" is the scourge of the development
community, and there has been no dearth of explanations for the
problem. The most frequently heard explanation is that aid impedes
the growth of indigenous institutions, and consequently little local

capacity develops to use aid for anything but limited-horizon, immediate solutions.

The same is true for international justice. In many states, it seems that international justice has created, or threatens to create, "legal" dependency, a disability that operates much like aid dependency—once states are allowed the luxury of "outsourcing" their justice to the international community, they lose the capacity, and the belief in their capacity, to engage in difficult matters of justice on their own. *The Economist* has dubbed this larger problem as "Balkan Dependency Syndrome," which it describes as "a form of behavior . . . whereby local leaders let foreigners do what should be their own work, handing over responsibility for unpopular decisions and, naturally, failures."[12]

This dependency tends to be exacerbated by many bureaucratic problems. "Bureaucratic inertia," for instance, propels organizations forward even if their direction is misguided. Once institutions that provide specific kinds of aid are established, they seek out places to disburse that aid. Problems arise, however, when the headlong rush to disburse aid means that there is inadequate time to coordinate with local and international actors, resulting in aid provided at cross purposes.

An equally unfortunate consequence of the bureaucratic aspect of international aid is that in order to validate themselves, organizations providing aid are often willing to find a "need" where none may exist. In the judicial sphere, this has seen the international community look critically at domestic courts conducting local trials and claim, in the face of evidence to the contrary, that such domestic trials cannot possibly occur. This has been rife in the Balkans.

There have been similar occurrences in Africa. Concerning the trial of Charles Taylor, the international community seems to be engaging in a more basic denigration of African justice: the often-repeated claim that Taylor is the first African head of state to be arraigned for serious crimes committed in office[13] makes the proceedings seem unique and perhaps leads people to conclude that such proceedings need to have more institutional, political, and economic support than is available in the African domestic sphere. Yet the novelty of Taylor's trial for Africa only seems real if one ignores the difficult, successful cases in which similarly poor, and equally seemingly incapable Equatorial Guinea, Mali, and the Central African Republic brought their leaders to court and to justice in the domestic arena.

The last part of the problem of aid is that upon finding a "need," international assistance regularly prescribes a specific solution that has all too often aggravated the problem that created the need. For instance, in the 1960s, a movement in development circles emerged that linked poverty in the developing world to an absence of robust legal structures. "Legal development" theorists posited that law, and in particular legal institutions, were the key to economic growth. Led by the US Agency for International Development, the Ford Foundation, and other NGOs, supporters of this theory embarked on a comprehensive effort to fill the "legal gap" that existed in poor countries. Unfortunately, despite its intentions, the effort failed, with many blaming its poor outcome on its focus on formal legal systems to the exclusion of "informal and customary ways in which many in developing nations order their lives."[14] It has since been widely recognized that the effort to bring law to the developing world was actually counterproductive to real economic, political, institutional, and even *legal* development. The "legal gap" was larger and more destructive to development after the legal development efforts than before.

A similarly counterproductive outcome can be seen in some attempts to bring justice to war-torn states. For instance, in Bosnia, even in the initial "fog of war" during the early 1990s, domestic courts successfully tried several war crimes cases. Moreover, inasmuch as domestic trials slowed down, or, in some areas ceased as the war continued, it was not necessarily due to a renunciation of legal repercussions for battlefield wrongs. Rather, as observers on the ground reported at the time, it was the

> loss of skilled members of the legal profession and the judiciary, as well as the physical destruction and lack of proper equipment or facilities . . . [that] hampered the ability of the courts to administer justice.[15]

This lack of capability had an obvious solution—investment in training and infrastructure rebuilding. However, the aid that was given exacerbated the problem by largely ignoring domestic institutions—allowing them to deteriorate and then eventually removing war crimes jurisdiction and cases from the state, thus causing domestic systems to dilapidate further.

These common traps of development institutions may yet befall the ICC. However, given its financially and statutorily limited charter, it may have to be more selective in its targeting and more cautious in its finding of "need" than its development aid cousins—or even its international judicial parents in The Hague and Arusha. The ICC will in all likelihood grow to be a far leaner organization than either the Yugoslavia or Rwanda tribunal, and will necessarily be spread more thinly, given its geographic coverage. For these reasons, it will hopefully have less ability and desire to crowd out local, domestic initiatives. And yet, even in those cases in which the ICC will fully engage, the problems international justice shares with foreign aid will mean that domestic assistance for establishing long-term solutions will be needed regardless. Again, supporters of true war crimes justice will have no choice but to assist states on the domestic level.

THE ROAD AHEAD

Turning the ICC primarily into a supporter and facilitator of international justice rather than a provider of justice will require a rethinking of the Court. Though some believe that such a refocus could be done within the confines of the ICC Treaty, others are not so sure. Regardless, pragmatics suggest that retooling of the Court would be required. Prosecutor Ocampo concedes that his organization is neither designed for nor funded to help build domestic judicial capacity. Even if states that are ardent supporters of international justice are unconcerned with the problems for "justice" imposed by international provision, there are several benefits to such a refocusing that may sway even those committed to the idea of international courts.

A key gain, not to be underestimated, is that the further the ICC moves from being a tool of prosecution, the more acceptable it will be to the key countries that have refused to join it—a group that represents nearly half of the world's population. If the Court transforms into being primarily a source of judicial wisdom, a supporter of domestic justice, and a form of global conscience to push states to prevent crimes as well as to deal with their aftermaths, the Court will become less threatening to those states who still fear it.

This blueprint for cooperating and working with the ICC dovetails nicely with several ideas proposed in the United States and elsewhere. For example, in May 2005, President Bush inaugurated the Active Response Corps, a "rapid reaction team," set to be deployed as civilian first responders to areas of the world in need of governance assistance.[16] The Bush administration originally planned to compose the corps of foreign and civil service officers. However, since the announcement, plans for the corps have expanded to include judges, lawyers, and corrections officers. Though still nascent, the State Department's coordinator for the Office of Reconstruction and Stabilization says that the idea is to be able to quickly deploy "people who can oversee or actually provide basic government services in a pinch."[17] The corps could go into countries like Rwanda in the wake of conflict, bringing experience and financing in order to help countries rebuild or enhance their own justice systems. The State Department is even planning to make the corps capable of being inserted into ongoing conflict zones. Though presumably state cooperation would still be needed, such a capability opens the possibility for the corps to provide on-the-ground support to countries like Uganda, the Democratic Republic of the Congo, and the Central African Republic.

A specifically judicial rapid-reaction corps—"JRR: Justice Rapid Response"—is also under discussion between several states and NGOs.[18] There seems little reason not to include ICC experts and expertise in such efforts.

Though both JRR and the Active Response Corps have yet to be realized, there is already an example of how an internationally backed, domestic justice promotion effort would work. In spring 2008, elements of the international community began to work toward the prosecution of former Chadian strongman Hissène Habré. Habré's eight-year dictatorship in Chad was marked by the torture and murder of tens of thousands of his countrymen. His acts earned him the unfortunate epithet, "Africa's Pinochet." He was overthrown in 1990 by Idress Déby, and, after receiving asylum in Senegal, fled to Dakar. After a decade-long odyssey in which evidence of Habré's crimes while in office came to light and Chadian victims came together, Senegalese officials indicted him in February 2000 and placed him under house arrest. There was much legal wrangling. While Senegal was uncertain about the propriety of prosecuting Habré, Belgium (the jurisdiction in which some Chadian victims had filed suit against Habré) demanded Habré's extradition. The Senegalese president asked the African Union to rule on the question of what should be done with Habré, and in July 2006, a Committee of Eminent African Jurists concluded that Senegal should prosecute Habré "on behalf of Africa." Senegal agreed.[19]

The wider international community, which had watched from the sidelines as the African Union and Senegal slowly came to the conclusion that a trial would be held, now became involved. With Habré serving as at least a partial catalyst, in December 2007, during the Lisbon EU Summit, the EU signed a Strategic Partnership agreement with African states, which included a provision that "crimes against humanity, war crimes, and genocide should not go unpunished and their prosecution should be ensured."[20] This followed an April 2007 resolution of the European Parliament that invited the EU "to encourage and assist the government of Senegal in preparing for the prompt and fair trial of Hissène Habré, in order to answer accusations of mass violations of human rights."[21]

Though the EU's support for international justice may make one assume that the language of both the partnership agreement and the parliamentary resolution spoke to the necessity of bringing violators to the international dock, this is not what has transpired in this case. Rather, preparations for the Habré trial may provide an effective model for how the ICC may reinvent itself to support domestic proceedings.

In their support for the Habré trial, the EU has simultaneously recognized the difficulties of international justice, alongside the potential of effective, nuanced domestic justice. Equally importantly, the Europeans have figured out a way to help make domestic justice a reality. The first critical element in the Habré case was the quick recognition, on behalf of Africans originally and then of the Europeans, that an international court was an inappropriate venue for the trial. Looking at the Yugoslavia, Rwanda, and Sierra Leone tribunals, the African Union and others promptly dismissed establishing a free-standing tribunal for Habré. Reed Brody of Human Rights Watch estimated that such a tribunal would cost more than $100 million and take several years to erect.[22] Rather, the African Union, and then quickly the Europeans, set upon a domestic court for conducting this trial.

There was some discord about whether the trial would take place in Africa or Belgium, with some members of the international community proceeding down the well-worn path of doubting the ability of poor states to manage the complexity of a case like Habré's. In June 2003, the Belgian minister of justice made this explicit, and claimed that neither Senegal nor Chad was in a position to take the case.[23]

Fortunately, cooler heads prevailed, with some stating their concerns about the image of sending a former African leader to a former African colonial power for trial. Even if the ICC could have heard the case (which it could not because Habré's crimes occurred prior to the Court's establishment), this concern, amongst others, seems as though it would have compelled the Europeans to proceed with the domestic course. Clearly the Europeans had learned some of the difficult lessons arising from international justice's unfortunate recent penchant for setting up tribunals in emotively laden locations, such as The Hague and Arusha. Though the trial will not be held where it should be, in Chad, a Senegalese trial conducted "in the name of Africa" is nonetheless much closer to home for victims, survivors, and perpetrators, than would be an international trial conducted on a different continent, and likely conducted in the name of the "world community."

In January 2008, the EU sent a mission to Senegal to evaluate the country's judicial system and any shortcomings it might have had in hosting such a trial. Alongside the Senegalese government the mission assessed the cost of the trial estimating that it would be about 30 million Euros (approximately $45 million). Individual European states, such as France and Switzerland, have pledged to support the trial, and the EU as a whole has become engaged in furthering the proceedings. The EU mission sent to Senegal was emphatic that the proceedings planned were "*not* [to be] an international trial."[24]

In signing off on and agreeing to support a domestic trial in Senegal, the EU consented to aiding a proceeding that promises to be far more flexible and expansive than an international case would be. For instance, though Habré will likely be charged with "crimes against humanity," he will also likely have to respond to broader claims including barbarity and plunder. Habré had arrived in Dakar with $14 million in his suitcases, and by all accounts he had lived a comfortable life in the capital.[25] His questionable financial gains can be scrutinized in a domestic case, an impossibility in international justice. The domestic trial will be able to respond to the findings of a Truth and Reconciliation Commission set up in Chad in 1992 and to the demands of victims, both of which have demanded reparations from the defendant.

Secondly, though international courts would be limited in the temporal scope of their prosecution—with international courts' statutes invariably restricting the examination of crimes to a specific timeframe—the same is not true for domestic courts. All of Habré's wrongs can be placed under scrutiny. Finally, dulling the impact of the distance of a Senegalese trial instead of Chadian trial (the two countries may share a French colonial history but are more than two thousand miles apart) is an important aspect of the French legal system, the system that Senegal adopted upon independence. French law (and that of many other civil law countries) allows civil parties to join a criminal case as coparties against a defendant.[26] Thus a prosecution becomes not just the "state" versus a defendant, but rather the state and all those who have claims against the defendant against him. One of the better-known instances in which this allowance was exploited occurred in France in the 1987 case against Nazi Klaus Barbie. There, survivors, victims' family members, and even organizations joined in the suit. This process, if maintained for the Habré trial, will provide Chadian victims—who first organized into the Chadian Association of Victims of Political Repression and Crime in 1991 and have militated for justice ever since—a measure of control and power in the system. Though the ICC permits the "views . . . of the victims" to be presented as "appropriate,"[27] international justice does not afford a similar measure of ownership to victims.

While the EU's efforts are promising, perhaps the most promising aspect of the EU's support was the makeup of the mission that it sent to Dakar in January 2008. Bruno Cathala, a French jurist, who at the time was also the registrar (chief administrative officer) of the ICC, headed the delegation. It was he who was emphatic that the potential trial that his mission had come to assist was not to be an international proceeding. This demonstrates that there has been experience within the highest reaches of the ICC hierarchy in moving the ICC and wider international justice toward new ends.

SOLVING THE "PROBLEM FROM HELL"

Despite the promise in the potential of the EU, the ICC, and perhaps the wider international community responding to the difficulties inherent in today's international justice and moving forward in new ways, I recognize that this conclusion does not *solve* the "Problem from Hell." It will not stop genocide or mass crimes, and indeed takes as an unfortunate premise that such reforms are needed because atrocities will continue.

I wish it were otherwise, but there is no sign that peoples of the world are becoming any kinder or tolerant of one another, nor is there any indication that the international community is ready to make "never again" really "never again." Stopping crimes before they occur and arresting them as soon as they start are by far the preferable means of dealing with such horrors. There has been no shortage of proposals made by academics, multilaterals, think tanks, and major states as to how to do so. Solely since 2000 we have seen the publication of John G. Heidenrich's rightly lauded, comprehensive guide *How to Prevent Genocide*;[28] the UN secretary general's publication of an Action Plan to Prevent Genocide and inauguration of the post of Special Advisor on the Prevention of Genocide and Mass Atrocities;[29] and, most recently, in December 2008, the publication of an extensive, intelligent report on preventing mass crimes from the Genocide Prevention Taskforce— a group led by former US secretary of state Madeleine Albright and former US secretary of defense William Cohen.[30]

While each effort has been promising and worthy of support, recent history is sobering. The number of times that the international community has actually stepped in to stop crimes is distressingly small, and is far outweighed by the continuing crises in which the international community has chosen to sit on its hands. As seen in Darfur, this complacency now seems to include the resort to international justice as a "solution," often seemingly in lieu of undertaking the effort, expense, and risk of forcibly acting to stop violations. Moreover, even if the international community actively took on its responsibility for preventing mass crimes, it could not hope to forcibly stop all crimes—much as the ICC could not hope to prosecute all potential defendants.

Though the combination of pragmatics and politics means that the international community will likely remain largely on the sidelines as crimes unfold, this does not mean that the international community should not be involved in the aftermath. The question becomes how best to leverage the international community's increasingly uniform desire to do "something." What are the international community's comparative advantages? And, just as importantly, what can the international community develop the political will to do—either as individual states or as a collective? If a judicial solution is chosen, we have some clarity as to where the international community can contribute in the most meaningful ways, thanks to the paths forged by the courts in The

Hague, Arusha, and Freetown. Internationals have, from the beginning of the UN tribunals, proven very capable in investigating crimes and engaging in sophisticated forensic investigations. They also have expertise in providing security to courts, witnesses, and investigators; integrating technology into judicial processes; and providing needed physical, monetary, and intellectual capital to countries in need. It is to these ends that the international community ought to direct its energies. Canada, for example, is being lobbied to help with "trial preparation, research, forensic investigations, legal advice, as well as financing," for the Habré case.[31] Ottawa would do well to heed these requests.

Though we assume the unfortunate fact that mass crimes will likely continue, a focus on effective domestic responses to war crimes can provide a clear benefit concerning future violations. Supporting domestic rule of law has a far greater chance of encouraging true deterrence and cultural change that might prevent a repetition of violence than does the imposition of a paternalistic justice from afar. A concerted focus on the domestic arena may make recurrence—and a return to "Hell"—that much rarer. It does not quite reach "never again," but it hopefully can move us away from "again and again."

NOTES

CHAPTER 1
FROM BUDAPEST TO BONDI TO BOSNIA:
AN UNLIKELY WAR CRIMES JOURNEY

1. US Embassy, *Survey on Opinions Regarding ICTY and Domestic Justice* (Belgrade, 2004). See also generally, Vojin Dimitrijevic, "The War Crimes Tribunal in the Yugoslav Context," *East European Constitutional Review* 5 (1996): 85; Daniel Simpson, "Milosevic Trial Leaves Most Serbs Cynical," *New York Times*, August 9, 2002, p. 8.

2. International IDEA, *South-East Europe Public Agenda Survey*, 2002, http://www.idea.int/press/pr20020404.htm.

CHAPTER 2
AN ODD, MISGUIDED DEBATE:
IS IT REALLY INTERNATIONAL JUSTICE OR NO JUSTICE?

1. Samantha Power, "It's Not Enough to Call it Genocide," *Time Magazine*, October 4, 2004, pp. 36, 59 (citing Colin Powell, US secretary of state, testimony before Congress on September 9, 2004); see also Paul Richter and Maggie Farley, "US Declares Darfur Crisis is Genocide," *Los Angeles Times*, September 10, 2004, p. A3.

2. Jay Goodliffe and Darren Hawkins, "A Funny Thing Happened on the Way to Rome: Explaining International Criminal Court Negotiations," *Brigham Young University School of Law*, December 29, 2006. Paper delivered at the Forty-Seventh Annual International Studies Association Convention, San Diego, CA, March 22–25, 2006.

3. Jesse Helms, "Remarks to the UN Security Council," *FDCH Media*, January 20, 2000.

4. Richard H. Curtiss, "Vote Postponed After Acrimonious Bolton Confirmation Hearing," *Washington Report on Middle East Affairs* 14, no. 4 (2005): 16–17.

5. Ibid.

6. David J. Scheffer, *Developments at the Rome Treaty Conference*, Department of State dispatch, August 1998, p. 19.

7. "I will not, and do not recommend that my successor submit the treaty to the Senate for advice and consent until our fundamental concerns are satisfied." President William Jefferson Clinton, "Statement on the Rome Treaty on the International Criminal Court," *Weekly Compilation of Presidential Documents* (Washington, DC: Federal Register, December 30, 2000), p. 4.

8. Joshua Rozenberg, "Will Bush Invade Cambridgeshire?" *Daily Telegraph* (London), September 5, 2002, p. 23; Bob Egelko, "Candidates' Views on War Court Differ on U.S.'s Global Duty; U.S.'s Global Duty Defined in Presidential Hopefuls' Opinions," *San Francisco Chronicle*, January 2, 2008, p. A1.

9. Philip Stephens, "America Breaks the Global Ties," *Financial Times* (London), July 5, 2002, p. 19.

10. Letters to the Editor, *Topeka Capital-Journal* (Kansas), August 1, 1998.

11. "No to a World Court," *Omaha World Herald* (Nebraska), December 30, 2000, p. 21.

12. Letters to the Editor, *Burlington Free Press* (Vermont), December 24, 2000.

13. Letters to the Editor, *Sarasota Herald Tribune*, (Florida) January 21, 2001.

14. "Flawed War-Crimes Treaty," *Kansas City Star* (Kansas & Missouri), February 1, 2001, p. B6.

15. Letters, *El Paso Times* (Texas), August 4, 2000, p. 14A.

16. "Sometimes Treaties are Worthless," *The State Journal-Register* (Springfield, IL), April 11, 2001, p. 6.

17. Letters to the Editor, *Bismarck Tribune* (North Dakota), September 19, 2000.

18. "Threat to Constitution," *Augusta Chronicle* (Georgia), July 27, 1998, p. A4.

19. "Stop the Global Monster Taking Shape in Rome," *Augusta Chronicle* (Georgia), June 22, 1998, p. A5.

20. State of Utah, Joint Resolution (Utah House of Representatives), May 4, 2004, POM 408.

21. "War Crimes: The World Needs a New Court," *Roanoke Times* (Virginia), February 26, 1995, p. G2.

22. Letters to the Editor, *Dayton Daily News* (Ohio), June 27, 2001.

23. Letters to the Editor, *The Oregonian*, August 25, 2001.

24. David Held, "Globalization: The Dangers and the Answers," May 26, 2004. http://www.opendemocracy.net/globalization-vision_reflections/article_1918.jsp (accessed May 18, 2008).

25. Ibid.

26. Gustavo Gonzalez, "Politics: Attacks on US Worry Anti-Globalization Forces," Inter Press Service, October 1, 2001.

27. Ibid.

28. Global Exchange, World Bank, IMF, http://www.globalexchange .org/campaigns/wbimf/ (accessed May 18, 2008).

29. "September 11: Roundtable," *Tikkun Magazine*, December 31, 2001, p. 15.

30. Declan Walsh, "The Country Where 'Di Wor is Don Don'—Tony Blair Arrives Today in Sierra Leone, Hoping to Cement a Fragile Peace There," *Irish Times*, February 9, 2002, p. 11.

31. Remarks made by Eleanor Roosevelt at a ceremony at the UN, New York, March 27, 1958, cited in Ethel C. Phillips, *You in Human Rights* (New York: US National Commission for UNESCO, 1967), p. 2.

32. Daniel Goleman, "The Group and the Self: New Focus on a Cultural Rift," *New York Times*, December 25, 1990, p. 41.

33. David Willman, Letters to the Editor, *Bismarck Tribune*, November 1, 2002.

34. Rich Lopiccolo, "America Should Avoid Global Entanglements and Absorption," *Pittsburgh Post-Gazette*, May 29, 2001.

35. Ralph Zacklin, "The Failings of Ad Hoc International Tribunals," *Journal of International Criminal Justice* 2 (2004): 541.

36. ICTR, *Prosecutor v. Kambanda*, Case ICTR-97-23-DP (1998).

37. ICTR, *Prosecutor v. Barayagwiza*, Case ICTR-97-19-I (1999).

38. ICTR, *Prosecutor v. Akayesu*, Case ICTR-96-4-T (1998).

CHAPTER 3
LEFT BEHIND

1. Christopher Solomon, "Sarajevo," *New York Times*, February 5, 2006, p. 1(5); William Oscar Johnson, "The Killing Ground," *Sports Illustrated*, February 14, 1994, p. 44.

2. Charles G. Boyd, "Making Peace with the Guilty: The Truth about Bosnia," *Foreign Affairs* (September/October 1995): 22.

3. Daniel McLaughlin, "Croatia Marks Crushed Uprising," *Irish Times*, August 6, 2005, p. 8.

4. Valerie Talacko, "Croatian Leaders Praise Operation Storm, Say War Crimes were 'Individual' Acts," *World Markets Analysis*, August 8, 2005.

5. "Croatia Lacks Courage to Face its Past," Primorske (Ljubljana, Slovenia), *BBC Monitoring International Reports*, December 12, 2005.

6. Vladimir Seks, "Storm as Pure as Driven Snow," Speaker, HRT1 TV (Zagreb), *BBC Monitoring International Reports*, August 5, 2005.

7. Daniel McLaughlin, "Croatia Honours Day Serbs Recall with Bitterness," *Irish Times*, August 5, 2005, p. 10.

8. Dejan Anastasijevic, "Karadzic Arrest: A Boost for Serbia," *Time*, July 22, 2008.

9. "Balkan End-Game," *Economist*, May 17, 2008, p. 66.

10. "Ex-Kosovo PM Pleads Not Guilty to War Crimes," *Turkish Daily News*, March 15, 2005.

11. See generally, Tim Judah, "Kosovo's Moment of Truth," *Survival* 47 (2005): 73.

12. OSCE Mission in Kosovo, *Human Rights Challenges Following the March Riots* (Pristina: OSCE, 2004).

13. Andrew Rosenbaum, "An Ethnic War that Still Rages," *New York Times*, October 14, 2003, p. A25.

14. David Charter, "Mitrovica Bridge Becomes Wall Between Two Worlds as Serbs Prepare for Long Fight," *Times* (London), March 19, 2008, p. 50.

15. Gary T. Dempsey, "Hague Mania," *National Review*, April 18, 2002.

16. Date-limited LEXIS Search for "international justice," "international criminal law," or "international humanitarian law," in the *Harvard Law Review*, *Yale Law Journal*, and *Columbia Law Review*.

17. Ian Brownlie, *Principles of Public International Law*, 4th ed. (Oxford: Clarendon Press, 1990), pp. 563–64, cited in Robert Cryer, *Prosecuting International Crimes* (Cambridge: Cambridge University Press, 2005), p. 51.

18. Date-limited LEXIS-NEXIS search of selected publications for "international justice," "international criminal law," or "international humanitarian law."

19. Ibid.

20. Jonathan D. Glater, "Harvard Law Decides to Steep Students in 21st-Century Issues," *New York Times*, October 7, 2006, p. 10; Jeri Zeder, "At Home in the World," *Harvard Law Bulletin* (Winter 2008), http://www.law.harvard .edu/news/bulletin/2008/winter/feature_3.php (accessed May 26, 2008).

21. Roy S. Lee, *The International Criminal Court: The Making of the Rome Statute* (The Hague: Kluwer Law International, 1999), p. 392.

22. The SCSL is unique among these courts in that it has operated alongside a Truth and Reconciliation Commission, which officially ended in 2004. In large part because the commission did not pursue prosecutions, the relationship between the two was at times fraught with controversy. This book solely focuses on the Court (which continues) and not on the commission, but acknowledges that the commission has had an impact on the Court's operations. See, William A. Schabas, "A Synergistic Relationship: The Sierra Leone Truth and Reconciliation Commission and the Special Court for Sierra Leone," *Criminal Law Forum* 15 (2004): 3–54; Hans Nichols, "Truth Challenges Justice in Freetown," *Washington Times*, January 5, 2005.

23. UN, *Security Council Resolution 827* passed the ICTY unanimously; *Security Council Resolution 955* passed the ICTR with 13 "yes" votes, 1 "no" vote, and 1 abstention; *Security Council Resolution 1664* passed the Lebanon tribunal unanimously.

24. James Bucyana, "The International Penal Tribunal for Rwanda and National Reconciliation," *International Journal of Refugee Law* 8 (1996): 622.

25. Amnesty International, *Rwanda: The Hidden Violence: "Disappearances" and Killings Continue* (New York: Amnesty International, 1998).

26. Kevin Whitelaw, "Rwanda Reborn," *US News & World Report*, April 23, 2007, p. 43.

27. Judith Miller, "Killing Again," *New York Sun*, January 29, 2007, p. 8.

28. Whitelaw, "Rwanda Reborn," p. 43.

29. Aloys Habimama, "Judicial Responses to Mass Violence: Is International Criminal Tribunal for Rwanda Making a Difference toward Reconcili-

ation in Rwanda," in *International War Crimes Trials: Making a Difference*, ed. Steven Ratner and James Bischoff (Austin: University of Texas Press, 2003), p. 86. Stating that "constantly exposed to such bitter criticisms highlighting the imperfections of the tribunal, many Rwandans tend to hold an overwhelmingly negative opinion of international justice."

30. The Appeals Chamber of the Special Court for Sierra Leone dismissed a motion brought by Hinga Norman claiming that his right to a fair trial was abrogated due to the funding arrangement. Special Court for Sierra Leone, *Prosecutor v. Hinga Norman*, Case SCSL-2004-14-AR72 E.

31. Tim Reid, "Donations Shortage Threatens Sierra Leone War Crimes Trial," May 31, 2007, p. 40.

32. Ibid.; IRIN, "Special Court Needs $30 Million to See War Crimes Trials Through," *IRIN Africa*, May 25, 2005, http://www.irinnews.org/report .aspx?reportid=54639 (accessed May 26, 2008).

33. "The Problems with the Special Court for Sierra Leone," *Standard Times* (Freetown), July 5, 2004.

34. International Crisis Group, "Sierra Leone: The Election Opportunity," *Africa Report* 129 (July 12, 2007): 1.

35. International Crisis Group, "Sierra Leone: Delicate Peace as Elections Approach–Report," *AllAfrica*, July 12, 2007.

36. "Life on 70 Cents a Day," *Economist*, December 13, 2008, p. 55.

37. Gary Jonathan Bass, *Stay the Hand of Vengeance* (Princeton, NJ: Princeton University Press, 2000), p. 310.

38. William Montgomery, "The Arrest of Ratko Mladic and Radovan Karadzic," p. B92, http://www.b92.net/feedback/misljenja/press/william06-02-27.php (accessed May 18, 2008).

39. See, for instance, most recently, "South African Clarifies Apartheid Era Crimes," Xinhua News Agency (Beijing), January 17, 2006 (reporting that the country's chief prosecutor only has a "few cases" arising from the Apartheid era/Truth and Reconciliation Commission).

40. William F. Buckley Jr., "East Germany's Biggest Spy on Trial," *Buffalo News*, May 10, 1993, p. 3.

41. See, for example, Natalia Letki, "Lustration and Democratization in East-Central Europe," *Europe-Asia Studies* 54 (2002): 529.

42. Reuters, "Purge of Army Officers Is Begun in El Salvador," *New York Times*, May 5, 1993, p. A10.

43. "Bringing the Wicked to the Dock—War Crimes," *Economist*, March 11, 2006.

44. See, for example, Jamie O'Connell, "Gambling with the Psyche: Does Prosecuting Human Rights Violators Console Their Victims?" *Harvard International Law Journal* 46 (2005): 295.

45. Martha Minow, *Between Vengeance and Forgiveness* (Boston: Beacon Press, 1998). See also, Diane F. Orentlicher, "Settling Accounts: The Duty To Prosecute Human Rights Violations of a Prior Regime," *Yale Law Journal* 100 (1991): 2537.

46. *Rome Statute of the International Criminal Court*, July 17, 1998, pmbl., 2187 UNTS 90, UN Doc. A/CONF.183/9 (1998), at article 17. See also John T. Holmes, "The Principle of Complementarity," in *The International Criminal Court: The Making of the Rome Statute*, ed. Roy S. Lee (The Hague: Kluwer Law International, 1999), p. 77.

47. According to the UN Database on "Multilateral Treaties Deposited with the Secretary General," there are 139 states party to the treaty (though only 106 have ratified the treaty), http://untreaty.un.org/ENGLISH/bible/english internetbible/partI/chapterXVIII/treaty11.asp (accessed May 18, 2008).

48. Robert M. Press, "In Rwanda's 'Slave Ship' Prisons, Life is Grim for Suspected Killers," *Christian Science Monitor*, November 18, 1994, pp. 1.

49. Dina Temple-Raston, *Justice on the Grass* (New York: Simon and Shuster, 2005), pp. 71–72.

50. Reuters, "Bosnia Verdict Stands Though Victims Live," *New York Times*, June 15, 1997, p. 12. See also Jonathan C. Randal, "Serb Convicted of Murders Demanding Retrial After 2 'Victims' Found Alive," *Washington Post*, March 15, 1997, p. A17.

51. Zelijka Aleksic, Editorial, *Srpski Nacional* (Belgrade), July 8, 2005, http://www.globalsecurity.org/military/library/news/2005/07/wwwh70519.ht m (accessed June 1, 2008).

52. Livia Klingl, Editorial, *Kurier* (Vienna), July 12, 2005.

53. Zarko Korac, "Srebrenica—The Day After," *Nezavisne Novine* (Banja Luka), July 12, 2005. (Translated US Department of State, International Information Programs, at GlobalSecuirty.org), http://www.globalsecurity.org/military/library/news/2005/07/wwwh70519.htm (accessed May 27, 2008).

54. Ruzdija Adzovic, *Jutarnje Novine*, July 9, 2005. (Translated at ibid.).

55. Editorial, *Slobodna Dalmacija*, July 12, 2005. (Translated at ibid.).

CHAPTER 4
THE POLITICS OF HELL: WHAT HAPPENED?

1. Samantha Power's book, *A Problem from Hell: America and the Age of Genocide* (New York: Perennial, 2003) served as the starting point for much of my thinking and work.

2. See generally, Edmond Paris, *Genocide in Satellite Croatia, 1941–1945: A Record of Racial and Religious Persecutions and Massacres* (Chicago: American Institute for Balkan Affairs, 1961).

3. J. F. O. McAllister, "Atrocity and Outrage," *Time Magazine*, August 17, 1992, p. 20.

4. Power, *A Problem from Hell*, p. 306.

5. Ibid.

6. Ibid.

7. V. P. Gagnon Jr. notes that Serbs and Croats never fought before the twentieth century, "intermarriage rates were quite high . . . and sociological polling as late as 1989–90 showed high levels of tolerance, especially in [the ethnically] . . . mixed regions." V. P. Gagnon Jr. "Ethnic Nationalism and International Conflict: The Case of Serbia," *International Security* 19 (1994): 134. However, Ilana Bet-El notes that, at least in regard to the Croat-Serb enmity, "their conflict dates to the late 19th century, when both began to emerge from within empires as distinct states. But rather than becoming established as such, it was their fate to be constantly flung together in untenable frameworks throughout the 20th century." Ilana Bet-El, "Balkan Bloodbaths," *Financial Times* (London), February 21, 1998, p. 6. Neither, however, concur with Christopher's assessment of "perpetual" animosity and violence between any of the ethnic groups present in the Balkans.

8. Janine di Giovanni, "The Family from Hell," *Times* (London), January 29, 2000.

9. Melanie Reid, "Bride From Hell: Warlord's Pop Star Wife is Evil Genius Behind Bloodshed," *Sunday Mail* (Edinburgh), March 28, 1999, p. 26.

10. "Dark Pages of Human History," *News24.com* (South Africa), July 23, 2008, http://www.news24.com/News24/World/News/0,2-10-1462_2361887,00.html. (accessed November 25, 2008).

11. Ian Traynor, "Muslims Regain Srebrenica–For a Day," *Guardian* (London), July 15, 2005, p. 7.

12. Power, *A Problem from Hell*, p. 449; see also, Steve Crawshaw, "Pristina Diary: A Land Divided by Hatred and Schnitzels," *The Independent* (London), March 30, 1998, p. 10.

13. Mark Etherington, "Coherence is the First Need for Intervention and State-Building," *Financial Times* (London), August 19, 2005, p. 15. Christopher's views are perhaps even clearer in other renditions of his speech—other versions have him modify "problem" with "intractable." Thomas L. Friedman, "Bosnia Reconsidered," *New York Times*, April 8, 1993, p. A1.

14. Ralph Zacklin, "The Failings of Ad Hoc International Tribunals," *Journal of International Criminal Justice* 2 (2004): 541.

15. Bernard D. Kaplan, "War Trials Call Just Rhetoric," *Seattle Post-Intelligencer*, December 20, 1992, p. P-1.

16. Mats Berdal, "The United Nations, Peacebuilding and Genocide in Rwanda," *Global Governance* 11, no. 1 (2005): 115.

17. Ian Fisher, "Ideas & Trends: If Only the Problem Were As Easy as Old Hatreds," *New York Times*, January 2, 2000, p. 10.

18. "The Pulitzer Prizes: Journalism and the Arts Bestow a Most Prestigious Honor," *New York Times*, April 19, 1995, p. B7; Roméo Dallaire, *Shake Hands with the Devil: The Failure of Humanity in Rwanda* (New York: Carroll & Graff, 2005).

19. Editorial, "Hell's Other Name is Sierra Leone," *Chicago Tribune*, February 18, 1999, p. 14.

20. Nicholas Wood, "The Hero of Hell City," *Times* (London), May 4, 1998.

21. J. T. Nguyen, "Security Council Votes to Form War Crimes Tribunal for Yugoslavia," *United Press International* (BC Cycle), February 23, 1993.

22. See the following chapters for further discussion and details.

23. ICTY, *Prosecutor v. Tadic*, opening statement. Cited in Barbar Demick, "As War Crimes Trial Opens, a Minor Figure Looms Large," *Philadelphia Inquirer*, May 8, 1996, p. A1.

24. B. V. A. Röling, "The Law of War and the National Jurisdiction since 1945," in The Hague Academy of International Law, Collected Courts, 1960-II, 354 (1961), quoted in Antonio Cassese, "Reflections on International Criminal Justice," *The Modern Law Review* 61 (1998): 7 n.11.

25. See Adam M. Smith, "Balkan Justice," *New Republic*, May 1, 2006, pp. 14–15.

26. Anna Merritt and Richard Merritt, *Public Opinion in Occupied*

Germany—The OMGUS Surveys (Urbana: University of Illinois Press, 1970), p. 31.

27. Ibid.

28. Samuel H. Barnes, "The Contribution of Democracy to Rebuilding Post-Conflict Societies," *American Journal of International Law* 95 (2001): 90.

29. Anna Merritt and Richard Merritt, *Public Opinion in Semi Sovereign Germany—The HICOG Surveys* (Urbana: University of Illinois Press, 1980), p. 7.

30. Frank Buscher, *The U.S. War Crimes Program in Germany, 1946–1955* (New York: Greenwood Press, 1989), p. 91.

31. Merritt and Merritt, *Public Opinion in Semi Sovereign Germany— The HICOG Surveys*, p. 8.

32. Ibid.

33. Fritz Weinschenk, "'The Murderers Among Them'—German Justice and the Nazis," *Hofstra Law & Policy Symposium* 3 (1999): 140.

34. John F. Kennedy, *Profiles in Courage* (New York: Harper Collins, 2004), p. 199.

35. "Democrats Assail Taft View on Nazis," *New York Times*, October 8, 1946, p. 45.

36. Kennedy, *Profiles in Courage*, p. 198. See also See Richard J. Goldstone and Adam M. Smith, *International Judicial Institutions: The Architecture of International Justice at Home and Abroad* (London: Routledge, 2009), chapter 4.

CHAPTER 5
FALLING ON DEAF EARS (PART I):
INTERNATIONAL JUSTICE FROM THE GROUND UP

1. "Hotel Rwanda Hero Urges Justice—Letter to UN Secretary General," *BBC News*, June 27, 2007.

2. "Rwanda; Thousands Demonstrate Against UN Tribunal," *Africa News*, February 29, 2004.

3. *New Times* (Kigali), "Rwanda Lauds ICTR Action on Suspect Staff," *AllAfrica*, July 2, 2006.

4. "Case of Rwandan Lawyer Revives Tension Between Kigali and the ICTR," Hirondelle News Agency, March 7, 2006.

5. Rwanda News Agency, "UN Court 'Behaving Arrogantly,'" *Financial Times Information*, January 25, 2008.

6. *New Times* (Kigali), "Rwanda: Registrar Blamed for UN Tribunal's Staff Defiance," *BBC Summary of World Broadcasts*, November 26, 2004.

7. Vojin Dimitrijevic, "Justice Must Be Done and Be Seen to Be Done: The Milosevic Trial," *Eastern European Constitutional Review* 11 (2002): 62.

8. Nina Bang-Jensen in Kristen Cibelli and Tamy Guberek, *Justice Unknown, Justice Unsatisfied?* (Medford, MA: Education and Public Inquiry and International Citizenship at Tufts University, 1999).

9. Chandra Lekha Sriram, "Wrong-Sizing International Justice?" *University of Maryland School of Law Legal Studies Research Paper* 49 (2006): 14.

10. In his first appearance before the international tribunal seeking to try him for war crimes, Charles Taylor, the former Liberian president, refused to recognize the Special Court's jurisdiction and accused it of attempting to meddle in the region's affairs; he then pled not guilty to eleven counts of war crimes. Hans Nichols and Lydia Polgreen, "Ex-Liberian Leader Pleads Not Guilty; Taylor at First Refuses to Recognize Court," *International Herald Tribune*, April 4, 2006, p. 5.

11. Ibid.; Georg Schwarzenberger, *International Law as Applied by International Courts and Tribunals*, vol. 2: *The Law of Armed Conflict* (London: Stevens, 1968), p. 464.

12. John Wilson, *Switzerland* (New York: Carey and Lea, 1832), p. 123.

13. Slobodan Milosevic, "Statement of President Slobodan Milosevic on the Illegitimacy of The Hague 'Tribunal,'" (August 31, 2001), *Alternative Press Review* 7, no.1 (Spring 2002), http://www.blythe.org/nytransfer-subs/2001 -Eastern_Europe/The_Statement_Milosevic_Was_Not_Allowed_to_Read (accessed May 24, 2008).

14. Robert Cryer, *Prosecuting International Crimes* (Cambridge: Cambridge University Press, 2005), p. 53.

15. UN, *Security Council Debate*, S/PV.3217 (May 25, 1993), para. 33, in Daniel L. Bethlehem and Marc Weller, *The 'Yugoslav' Crisis in International Law* (Cambridge: Cambridge University Press, 1997), p. 281.

16. UN, *Security Council Debate*, S/PV.3217 (May 25, 1993), para. 36, in Bethlehem and Weller, *'Yugoslav' Crisis*, p. 282.

17. Louis Henkin, *How Nations Behave: Law and Foreign Policy* (New York: Columbia University Press, 1979), p. 33. Arguing that customary international law is law "made over time by widespread practice of governments acting from a sense of legal obligation."

18. Jose E. Alvarez, "Trial of the Century? Assessing the Case of Dusko Tadic before the International Criminal Tribunal for the former Yugoslavia: The Likely Legacies of Tadic," *ILSA: Journal of International and Comparative Law* 3 (1997): 616; see generally, Ibrahim F. I. Shihata, *The Power of the International Court to Determine its Own Jurisdiction* (The Hague: M. Nijhoff, 1965), pp. 25–26.

19. ICTY, *Prosecutor v. Tadic*, Case IT-94-1-AR72 (October 2, 1995), paras. 6–11, 18–22 held that the ICTY has the jurisdiction to determine its own jurisdiction, in accordance with the principle of "Kompetenz-Kompetenz" or "competence de la competence."

20. ICTR, *Prosecutor v. Kanyabashi*, Decision on Jurisdiction, Case ICTR-96-15-T (June 18, 1997).

21. Yugoslav Telegraph Service (Belgrade), "Yugoslav Experts Say UN War Crimes Tribunal Legal, but Difficult in Practice," *BBC Summary of World Broadcasts*, February 26, 1993.

22. Yutaka Arai-Takahashi, *The Margin of Appreciation Doctrine and the Principle of Proportionality in the Jurisprudence of the ECHR* (The Hague: Intersentia Uitgevers, 2002), p. 4. See also generally, Eyal Benvenisti, "Margin of Appreciation, Consensus, and Universal Standards," *New York University Journal of International Law and Policy* 31 (1999): 845. For a discussion of the importance of the margin in securing national compliance, see Adam M. Smith, "Good Fences Make Good Neighbors? The 'Wall Decision' and the Troubling Rise of the ICJ as a Human Rights Court," *Harvard Human Rights Journal* 18 (2005): 255–63.

23. "Human Rights Act: How it Works," *BBC News*, http://news.bbc.co.uk/1/hi/uk/946390.stm (accessed May 24, 2008).

24. Adam M. Smith, "'Judicial Nationalism' in International Law: National Identity and Judicial Autonomy at the ICJ," *Texas International Law Journal* 40 (2005): 205–206. See, for example, ICJ, *Statute of the International Court of Justice*, article 31(1), June 26, 1945, which provided a right for "judges of the nationality of each of the parties . . . to sit in the case before the Court." Stephen M. Schwebel, "National Judges and Judges Ad Hoc of the International Court of Justice," *International and Comparative Law Quarterly* 48 (1999): 891. The rules of the International Center for the Settlement of Investment Disputes (ICSID), one of the main bodies of private international arbitration, also allow the party appointment of adjudicators (ICSID, Arbitration Rules, chapter 1, rule 3).

25. *Procès-Verbaux of the Proceedings of the Advisory Committee of Jurists*, Twenty-fourth Meeting, July 14, 1920, p. 532.

26. *European Convention for the Protection of Human Rights and Fundamental Freedoms*, 213 UNT. S. 222 (November 4, 1950), article 36, para. 1; and *Rules of the European Court of Human Rights*, rule 44.

27. The ten cases of "Legality of Use of Force" were (*Serbia and Montenegro v. Belgium*), (*Serbia and Montenegro v. Canada*), (*Serbia and Montenegro v. France*), (*Serbia and Montenegro v. Germany*), (*Serbia and Montenegro v. Italy*), (*Serbia and Montenegro v. Netherlands*), (*Serbia and Montenegro v. Portugal*), (*Serbia and Montenegro v. United Kingdom*), (*Serbia and Montenegro v. United States*), and (*Serbia and Montenegro v. Spain*). The cases against the United States and Spain were dismissed in 1999—Legality of Use of Force (*Serbia and Montenegro v. United States*), Provisional Measures, 1999 ICJ REP. 916 (June 2); Legality of Use of Force (*Serbia and Montenegro v. Spain*), Provisional Measures, 1999 ICJ REP. 761 (June 2)—and those against the remaining eight were dismissed in 2004. See generally, John H. Crook, "Current Development: The 2004 Judicial Activity of the International Court of Justice," *American Journal of International Law* 99 (2005): 454–57.

28. Nebojsa Bugarinovic, "Beograd: 37 Posto Gradana Smatra da Milosevic u Hagu Brani Srbiju I Srpski Narod," *Danas*, February 20, 2002. Cited/translated in: Emily Shaw, "The Role of Social Identity in Resistance to International Criminal Law: The Case of Serbia and the ICTY," Abstract, *Berkeley Program in Soviet and Post-Soviet Studies* (2003).

29. Conflict and competition between Serbs and Croats was largely responsible for the delegitimization of the official World War II Yugoslav government in exile, and the rise of Tito as an alternate leader. See Laurie West Van Hook, "Ethnicity in Exile: Coping with the Yugoslavs in World War II," *Woodrow Wilson International Center for Scholars*, Meeting Report 230, March 14, 2001.

30. Author's confidential discussions with Serb judges, Belgrade (March 2005); Croatian judges, Zagreb (July 2005).

31. US Embassy, *Survey on Opinions Regarding ICTY and Domestic Justice* (Belgrade, 2004). See also generally, Vojin Dimitrijevic, "The War Crimes Tribunal in the Yugoslav Context," *Eastern European Constitutional Review* 5 (1996): 85; Daniel Simpson, "Milosevic Trial Leaves Most Serbs Cynical," *New York Times*, August 9, 2002, p. 8.

32. International IDEA, *South-East Europe Public Agenda Survey*, (2002). 83 percent of Kosovars, 51 percent of Bosnians in the Federation, and only 21 percent of Croatians, and 4 percent of the residents of Republika Srpska express any trust in the tribunal.

33. Institute for War and Peace Reporting, "Sierra Leone; Dispute at Charles Taylor Trial Over Defence Resources," *Africa News*, June 9, 2007.

34. Mary Kimani, "Former US Attorney General Slams Tribunal," *InterNews Reports: The International War Crimes Tribunal for Rwanda Current Reports*, April 2, 2001.

35. Jamil Mujuzi, "The Special Court for Sierra Leone—Enforcing Law Or Politics?" *Monitor* (Uganda), October 15, 2006.

36. David Cohen, "Indifference and Accountability: The United Nations and the Politics of International Justice in East Timor," *East-West Center Special Reports*, no. 9, 2006.

37. Amnesty International, *Amnesty International and Judicial System Monitoring Programme. Indonesia and Timor-Leste. Justice for Timor-Leste: The Way Forward* (April 2004).

38. Erica Kinetz, "Cambodian Justice Moves Forward," *Christian Science Monitor*, November 21, 2007, p. 6.

39. Judge McDonald, interview with Eric Stover and Christopher Joyce, The Hague, the Netherlands, July 26, 1999; cited in International Human Rights Law Clinic, *Justice, Accountability and Social Reconstruction* (Berkeley: University of California Human Rights Center, 2000), p. 43, n. 37.

40. Francis Fukuyama, *The End of History and the Last Man* (New York: Harper, 1993).

41. See generally, UN, *The Path to The Hague* (New York: United Nations, 2001).

42. Mirko Klarin, "Nuremberg Now!" *Borba*, May 16, 1991, in UN, *The Path to The Hague*.

43. UN, *Security Council Debates*, S/PV.3217 (May 25, 1999), para. 33, in Bethlehem and Weller, '*Yugoslav*' *Crisis*, p. 281.

44. The conclusion of the first Gulf War in April 1991 provided support for the revived notion of judicial responses to massive humanitarian crimes, as some participants moved for the establishment of a tribunal to prosecute Iraqi leaders responsible for the slaughter of thousands of Iraqi Kurds. Such discussions reached as high as the UN secretary general (at the time, Peruvian Javier Perez de Cuellar), and the French and German governments both became heavily involved. However, nothing was to come of it, though the support for such international criminal justice was clearly growing. Frederic L. Borch, *Judge Advocates in Combat: Army Lawyers in Military Operations from Vietnam to Haiti* (Washington, DC: Office of the Judge Advocate General, 2001), pp. 135–36.

45. Garrett Fitzgerald, "Bosnian Conflict Highlights Trans-Atlantic Policy Gap," *Irish Times*, May 15, 1993, p. 12.

46. See, for example, Elie Wiesel, "Shadows in the Camps," *New York Times*, February 25, 1993, p. A19.

47. UN, *Security Council Debates*, S/PV.3217 (May 25, 1999), para. 33, in Bethlehem and Weller, '*Yugoslav' Crisis*, p. 281.

48. Dina Temple-Raston, *Justice on the Grass* (New York: Free Press, 2005), p. 72.

49. Thierry Cruvellier, "The United States on All Fronts," *International Justice Tribune*, February 9, 2002.

50. *Salone Times* (Freetown), April 8, 2003. Cited in International Crisis Group—Africa Briefing, *The Special Court for Sierra Leone and the Pitfalls of a "New Model*," August 4, 2003, p. 16, n. 98.

51. Abid Aslam, "Liberia: Capture Puts Ex-Warlord in Jail, New President in a Bind," Inter Press Service, March 29, 2006; Simon Robinson, "Trial and Error," *Time International*, June 6, 2005, p. 13.

52. Douglas Farrah, "Report Says Africans Harbored Al Qaeda," *Washington Post*, December 29, 2002, p. A01.

53. International Crisis Group—Africa Briefing, *The Special Court for Sierra Leone and the Pitfalls of a "New Model*," August 4, 2003, p. 17, n. 105.

54. Damien Lewis, "Diamonds are for Terror," *Mail on Sunday* (London), June 25, 2006, p. 24.

55. International Crisis Group—Africa Briefing, *The Special Court for Sierra Leone and the Pitfalls of a "New Model*," August 4, 2003, p. 17.

56. Judge Howard Morrison, "Human Rights Challenges in Trying Grave Crimes," Public Lecture, Monash University Law Chambers (Melbourne, Australia), March 8, 2007, http://www.law.monash.edu.au/castancentre/events/2007/morrison-paper.html (accessed May 18, 2008).

57. Aminatta Forna, "Back to My Shattered Home," *Sunday Times* (London), March 14, 2004, p. 9.

58. Stephen Ellis, *The Mask of Anarchy: The Destruction of Liberia and the Religious Dimensions of an African Civil War* (New York: New York University Press, 2001), p. 71. See also, Lansana Gberie, *A Dirty War in West Africa* (Bloomington: Indiana University Press, 2005), p. 52.

59. Special Court for Sierra Leone, *Prosecutor v. Foday Saybana Sankoh*, Case SCSL-03-I, Indictment (March 3, 2003), para. 18.

60. Barbara Crossette, "US Recalls Envoy to Burkina Faso," *New York Times*, November 6, 1992.

61. Special Court for Sierra Leone, *Prosecutor v. Charles Ghankay Taylor*, Case SCSL -03-I (March 3, 2003), para. 23.

62. David M. Crane, "A Just Ending: War Crimes I," *International Herald Tribune*, July 9, 2007, p. 6.

63. The SCSL was forced to cut off Samuel Hinga Norman's communication privileges for two weeks after he was overheard on the phone planning to incite civil unrest.

64. Sierra Leone Truth and Reconciliation Commission, *Final Report* (Freetown: Government of Sierra Leone), paras. 278, 283.

65. Human Rights Watch, Letter to President John Kufuor, "Liberia: ECOWAS Troops Must Respect Human Rights," July 21, 2003.

66. See, for example, Zarko Modric, "Tudjman's Dark Secrets Surfacing," *Yomuri Shimbun* (Tokyo), May 22, 2000.

67. See for example, Peter Maass, "Let's Not Forget Milosevic's Partner in Crime: To Insure Fairness, Tudjman Should be Indicted Too," *New York Times*, May 31, 1999, p. A13.

68. Though it has left out their leader, the ICTY has brought war crimes charges against numerous Bosnian Muslim military leaders: Enver Hadzihasanovic, Amir Kubura, Mehmed Alagic, Sefer Halilovic (the chief of the supreme command of the Bosnian Muslim Army, who is charged with command responsibility for the murder of sixty-two Bosnian Croat civilians in 1993), Naser Oric, the Bosnian Muslim military commander of Srebrenica, and, Rasim Delic, the wartime commander of the Bosnian Muslim army. Camp guards Hazim Delic and Esad Landzo were convicted for war crimes against Bosnian Serbs at the Celebici camp. For some of the resulting cases, see, for example, ICTY, *Prosecutor v. Enver Hadzihasanovic and Amir Kubura*, Case IT-01-47; ICTY, *Prosecutor v. Sefer Halilovic*, Case IT-01-48. Note, at least one Bosnian Muslim indictee, Zejnil Delalic, has been acquitted. ICTY, *Prosecutor v. Delalic et al.*, Case IT-96-21-A, Appeals Chamber Judgment (February 20, 2001).

69. The spokeswoman for the ICTY, Florence Hartmann, stated that "Izetbegovic was one of the suspects under investigation" but did not reveal the status of any investigation, the nearness of any potential indictment, nor even the crimes for which the former leader was being investigated. See, "Bosnia Leader was War Crimes Suspect," *BBC News*, October 22, 2003, http://news.bbc.co.uk/2/hi/europe/3203323.stm (accessed May 24, 2008).

70. See for example, (English Translation) Augustin Palokaj, "Justice of The Hague Tribunal," *Koha Ditore* (Pristina, Kosovo), October 27, 2003, http://www.unmikonline.org/press/2003/mon/Oct/lmm271003.pdf. (accessed May 24, 2008).

71. See, "Bosnia Leader Was War Crimes Suspect," *BBC News*, October 22, 2003.

72. Elaine Sciolino, "US Names Figures It Wants Charged With War Crimes," *New York Times*, December 17, 1992, p. A6.

73. US House of Representatives, *Expressing the Sense of the Congress Regarding the Culpability of Slobodan Milosevic for War Crimes, Crimes Against Humanity, and Genocide in the Former-Yugoslavia, and For Other Purposes*, House Concurrent Resolution 105 (Passed September 14, 1998). See also, "Resolution Calls for Immediate 'Indictment and Trial' of Milosevic," PR Newswire, August 7, 1998.

74. Vojin Dimitrijevic, interview with author, Belgrade, March 2005. See also, Dimitrijevic, "The Milosevic Trial," p. 59.

75. Elizabeth Sullivan, "Envoy Warns Albanian Rebels on Kidnapping," *Plain Dealer* (Cleveland), July 26, 1998, p. 6A.

76. Peter Maass, "Tribunal Should Pursue Tudjman," *Plain Dealer* (Cleveland), June 3, 1999, p. 9B.

77. Raymond Bonner, "A Would-Be Tito Helps to Dismantle His Legacy," *New York Times*, August 20, 1995, p. 12.

78. See, for example, Carl Savich, *Celebici*, http://www.serbianna.com/columns/savich/047.shtml (accessed November 11, 2003).

79. Chris Stephen, "War Crimes Tribunal Faces Crisis as Suspects Elude Their Captors," *Scotsman*, January 23, 2001, p. 12.

80. Celestine Bohlen, "Russians See and Read Another Slant to the War, With Milosevic as a Patriot," *New York Times*, April 4, 1999, p. 9.

81. See, for example, Gregory Katz, "Anger of NATO Bombing is Widespread in Greece," *Dallas Morning News*, May 29, 1999, p. 27A; "Demonstrators in Many Cities Demand Halt to Air Strikes," *New York Times*, March 29, 1999, p. A11; Howard Zinn, "The Deadly Semantics of NATO Bombings," *Boston Globe*, May 28, 1999, p. A19.

82. "NATO Intensifies Bombing Despite Russian, Chinese Objections," *Bulletin's Frontrunner*, May 12, 1999.

83. Emma Daly, "Dossier of NATO 'Crimes' Lands in Prosecutor's Lap," *Observer* (London), December 26, 1999, p. 15; Associated Press, "War Crimes

Prosecutor is Reviewing NATO Strikes on Yugoslavia," *St. Louis Post-Dispatch*, December 29, 1999, p. A6.

84. Special Court for Sierra Leone, "Article 1: Competence of the Court," *Statute of the Special Court for Sierra Leone.*

85. UN, *Preliminary Report of the Independent Commission of Experts Established in Accordance with Security Council Resolution 935*, UN Doc. S-1994-1125 (1994).

86. "The International Criminal Tribunal for Rwanda Must Rise Above the Politics," Press Release no. 12 (2001)—Rassemblement pour le Retour des Réfugiés et la Démocratie au Rwanda, July 23, 2001, http://www.inshuti .org/rdr35a.htm (accessed May 27, 2008).

87. UN representative from Venezuela, *Security Council Debates*, S/PV.3217, para. 8, in Bethlehem and Weller, *'Yugoslav' Crisis*, p. 275.

88. Yugoslav Telegraph Service (Belgrade), "UN Resolution on War Crimes is Aimed at Punishing One State," *BBC Summary of World Broadcasts*, April 14, 1993.

89. Yugoslav Telegraph Service (Belgrade), "FRY Opposes Setting up of War Crime Tribunal," *BBC Summary of World Broadcasts*, May 27, 1993.

90. Yugoslav Telegraph Service (Belgrade), "FRY Human Rights Minister on Pitfalls of UN Resolution on War Crimes Tribunal," *BBC Summary of World Broadcasts*, February 23, 1993.

91. Yugoslav Telegraph Service (Belgrade), "Prince Karadjordjevic Appeals to UN to Ensure Balanced War Crimes Investigations," *BBC Summary of World Broadcasts*, February 24, 1993.

92. Klaus Kinkel, "The London Conference Statement," August 26, 1992, in UN, *The Path to The Hague*. Michael Libal, the former head of the German foreign ministry's South-East European Department, discusses the broad-based support within the German government for something to be done to stem the tide of war, with many members of the Bundestag particularly aghast at what they viewed were Serb excesses against civilians in Croatia. See Michael Libal, *Limits of Persuasion: Germany and the Yugoslav Crisis, 1991–1992* (London: Praeger, 1997), p. 105.

93. "Food Flights can Resume," *Herald Sun* (Sydney, Australia), August 20, 1992.

94. Paul Lewis, "Security Council Establishes War-Crimes Tribunal for the Balkans," *New York Times*, May 26, 1993, p. A13. See also, for example UN,

Security Council Resolution 1034 (December 21, 1995), which singled out Bosnian Serbs for reprobation.

95. See generally the website of the ICTY at http://www.icty.org.

96. Neil MacDonald, "Hunt for Justice Reopens Wounds," *Financial Times* (London), February 20, 2006, p. 15.

97. Charles G. Boyd, "Making Peace with the Guilty: The Truth about Bosnia," *Foreign Affairs* 74 (1995): 23.

98. Susan L. Woodward, "Genocide or Partition: Two Faces of the Same Coin?" *Slavic Review* 55 (1996): 755.

99. See, for example, UN, *Security Council Resolution 1019* (November 9, 1995), which notes "serious violations of international humanitarian law . . . in the Republic of Croatia."

100. Norman Kempster, "All Sides Share Guilt in Bosnia, Christopher Says," *Los Angeles Times*, May 19, 1993, p. A1.

101. "Nuremberg in Bosnia: The US Proposed War-Crimes Trials of Serbs and Croats," *Time Magazine*, December 28, 1992, p. 15.

102. UN, *Commission on Human Rights Inquiry*, E-CN.4-1993-50 (February 10, 1993). See also, Alan Ferguson, "Croat Forces, Muslims Guilty of Atrocities, UN Reports," *Star* (Toronto), May 20, 1993, p. A18.

103. Ibid.

104. Florence Hartmann, the former spokeswoman for the ICTY, notes that these figures very closely match estimates drawn up by the CIA. See Florence Hartmann, "Bosnia," in *Crimes of War: The Book*, http://www.crimesofwar.org/thebook/bosnia.html (accessed May 18, 2008).

105. See, for example, Robert Block, "UN Condemns Belgrade Over War Crimes," *Independent* (London), March 10, 1995, p. 14.

106. Stacy Sullivan, "Milosevic's Willing Executioners," *New Republic*, May 10, 1999, p. 26.

107. Michael P. Scharf, *Balkan Justice: The Story Behind the First International War Crimes Trial Since Nuremberg* (Durham, NC: Carolina Academic Press, 1997), p. 24.

108. Boyd, "Making Peace with the Guilty," p. 25.

109. Blaine Harden and Mary Battiata, "East Europeans Weigh Costs of Change: Move Away From Communism More Difficult Than Many Expected," *Washington Post*, December 24, 1990, p. A1.

110. The figure of 70 percent is also heard. See, for example, Judy

Dempsey, "The Centre Slowly Loses its Hold," *Financial Times* (London), December 19, 1990, p. 17.

111. John Pomfret, "Atrocities Leave Thirst for Vengeance in Balkans," *Washington Post*, December 18, 1995, p. A01.

112. International Crisis Group—Africa Briefing, *The Special Court for Sierra Leone and the Pitfalls of a "New Model,"* August 4, 2003, p. 17.

113. Laura Barbanel and Robert J. Sternberg, *Psychological Interventions in Times of Crisis* (New York: Springer, 2006), p. 227.

114. Joshua Wallenstein, "Punishing Words," *Stanford Law Review* 54, no. 2 (2001): 351, n. 7.

115. David Kindred, "Atlanta Games; Day 9—Quick Read—Burundi Athletes Happy to Be Here," *Atlanta Journal and Constitution*, July 27, 1996.

116. Christian Scherrer, *Genocide and Crisis in Central Africa: Conflict Roots, Mass Violence and Regional War* (Westport, CT: Greenwood, 2002), p. 29.

117. International Crisis Group, *Conflict History: Burundi*, http://www .crisisgroup.org/home/index.cfm?action=conflict_searchandl=1andt=1andc _country=20 (accessed May 18, 2008).

118. Warren Weinstein and Robert Schrire, *Political Conflict and Ethnic Strategies: A Case Study of Burundi* (Syracuse, NY: Syracuse University Press, 1976), p. 19.

119. Stephen R. Weissman, *Preventing Genocide in Burundi* (Washington, DC: United States Institute of Peace, 1998), p. 5.

120. See UN, *Security Council Debates*, Forty-ninth session, 3,453d meeting, UN Doc. S-PV.3453, at 14–15 (1994).

121. John A. Armstrong, "Collaborationism in World War II: The Integral Nationalist Variant in Eastern Europe," *Journal of Modern History* 40 (1968): 400–409. See also generally, Ladislus Hory and Martin Broszat, *Der Kroatische Ustascha-Staat, 1941–1945* (Stuttgart, West Germany: Institut fur Zeitgeschichte, 1964).

122. Srdjan Trifkovic, "Rivalry Between Germany and Italy in Croatia, 1942–1943," *The Historical Journal* 36 (1993): 879; Armstrong, "Collaborationism in World War II," p. 401.

123. "Ustasa," in *Encyclopedia Britannica*, http://search.eb.com/eb/ article-9074533 (accessed December 1, 2008). So brutal were some attacks that the Italians were obliged to intervene in order to mitigate some of the violence. See also Mark Aarons and John Loftus, *Unholy Trinity: The Vatican, The Nazis, and the Swiss Banks* (New York: MacMillan, 1991), p. 73; Florence

Hamlish Levinsohn, *Belgrade: Among the Serbs* (Chicago: Ivan R. Dee, 1994), p. 36.

124. John Pomfret, "Atrocities Leave Thirst for Vengeance in Balkans," *Washington Post*, December 18, 1995, p. A01.

125. UN, *Convention on the Non-Applicability of Statutory Limitations to War Crimes and Crimes Against Humanity* (1968).

126. Bosnian Serb leader, and indicted war criminal, Radovan Karadzic forcefully made this argument when, upon hearing of the establishment of the ICTY he asked why the UN did not erect a "permanent international court for war crimes which would treat those crimes of World War II that have escaped justice and also all those war crimes since World War II up to now." He argued that by setting up the ICTY with so limited a temporal mandate, the UN made the tribunal look "more like revenge by the German lobby for the Nuremberg trial and as an attempt to choose a side to be declared guilty in the Yugoslav conflict." "Bosnian Serbs Refuse to Cooperate with War Crimes Tribunal," *United Press International* (BC Cycle), May 26, 1993. Milan Bulajic, a former Yugoslav diplomat and chair of the Yugoslav State Commission for War Crimes and Crimes of Genocide, made a similar argument questioning why the ICTY would be so limited in jurisdiction when war crimes had no statute of limitations. See Yugoslav Telegraph Service (Belgrade), "Yugoslav Official: UN Resolution on War Crimes is Aimed at Punishing One State," *BBC Summary of World Broadcasts*, April 14, 1993. Finally, in May 1993, shortly after the Security Council approved the tribunal, "Yugoslav Deputy President and Foreign Minister Vladislav Jovanovic said the Federal Republic of Yugoslavia had for quite some time urged the setting up of a standing international court for war crimes and saw no justification for a selective and not a universal approach to the matter." Yugoslav Telegraph Service (Belgrade), "Yugoslav Foreign Minister Criticizes 'Selective' Approach to War Crimes," *BBC Summary of World Broadcasts*, May 29, 1993.

127. County Court of Zagreb, Press Release "Sakic Found Guilty as Charged and Sentenced to 20 Years in Prison," http://public.carnet.hr/sakic/hinanews/arhiva/9910/hina-04-h.html (accessed May 27, 2008).

128. Ian Traynor, "War Crimes: Austria Stalls on Extradition after Nazi Hunter Highlights Actions of 92-Year Old in Wartime Croatia," *Guardian* (London), November 25, 2005, p. 23.

129. Benjamin Wittes, "For An Accused War Criminal, A 50-Year Haven in America," *Washington Post*, September 20, 1999, p. A15.

130. See, generally, Milovan Djilas, *Wartime* (Fort Washington, PA: Harvest Books, 1980), chap. 2; "Tito's Men Seize Gen. Mikhailovitch in Yugoslav Cave: Arrest of the Chetnik Leader," *New York Times*, March 25, 1946, p. 1.

131. See, generally, George Lepre, *Himmler's Bosnian Division: The Waffen-SS Handschar Division 1943–1945* (Algen, PA: Schiffer, 1997); Antonio J. Munoz, eds. *The East Came West: Muslim, Hindu and Buddhist Volunteers in the German Armed Forces* (London: Europa Books, 2002), chapters 2, 13.

132. John Kifner, "An Outlaw in the Balkans is Basking in the Spotlight," *New York Times*, November 23, 1993, A1.

133. Charles Krause, *MacNeil/Lehrer Newshour*, PBS, October 6, 1992.

134. Marguerite Feitlowitz, "UN War Crimes Court Approved for Sierra Leone," *Crimes of War*, January 8, 2002, http://www.crimesofwar.org/onnews/news-sierra.html (accessed May 24, 2008).

135. Catherine Maddux, "Hague Trial Could Mean Justice for More West African War Victims," *Voice of America*, April 10, 2006. Citing Phillip Banks, who led the drafting of Liberia's postwar constitution.

136. Both 1993 resolutions on the matter, *Security Council Resolutions 808* and *827*, are nebulous on the question of who should be prosecuted, speaking of only bringing to justice those "persons responsible for serious violations of international humanitarian law." However, there was a widespread assumption that only the most senior and most responsible ought to be brought into the dock. For example, UN lawyers who visited the Balkans after the ICTY resolution was passed but before the body was in operation, returned with concerns about the potential for trials, contending that "it is going to be very difficult to get a *senior* political figure or a *very senior* military figure before a court." John F. Burns, "Balkan War Trial in Serious Doubt," *New York Times*, April 26, 1993, p. A9 (emphasis added).

137. Keith Dovkants and Victor Sebestyn, "War Criminals Who May be Charged with Balkan Atrocities," *Evening Standard* (London), February 16, 1993, p. 16. See also, Tom Post, "A Pattern of Rape," *Newsweek*, January 4, 1993, p. 32.

138. See for example, Filip Svarm and Jovan Dulovic, "War Crimes—Witnesses and Victims," *Vreme News Digest Agency* no. 232, March 19, 1996.

139. Barbara Demick, "As War Crimes Trial Opens, A Minor Figure Looms Large," *Philadelphia Inquirer*, May 8, 1996, p. A01.

140. R. Bruce Hitchner, "Comment: The Tribunal's Own Failings," *Institute for War and Peace Reporting*, August/September 1997, p. 8. Hitchner said

that "[i]n contrast with the Nuremberg and Tokyo Tribunals which tried only the most senior Nazis and Japanese war criminals, the Tribunal has preferred to target low-level figures, including prison guards and foot soldiers, rather than those primarily responsible for orchestrating ethnic cleansing and genocide in Bosnia and Croatia." See also, "War Crimes Sentence Stokes Serb Defiance," *New York Times*, July 15, 1997, p. A1.

141. Scharf, *Balkan Justice*, p. 225.

142. See, for example, "One Brought to Justice, Many at Large—Balkans War Crimes," *Economist*, February 9, 2002. The report states that some of those responsible for the Srebrenica massacre remain serving on the local police force.

143. Chandra Lekha Sriram, "Wrong-Sizing International Justice? The Hybrid Tribunal in Sierra Leone," *Fordham International Law Journal* 29 (2006): 472.

144. "Bringing Justice: The Special Court for Sierra Leone," *Human Rights Watch* 16, no. 8(a) (2004): 5–6, http://www.hrw.org/reports/2004/sierraleone0904/sierraleone0904.pdf (accessed May 27, 2008).

145. Tim Weiner, "Taylor Stole $100 Million from Liberia, Records Show" *New York Times*, September 18, 2003, p. 3.

146. "Marshals Seeking Ex-Official Of Liberia After His Escape," *New York Times*, September 17, 1985, p. A20.

147. "Inmate Surrenders to Authorities," *United Press International*, September 19, 1985.

148. Emira Woods, "Can Africa's First Woman President get Liberia back on Track?" *Christian Science Monitor*, January 17, 2006, p 9.

149. Carlotta Gall, "A Dark Secret Comes to Light in Serbia," *New York Times*, June 1, 2001, p. 10. There was talk of also trying Milosevic on a specific charge of electoral fraud. See Steve Crenshaw, "Milosevic is Warned He May Go on Trial in Belgrade for Rigging Election Ballot," *Independent* (London), October 9, 2000, p. 1.

150. Reuters, "Serbs Insist Any Trial of Milosevic be in Yugoslavia," *Chicago Tribune*, January 25, 2001, p. 6.

151. Thierry Cruvellier, "Africa: The Laboratory of Justice," *Crimes of War*, October 2004.

CHAPTER 6
FALLING ON DEAF EARS (PART II):
"UNFAIR AND UNHELPFUL"

1. Barbara Crossette, "Rwanda Asks Quick Start of Tribunal," *New York Times*, October 9, 1994, p. 19.

2. Jane Perlez, "For Sarajevans, A Very Hard-to-Grasp Day at the Beach," *New York Times*, August 5, 1996, p. A3.

3. Royal Netherlands Embassy–Sarajevo, http://bosniaherzegovina.nl embassy.org/consular_affairs (accessed May 17, 2008).

4. Serb per capita income per month computed via data from US Central Intelligence Agency, *World FactBook*, http://www.odci.gov/cia/publications/factbook/index.html (accessed May 24, 2008).

5. See, for example, in the United States, *Globe Newspaper Co. v. Superior Court*, 457 US 596, 606 (1982), which held that "the right of access to criminal trials plays a particularly significant role in the functioning of the judicial process and the government as a whole. Public scrutiny of a criminal trial enhances the quality and safeguards the integrity of the factfinding process, with benefits to both the defendant and to society as a whole"); in Russia, the 2002 Criminal Code, article 241, declared that "the judicial proceedings on criminal cases in all the Courts shall be open"; in the Inter-American System, the IACHR requires such public trials in article 8.5, as does the Universal Declaration of Human Rights, article 11(1).

6. ICTR, "Job Description," http://www.ictr.org (accessed May 17, 2008).

7. Jeffrey Gettleman, "Justice in Rwanda," *St. Petersburg Times*, May 1, 1998, p. 1A.

8. Ateesh Chanda, *Transitional Justice: The Case of East Timor* (senior thesis, Brown University, 2004), p. 88.

9. International Human Rights Law Clinic, *Justice, Accountability and Social Reconstruction: An Interview Study of Bosnian Judges and Prosecutors* (Berkeley: University of California Human Rights Center, 2000), p. 43. See also Kristin Cibelli and Tamy Guberek, *Justice Unknown, Justice Unsatisfied? Bosnian NGOs Speak about the International Criminal Tribunal for the Former Yugoslavia* (Medford, MA: Tufts University, 1999), pp. 14–16.

10. Balkan and UN personnel, interview with author, 2004–2006. See also, Ralph Zacklin, "The Failings of Ad Hoc International Tribunals," *Journal of International Criminal Justice* 2 (2004): 544.

11. Chandra Lekha Sriram, "Wrong-Sizing International Justice? The Hybrid Tribunal in Sierra Leone," *Fordham International Law Journal* 29 (2006): 472.

12. Thierry Cruvellier, "Africa: The Laboratory of Justice," *Crimes of War,* October 2004, http://www.crimesofwar.org/africa-mag/afr_06_cruvellier .html (accessed May 17, 2008).

13. International Crisis Group—Africa Briefing, *The Special Court for Sierra Leone and the Pitfalls of a "New Model,"* August 4, 2003, p. 11.

14. Craig Timberg, "Well-Funded but Selective War Crimes Probe Draws Resentment of Victims," *Washington Post,* March 26, 2008, p. A11.

15. Dina Temple-Raston, *Justice on the Grass* (New York: Free Press, 2005), p. 75.

16. Timberg, "Well-Funded but Selective War Crimes Probe," p. A11.

17. David Crane, press conference, Freetown, March 18, 2003, quoted in James Cockayne, "Hybrids or Mongrels? Institutionalized War Crimes Trials as Unsuccessful Degradation Ceremonies," *Journal of Human Rights* 4 (2005): 460, n. 33.

18. International Crisis Group—Africa Briefing, *The Special Court for Sierra Leone and the Pitfalls of a "New Model,"* p. 14.

19. Thierry Cruvellier, "Domino Effect," *International Justice Tribune,* June 11, 2002.

20. Ibid.

21. InterNews, "ICTR Prosecutor Seeks to Drop Charges Against Genocide Suspect," *AllAfrica,* August 14, 2002.

22. Cruvellier, "Domino Effect."

23. ICTY, *Prosecutor v. Karemera,* Karemera Decision on Judicial Notice, Case ICTR-98-44- AR73(C), Decision on Prosecutor's Interlocutory Appeal of Decision on Judicial Notice, (June 16, 2006), para. 35.

24. ICTY, *Prosecutor v. Milosevic,* Case IT-02-54, Kosovo Indictment issued May 24, 1999; Croatia Indictment issued October 8, 2001; Bosnia Indictment issued November 22, 2001.

25. Vojin Dimitrijevic, "Justice Must Be Done and Be Seen to Be Done: The Milosevic Trial," *Eastern European Constitutional Review* 11 (2002): 60.

26. Jon Silverman, "Worst Outcome for Milosevic Tribunal," *BBC News,* March 11, 2006.

27. Ibid.

28. "Trial Judges Formally Close Milosevic Case," *New York Times,* March 14, 2006.

29. Marlise Simons, "Milosevic Died of Heart Attack, Autopsy Shows," *New York Times*, March 13, 2006, p. A6.

30. Thierry Cruvellier, "Africa: The Laboratory of Justice."

31. Ibid.

32. See, for example, "Weekly Press Briefing," March 24, 1999, http://www.un.org/icty/briefing/PB240399.htm (accessed May 17, 2008). Deputy Prosecutor Blewitt admitted that leaks of sensitive documents on investigation "clearly started from within the [Office of the Prosecutor.]" See also, "Assessment of the Prosecutor on the Co-operation Provided by Croatia," October 3, 2005, http://www.un.org/icty/pressreal/2005/p1009-e.htm (accessed May 17, 2008). Details "leaks of sensitive information to the media" from a putatively "cooperating state."

33. Timberg, "Well-Funded but Selective War Crimes Probe," p. A11.

34. Ibid.

35. Quoted in Lydia Polgreen and Marlise Simons, "Sierra Leone Asks to Move Liberian's Trial," *New York Times*, March 31, 2006, p. A7.

36. Radio Rwanda, "UN Rwanda Tribunal Defence Lawyers to Hold Further Talks," *BBC Monitoring International Reports*, January 30, 2004.

37. David Aronofsky, "International War Crimes and Other Criminal Courts: Ten Recommendations for Where We Go from Here and How to Get there," *Denver Journal of International Law and Policy* 34 (2006): 17; Jacob Katz Cogan, "International Criminal Courts: Difficulties and Prospects," *Yale Journal of International Law* 27 (2002): 112.

38. Thierry Cruvellier, "Domino Effect."

39. See website of the ICTY, "ICTY At a Glance—Key Figures," http://www.un.org/icty/glance-e/index.htm (accessed May 17, 2008).

40. Ludovic Kennedy, "Why Are We So Wedded to a System That Fails Us at Every Turn?" *Times* (London), July 2, 2002, p. 3.

41. Ibid.

42. J. Mark Ramseyer and Eric B. Rasmusen, "Why is the Japanese Conviction Rate So High?" *Journal of Legal Studies* 30 (2001): 53; David H. Bayley, "Police, Crime and the Community in Japan," in *Institutions for Change in Japanese Society*, ed. George De Vos (Berkeley: Institute of East Asian Studies, University of California, 1982), p. 182.

43. Australian Institute of Criminology, *Australian Crime: Facts and Figures 2003, Defendants' Cases Finalized in Higher Courts*, http://www.aic.gov.au/publications/facts/2003/fig074.html (accessed May 17, 2008).

44. "Journalists' Guide to the Federal Courts, Criminal Case—Plea Bargains and Sentencing," http://www.uscourts.gov/journalistguide/district _criminal.html (accessed May 17, 2008).

45. Ian Fisher, "Trial of Milosevic Will Peel Layers of Balkan Guilt, Too," *New York Times,* February 11, 2002, p. 1.

46. Barry Schweid, "New US Efforts to Rid Serbia of Milosevic," *Advertiser,* June 30, 2000, p. 29.

47. David Rohde, *End Game* (Boulder, CO: Westview Press, 1997), pp. 137–80.

48. Marlise Simons, "Dutch Cabinet Resigns Over Failure to Halt Bosnian Massacre," *New York Times,* April 17, 2002, p. 3.

49. Eve-Ann Prentice, "Oxfam Condemns UN for Rwanda 'Complacency,'" *Times* (London), October 14, 1994.

50. *East African,* "Rwanda: Thou Shalt Kill," *Africa News,* April 1, 2002.

51. "Rwanda: Tough Year Ahead for Semi-Traditional Gacaca Courts," *Africa News,* February 22, 2006.

52. "Rwanda: An ICTR Witness is Refused Protection Measures," *Africa News,* November 30, 2007.

53. Ian Fisher, "Peace in Burundi Still Elusive as Africa Readies for Clinton," *New York Times,* August 26, 2000, p. A1.

54. "A Tale of Two Homecomings," *Economist,* December 21, 1996.

55. Rosemary Righter, "France's Killing Fields," *Times* (London), July 6, 1994.

56. "Official Website for H. E. Paul Kagame," http://www.gov.rw/ government/president/index.html (accessed December 6, 2008) (indicating that his spoken languages are English, Kinyarwanda, and Swahili).

57. Herbert M. Howe, *Ambiguous Order: Military Forces in African States* (Boulder, CO: Lynne Rienner, 2004), p. 6.

58. Nile Gardiner, "Law of the Jungle," *Daily Standard,* April 29, 2008.

59. "Rwanda: UN Report Reveals Corruption at Genocide Tribunal," *Hirondelle Foundation-BBC Monitoring Africa,* March 14, 2002.

60. "Whistle Blowing at the UN," *National Journal* 37 (March 12, 2005).

61. "Barred in New York and Litigating in Arusha," *International Justice Tribune,* May 3, 2004.

62. Ibid.

63. Ibid.

64. *Arusha Times,* "Suspected Criminal Working for ICTR Uncovered, Flees to Kenya," *All Africa,* June 18, 2005.

65. Geoffrey Robertson, *Crimes Against Humanity* (New York: New Press, 2000), p. 301.

66. Thierry Cruvellier, "Africa: The Laboratory of Justice."

67. ICTY, *Prosecutor v. Tadic,* Case IT-94-1-1, Appeals Chamber (July 15, 1999), para. 44.

68. Regarding "presumption of innocence," see for example England and Australia, where the presumption of innocence is an "integral element of the notion of a fair trial." See Ben Fitzpatrick, "Double Jeopardy: One Idea and Two Myths from the Criminal Justice Bill 2002," *Journal of Criminal Law* 67 (2003): 156, along with the United States, *Coffin v. United States,* 156 US 432, 453 (1895), which holds that the presumption is "axiomatic and elementary, and its enforcement lies at the foundation of the administration of our criminal law," and France, where the presumption is found in article 9 of the Declaration of 1789. The European Convention of Human Rights, article 6, similarly demands that "everyone charged with a criminal offense shall be presumed innocent," ECHR, article 6(2). The requirement for a high burden of proof for conviction can also be found in several states. United States, *In re Winship,* 397 US 358, 373 (1970) reaffirmed "the requirement that guilt of a criminal charge be established by proof beyond a reasonable doubt," arguing that the "demand for a higher degree of persuasion in criminal cases was recurrently expressed from ancient times." Regarding Provision of Counsel, see the United States, *Gideon v. Wainwright,* 372 US 335 (1963), and Europe, ECHR, article 6(3). Regarding Provision of Exculpatory Evidence see, for example, Canada, where *R. v. Stinchcombe* (1991), 68 CCC (3d) 1 (SCC) holds that the state must provide all "relevant" information to the defense, the United States where *Brady v. Maryland* 373 US 83, 86–87 (1963) holds that "suppression of evidence favorable to an accused upon request violated the due process clause, US Constitution, Amendment 14, where the evidence was material to guilt or punishment, regardless of the State's good or bad faith."

69. Elise Groulx, "The Position of the Defense at the International Criminal Court," Hague Conference Presentation by International Criminal Defense Attorneys Association, November 3, 2000. Tiphaine Dickson, a lawyer who practiced before the ICTY and ICTR for several years is even more direct in her assessment of this inequality:

> The precedents set by the Rwanda and Yugoslav courts are shocking
> for defense lawyers who arrive to defend a client at The Hague or

Arusha. Indictments with little or no evidence, disregard for extradition procedures, piecemeal disclosure, third hand hearsay, drastically limited cross examination, and modification of rules by judges in collaboration with the prosecution as trials go along, not to mention US pressure to speed up the process.

John Steppling, "Debacle at The Hague," *Swans Commentary*, August 16, 2004. http://www.swans.com/library/art10/johns03.html (accessed May 17, 2008).

70. ICTY, "Article 21(3): Rights of the Accused," *Statute of the International Criminal Tribunal for the Former Yugoslavia*, http://www.un.org/icty/legaldoc-e/index.htm.

71. Slobodan Milosevic, "Statement," August 30, 2001, http://www3.sympatico.ca/sr.gowans/milosevic.html (accessed May 24, 2008).

72. Report by Justice Jackson to US President Harry Truman, October 7, 1946, http://www.yale.edu/lawweb/avalon/imt/jackson/jack63.htm. (accessed May 24, 2008).

73. Richard Goldstone, "Advancing the Cause of Human Rights," in *Realizing Human Rights*, ed. Samantha Power and Graham Allison (New York: Palgrave MacMillan, 2006), pp. 206–207.

74. Cf. Amy Colton, "Eyes to the Future, Yet Remembering the Past: Reconciling Tradition with the Future of Legal Education," *University of Michigan Journal of Law Reform* 27 (1994): 964–66.

75. Robert Mount, Doug Cassel, and Jeff Bleich, "War Crimes and Human Rights Abuses in the Former Yugoslavia," *Whittier Law Review* 16 (1995): 407.

76. Ibid.

77. ICTY, "Article 15: Rules of Procedure and Evidence," *Statute of the International Criminal Tribunal for the Former Yugoslavia*, http://www.un.org/icty/legaldoc-e/index.htm (accessed December 5, 2008).

78. Ibid.

79. Anthony D'Amato, "Defending a Person Charged with Genocide," *Chicago Journal of International Law* 1 (2000): 468–69.

80. See generally, Felicity Nagorcka, Michael Stanton, and Michael Wilson, "Stranded Between Partisanship and the Truth? A Comparative Analysis of Legal Ethics in the Adversarial and Inquisitorial Systems of Justice," *Melbourne University Law Review* 29 (2005): 448.

81. Danner and Martinez note:

The [ICTY and the ICTR] . . . for example, take from common law systems an adversarial system for the presentation of evidence, including cross-examination. Drawing on civil law traditions, however, [they] . . . also employ judges rather than juries, incorporate a more active role for the judges in questioning witnesses (and even in calling their own witnesses), draw more heavily on written evidence prepared in a pretrial dossier, and allow for appeals by the prosecution.

Allison Marston Danner and Jenny S. Martinez, "Joint Criminal Enterprise, Command Responsibility, and the Development of International Criminal Law," *California Law Review* 93 (2005): 75, n.1.

82. Sir Anthony Mason, "The Future of Adversarial Justice," paper presented at the Seventeenth AIJA Annual Conference, Adelaide, August 7, 1999, p. 4. A similar point was made by Lord Denning in a Privy Council case, *Air Canada v. Secretary of State for Trade* (2), in which he argued that "when we speak of the due administration of justice this does not always mean ascertaining the truth of what happened." (1983) 2 AC 394, 411.

83. Alan Dershowitz, *Reasonable Doubts* (New York: Simon & Schuster, 1996), p. 166.

84. See ICTY, *Prosecutor v. Milosevic*, Case IT-02-54, Decision on Interlocutory Appeal of the Trial Chamber's Decision on the Assignment of Defense Counsel (November 5, 2004).

85. John Laughland, "The Anomalies of the International Criminal Tribunal are Legion," *Times* (London), June 17, 1999.

86. Freedom House, "Freedom in the World—Paraguay" (2007), http://www.freedomhouse.org/inc/content/pubs/fiw/inc_country_detail.cfm?year=2007&country=7251&pf (accessed December 5, 2008).

87. Adam M. Smith, "Balkan Legal," *New Republic*, May 1, 2006, p. 14.

88. David Cohen, "Seeking Justice on the Cheap: Is the East Timor Tribunal Really a Model for the Future?" *East-West Center, Asia Pacific Issues* 61 (August 2002): 1.

89. John Cockayne, cited in Keven Jon Heller, "(In)equality of Arms at the International Tribunals," February 7, 2006, http://www.opiniojuris.org (accessed May 17, 2008).

90. Institute for War & Peace Reporting, "Sierra Leone; Dispute at Charles Taylor Trial Over Defence Resources," *Africa News–All Africa*, June 9, 2007.

91. Cited in Keven Jon Heller, "(In)equality of Arms at the International Tribunals."

92. "Registrar Visits ICTR Facilities, Meets Detainees," *Africa News–All Africa*, November 24, 1998.

93. Ibid.

94. See UN, *Report of the Expert Group to Conduct a Review of the Effective Operation and Functioning of the ICTY and the ICTR*, UN document A-54-634 (1999), para. 210.

95. Ibid. See also Sienho Yo, "The Erdemovic Sentencing Judgment: A Questionable Milestone for the International Criminal Tribunal for the Former Yugoslavia," *Georgia Journal of International and Comparative Law* 26 (1997): 263.

96. David Cohen, "'Justice on the Cheap'" Revisited: The Failure of Serious Crimes Trials in East Timor," *Asia Pacific Issues, East West Center* 80 (May 2006): 5.

97. For example, on January 31, 2000, the tribunal imposed a fine of approximately $2,000 on Belgrade lawyer Milan Vujin for manipulating witnesses with bribes and other forms of persuasion in the ICTY case against Dusan Tadic. Vujin was also barred from further practice in front of the tribunal. It is unclear, however, whether the fine was ever collected or if there were more severe penalties (such as incarceration) available to the tribunal. See, "Belgrade Lawyer Fined," *New York Times*, February 1, 2000, p. A10.

98. The confusion on this matter stems from the fact that while the ICTY is not explicitly empowered to impose fines, it has adopted provisions for fines as penalties for procedural misconduct, such as contempt. Valerie Oosterveld, Mike Perry, and John McManus, "How the World Will Relate to the Court: The Cooperation of States with the International Criminal Court," *Fordham International Law Journal* 25 (2002): 822, n. 348.

99. "Rwanda: Case of Rwandan Lawyer Revives Tensions Between Kigali and the ICTR," *Africa News*, March 7, 2006.

100. Ibid.

101. Dean M. Murphy, "Balkan Peace Treaty: With Peace at Hand, is Justice Beyond Reach?" *Los Angeles Times*, December 15, 1995, p. 17.

102. ICTY, *Prosecutor v. Blaskic*, Case IT-95-14, Trial Chamber, Disposition (March 3, 2000).

103. ICTY, *Prosecutor v. Blaskic,* Case IT-95-14, Appellate Chamber, Disposition (July 24, 2004).

104. Cogan, "Problem of Obtaining Evidence for International Criminal Courts," p. 412.

105. Henry Porter, "This War Criminal Must be Brought to Justice," *Observer* (London), October 4, 1998, p. 15.

106. Cogan, "Problem of Obtaining Evidence for International Criminal Courts," p. 412.

107. Peter Maass, "Let's Not Forget Milosevic's Partner in Crime: To Insure Fairness, Tudjman Should be Indicted Too," *New York Times,* May 31, 1999, p. A13.

108. Raymond Bonner, "War Crimes Panel Finds Croat Troops 'Cleansed' the Serbs," *New York Times,* March 21, 1999, p. 1.

109. See generally, Mark Thieroff and Edward A. Amley Jr., "Proceeding to Justice and Accountability in the Balkans: The International Criminal Tribunal for the Former Yugoslavia and Rule 61," *Yale Journal of International Law* 23 (1998): 231.

110. HINA News Agency (Zagreb), "Parliamentary Committee Supports Government Over Hague Tribunal," *BBC Summary of World Broadcasts,* July 31, 1997.

111. ICTY, *Prosecutor v. Blaskic,* Case IT-95-14, Judgment on the Request of the Republic of Croatia for Review of the Decision of Trial Chamber II of 18 July 1997 (October 29, 1997). The tribunal held that "the ICTY cannot issue binding orders to specific officials of a state when acting in their official capacity, since it is for the state itself to determine which officials are responsible for the requested documents." See also, Ambassador Mihomir Zuzul, quoted in Tom Gjelten, "US and Croatia," *All Things Considered,* transcript no. 97030708-212 ; Croatian Radio (Zagreb) "Government Refuses to Act on Hague Tribunal's Request," *BBC Summary of World Broadcasts,* July 23, 1997.

112. ICTY, "Rule 68: Disclosure of Exculpatory and Other Relevant Material," *Rules of Procedure and Evidence,* http://www.un.org/icty/legaldoc-e/basic/rpe/IT032Rev38e.pdf (accessed December 5, 2008).

113. ICTY, "Rule 70: Matters not Subject to Disclosure," *Rules of Procedure and Evidence,* http://www.un.org/icty/legaldoc-e/basic/rpe/IT032Rev38e .pdf (accessed December 5, 2008).

114. Ralph Zacklin, "The Failings of Ad Hoc International Tribunals," *Journal of International Criminal Justice* 2 (2004): 541.

115. ICTY, "ICTY At a Glance, General Information," http://www.un .org/icty/glance-e/index.htm (accessed May 17, 2008).

116. G. S. Yacoubian, "Evaluating the Efficacy of the International Criminal Tribunals for Rwanda and the Former Yugoslavia: Implications for Criminology and International Criminal Law," *World Affairs* 3 (2001): 133.

117. Allison Marston Danner, "When Courts Make Law: How the International Criminal Tribunals Recast the Laws of War," *Vanderbilt Law Review* 59 (2006): 25.

118. Marlise Simons, "Liberian Ex-Leader's War Crimes Trial Is Stalled," *New York Times*, August 27, 2007, p. 6.

119. Individual state GDPs from US Central Intelligence Agency, *World FactBook*.

120. "Special Court Takes Over Prison Camp," *Africa News*, October 2, 2002; Sriram, "Wrong-Sizing International Justice?" p. 499.

121. Ibid., p. 472.

122. Timberg, "Well-Funded but Selective War Crimes Probe," p. A11.

123. "Inquiry Fine, But Will the Answers Hold," *New Times*, July 2, 2006.

124. Hans Nichols, "UN Court Makes Legal Mischief," *Insight on the News*, January 20, 2003, p. 34.

125. Christian P. Sherrer, *Genocide and Crisis in Central Africa* (Westport, CT: Praeger, 2002), p. 104.

126. ICCPR, article 9 and ECHR, article 5(3) both demand those arrested to "be brought promptly before a judge." Bass also notes the "grinding" slowness of justice at the tribunal. Gary Jonathan Bass, *Stay the Hand of Vengeance* (Princeton, NJ: Princeton University Press, 2001), p. 36.

127. Vesna Peric-Zimonjic, "Deaths in The Hague 'Justify' Belgrade's Stance," Inter Press Service, September 22, 1998.

128. See, for example, HRT1 TV (Zagreb), "Croatia is Unhappy with Hague Tribunal, Ruling Party Spokesman Says," *BBC Worldwide Monitoring*, February 2, 1999.

129. See generally, Fritz Weinshenk, "The Murderers Among Them— German Justice and the Nazis," *Hofstra Law and Policy Symposium* 3 (1999): 137.

130. Anna J. Merritt & Richard L. Merritt, *Public Opinion in Occupied Germany: The OMGUS Surveys, 1945–1949* (Urbana: University of Illinois Press, 1970), p. 34.

131. Ibid., pp. 34–35, 121–22.

132. ICTY, *Prosecutor v. Delalic*, Case IT-96-21-T, Appeals Chamber

(February 20, 2001), para 756 (emphasis added); See also, generally, Allison Marston Danner, "Constructing a Hierarchy of Crimes in International Criminal Law Sentencing," *Virginia Law Review* 87 (2001): 415.

133. Mark A. Drumbl and Kenneth S. Gallant, "Sentencing Policies and Practices in the International Criminal Tribunals," *Federal Sentencing Reporter* 15 (2002): 140.

134. Mark A. Drumbl, "Collective Violence and Individual Punishment: The Criminality of Mass Atrocity," *Northwestern University Law Review* 99 (2005): 582, n. 230; Andrew N. Keller, "Punishment for Violations of International Criminal Law: An Analysis of Sentencing at the ICTY and ICTR," *Indiana International and Comparative Law Review* 12 (2001): 63. See also, ICTY, "Article 24: Penalties," *Statute of the International Criminal Tribunal for the Former Yugoslavia*, http://www.un.org/icty/legaldoc-e/index.htm (accessed May 17, 2008), which states that the tribunal "shall have recourse" to the Yugoslav code when designing penalties, but not compelling such recourse.

135. ICTY, "Article 27: Enforcement of Sentences," *Statute of the International Criminal Tribunal for the Former Yugoslavia*, http://www.un.org/icty/legaldoc-e/index.htm (accessed May 17, 2008).

136. Virginia Morris and Michael P. Scharf, *An Insider's Guide to the International Criminal Tribunal for the Former Yugoslavia* (Irvington-on-Hudson, NY: Transnational, 1994), p. 304.

137. See ICTR, "Basic Legal Texts, Bi-Lateral Agreements," http://65 .18.216.88/ENGLISH/agreements/index.htm (accessed May 17, 2008).

138. "Report on Prison Conditions in Benin from Freedom House, 2005," *Freedom in the World*, http://www.freedomhouse.org (accessed May 17, 2008).

139. "Report on Prison Conditions in Mali from Freedom House, 2005," *Freedom in the World*, http://www.freedomhouse.org (accessed May 17, 2008).

140. Jack Snyder and Leslie Vinjamuri, "Trials and Errors: Principles and Pragmatism in Strategies of International Justice," *International Security* 28 (2003): 22.

141. Laurel E. Fletcher and Harvey M. Weinstein, "A World Unto Itself? The Application of International Justice in the Former Yugoslavia," in *My Neighbor, My Enemy: Justice and Community in the Aftermath of Mass Atrocity*, ed. Eric Stover and Harvey M. Weinstein (Cambridge: Cambridge University Press, 2004), p. 46.

142. Snyder and Vinjamuri, "Trials and Errors," p. 22.

143. See Roman David, "Lustration Laws in Action: The Motives and Evaluation of Lustration Policy in the Czech Republic and Poland (1989–2001)," *Law and Social Inquiry* 28 (2003): 405–407. Describing how lustration programs sought to restore public trust in state institutions by purging most serious wrongdoers among civil servants. See also, Roman Boed, "An Evaluation of the Legality and Efficacy of Lustration as a Tool of Transitional Justice Success of Lustration in Eastern Europe," *Columbia Journal of Transnational Law* 37 (1999): 357.

144. Herman Schwartz, *Trials in Absentia, Human Rights Brief* (Washington, DC: Center for Human Rights and Humanitarian Law at Washington College of Law, American University, 1996).

145. See, for example, Jakob Finci, "Exchange: Bosnia Needs a Truth Commission," *Institute for War and Peace Reporting*, May 21, 2001. Herman Schwartz, "What Can We Do About Balkan Atrocities," *New York Times*, April 9, 1993, p. A27, in which he argues that "a Truth Commission is the best answer" to address the atrocities; "Balkans: Truth and Reconciliation," *Peace Watch* 6 (2000): 6.

146. Martha Minow is one such scholar. See Martha Minow, *Between Vengeance and Forgiveness: Facing History After Genocide and Mass Violence* (Boston: Beacon Press, 1998): 47, 58–59, 78.

CHAPTER 7
THE INTERNATIONAL CRIMINAL COURT
AND THE LIMITS OF INTERNATIONAL JUSTICE

1. Current numbers of states having signed and ratified the Rome Treaty can be found at the website of the Coalition for the International Criminal Court, http://www.iccnow.org (accessed May 18, 2008).

2. Biographies of ICC Judges, http://www.icc-cpi.int/chambers/judges.html (accessed May 17, 2008).

3. Caitlin Reiger and Marieke Wierda, "The Serious Crimes Process in Timor-Leste: In Retrospect," *Prosecutions Case Studies Series—International Center for Transitional Justice* (New York: ICTJ, 2006), p. 23.

4. ICC, "Article 36 (8, iii): A Fair Representation of Female and Male Judges," *Rome Statute of the International Criminal Court*. See also, Cherie

Booth, "Prospects and Issues for the International Criminal Court," in *From Nuremberg to The Hague: The Future of International Criminal Justice*, ed. Philippe Sands (Cambridge: Cambridge University Press, 2003), p. 164.

5. Biographies of ICC Judges, http://www.icc-cpi.int/chambers/ judges.html (accessed May 17, 2008).

6. "ICTY At-a-Glance, Organs of the Court," http://www.un.org/ icty/glance-e/index.htm (accessed May 17, 2008).

7. Pascal Kambale and Anna Rotman, "The International Criminal Court and Congo: Examining the Possibilities," *Crimes of War*, October 2004, http://www.crimesofwar.org/africa-mag/afr_05_kambale.html (accessed May 17, 2008).

8. Jacob Katz Cogan, "The Problem of Obtaining Evidence for International Criminal Courts," *Human Rights Quarterly* 22 (2002): 404.

9. US Ambassador-at-large for War Crimes Pierre-Richard Prosper, debate on the ICC with Kenneth Roth (executive director of Human Rights Watch), Harvard Law School, October 7, 2005.

10. Chandra Sriram, "The ICC Africa Experiment: Darfur, Northern Uganda, and the DRC," paper presented at the annual meeting of the ISA's Forty-Ninth Annual Convention, San Francisco, CA, March 26, 2008, abstract available at http://www.allacademic.com/meta/p251725_index.html (accessed May 26, 2008).

11. Nikki Tait, "ICC's First Inquiry to Focus on Congo War," *Financial Times* (London), June 24, 2004, p. 10.

12. See e.g., Silas Chekera, "The Charles Taylor Case and Idiosyncrasies of International Criminal Law, *Sierra Leone Court Monitoring Programme* (June 2006) http://www.slcmp.org/drwebsite/manager/uploads/1/14th _edition_newsletter.pdf (accessed December 9, 2008); "Museveni: General in His Labyrinth," Blackstar News, June 13, 2008 http://blackstarnews.com/ ?c=122&a=4609 (accessed December 9, 2008).

13. ICJ, *Democratic Republic of the Congo v. Uganda*, In the Case Concerning Armed Activities on the Territory of the Congo, (December 19, 2005).

14. Human Rights Watch, "Uganda: New Accord Provides for War Crimes Trials," *AllAfrica*, February 19, 2008; Adam Branch, "Uganda's Civil War and the Politics of ICC Intervention," *Ethics and International Affairs* 21 (2007).

15. Branch, "Uganda's Civil War and the Politics of ICC Intervention," p. 187; Mahnoush H. Arsanjani and W. Michael Reisman, "The Law-in-Action

of the International Criminal Court," *American Journal of International Law* 99 (2005): 397.

16. Newton writes:

Article 1 of the Rome Statute promulgates in simple language that the court will "be a permanent institution and shall have the power to exercise its jurisdiction over persons for the most serious crimes of international concern . . . and shall be *complementary* to national criminal jurisdictions." The Rome Statute nowhere defines the term "complementarity," but the plain text of Article 1 compels the conclusion that the International Criminal Court is intended to supplement the foundation of domestic punishment of international violations, rather than supplant domestic enforcement of international norms.

Michael A. Newton, "Comparative Complementarity: Domestic Jurisdiction Consistent with the Rome Statute of the International Criminal Court," *Military Law Review* 167 (2001): 26.

17. Arsanjani and Reisman, "The Law-in-Action of the International Criminal Court," p. 397.

18. David J. Scheffer, "International Judicial Intervention," *Foreign Policy* 102 (March 22, 1996): 34.

19. See generally, Peter G. Fischer, "The Victims' Trust Fund of the International Criminal Court: Formation of a Functional Reparations Scheme," *Emory International Law Review* 17 (2003): 187.

20. David Adams, "Chile to Pay Survivors of its 'Dirty War,'" *St. Petersburg Times*, December 11, 2004, p. 4A; Larry Rohter, "After Decades, Nations Focus on Rights Abuses," *New York Times*, September 1, 2005, p. 4.

21. "Civil Society Organizations Express Concerns About the Upcoming Election to International Criminal Court," M2 Presswire, August 1, 2002, in Adam M. Smith, "'Judicial Nationalism' in International Law: National Identity and Judicial Autonomy at the ICJ," *Texas International Law Journal* 40 (2005): 204, n. 40.

22. "South Korean President Returns Home," *BBC News*, September 16, 2005.

23. Other than the Netherlands, Germany, France, and Italy also lobbied to be host of the Court. Hans Bevers, Niels Blokker, and Jaap Roording, "The

Netherlands and the International Criminal Court: On Statute Obligations and Hospitality," *Leiden Journal of International Law* 16 (2003): 136.

24. ICJ, *Proposed Program Budget for 2006 of the International Criminal Court* (October 12, 2005), http://www.icc-cpi.int/library/asp/ICC-ASP-4-5-Corr1*_English.pdf (accessed May 17, 2008).

25. Individual state GDPs from US Central Intelligence Agency, *World FactBook*, 2005.

26. The ICTR only moved to Arusha, Tanzania, four months after the establishment of the tribunal. See UN, *Security Council Resolution 977* (February 22, 1995). Regarding the prohibition on the death penalty in international criminal justice see generally Jens David Ohlin, "Applying the Death Penalty to Crimes of Genocide," *American Journal of International Law* 99 (2005): 747.

27. Individual state GDPs from US Central Intelligence Agency, *World FactBook*, 2005.

28. UN, *Security Council Resolution 1593* (March 31, 2005).

29. "U.S. Calls Sudan Conflict Genocide," *Chicago Tribune*, September 12, 2004, p. 12.

30. Nat Hentoff, "World Has Ignored Genocide Long Enough," *Chicago Sun Times*, January 7, 2006, p. 10; Farah Stockman, "Shortfalls Seen in Darfur Peace Force," *Boston Globe*, November 12, 2005, p. A6. Reports that the "6,700-member African Union force sent to help prevent genocidal attacks in the Darfur region of Sudan has been unable to protect its own soldiers [due to financial shortfalls leading to a dearth of soldiers and material], let alone the 2 million displaced people living in camps."

31. See Nicholas Thompson, "Adopt-a-Peacekeeper," *Boston Globe*, March 6, 2005, p. D4.

32. Hans Nichols, "Search for Justice Stalls in Rwanda, Government at Odds with U.N. Court," *Washington Times*, January 2, 2003, p. A08.

33. Tanja Hohe, "Justice Without Judiciary in East Timor," *Conflict, Security & Development* 3 (2003): 340.

34. Marc Lacey, "Victims of Uganda Atrocities Choose A Path of Forgiveness," *New York Times*, April 18, 2005, p. A1.

35. Hohe, "Justice Without Judiciary in East Timor," p. 347; in Ateesh Chanda, *Transitional Justice: The Case of East Timor* (senior thesis, Brown University, 2004), p. 95.

36. Adam M. Smith, "From Nuremberg to the Hague (Book Review)," *Harvard International Law* Journal 45 (2004): 573–74.

37. "Hunting Uganda's Child-Killers: Justice Versus Reconciliation," *Economist*, May 7, 2005; Blake Lambert, "Court Pursues Fugitive Uganda Rebel Leaders," *Washington Times*, November 10, 2005, p. A16; Katherine Southwick, "When Peace and Justice Clash," *International Herald Tribune*, October 15, 2005, p. 6.

38. Steven Erlanger, "Word of Indictment Stuns Serbs and Blights Hopes," *New York Times*, May 27, 1999, p. A12; Candice Hughes, "UN Indictments Worry Battered Serb Opposition," *Chicago Tribune*, May 29, 1999, p. 3.

39. Jiri Dienstbier, quoted in Jolyon Naegele, "Yugoslavia: UN Envoy Dienstbier Advocates Deal for Milosevic," Radio Free Europe/Radio Liberty, October 4, 2000. Cited in Pierre Hazan, *Justice in a Time of War*, trans. James Thomas Snyder (College Station: Texas A & M University Press, 2004), p. 153.

40. Radio Bosnia-Herzegovina (Sarajevo), "Bosnian Premier Calls on Bildt to Curtail Aid to Serb Entity," *BBC Summary of World Broadcasts*, March 31, 1996.

41. David B. Ottaway, "Bosnia Convicts 2 Serbs in War Crimes Trial: UN Officer Seeks Amnesty to Promote Peace," *Washington Post*, March 31, 1993, p. A21.

42. Colin Soloway and Stephen J. Hedges, "How Not to Catch a War Criminal," *U.S. News & World Report*, December 9, 1996, p. 63.

43. Gordon Brown and Nicolas Sarkozy, "We Are Pushing and Pushing to Save the Darfuris," *Times* (London), August 31, 2007, p. 19. Justice Richard Goldstone noted this curiosity in his Hart Lecture at Georgetown University Law Center, March 24, 2008.

44. Sian Powell, "Justice Loses out on Timor Abuses," *Australian*, May 24, 2004, p. 11.

45. "L'Afrique est une tache sur la conscience occidentale," *Jeune Afrique L'intelligent*, 29 October 2003. In Pascal Kambale and Anna Rotman, "The International Criminal Court and Congo: Examining the Possibilities," *Crimes of War*, October 2004, http://www.crimesofwar.org/africa-mag/afr_05_kambale.html (accessed May 17, 2008).

46. "Hunting Uganda's Child Killers—Justice Versus Reconciliation," *Economist*, May 7, 2005.

47. See e.g., Jonathan Fanton, President of the MacArthur Foundation, National Press Club Luncheon (Federal News Service), December 10, 2007.

48. *When the War Ends: A Population Based Survey on Attitudes about Peace, Justice, and Social Reconstruction in Northern Uganda* (Berkeley: University of California Human Rights Center, 2007).

49. Andrew Natsios, "A Disaster in the Making," SSRC Blog, Making Sense of Darfur, July 12, 2008, http://www.ssrc.org/blogs/darfur/2008/07/12/a-disaster-in-the-making/ (accessed July 23, 2008).

50. Rony Brauman, "The ICC's Bashir Indictment: Law Against Peace," July 23, 2008, http://worldpoliticsreview.com/Article.aspx?id=2471 (accessed July 23, 2008).

51. ICC, "Article 15: Prosecutor," *Rome Statute of the International Criminal Court.*

52. "ICC Could Suspend Northern Investigations—Spokesman," *IRIN-News*, April 18, 2005 in Katherine Southwick, "Negotiating War in Northern Uganda: Dilemmas for the International Criminal Court," *Yale Journal of International Affairs* 1 (2005): 112.

53. Richard Holbrooke, *To End a War* (New York: Random House, 1998), pp. 368–69.

CHAPTER 8
THEY SAY IT CAN'T BE DONE

1. Kenneth Roth (executive director of Human Rights Watch), debate on the ICC with US Ambassador-at-Large for War Crimes Pierre-Richard Prosper, Harvard Law School, October 7, 2005.

2. European Commission, *Opinion: On the Application of Croatia for Membership in the European Union* (April 20, 2004), http://www.mvpei.hr/ei/Download/2004/05/31/cr_croat.pdf (accessed December 11, 2008).

3. Ian Traynor, "Torturer's Confession Rocks Croatia," *Guardian* (London), September 8, 1997, p. 5.

4. HINA News Agency (Zagreb) "Croatia: War Crimes Trial in 'Pakracka Poljana' Case Starts," *BBC Worldwide Monitoring* (May 29, 2002).

5. US Department of State, *Croatia: Country Report on Human Rights* (1999), http://www.state.gov/g/drl/rls/hrrpt/1999/323.htm (accessed May 25, 2008). Though, it must be said that this was not the end of the saga; the retrials were wracked with problems, and may very well have resulted in a miscarriage of justice that has, to this day, unfortunately stuck. See Amnesty International, *Short-Changing Justice—The Sodolovci Group*, EUR 64-006-1999 (December 1, 1999), http://web.amnesty.org/library/pdf/EUR64006 1999ENGLISH/$File/EUR6400699.pdf (accessed May 25, 2008).

6. Maurice H. Keen, *The Law of War in the Late Middle Ages* (Aldershot, UK: Gregg Revivals, 1965), p. 50.

7. Hiller Zobel, *The Boston Massacre* (New York: W. W. Norton, 1970).

8. T. L. H. McCormack, "Selective Reaction to Atrocity: War Crimes and the Development of International Criminal Law," *Albany Law Review* 60 (1997): 694.

9. Jordan J. Paust, "My Lai and Vietnam: Norms, Myths, and Leader Responsibility," *Military Law Review* 57 (1972): 117; David Glazier, "Kangaroo Court or Competent Tribunal: Judging the 21st Century Military Commission," *Virginia Law Review* 89 (2003): 2005.

10. Glazier, "Kangaroo Court or Competent Tribunal," p. 2031, n. 103.

11. Thomas P. Lowry, *Tarnished Eagles: The Court-Martial of Fifty Union Colonels and Lieutenant Colonels* (Mechanicsburg, PA: Stackpole Books, 1997), p. 7.

12. Howard S. Levie, "Penal Sanctions for the Maltreatment of Prisoners of War," *American Journal of International Law* 56 (1962): 433.

13. Nagao Ariga, *La Guerre Sino-Japonaise au Point de Vue du Droit International* (Paris: A. Pedone, 1896), p. xiii, 9.

14. Percy Bordwell, *The Laws of War between Belligerents: A History and Commentary* (Chicago: Callaghan & Col, 1908), pp. 173–74, 332–44.

15. Elbridge Colby, "War Crimes," *Michigan Law Review* 23 (1924–1925): 498.

16. Tokichi Masao, "The Kowshing, In the Light of International Law," *Yale Law Journal* 5 (1896): 247.

17. Alejandro Alvarez, "Latin America and International Law," *American Journal of International Law* 3 (1909): 304.

18. Geoffrey Best, "Restraints on War by Land Before 1945," in *Restraints on War*, ed. Michael Howard (Oxford: Oxford University Press, 1979), p. 18.

19. British Parliament, *German War Trials*, [Cd. 1450], 1921, pp. 8, 25.

20. Keith Ewing and John Fisher, *Czechoslovak Military Justice Abroad During the Second World War* (New York: Czechoslovak Society of Arts and Sciences in America, 1975), p. 10.

21. Ian Hurd, "Why Iraq, and Not the US, Should Prosecute Hussein's Pals," *Chicago Tribune*, May 19, 2003, p. 15; Benjamin Frommer, *National Cleansing* (Cambridge: Cambridge University Press, 2004), p. 112.

22. "Poles" pamphlet published by US Holocaust Memorial Museum, http://www.ushmm.org/education/resource/poles/poles.pdf (accessed May 25, 2008).

23. Alfred de Zayas, *The Wehrmacht War Crimes Bureau, 1939–1945* (Lincoln: University of Nebraska Press, 1989), p. 109.

24. Ibid.

25. Ibid., p. 18.

26. Ibid., p. 19.

27. Ibid.

28. Ibid.

29. Ibid., p. 20.

30. Ibid., pp. 93, 94.

31. Ibid.

32. Ibid., p. 94.

33. Ibid., p. 95.

34. Ibid., p. 97.

35. Ibid., p. 101.

36. Ibid., p. 20.

37. Ibid.

38. Ibid.

39. Michael Walzer, *Just and Unjust War* (New York: Basic Books, 1977), p. 38; Ronald Lewin, *Rommel as Military Commander* (London: Batsford, 1968), pp. 310–11.

40. Gary D. Solis, "Military Justice, Civilian Clemency: The Sentences of Marine Corps War Crimes in South Vietnam," *Transnational Law and Contemporary Problems* 10 (2000): 61–62.

41. "Trial of Dictator Opens," *Globe and Mail* (Toronto), September 25, 1979.

42. Leo Kuper, *The Prevention of Genocide* (New Haven, CT: Yale University Press, 1986), pp. 16–17.

43. *The Trial of Macias in Equatorial in Guinea* (Geneva: International Commission of Jurists, 1979).

44. See Richard J. Goldstone and Adam M. Smith, *International Judicial Institutions: The Architecture of International Justice at Home and Abroad* (London: Routledge, 2009), chapter 5.

45. Mark Osiel, "The Making of Human Rights Policy in Argentina: The Impact of Ideas and Interests on a Legal Conflict," *Journal of Latin American Studies* 18 (1986): 135; Alejandro M. Garro, "Nine Years of Transition to Democracy in Argentina: Partial Failure or Qualified Success?" *Columbia Journal of Transnational Law* 31 (1993–1994): 10.

46. "Decree 158," Argentine Presidential Order to Proceed Against the Military Juntas, December 1983.

47. Shirley Christian, "Argentina Frees Ex-Junta Leaders," *New York Times*, December 30, 1990.

48. Evan W. Gray, "Human Rights: Conviction of Former Argentine Military Commanders for Human Rights Abuses Committed by Subordinates," *Harvard International Law Journal* 27 (1986): 688.

49. Luis Moreno Ocampo, "Beyond Punishment: Justice in the Wake of Massive Crimes in Argentina," *Journal of International Affairs* 52 (1999): 1.

50. Jack Chang, "Death, Kidnappings Plague Argentina's Human-Rights Trials," *Knight Ridder* (Washington Bureau), February 27, 2008.

51. Marcela Valente, "Cyanide Kills Torture Suspect, Days Before Verdict," Inter Press Service, December 14, 2007.

52. Jonathan Randal, "Bokassa Stumbles in Idi Amin's Bloody Footsteps," *Sydney Morning Herald*, January 31, 1987, p. 21.

53. Associated Press, "Bokassa Doomed by Bangui Court," *New York Times*, June 13, 1987, p. 5.

54. Randal, "Bokassa Stumbles," p. 21.

55. Ron Christenson, ed. *Political Trials in History* (New Brunswick, NJ: Transaction Publishers, 1992), pp. 36–37; "Bokassa Doomed by Bangui Court," *New York Times*, June 13, 1987.

56. News Services, "Emperor Sentenced to Death," *San Diego Union Tribune*, June 13, 1987, p. A2.

57. Drago Hedl, "Regional Report: Vukovar Serb Killings Investigated," *Institute for War and Peace Reporting*, November 25–29, 2002, http://www.iwpr.net/?p=tri&s=f&o=163221&apc_state=henitri2002 (accessed May 27, 2008).

58. Marc Weller, "Soldiers Charged by a State in Limbo," *Times* (London), July 21, 1992.

59. John F. Burns, "His Bosnia Trial Ending, Serb Asks Death Penalty," *New York Times*, March 28, 1993, p. 8.

60. Burns, "His Bosnia Trial Ending," p. 8.

61. "This Week on Court TV (Scheduling of Programs)," *Legal Times*, May 3, 1993, p. 37.

62. Lee Michael Katz, "Bosnia Vote Pivotal for US Forces," *USA Today*, May 6, 1993, p. 1A.

63. Yugoslav Telegraph Service (Belgrade), "Montenegrin Court Sen-

tences Five Bosnian Serb Soldiers for Killing Muslim Family," *BBC Summary of World Broadcasts*, May 8, 1993.

64. Yugoslav Telegraph Service (Belgrade), "Trebinje Authorities Charge 66 People for 'War Crimes Against Civilians,'" *BBC Summary of World Broadcasts*, May 8, 1993.

65. Yugoslav Telegraph Service (Belgrade), "FRY Commission Prepares Report on Muslim War Crimes Against Serbs in East Bosnia," *BBC Summary of World Broadcasts*, May 28, 1993.

66. Yugoslav Telegraph Service (Belgrade), "Gathering of Evidence of War Crimes Against Serbs in Northern Bosnia Continues," *BBC Summary of World Broadcasts*, May 31, 1993.

67. Jonathan Silvers, "The Worst Man on Earth," *Star* (Toronto), March 30, 1996, p. B1.

68. Roger Cohen, "Serbs Put a Serb on Trial for War Crimes," *New York Times*, June 12, 1994, p. 14.

69. Silvers, "The Worst Man on Earth," p. B1.

70. Ibid.

71. Tanjug News Agency (Belgrade), "Court Sentences Two for War Crimes in Bosnia," *BBC Summary of World Broadcasts*, July 9, 1996.

72. OSCE—Mission to Serbia and Montenegro, *War Crimes Before Domestic Courts* (Vienna: Organization for Security and Cooperation in Europe, October 2003), p. 8.

73. Ibid.

74. "NATO/SFOR Joint Press Conference (Sarajevo)," M2 Presswire, October 27, 1997.

75. "Bosnia Serbs Prosecute Halilovic for War Crimes While Observers Question Fairness of National War Crime Trials," *International Enforcement Law Reporter*, July 1997.

76. US Department of State, *Human Rights Report for 1999, Bosnia & Herzegovina.*

77. Tracy Wilkinson, "Bosnian Case Pours Salt on a War Wound," *Los Angeles Times*, October 25, 1997, p. A2.

78. Habena News Agency (Mostar), "Opposition Politician Warns of Influx of Yugoslav Muslims," *BBC Summary of World Broadcasts*, October 14, 1998.

79. Bosnian Croat Radio, "Bosnia: Sarajevo Court Frees War Crimes Suspect for Lack of Evidence," *BBC Worldwide Monitoring*, March 27, 2000.

80. Nicholas Wood, "The War Crimes Cases, To-and-Fro in Serbia," *International Herald Tribune,* April 14, 2007, p. 3.

81. UN Secretary General, *Fifth Report of the Secretary General on the Situation in Sierra Leone,* S-1998-486 (June 9, 1998), para. 41.

82. Associated Press, "Former Paramilitary Fighters Charged With War Crimes in Kosovo," *International Herald Tribune,* April 21, 2008.

83. Ori Nir, interview with author, October 25, 2005.

84. Kate Zernike and Sheryl Gay Stolberg, "Differences Settled in Deal Over Detainee Treatment," *New York Times,* September 23, 2006, p. 9.

85. Theodor Meron, "Shakespeare's Henry the Fifth and the Laws of War," *American Journal of International Law* 86 (1992): 3.

86. James Neagles, *Summer Soldiers: A Survey and Index of Revolutionary War Courts-Martial* (Salt Lake City, UT: Ancestry, 1986), p. 67.

87. James Kent, *Kent's Commentary on International Law* (Cambridge: Deighton, 1878), p. 30, in Paust, "My Lai and Vietnam," p. 112.

88. Lowry, *Tarnished Eagles: The Court-Martial of Fifty Union Colonels and Lieutenant Colonels,* p. 7.

89. James B. Roan and Cynthia Buxton, "The American Military Justice System in the New Millennium," *Air Force Law Review* 52 (2002): 187.

90. W. Hays Parks, "Crimes in Hostilities," *Marine Corps Gazette,* August 1976, p. 17.

91. *US v. Griffen* 39 CMR 586 (1968), convicted Griffen for killing a POW.

92. *US v. Passantino,* Hq. First Infantry Division Special Court-Martial Order No. 11, February 11, 1968, found the defendant guilty of conduct a discredit to the armed forces and a violation of Laws of War.

93. *US v. Bumgarner* 43 CMR 559 (1970), held the defendant guilty of murdering three Vietnamese soldiers; *US v. Keenan* 18 USCMA 108, 39 CMR 108 (1969), found Keenan guilty of killing an unarmed Vietnamese.

94. Jordan J. Paust, "My Lai and Vietnam," p. 118.

95. Robert Cryer and Olympia Bekou, "International Crimes and ICC Cooperation in England and Wales," *Journal of International Criminal Justice* 5, vol. 2 (2007): 441, n. 29.

96. US Department of State, "Seventh Report on War Crimes in the Former Yugoslavia," *Department of State Dispatch,* vol. 4, April 19, 1993.

97. Barbara Donagan, "Atrocity, War Crime, and Treason in the English Civil War," *American Historical Review* 99 (1994): 1138–39.

98. George L. Coil, "War Crimes and the American Revolution," *Military Law* Review 82 (1978): 185.

99. M. Angulu Onwuejeogwu, *A Study in Military Sociology: The Biafran Army* (Lagos: UTO, 2000).

100. Paul Peachey, "Cleared: Colonel Accused of Mistreating Prisoners," *The Independent* (London), September 2, 2003, p. 2.

101. Thomas Harding, "Colonel Is Cleared," *Daily Telegraph* (London), February 15, 2007, p. 1.

102. Max Hastings and Simon Jenkins, *The Battle for the Falklands* (New York: Norton, 1983), p. 313.

103. Ibid., p. 325.

104. Nicholson Baker, *Human Smoke: The Beginnings of World War II, the End of Civilization* (New York: Simon and Schuster, 2008), p. 157.

105. De Zayas, *The Wehrmacht War Crimes Bureau*, p. 141.

106. Sol Gittleman, "Single Minded and Boring, Himmler was Perfect Tool for Hitler," *Times* (Washington), May 13, 1991; John C. Fredriksen, *America's Adversaries: From Colonial Times to Present* (Santa Barbara, CA: ABC-CLIO, 2001), pp. 57–58.

107. Michael Evans, "Croats Try to Ward Off War Crimes Retribution," *Times* (London), May 25, 1993.

108. Anthony Dworkin, "Rwanda Tribunal Finds Media Executives Guilty of Genocide," *Crimes of War*, December 9, 2003, http://www.crimesof war.org/onnews/news-rwanda.html (accessed May 25, 2008).

109. Paust, "My Lai and Vietnam," p. 163.

110. See generally, Henry F. Graff, ed. *American Imperialism and the Philippines Insurrection* (Boston: Little, Brown, 1969).

111. Steven Keeva, "Lawyers in the War Room," *ABA Journal* 77 (1991): 52.

112. Joshua Kucera, "Serbia Pursues Route to Exoneration: Targets Own Past, War Crimes to Restore its National Honor," *Washington Times*, November 4, 2001, p. A8.

113. "Black Flag Order," *Economist*, June 23, 1990, p. 37.

114. Isabel Vincent, *National Post Online*, September 14, 2002.

115. Radhabinod Pal, "Judgment," in *The Tokyo Judgment: The International Military Tribunal for the Far East (IMTFE) 29 April 1946–12 November 1948*, ed. B. V. A. Röling and C. F. Rüter (Amsterdam: University Press Amsterdam, 1977).

116. Seth Stern, "Race for Order in Iraq," *Christian Science Monitor,* April 24, 2003, p. 11.

117. "Fact Sheet: Department of Justice Efforts in Iraq," States News Service, August 11, 2007.

118. David Cohen, *Intended to Fail: The Trials Before the Ad Hoc Human Rights Court in Jakarta* (New York: International Center for Transitional Justice, 2003), p. iii.

119. Vesna Peric-Zimonjic, "The Serbian Judiciary, A Law Unto Itself," Inter Press Service, September 3, 1998.

120. "Clearing Path to Arrest of Milosevic, Judges He Picked Are Fired," *New York Times,* February 15, 2001, p. A11.

121. De Zayas, *The Wehrmacht War Crimes Bureau,* p. 22.

122. Ibid., p. xvii.

123. Ibid., p. 24; M. Balfour and J. Frisby, *Helmuth James von Multke* (Stuttgart: Deutsche Verlags-Anstalt, 1975), pp. 282–83; Detlev Vagts, "International Law in the Third Reich," *American Journal of International Law* 84 (1990): 661.

124. De Zayas, *The Wehrmacht War Crimes Bureau,* p. 24.

125. Robert Aitken and Marilyn Aitken, *Law Makers, Law Breakers and Uncommon Trials* (Washington, DC: American Bar Association, 2008), p. 10.

126. Ian Fisher, "If Only the Problem Were As Easy As Old Hatreds," *New York Times,* January 2, 2000, p. 10.

127. Ibid.

128. Abid Aslam, "Liberia: Capture Puts Ex-Warlord in Jail, New President in Bind," Inter Press Service, March 29, 2006.

129. See Goldstone and Smith, *International Judicial Institutions,* conclusion. See also, Adam M. Smith, "Good Fences Make Good Neighbors? The Wall Decision and the Troubling Rise of the ICJ as a Human Rights Court," *Harvard Human Rights Journal* 18 (2005): 251.

130. Goldstone and Smith, *International Judicial,* chapter 5. See also The Nizkor Project, "The Demjanjuk Case: Factual and Legal Details," http://www.nizkor.org/hweb/people/d/demjanjuk-john/israeli-data/ (accessed May 26, 2008).

131. Marcela Valente, "Argentina: One Officer Guilty in the 'Dirty War' Pays—Literally," Inter Press Service, August 24, 2004.

132. Uli Schmetzer, "Japanese Firm Offers $4.6 Million to War Slaves," *Chicago Tribune,* November 30, 2000, p. 1.

133. Alex Boraine, "Reconciliation in the Balkans?" *New York Times*, April 22, 2001, p. 17.

134. Daniel Williams, "On Belgrade's Streets, Doubts About Fair Trial: Many Wanted Milosevic Judged at Home," *Washington Post*, February 13, 2002, p. A23.

135. Blaine Harden, "The Unrepentant," *New York Times Magazine*, January 20, 2002, p. 24.

136. Romesh Ratnesar, "The End of the Line," *Time*, July 9, 2001, p. 18.

137. Editorial, "Let Milosevic Face UN Court," *Herald* (New Zealand), April 3, 2001.

138. Ibid.

139. See for example, Wire Reports, "Four Found Guilty of Bosnia War Crimes," *Plain Dealer* (Cleveland), May 6, 1993, p. 13A.

140. Marcus Tanner, "Serbs Fear War Crimes Trials," *Independent* (London), October 9, 1992, p. 10.

141. Elizabeth S. Kopelman, "Ideology and International Law: The Dissent of the Indian Justice at the Tokyo War Crimes Trial," *New York University Journal of International Law and Politics* 23 (1990–1991): 443.

142. Ratnesar, "The End of the Line," p. 18.

143. *Africa News*, "Liberia: Capture Puts Ex-Warlord in Jail, Liberia in a Bind," Inter Press Service, March 29, 2006.

144. Morris Amchan, former deputy Nuremberg prosecutor, "Letters to the Times," *New York Times*, January 28, 1965, p. 28.

145. Yigal Chazan, "Serbs Face War Crimes Trial," *Guardian* (London), December 7, 1991.

146. Robert A. Pape, "Why Economic Sanctions Do Not Work," *International Security* 22 (1997): 93.

147. I am indebted to a colleague, Andrew Kim, for bringing this example to my attention.

148. UN, *Security Council Resolution 837* (1993), para. 5.

149. Adam M. Smith, review of *From Nuremberg to The Hague: The Future of International Criminal Justice*, Philippe Sands, ed. *Harvard International Law Journal* 45 (2004): 566.

150. Kay Rala Xanana Gusmao, "Statement by His Excellency Kay Rala Xanana Gusmao on the Indictment by the Deputy General Prosecutor for Serious Crimes of Indonesian Officers for Events in Timor-Leste during 1999," quoted in Sylvia de Bertodano, "East Timor: Trials and Tribulations,"

Internationalized Criminal Courts, ed. Cesare P. R. Romano et al., (Oxford: Oxford University Press, 2004), p. 85, n. 17.

151. Kingsley Chiedu Moghalu, "Saddam Hussein's Trial Meets a 'Fairness' Test," *Ethics and International Affairs* 20, no. 4 (2006): 517–25; see also Anne Applebaum, "Justice in Iraq: How to Judge the Trial of Saddam Hussein," *Washington Post*, November 7, 2006, p. A21.

152. Larry K. Wentz, "Peace Operations and the Implications for Coalition Information Operations: The IFOR Experience," Command and Control Research Program, National Defense University, Fort Leslie J. McNair, Washington, DC (1998), http://www.dodccrp.org/files/wentz_info_operations _2.htm (accessed May 27, 2008).

153. Cited in James Kitfield, "Humanity's Court," *National Journal*, May 13, 2000, p. 1508.

154. See Theodor Meron, "Answering for War Crimes: Lessons from the Balkans," *Foreign Affairs* (January 1997): 2.

CHAPTER 9
CROATIA: JUSTICE IN THE SHADOW OF THE HAGUE

1. "Battle in Bosnia," *Time Magazine*, July 24, 1972, http://www.time .com/time/magazine/article/0,9171,906151,00.html (accessed May 25, 2008).

2. Marcus Tanner, *Croatia: A Nation Forged in War* (New Haven, CT: Yale University Press, 1997), p. 142.

3. Uki Goni, *The Real Odessa* (London: Granta, 2002), p. 202; Report to Reichsfuhrer SS Heinrich Himmler from the Geheime Staatspolizei— Gestapo (February 17, 1942).

4. David Binder, "Tudjman is Dead: Croat Led Country Out of Yugoslavia," *New York Times*, December 11, 1999, p. A1.

5. Jasminka Udovicki and James Ridgeway, *Burn This House: The Making and Unmaking of Yugoslavia* (Durham, NC: Duke University Press, 2000), p. 288.

6. Chris Hedges, "Fascists Reborn as Croatia's Founding Fathers," *New York Times*, April 12, 1997, p. 3.

7. Chris Hedges, "War Crimes Horrors Revive As Croat Faces Possible Trial," *New York Times*, May 2, 1998, p. A1.

8. Michael Parenti, *To Kill a Nation: The Attack on Yugoslavia* (New York: Verso, 2000), p. 45.

9. Slavenka Drakulic, "Croatia Puts Itself on Trial," *New York Times*, March 16, 1998, p. A1.

10. Editorial, "Selective Memory In Croatia," *Boston Globe*, April 12, 1998, p. D6.

11. Gregory Elich, "Odious, Racists Croatia Gets U.S. Support," *Columbus Dispatch*, September 14, 1995, p. 11A.

12. Drakulic, "Croatia Puts Itself on Trial," p. A1.

13. Ian Traynor, "Franjo Tudjman: Authoritarian Leader Whose Communist Past and Nationalist Obsessions Fuelled His Ruthless Pursuit of an Independent Croatia," *Guardian* (London), December 13, 1999, p. 18.

14. Raymond Bonner, "A Would-Be Tito Helps to Dismantle His Legacy," *New York Times*, August 20, 1995, p. 12.

15. Tom Hundley, "Croatia's New Regime Sheds Extravagance of Tudjman Era," *Chicago Tribune*, August 16, 2000, p. 8C.

16. Alison Smale, "US Backs Bold Croat Leader," *Chicago Sun-Times*, May 19, 1996, p. 46.

17. Laura Pitter, "Croatia: Free Press a Victim of a Rigid Regime, Charge Critics," Inter Press Service, May 6, 1993.

18. Jelena Pejic, "Yugoslavia: Presidency Meets Behind Closed Doors," Inter Press Service, July 18, 1991.

19. Drago Hedl, "How to Tell it Like it Isn't," *Guardian* (London), July 5, 1993, p. 18.

20. Editorial, "Croatia's Censor-in-Chief," *International Herald Tribune*, August 3, 1996.

21. UN, *Situation of Human Rights in Bosnia and Herzegovina, The Republic of Croatia, and the Federal Republic of Yugoslavia (Serbia and Montenegro)*, A-54-396, S-1999-1000 (October 24, 1999), para. 101. Discussing the forced conscription of journalists in Montenegro.

22. Michael Foley, "Tudjman Keeps Media Under His Thumb," *Irish Times*, December 15, 1998, p. 12.

23. Pitter, "Croatia: Free Press a Victim of a Rigid Regime."

24. Vladimir Gotovac, quoted by Radio 101 (Zagreb) "Presidential Candidate Says Media, Army and Police Have Political Aims," *BBC Summary of World Broadcasts*, June 16, 1997.

25. Vesna Peric-Zimonjic, "Croatia Information: Don't Insult the President!" Inter Press Service, September 30, 1996.

26. Michael Evans, "Croats Try to Ward Off War Crimes Retribution," *Times* (London), May 25, 1993.

27. Yugoslav News Agency (Belgrade), "Criminal Charges Brought Against Plitvice Rebels," *BBC Summary of World Broadcasts*, April 3, 1991.

28. Marcus Tanner, "Serbs Fear War Crimes Trials," *Independent* (London), October 9, 1992, p. 10.

29. Yugoslav News Agency (Belgrade), "Reports on Conflict in Croatia: Belgrade Daily says 20,000 Serbs in Croatia Are to be Tried for War Crimes," *BBC Summary of World Broadcasts*, May 22, 1992.

30. Croatian Radio (Zagreb), "Croatian Opposition Parliamentary Parties Form Human Rights Committee," *BBC Summary of World Broadcasts*, January 8, 1992.

31. "Croats Face War Crimes Probe," *Herald Sun* (Australia), May 27, 1993.

32. Yigal Chazan, "Assaults on Serbs 'Mock Croatia's Democratic Status,'" *Guardian* (London), May 24, 1993, p. 6; the Helsinki Committee would also come to publicize the lack of support Tudjman had for some of his more outlandish and ethnically exclusive programs—many soldiers refused to be transferred to Bosnia to aid the Bosnian Croats (it would no longer be a "Homeland" War), and others refused to participate in the mass expulsion of Serbs from the Krajina in Operation Storm. In both cases, Tudjman's generals were forced to also resort to law, threatening court-martials for those unwilling to follow orders. See, for example, Croatian Radio (Zagreb), "Croatian Radio Says Recruits Forced to Fight in Bosnia-Herzegovina," *BBC Summary of World Broadcasts* (January 1, 1994).

33. OSCE—Mission to Croatia, *Supplementary Report: War Crime Proceedings in Croatia and Findings from Trial Monitoring* (Vienna: Organization for Security and Cooperation in Europe, June 22, 2004), pg. 3.

34. Croatian Radio (Zagreb), "Croatian Supreme Court Denies Trying Large Numbers of Serbs," *BBC Summary of World Broadcasts*, December 10, 1993.

35. Ibid.

36. Ibid.

37. Tanjug News Agency (Belgrade), "Serb Prisoners Unaccounted for After Release from Croatian Prisons," *BBC Summary of World Broadcasts*, December 20, 1995.

38. Dean E. Murphy, "With Peace at Hand, Is Justice Beyond Reach?" *Los Angeles Times*, December 15, 1995, p. A17.

39. HINA News Agency (Zagreb), "Prominent Ethnic Serbs Granted Croatian Citizenship," *BBC Summary of World Broadcasts*, June 17, 1995.

40. HINA News Agency (Zagreb), "Serb Candidates Stage Election Rally in Western Slavonia," *BBC Summary of World Broadcasts*, October 24, 1997.

41. Smale, "US Backs Bold Croat Leader," p. 46.

42. Viktor Ivancic, "Croatia's Mock Shock Therapy: Public Horror at a Graphic Account Against Serbs Misses the Main Point," (trans. Ivanka Anicic), *Guardian* (London), September 10, 1997, p. 14.

43. See e.g. Dan Bilefsky, "Fears of Ethnic Conflict in Bosnia," *New York Times*, December 13, 2008.

44. President Tudjman condemned instances of starting court proceedings contrary to the general amnesty act. See HINA News Agency (Zagreb), "President Tudjman Receives Delegation of Serbs," *BBC Summary of World Broadcasts*, December 8, 1997. See also *NATO Report on Situation of Human Rights in Croatia, Presented to the UN Security Council, Pursuant to Resolution 1019 §5*, December 10, 1996.

45. Editorial, "Selective Memory in Croatia," p. D6.

46. "Croatia Seeks Extradition of Wartime Camp Chief," *New York Times*, April 11, 1998, p. A6.

47. Elli Wohlgelernter, "Sakic Found Guilty, Gets 20-year Maximum Sentence," *Jerusalem Post*, October 5, 1999, p. 1; HINA News Agency (Zagreb), "Croatia's Efforts to Investigate Nazi Crimes Insufficient—Wiesenthal Centre,", *BBC Worldwide Monitoring*, April 10, 2002.

48. "Camp Commandant Gets Prison," *Los Angeles Times*, October 5, 1999, p. A8.

49. HINA News Agency (Zagreb), "Supreme Court Upholds 20-year Sentence for War Criminal," *BBC Summary of World Broadcasts*, October 10, 2000.

50. Slavenka Drakulic, "Croats Should Confront Shameful Past, Present During Dinko Sakic Trial," *Seattle Post-Intelligencer*, March 19, 1999, p. A13.

51. Hedges, "War Crimes Horrors Revive as Croat Faces Possible Trial," p. A1.

52. Drakulic, "Croatia Puts Itself on Trial," p. A1.

53. HINA News Agency (Zagreb), "Trial of Concentration Camp Commander Reopens, Then Adjourned," *BBC Summary of World Broadcasts*, September 1, 1999.

54. Associated Press, "Croatian Suspect in World War II Torture is Freed," *New York Times*, February 2, 1999, p. A3.

55. Ibid. p. A3.

56. Drazen Tripalo, *Curriculum Vitae*, Supreme Court of the Republic of Croatia. http://www.vsrh.hr/EasyWeb.asp?pcpid=532 (accessed May 17, 2008).

57. Anthony Robinson and Guy Dinmore, "Croatia: National Dream Close to Reality," *Financial Times* (London), May 28, 1997, p. 01.

58. Editorial, "The Balkans' Long Haul," *Christian Science Monitor*, October 8, 1997, p. 20.

59. Tribune New Services, "Nine War Crimes Suspects Agree to Face Trial Before Hague Panel," *Chicago Tribune*, October 5, 1997, p. C6.

60. HINA News Agency (Zagreb), "US Envoy: Croatia Must Comply With Dayton On Pain Of Economic Sanctions," *BBC Summary of World Broadcasts*, September 20, 1997.

61. Nicholas Wood, "Croatian Turnaround Led to Arrest of General," *International Herald Tribune*, December 29, 2005, p. 2.

62. Chris Hedges, "Croatian's Confession Describes Torture and Killing on Vast Scale," *New York Times*, September 5, 1997, p. A1.

63. Chris Hedges, "A War-Bred Underworld Threatens Bosnia Peace," *New York Times*, May 1, 1996, p. A8.

64. Ibid.

65. HINA News Agency (Zagreb), "Government Criticizes US Report on Human Rights in Croatia," *BBC Summary of World Broadcasts*, February 7, 1998.

66. Ambassador Mihomir Zuzul, quoted in Tom Gjelten, "US and Croatia," *All Things Considered* (transcript no. 97030708-212), March 7, 1997.

67. Raymond Bonner, "Croatia Branded as Another Balkan Pariah," *New York Times*, March 3, 1999, p. A6.

68. HINA News Agency (Zagreb), "US Envoy Holbrooke Discusses War Crimes Extradition With President," *BBC Summary of World Broadcasts*, September 6, 1999.

69. Croatian Radio (Zagreb), "Croatian Christian-Democrats Want British Commanders to be Tried at The Hague," *BBC Worldwide Monitoring*, February 2, 1999. However, some figures in Croatian politics vehemently opposed such oversight, but perhaps only if it came from the ICTY (as opposed to other international bodies). See, for example, HINA News Agency (Zagreb),

"Croatian Justice Minister: Hague Tribunal Not Empowered to Supervise Croatian Courts," *BBC Summary of World Broadcasts*, February 27, 1998.

70. Hedges, "A War-Bred Underworld Threatens Bosnia Peace," p. A8.

71. "Periscope: The Fugitives," *Newsweek*, March 10, 1997, p. 3.

72. Croatian Radio (Zagreb), "Bosnian Croat War Crimes Suspect is Croatian Citizen, Court Rules," *BBC Summary of World Broadcasts*, November 22, 1997.

73. Croat Radio Herceg-Bosna (Mostar), "Bosnian Croat Commander's Trial Adjourned as Witnesses Fail to Appear," *BBC Summary of World Broadcasts*, January 16, 1998.

74. HINA News Agency (Zagreb), "Hague War Crimes Tribunal Indicts Two Bosnian Croats," *BBC Summary of World Broadcasts*, December 24, 1998.

75. ICTY, *The Prosecutor v. Mladen Naletilic and Vinko Martinovic*, Case IT-98-34-1 (December 21, 1998).

76. HINA News Agency (Zagreb), "Bosnian Croat War Crimes Suspect Might be Put on Trial in Croatia," *BBC Summary of World Broadcasts*, March 10, 2000.

77. HINA News Agency (Zagreb), "Croatian Law Does Not Allow Interruption of Trial for Hague Tribunal—Lawyer," *BBC Worldwide Monitoring*, October 14, 1999.

78. Ibid.

79. HINA News Agency (Zagreb), "Bosnian Croat War Crimes Suspect Threatens to Sue Croatia," *BBC Summary of World Broadcasts*, October 21, 1999.

80. Robert Wright, "Croatia's Line on War Crimes Trials Strains Ties with EU," *Financial Times* (London), March 10, 2000, p. 3.

81. HINA News Agency (Zagreb), "Croatia Says UN Non-Cooperation Report Not Founded On Facts," *BBC Summary of World Broadcasts*, August 28, 1999.

82. Bonner, "Croatia Branded as Another Balkan Pariah," *New York Times*, March 3, 1999, p. A6.

83. HINA News Agency (Zagreb), "Croatia To Extradite War Crimes Suspect," *BBC Summary of World Broadcasts*, September 3, 1999.

84. See ICTY, "Decision of the Zagreb County Court," KV-I 200-99 (June 8, 1999). Official translation online: http://www.un.org/icty/naletilic/trialc/decision-e/990811.pdf (accessed May 17, 2008).

85. HINA News Agency (Zagreb), "Croatian Constitutional Court

Rejects War Crime Suspect's Appeal," *BBC Worldwide Monitoring*, October 21, 1999; HINA News Agency (Zagreb), "Court Rejects Appeal to Stop Extradition of War Crimes Suspect," *BBC Summary of Worldwide Broadcasts*, July 14, 1999.

86. Radio Mostar (Mostar), "Croatian Court Sentences Former Bosnian Croat Warlord for Murder," *BBC Worldwide Monitoring*, December 2, 1998.

87. Ibid.

88. See ICTY, *Naletilic and Martinovic*, IT-98-34, Case Information Sheet, http://www.un.org/icty/cases-e/index-e.htm (accessed May 17, 2008).

89. HINA News Agency (Zagreb), "Croatian Opposition Slates President's Claim That All Sides Bear War Guilt," *BBC Worldwide Monitoring*, September 22, 2000. (Emphasis added).

90. HINA News Agency (Zagreb), "Croatian Veterans Threaten to Take Up Arms over Hague Tribunal Declaration," *BBC Worldwide Monitoring*, April 14, 2000; HINA News Agency (Zagreb), "Croatian Veterans' Leader Conciliatory on Hague Cooperation After Meeting President," *BBC Worldwide Monitoring*, April 20, 2000.

91. HINA News Agency (Zagreb), "Croatia Allows Hague War Crimes Tribunal to Investigate Alleged Mass Grave," *BBC Worldwide Monitoring*, April 9, 2000.

92. Jonathan Steele, "Croatia's President Gives Seven Generals Their Marching Orders," *Guardian* (London), September 30, 2000, p. 19.

93. "Domestic War Crimes Trials Planned," *World Markets Analysis*, September 14, 2000.

94. Croatian Radio (Zagreb), "President Urges Courts to Process War Crimes Cases Committed by Croats," *BBC Summary of World Broadcasts*, December 30, 2000.

95. "No Strategic Differences on Cooperation with ICTY; Mesic, Racan," ONASA News Agency (Belgrade), December 14, 2000.

96. *Jutarnji List*, February 23, 2003, p. 5, 23.

97. Croatian Radio (Zagreb), "President Says Law Exempting War Veterans from Prosecution Not Right," *BBC Summary of World Broadcasts*, March 1, 2001.

98. HRT1 TV (Zagreb), "Premier Regrets Past Decision Not to Hold War Crimes Trials in Croatia," *BBC Monitoring Europe*, July 8, 2001.

99. Chief State Prosecutor, "Instructions to all County State Prosecutors in Organization for Security and Cooperation in Europe—Mission to

Croatia," *Supplementary Report: War Crime Proceedings in Croatia and Find-ings from Trial Monitoring* (June 22, 2004), p. 2, n. 2, http://www.osce.org/documents/mc/2004/06/3165_en.pdf (accessed May 17, 2008).

100. OSCE, Mission to Croatia, *Background Report: Domestic War Crime Trials*, (2002), p. 3, http://www.osce.org/documents/mc/2004/03/2185_en.pdf (accessed May 17, 2008).

101. "Southeast European Media Roundup on EU-Related Issues," *BBC Monitoring International Reports*, December 24, 2004.

102. Jeffrey Smith, "Death of a Man Who Knew Too Much; Croatian Bomb Victim Refused to Be Silent About War Crimes in His Home Town," *Washington Post*, September 14, 2000, p. A24.

103. "Southeast European Media Roundup on EU-Related Issues," *BBC Monitoring International Reports*, December 24, 2004.

104. HINA News Agency (Zagreb), "Croatia: Six Ex-policemen Sus-pected of War Crimes Arrested in Split," *BBC Worldwide Monitoring*, Sep-tember 27, 2001.

105. HINA News Agency (Zagreb), "Croatia: Witness in Serb Prisoner Murder Case Attacked Outside Judge's Office," *BBC Worldwide Monitoring*, October 10, 2001.

106. HINA News Agency (Zagreb), "Trial Starts of Eight Croatian Ex-policemen Accused of War Crimes," *BBC Worldwide Monitoring*, June 10, 2002.

107. Croatian Radio (Zagreb), "Croatian Radio Report Slams Judge, Pro-ceedings at Split War Crimes Trial," *BBC Monitoring International Reports*, June 13, 2002.

108. Ibid.

109. Ibid.

110. Ibid.

111. Ibid.

112. Ibid.

113. Croatian Radio (Zagreb), "Croatia: Split County Court Adjourns Lora Trial Ahead of Relocation Decision," *BBC Worldwide Monitoring*, June 20, 2002.

114. HINA News Agency (Zagreb), "Croatian State Prosecutor Agrees To Transfer of War Crimes Trial," *BBC Worldwide Monitoring*, June 20, 2002.

115. HINA News Agency (Zagreb), "Croatian Supreme Court Refuses to Move War Crimes Trial from Coastal Town," *BBC Worldwide Monitoring*, July 2, 2002.

116. HINA News Agency (Zagreb), "Croatian Defense Attorneys Say War Crimes Retrial 'Unnecessary,'" *BBC Worldwide Monitoring*, August 19, 2004.

117. HINA News Agency (Zagreb), "Croatian Local NGOs Dissatisfied with Verdict in Lora War Crimes Trial," *BBC Monitoring International Reports*, November 24, 2002.

118. Radio B92 (Belgrade), "Serbia: Acquittal of Former Croatian Policemen Met with Severe Criticism," *BBC Worldwide Monitoring*, November 23, 2002.

119. Stefan Bos, "Croatian Court Orders Retrial of Eight Croatian War Crimes Suspects," *Voice of America News*, August 19, 2004.

120. Ibid.

121. HINA News Agency (Zagreb), "Croatian Supreme Court Orders Custody for Accused in Lora War Crimes Case," *BBC Worldwide Monitoring*, October 12, 2004.

122. HINA News Agency (Zagreb), "Croatian Court Rejects Plea for Arrest of Ex-Policemen Charged with Ethnic Crime," *BBC Worldwide Monitoring*, September 8, 2004.

123. "Croatia Reopens War Torture Trial," *UPI*, September 12, 2005.

124. Croatian Radio (Zagreb), "Croatian Ex-policemen in Lora Prison Trial Convicted of War Crimes," *BBC Worldwide Monitoring*, March 2, 2006.

125. Croatian Radio (Zagreb), "Croatia: Split Court Releases All Defendants in War Crimes Trial," *BBC Monitoring International Reports*, November 22, 2002.

126. Radio B92 (Belgrade), "Croatian Veterans Want Film about War Crimes Against Serbs Withdrawn," *BBC Worldwide Monitoring*, October 14, 2004.

127. Nesho Djuric, "Feature: War Criminal, But Still Running," *UPI*, August 1, 2002.

128. "Southeast European Media Round Up," *BBC Monitoring International Reports*, March 10, 2005.

129. OSCE, Mission to Croatia, *Background Report: Domestic War Crime Trials* (2002), p. 4. http://www.osce.org/documents/mc/2004/03/2185_en.pdf (accessed May 17, 2008).

130. Ibid., p. 3.

131. HINA News Agency (Zagreb), "Croatia: Whereabouts of War Crimes Suspect Norac Unknown to Zagreb Police," *BBC Worldwide Monitoring*, February 8, 2001.

132. Associated Press, "Crowd Protests War-Crime Probe of Former Croat General," *Telegraph Herald* (Dubuque), February 12, 2001, p. A5.

133. Tribune News Services, "100,000 Protest Inquiry of Atrocities in '91 War," *Chicago Tribune*, February 12, 2001, p. 10.

134. HINA News Agency (Zagreb), "International Tribunal to Allow Croatia to Try General Suspected Of War Crimes," *BBC Summary of World Broadcasts*, February 23, 2001.

135. Combined News Services, "Croatia Indicts 5 Military Men," *Newsday* (New York), March 6, 2001, p. A53.

136. HINA News Agency (Zagreb), "Croatia: Gospic Group War Crimes Trial Adjourned As Soon As It Starts," *BBC Worldwide Monitoring*, June 25, 2001.

137. HINA News Agency (Zagreb), "Croatian War Crimes Trial Delayed Over Request to Drop Prosecution," *BBC Worldwide Monitoring*, July 3, 2001.

138. Reuters, "Is Croatia Dragging its Heels on War Crimes?" *IPR Strategic Business Information Database*, November 28, 2001.

139. HINA News Agency (Zagreb), "Croatia: War Crimes Suspect Norac Elected Honorary Citizen of Sinj," *BBC Worldwide Monitoring*, August 1, 2001.

140. Nesho Djuric, "Analysis: Croat War-Crime Trial Begins," *UPI*, January 27, 2002.

141. HINA News Agency (Zagreb), "Croatia: Gospic Group Trial Hears 1991 Report on Responsibility for Killings," *BBC Worldwide Monitoring*, September 30, 2002.

142. HRT1 TV (Zagreb), "Croatian War Crimes Trial Hears of General Ordering Killing of Serb Civilians," *BBC Worldwide Monitoring*, September 5, 2002.

143. HINA News Agency (Zagreb), "Croatia, Serbia to Step Up Cooperation on War Crimes Investigations," *BBC Monitoring International Reports*, July 21, 2003. Cooperation would become even stronger the following year when judges from Bosnia, Croatia and Serbia were provided joint training on criminal procedure and war crimes trials. SRNA News Agency, "Croatia, Bosnian, SCG Judiciary Receiving Same Training for War Crimes—NGO," *BBC Monitoring International Reports*, November 9, 2004.

144. HINA News Agency (Zagreb), "Witnesses in Croatian Gospic Group Trial Take Stand in Serbian Court," *BBC Worldwide Monitoring*, September 23, 2002.

145. HINA News Agency (Zagreb), "Yugoslav Army Pathologist Testifies at Croatian War Crimes Trial," *BBC Worldwide Monitoring*, October 17, 2002.

146. HINA News Agency (Zagreb), "Croatia: Another War Crimes Suspect Released from Custody," *BBC Worldwide Monitoring*, September 12, 2002.

147. HINA News Agency (Zagreb), "Defense Witnesses in Croatian War Crimes Trial Deny Knowledge of Murder of Serbs," Global News Wire, November 19, 2002.

148. HINA News Agency (Zagreb), "Croatia: Serb Witnesses Testify at Gospic Trial They Felt Safe During War," *BBC Worldwide Monitoring*, October 2, 2002.

149. "Croatia Jails General for Killing Serbs," *Morning Star,* March 25, 2003, p. 2; "Croatia: War Crimes Convictions," *Facts on File World Digest*, March 24, 2003, p. 251D2.

150. Radio B92, "Serb Official from Croatia Welcomes Sentences for Gospic War Crimes Group," *BBC Monitoring International Reports*, March 25, 2003.

151. HINA News Agency (Zagreb), "Appeal Process in Gospic War Crime Case Starts Before Croatian Court," *BBC Worldwide Monitoring*, May 31, 2004.

152. HINA News Agency (Zagreb), "Croatian Supreme Court Confirms Guilty Verdict for War Crimes Against Serbs," *BBC Worldwide Monitoring*, June 24, 2004.

153. HINA News Agency (Zagreb), "Croatian General to Enter Plea for Crimes Against Humanity 8 July," *BBC Worldwide Monitoring*, July 7, 2004.

154. HINA News Agency (Zagreb) "Gen. Norac Back in Croatian Jail after Pleading Not Guilty in Hague," *BBC Worldwide Monitoring*, July 9, 2004.

155. "UN War Crimes Court Transfers First Case for Trial in Croatia," *ONASA News Agency*, November 1, 2005.

156. HINA News Agency (Zagreb), "Croatian Foreign Minister Says Planned Reforms Depend on International Support," *BBC Worldwide Monitoring*, March 23, 2000.

157. "Domestic War Crimes Trials Planned," *World Markets Analysis*, September 14, 2000.

158. HINA News Agency (Zagreb), "International War Crimes Tribunal Rejects Idea of Holding Trial in Croatia," *BBC Monitoring International Reports*, March 13, 2000.

159. HINA News Agency (Zagreb), "Croatia Can Take Over ICTY Trials, But Must Train Judges First—OSCE Official," *BBC Monitoring International Reports*, June 22, 2004.

160. SRNA News Agency, "Human Rights Watch Says Croatian War Crimes Trials 'Ethnically Biased,'" *BBC Monitoring International Reports*, November 3, 2004.

161. ONASA News Agency, "Croatian Court Acquits Serb of War Crimes Charges," Europe Intelligence Wire, October 18, 2004.

162. HINA News Agency (Zagreb), "OSCE Calls on Croatia to Enhance Human Rights Protection," *BBC Monitoring International Reports*, June 3, 2004.

163. Valerie Mason, "Government Approves Judicial Reform Plan," *World Markets Analysis*, November 8, 2002.

164. HINA News Agency (Zagreb), "Croatian Agency Notes Local War Crimes Court Gets Video Link System," *BBC Monitoring International Reports*, January 27, 2005.

165. Vlado Rajic, "Is The Hague Severing Cooperation with Croatia," *Zagreb Vjesnik*, November 24, 2002. English trans. Global News Wire/NTIS, US Department of Commerce.

166. Mark Beunderman, "Del Ponte Angers UN Staff over Croatia Move," *EUObserver.com*, October 5, 2005.

167. OSCE, Mission in Bosnia and Herzegovina, *War Crimes Trials Before the Domestic Courts of Bosnia and Herzegovina* (March 2005), p. 47.

168. Ibid.

CHAPTER 10
CONCLUSION: IS IT TOO LATE TO
LISTEN TO THE CANARY IN THE MINE?

1. Joshua Kucera, "Serbia Pursues Route to Exoneration: Targets Own Past, War Crimes to Restore its National Honor," *Washington Times*, November 4, 2001, p. A8.

2. Editorial, "Milosevic Must Answer For His Crimes," *Atlanta Journal-Constitution*, April 10, 2001, p. 18A.

3. Romesh Ratnesar, "The End of the Line," *Time*, July 9, 2001, p. 18.

4. Tanjug Serbian News Agency, cited in Alex Bivol, "Judge Rules on

Karadzic's Extradition to The Hague Tribunal," Sofia-Echo.com, July 22, 2008, http://www.sofiaecho.com/judge-rules-on-karad-I-263-s-extradition-to-the-hague-tribunal/id_30697/catid_68 (accessed July 23, 2008).

5. John Dower, *Embracing Defeat* (New York: W. W. Norton, 1999), chapter 15.

6. *Judgment of the International Military Tribunal for the Far East*, p. 1012, para. 2.

7. John A. Tucker, "The Nanjing Massacre: A Review Essay," *China Review International* 7 (2000): 321.

8. "Jewish Groups Condemn Nazi Funeral," Associated Press, July 29, 2008.

9. "One Brought to Justice, Many At Large—Balkans War Crimes," *Economist*, February 9, 2002.

10. *When the War Ends: A Population Based Survey on Attitudes about Peace, Justice, and Social Reconstruction in Northern Uganda* (Human Rights Center: University of California, at Berkeley, 2007).

11. Roger Riddell, *Does Foreign Aid Really Work?* (Oxford: Oxford University Press, 2007), pp. 253–54.

12. "The World's Newest State," *Economist*, February 23, 2008.

13. See e.g., Tony Cox, "News & Notes," *National Public Radio*, June 26, 2007; "Playing On," *Cable News Network*, April 3, 2006 (10:39 EST); Ian Traynor, "Taylor War Crimes Trial Begins," *Guardian* (London), January 7, 2008, http://www.guardian.co.uk/world/2008/jan/07/internationalcrime.warcrimes (accessed May 27, 2008).

14. Law and Development Movement, *The World Bank—Rule of Law and Development*, http://siteresources.worldbank.org/INTLAWJUSTINST/Resources/LawandDevelopmentMovement.pdf. (accessed May 17, 2008); see e.g., David M. Trubek and Marc Galanter, "Scholars in Self Estrangement," *Wisconsin Law Review* (1974): 1062.

15. Human Rights Watch, "Background to the Establishment and Mandate of the War Crimes Chamber," http://www.hrw.org/reports/2006/ij0206/2.htm (accessed May 17, 2008); OSCE, Mission in Bosnia and Herzegovina, *War Crimes Trials Before the Domestic Courts of Bosnia and Herzegovina* (March 2005), p. 4.

16. Times Wires, "Bush Proposes Democracy Corps," *St. Petersburg Times*, May 19, 2005, p. 3A.

17. Fawzia Sheikh, "U.S. Creating Civilian Corps to Deploy to Global Hot Spots," *Inside the Pentagon* 24 (February 21, 2008).

18. "JRR: Justice Rapid Response," http://www.justicerapidresponse.org/ (accessed May 31, 2008).

19. *Alwiha* (N'Djamena), "EU Said Urged to Support Senegal Prepare Former Chadian Head's Trial," *BBC Monitoring Africa*, April 29, 2007.

20. "Africa-EU Dialogue, The Africa-EU Strategic Partnership," Adopted at the Lisbon Summit, Portugal, December 9, 2007, para. 30.

21. European Parliament, "Resolution of 26 April 2007," *Annual Report on Human Rights in the World 2006 and the EU's Policy on the Matter* (April 2007), para. 96.

22. "Chad; AU Balks at Habré Extradition, Asks African Jurists to Study Case," *UN Integrated Regional Information Networks*, January 25, 2006, http://www.irinnews.org/Report.aspx?ReportId=57919 (accessed May 27, 2008).

23. *Human Rights Watch*, "Chronology of the Habré Case," http://hrw.org/english/docs/2004/10/29/chad9579.htm (accessed May 17, 2008).

24. "Chad; Former President Will Be Tried in Senegal, Says ICC Registrar," *Africa News*—Hirondelle News Agency, February 26, 2008.

25. "Africa's Many Pinochets-In-Waiting," *Economist*, February 12, 2000.

26. Code of Civil Procedure of the French Republic, Article 3 § 1.

27. UN, *Rome Statute of the International Criminal Court*, July 17, 1998, pmbl., 2187 UNTS 90, UN Doc. A-CONF.183-9 (1998), at article 68(3).

28. John G. Heidenrich, *How to Prevent Genocide: A Guide for Policymakers, Scholars, and the Concerned Citizen* (Westport, CT: Praeger, 2001).

29. UN Press Release, *Action Plan to Prevent Genocide*, SG-SM-9197 AFR-893 (April 7, 2004), http://www.preventgenocide.org/prevent/UNdocs/KofiAnnansActionPlantoPreventGenocide7Apr2004.htm (accessed December 13, 2008).

30. *Preventing Genocide: A Blueprint for U.S. Policymakers*, United States Holocaust Memorial Museum/American Academy of Diplomacy/United States Institute for Peace (December 2008), http://www.usip.org/genocide_taskforce/pdf/FINAL%20REPORT.pdf (accessed December 13, 2008); "Preventing Genocide," *Economist*, December 13, 2008, p. 43.

31. Stuart Laidlaw, "Canada Urged to Act on Dictator," *Toronto Star*, September 11, 2007, p. L05.

INDEX